AF663704

Vedic Concept of Man and Universe

Vedic Concept of Man and Universe

English Translation of

Vyākhyāna-Pañcakam

(Five Discourses)

of

Paṇḍit Motilal Shastri

by

Rishi Kumar Mishra

Shri Shankar Shikshayatan
New Delhi

DK PRINTWORLD
Publishers of Indian Traditions

Cataloging in Publication Data — DK
[Courtesy: D.K. Agencies (P) Ltd. <docinfo@dkagencies.com>]

Śarmmā, Motīlāla, 1908-1960, **author.**
[Vyākhyāna-pañcaka. English]
Vedic concept of man and universe : English translation of Vyākhyāna-pañcakam (five discourses) of Paṇḍit Motilal Shastri / translation, Rishi Kumar Mishra.
pages cm
Includes passages in Sanskrit (Devanagari and roman).
Translated from Hindi.
"Shri Shankar Shikshayatan, New Delhi."
ISBN 9788124612057

1. Vedas – Criticism, interpretation, etc. 2. Hinduism. I. Mishra, R.K., 1932-2009, translator. II. Shri Shankar Shikshayatan Trust. III. Title.

LCC BL1112.46.S27 2024 | DDC 294.5921046 23

ISBN 978-81-246-1205-7
First published in India in 2024
© Shri Shankar Shikshayatan, New Delhi

All rights reserved. No part of this publication may be reproduced or transmitted in any form or by any means, electronic or mechanical, including photocopying, recording or any information storage or retrieval system, without prior written permission of both the copyright owner, indicated above, and the publisher.

Published by:
Shri Shankar Shikshayatan
D-6/25, Vasant Vihar, New Delhi - 110057
Phone: 011- 26142604 Web: www.vediceye.org
e-mail: <ssst.2015@gmail.com>

and

D.K. Printworld (P) Ltd.
Regd. Office : "Vedaśrī", F-395, Sudarshan Park
ESI Hospital Metro Station, New Delhi - 110015
Phones : (011) 4172 2626, 98713 94815
e-mail : indology@dkprintworld.com
Web : www.dkprintworld.com

Printed by: D.K. Printworld (P) Ltd., New Delhi

Preface

INDIA's first President, Dr Rajendra Prasad, had an abiding interest in Vedic knowledge. He often invited learned scholars for discourses on ancient Indian texts. He was introduced by one such scholar to Pandit Motilal Shastri from Jaipur. Impressed by what he learnt of Shastri-ji, the President invited him to offer five discourses on Vedic Vijñāna at Rashtrapati Bhawan during 14-18 December 1956. The lectures were attended by well-known scholars and *ācārya*s (teachers) of Vedaśāstra.

Shastri-ji was a devout disciple of famous Vedic *guru*, Paṇḍit Madhusūdan Ojhā, the royal paṇḍit at the court of Mahārājā of Jaipur.

For the lectures, Shastri-ji chose the central theme of his *guru*'s profound knowledge and books – the mysteries of Creation. The five themes he selected for the discourse focused on five distinct *vidyā*s (knowledge systems), all of which offered a unique insight into the mysteries of Creation.

For each of the discourses, Shastri-ji chose to expound on select Vedic terms to reflect upon their deeper meanings which illuminate the mysteries of Creation and the universe.

These discourses were collected and preserved as Pañcavyākhyānam.

In his Preface to the book, President Rajendra Prasad wrote that he found Shastri-ji's lectures far more perceptive than expected. Not only were the discourses important from the Vedic viewpoint, they also illuminated wisdom from Purāṇas and other important texts. Shastri-ji revealed new insights into the mysteries of Creation and offered new definitions of well known Vedic terms.

Shastri-ji's chosen disciple was Rishi Kumar Mishra, a well-known author, writer and editor. As *guru-dakṣiṇā*, Shastri-ji asked Mishra-ji to translate works of Veda Vijñāna into English. However part of the fifth discourse has been translated by Wilson John, editor at Shri Shankar Shikshayatan.

This volume is one such offering from the disciple to the venerable teacher.

Paṇḍit Motilal Shastri

Paṇḍit Motilal Shastri was one of the disciples of renowned Vedic savant, Paṇḍit Madhusūdan Ojhā, who learnt at the feet of his *guru* in the age-old tradition of *ṛṣi*s (seer scientists).

Born in 1908, Motilal Shastri received his education in Sanskrit and displayed an extraordinary talent for learning from childhood. At the age of 12, he passed the Prathama examination from Kāśī (also known as Benares and Varanasi), a pre-eminent centre for Sanskrit learning in the country. He continued his studies at the Maharaja Sanskrit College of Jaipur.

At a conference in Varanasi, the young Motilal Shastri heard Paṇḍit Madhusūdan Ojhā speak on the Vedic sciences and thus had the first exposure to the great scholar. The young man made a firm resolve to become a disciple of Ojhājī and pursue studies in Vedic science on his return to Jaipur. This marked his "second birth" as a student of Vedaśāstra (Vedic science).

Under the tutelage of Ojhājī, he began a rigorous study of the Vedas which continued till his last breath. It also ensured the continuation of a new tradition of dissemination of knowledge of Vedic science, which Paṇḍit Madhusūdan Ojhā had rekindled after it had sunk into oblivion for several centuries.

Ojhājī's writings are mostly in the form of aphorisms and the subjects covered therein are intricate and complex. This makes it difficult even for accomplished Sanskrit scholars to fully decipher and comprehend his writings. Therefore, Shastriji opted to write in Hindi, although it was not an easy task to explain the meaning of the Vedas in Hindi. Shastriji invented his own unique adaptation of Hindi to explain Vedic science to lay readers.

He wrote about 80,000 handwritten pages on Vedic themes. Thus, he not only made a great contribution to the exposition of the

Vedas but also to the evolution of Hindi itself, vesting remarkable richness to the great language.

In Jaipur, the main centre of his activities, Shastriji established an *āśrama* in 1943 to continue his work. During the latter phase of his life, he devoted himself to self-study, writing, preserving and publishing his work. It was during this phase that Pandit Rishi Kumar Mishra had the great fortune of coming in contact with him which sparked a life-long passion for exploring the unprecedented richness of the Vedic wisdom.

Paṇḍit Motilal Shastri passed away at the age of 52.

Shri Shankar Shikshayatan

SHRI Shankar Shikshayatan was set up at the beginning of the millennium with the belief that the study of the Vedas, undertaken with humility and without prejudice, could advance the human quest to discover the truth of all truths and illuminate us with the profound meaning of life.

It is today a premium institute engaged in research and dissemination of Veda Vijñāna as propounded by the exceptional Vedic scholar and teacher, Paṇḍit Madhusūdan Ojhā.

For thousands of years, the Vedas, the oldest repository of humankind's understanding of the cosmic mysteries, remained buried in the dark recesses of time and history. It was only a little more than 100 years ago that Paṇḍit Madhusūdan Ojhā rescued these lost riches of humankind's attainments from the debris of ignorance, distortion and misrepresentation.

Years later, Paṇḍit Ojhā took Motilal Shastriji as his disciple and found him to be an illustrious student who would take forward this unparalleled work of rediscovering ancient truths. Both Paṇḍit Madhusūdan Ojhā and Paṇḍit Motilal Shastri wrote extensively on the wisdom contained in the Vedas with remarkable clarity and assurance. Shastriji, in turn, found in Rishi Kumar Mishra, a gifted disciple and torch bearer of Veda Vijñāna. With Shastriji as his *guru*, Mishraji embraced this enchanting and exciting realm of profound knowledge articulated by the *ṛṣi*s in the Vedas.

Shri Shankar Shikshayatan embodies the true spirit, purpose and wisdom of the three *guru*s and seeks to generate awareness about the invaluable treasures contained within the Vedas.

A comprehensive account of the institute and its variegated events and publications can be found easily at www.vediceye.com or www.shankarshikshayatan.org.

Paṇḍit Rishi Kumar Mishra

LIKE his *guru*, and his *guru*'s *guru* before him, Rishi Kumar Mishra belongs to the lineage of R̥ṣi Bharadvāja, the renowned seer-scientist who unravelled several mysteries of the cosmos several thousands of years ago and is cited extensively in the Vedas.

An atheist and a Marxist, editor of a number of daily newspapers and magazines, and a former member of Rajya Sabha, Paṇḍit Rishi Kumar Mishra was initiated into the mysteries of Vedic wisdom by Paṇḍit Motilal Shastri. In a reversal of the traditional *guru–śiṣya paramparā*, Shastriji chose him as his disciple. The result was an inner transformation and initiation into the scientific thought of the Vedas.

In the same way that Shastriji illuminated the Vedas in Hindi, he set his disciple the task of disseminating the Vedic knowledge in English. In fulfilment of his *guru*'s desire, Mishraji authored the following works:

- *Before the Beginning and After the End: Rediscovering Ancient Insights.*
- *The Cosmic Matrix: In the Light of the Vedas.*
- *The Realm of Supraphysics: Mind, Matter, Energy.*
- *The Ultimate Dialogue: Fusion of Knowledge, Intelligence and Action.*
- *The Whole Being: A Journey Towards Harmony and Happiness.*

All his books are available to scholars for their reading on www.shankarshikshayatan.org.

Contents

Second Discourse

Third Discourse

Abbreviations

ईश॰उप॰ (*ĪśaUp*)	ईशावास्योपनिषद् (*Īśāvāsyopaniṣad*)
ऐत॰ब्रा॰ (*AitaBrā*)	ऐतरेय ब्राह्मण (*Aitareya Brāhmaṇa*)
ऐत॰आ॰ (*AitaĀr*)	ऐतरेय आरण्यक (*Aitareya Āraṇyaka*)
ऋ॰ (*ṚV*)	ऋग्वेद संहिता (*Ṛgveda Saṁhitā*)
क॰उप॰ (*KaUp*)	कठ उपनिषद् (*Kaṭha Upaniṣad*)
के॰उप॰ (*KeUp*)	केन उपनिषद् (*Kena Upaniṣad*)
गीता (*Gītā*)	*Śrīmad Bhagavadgītā*
गो॰ब्रा॰ (*GoBrā*)	गोपथ ब्राह्मण (*Gopatha Brāhmaṇa*)
छा॰उप॰ (*ChāUp*)	छान्दोग्य उपनिषद् (*Chāndogya Upaniṣad*)
तै॰उप॰ (*TaiUp*)	तैत्तिरीय उपनिषद् (*Taittirīya Upaniṣad*)
तै॰ब्रा॰ (*TaiBrā*)	तैत्तिरीय ब्राह्मण (*Taittirīya Brāhmaṇa*)
पूर्व॰मी॰सू॰ (*PūMīSū*)	पूर्व-मीमांसा सूत्र (*Pūrva-Mīmāṁsā Sūtra*)
प्र॰उप॰ (*PraUp*)	प्रश्न उपनिषद् (*Praśna Upaniṣad*)
बृ॰उप॰ (*BṛUp*)	बृहदारण्यक उपनिषद् (*Bṛhadāraṇyaka Upaniṣad*)
ब्रह्मबिन्दु॰उप॰ (*BrahmabinduUp*)	ब्रह्मबिन्दूपनिषद् (*Brahmabindūpaniṣad*)
महा॰ (*MBh*)	महाभारत (*Mahābhārata*)
मनु॰ (*Manu*)	मनुस्मृति (*Manusmṛti*)
मु॰उप॰ (*MuUp*)	मुण्डक उपनिषद् (*Muṇḍaka Upaniṣad*)
शत॰ब्रा॰ (*ŚataBrā*)	शतपथ ब्राह्मण (*Śatapatha Brāhmaṇa*)
श्वेत॰उप॰ (*ŚvetaUp*)	श्वेताश्वतर उपनिषद् (*Śvetāśvatara Upaniṣad*)

वाचं देवा उपजीवन्ति विश्वे वाचं गन्धर्वा पशवो मनुष्याः ।
वाचीमा विश्वा भुवनान्यर्पिता सा नो हवं जुषतामिन्द्रपत्नी ॥१॥

वागक्षरं प्रथमजा ऋतस्य वेदानां माता अमृतस्य नाभिः ।
सा नो जुषाणोपयज्ञमागादवन्ति देवी सुहवा मेऽस्तु ॥२॥

प्राक्कर्मोदयतो हो यस्य मिथिला देशे शरीरोदयः
श्रीविश्वेशदयोदयाच्च समभूत् काश्यां सुविद्योदयः ।
राज्ञा प्रीत्युदयादभूज्जयपुरे सम्पत्तिभाग्योदयः
सिद्धस्तन्मधुसूदनाय गुरवे नित्यं प्रणामोदयः ॥३॥

ओष्ठापिधाना न कुली दन्तैः परिवृता पविः ।
सर्वस्यै वाच ईशान चारुमामिह वादयेत् ॥४॥

तद्दिव्यमव्ययं धाम सारस्वतमुपास्महे ।
यत्प्रसादात्प्रलीयन्ते मोहान्धतमसच्छटाः ॥५॥

First Discourse

Science of Agni-Soma

Mr President, ladies and gentlemen,

TODAY, in this seat of opulence and affluence of the great and grand Indian nation, Rashtrapati Bhawan, a glimpse of the science of Creation as enunciated in the Vedas is being offered.

This marks the fulfilment of a long-awaited dream, a dream which the Indian people have nursed for many centuries.

In the days of the renowned poet Kālidāsa, known as the Bhoja Age, those who studied the Vedas were "honourably" called dull-witted. Perhaps similar sentiments exist today, even when our country is a sovereign and independent nation.

For those of us who are reverential to the Vedas, the sum and essence of our duty is confined to the recitation of *mantra*s (chants) systematically, melodiously and rhythmically, conducting some rites and rituals with these *mantra*s for obtaining some mysterious gains in some other world and at the same time imagining some *ātma-brahma* and to remain absorbed in that mysterious and unknown process of self-realization.

When did this Dark Age dawn on us? There is no historical timescale to measure it. In any case, time is of no significance since the *ṛṣi*s (seer scientists) never attached any importance to a history dictated by fluctuating elements and feelings influenced by human mind and body. Modern anthropologists and historians deride us for not having a systematic record of history. We should accept these accusations as we do not consider mere functions of body and mind as history.

For us, *sāṁskṛtika* (cultural) history based on *ātmā* (core of a being) and *mana* (intellect) is the only history that matters. We have worshipped ancient texts like the Purāṇas, Śāstras and knowledge systems of Āgama and Nigama[1] which communicated a historical narrative that is eternal.

Here, I would like to humbly submit some thoughts on *agni-somātmaham jagat,* a history of Creation related to the profound and fundamental Vedaśāstra.

I would like to begin with *agni* (vital fire) and *soma* (vital fluid) in relation to *saṁvatsara yajña* (yearly process of Creation). It is not my aim to present all the dramatic and extraordinary characters and features related to *agni* but only to draw an outline of the science of *agni-soma.* It deals with *soma* which pacifies the awesome *agni.*

But before this submission, a new view of the Vedas will be presented which might make the believers assembled here to exclaim, "what mistaken notions are we hearing today about the Vedas?".

Vedas: The Popular Belief

The religious people of India believe that the Veda is divided into four Saṁhitās (collected works) – *Ṛk, Yaju, Sāma* and *Atharva* – and each of these is further divided into 21, 101, 1,000 and 9 branches. Thus, there are, in all, 1,131 books of the Vedas. Every branch has one Brāhmaṇa, one Āraṇyaka and one Upaniṣad. Among the Sanātanists (traditionalists), the Brāhmaṇa, Āraṇyaka and Upaniṣads put together are called the Brāhmaṇa Veda. If the auxiliary books of Brāhmaṇa *grantha*s (texts) are added together, their total number will rest at 3,393. If 1,131 collected works are added to them, the total will become 4,524 and these were named by sages in the following words: मन्त्रब्राह्मणयोर्वेद नामधेयम् (*mantrabrāhamaṇayorveda nāmadheyam*).

Vedic Books Are not the Veda

In complete contradiction to this belief, I am going to take this audacious view that these Vedic books are not the Veda. It is true that there is a widespread belief that compilation (for instance, *agnimīḷa purohitam*) of *mantra*s, letters and words is the Veda and this Vedic Śabdaśāstra is not the creation of any person, but is divine and eternal. It is true that there is some truth in this divine nature of the *śabdātmaka* (literal) Vedaśāstra.

---

1 *Āgama vidyā* and *nigama vidyā* are two principal types of knowledge (*vidyā*) which have always existed and are not created. *Āgama vidyā* emanates from Śiva and *nigama vidyā* from Brahmā.

The Basic Essence

The real meaning of the word *veda* is "basic essence" (and not knowledge contained in the books referred to earlier). These books are called the Vedas because they explain the basic phenomenon of Creation. Just as a book on electricity may be titled "Electricity" but in essence it is just a book and not the scientific phenomenon of electricity. Similarly, the Vedic texts are a treatise on the *veda-tattva* and they are not the Veda, a fact which has eluded the attention of the Indian thinkers for many centuries.

Therefore, there has been considerable confusion in understanding the meaning of the Vedas and analysing the *veda-tattva*. It is my intention to remove this misconception about the Vedas first and follow it with an elucidation of *agni-soma vidyā* related to the Vedic Saṁvatsara *yajña*.

What is the idea behind the term *tattvātmaka veda*? The *ṛṣi*s followed a special method, or say the everlasting method of use and construction of words. When *ṛṣi*s used a particular word for a specific phenomenon, idea or thought, the construction of that word was such that the definition and meaning of the phenomenon, thought or idea became self-explanatory and no other reference was required to understand the meaning of the word.

Thus, the answer to the question "What is Veda?" is inherent in the word *veda* itself, as will be explained later.

Self-explanatory Words

To explain this specific system of construction of words used by the *ṛṣi*s, the word *hṛdayam* can be taken as an example. This word is known to all. It is not *hṛdaya* as commonly understood, it is *hṛdayam*. There are three letters in it – one is *hṛ* and another *da* and the third is *yam*. Though there are many *varṇa*s (vowels) in this word, according to Prātiśākhya principles,[2] there are only three *akṣara*s (letters). The first letter *hṛ* is derived from the well-known *hṛ harṇe* root of Sanskrit grammar. The second letter *da* is derived from *da avakhaṇḍane* and *yam* becomes the *niyāmaka* of both. *Hṛ* means ingress, inflow, to gather together; *da* means egress, outflow, scattering away and *yam* means regulating or controlling.

The Three Motions

To explain further, the force which gathers together or intakes is called *hṛ*, the force which throws out, outflows, is called *da* and the force which

[2] Prātiśākhyas are manuals of precise and consistent pronunciation of words.

regulates these two forces in all-pervasive manner is known as *yam*. The force which functions as a base for the forces of inflow, outflow and all these three forces put together is known as *hṛdayam*.[3]

In the Vedas, the technical term for the outflowing force is *prāṇan* and the technical term for the inflowing force is *apānan*. Coming in is *apānan*, going out is *prāṇan*. Going from the centre towards the circumference is *prāṇan*; this is outflow. Coming from the circumference towards the centre is inflow, *apānan*. Going forward is *prāṇan*, coming backward is *apānan* and the central point where both of them are regulated is *niyāman*. This is the central *vyānan*.

न प्राणेन नापानेन मर्त्यो जीवति कश्चन।
इतरेण तु जीवन्ति यस्मिन्नेतावुपाश्रितौ॥ – *कठोपनिषद्* २.२.५

na prāṇena nāpānena martyo jīvati kaścana ।
itareṇa tu jīvanti yasminnetāvupāśritau ॥ – *Kaṭhopaniṣad* 2.2.5

ऊर्ध्वं प्राणमुन्नयति अपानं प्रत्यगस्यति।
मध्ये वामनमासीनं विश्वेदेवा उपासते॥ – *कठोपनिषद्* २.२.३

ūrdhvaṁ prāṇamunnyati apānaṁ pratyagasyati ।
madhye vāmanamāsīnaṁ viśvedevā upāsate ॥ – *Kaṭhopaniṣad* 2.2.3

The three words, *prāṇa*, *apāna* and *vyāna*, are well known. *Prāṇa* is *da* (द); *apāna* is *hṛ* (हृ) and *vyāna* is *yam* (यम्); and the integrated state of these triple *prāṇa*s is known as *hṛdayam*.

The Solar Sphere

Let us now draw our attention to the solar system. The entire solar sphere is simply a conflux of sunbeams. These sunbeams have thousandfold expressions and have thousand-dimensional brilliance. They are fastened together and regulated by the centre of the sun. This regulating force is *vyānan* and the same force comes into play while the sunbeams move outward. This is a serpentine motion. This is the inflow and outflow, indicative of *prāṇan* and *apānan*.

Draw a line between the sun-light and shade, you will see that the light projected by the sun's rays moves backward and then moves forward. Going back is *apānan* and moving forward is *prāṇan*. He, who cannot get back, cannot move forward. Rooted firmly on the central *vyāna* – the present – a man is successful in creating the future *prāṇan*.

---

[3] *Hṛdayam* literally means heart but in Vedic science terminology, it has a different meaning.

If he were to base himself between *prāṇan* and *apānan*, there would naturally be chaos. To illustrate, the axle of a railway engine moves forward while moving backward and thus produces momentum. All motions are regulated by this *prāṇan–apānan* movement, inflow and outflow. Keeping this in view, *ṛṣi*s have said:

आयं गौः पृश्निरक्रमीदसदन्मातरं पुरः ।
पितरं च प्रयन्त्स्वः ॥ १॥

अन्तश्चरति रोचनास्य प्राणादपानती ।
व्यख्यन्महिषो दिवम् ॥ २॥

त्रिंशद्धाम वि राजति वाक्पतङ्गाय धीयते ।
प्रति वस्तोरह द्युभिः ॥ ३॥ – ऋ० १०.१८९.१-३

āyaṁ gauḥ pṛśnirakramīdasadanmātaraṁ puraḥ ।
pitaraṁ ca prayantsvaḥ ॥1 ॥

antaścarati rocanāsya prāṇādapānati ।
vyakhyanmahiṣo divam ॥2 ॥

triṁśaddhāma vi rājati vākpataṅgāya dhīyate ।
prati vastoraha dyubhiḥ ॥3 ॥ – *ṚV* X.189.1-3

This moving many-coloured (sun) has arrived, he has sat down before his mother (earth) in the east, and advances to his father, heaven. His radiance penetrates internally, drawing (the air) down (through the lungs) after having sent it up, the mighty one beholds the sky. The thirty stations of the day and night shine with (the sun's) rays, the voice (of praise) is addressed to the sun.

Gāyatrī-Vidyā: A Meaningful Narrative

This inflow–outflow action has been clearly analysed in the well-known *gāyatrī-vidyā*. Vital forces with the characteristics of *agni* (*prāṇātmaka agneya annād dharma devatā*s) felt that they would not be able to maintain themselves in their real form unless some *soma* was poured into them as fuel. The *soma* was kept far away from the *devatā*s in the third *dyauloka*, which is even higher than the sun and is known as *parameṣṭhi*. This *soma* was guarded in *parameṣṭhi* by the mighty *vāyu* and *gandharva*s, who were in the form of *āpya-prāṇa* (vital forces of water).

The *devatā*s wanted to bring *soma* to the earth. The four-legged Jagatī said, "I shall kidnap *soma*". Jagatī went there only with *prāṇat* motion and due to this weakness she lost her three legs at the hands of *gandharva*s who were guarding *soma* and came back disappointed. Then the four-legged Triṣṭup went on the same mission. She was going with both *prāṇan* and *apānan*; but due to the gravitational force of *antarikṣa* (interspace), *apānan* could not be explicitly manifested. As a result, Triṣṭup lost one leg and came back disappointed.

Then Gāyatrī started with both motions in a serpentine way. The *gandharvas* of *parameṣṭhi* could not face the force of Gāyatrī. She swooped down on them, abducted *soma* and brought with her the lost legs of Jagatī and Triṣṭup. When the three-legged Triṣṭup came and demanded her fourth leg, Gāyatrī said, "It has become a part of me and if you wish, you too can merge in me". Triṣṭup of three letters (*akṣara*) merged in Gāyatrī of eight letters. The latter became eleven-lettered. And similarly, when the one-legged Jagatī merged with Gāyatrī, she became twelve-lettered. This narrative of the abduction of *soma* explains and analyses many basic phenomena of Creation in an indirect manner through the medium of *chandas* (metres) called Gāyatrī, Triṣṭup and Jagatī. This has been explained in detail in the Brāhmaṇa books, thus *etaddha sauparṇamākhyānamākhyānaviddha*.

Eight Categories of Narratives

This seemingly mysterious but meaningful narrative of the Vedaśāstra related to Gāyatrī has been detailed in the Purāṇas in the form of "Kadrū–Vinatā" narrative. The believers present here must be aware of the narrative related to the rivalry between Kadrū, mother of snakes, and of Vinata, mother of Garuḍa (falcon). Such narratives have been called in the Paurāṇic language as *asadākhyāna* (unreal) narratives.

The Paurāṇic narratives are divided into eight categories – *ādhyātmika* (related to body, with self as the base), *ādhibhautika* (physical), *ādhidaivika* (vital), *ādhyātmika–ādhidaivika* (vital and physical combined together), *ādhyātmika–ādhibhautika* (material and physical), *ādhidaivika–ādhyātmika–ādhibhautika* and *asat* (unreal).

The Kadrū–Vinatā narrative (in the *Mahābhārata*) falls under the eighth "non-real" category. Creative narrative is non-real narrative. In your favourite language, perhaps this is called mythology, which means apocryphal knowledge or narrative.

The *ṛṣis* had realized, with their foresight, that the fundamental history of man could never be permanently written on paper and therefore in their desire to make the history of human culture permanent, they inscribed it on the sheets of rivers, mountains and stars. Rivers and rivulets became the medium of historical events of a common nature, mountains became the medium of historical events and stars became the medium of the most preservable part of our history.

Please remember that the history of Indian culture is written on rivers, mountains and stars. The records of the eternal and permanent culture are also eternal and permanent. This is why despite many invaders throwing precious books of this land into fire, the Indian culture has remained alive through the medium of narratives connected with these rivers, mountains and stars, and will continue to exist as long as the sun and the moon exist. There is no doubt that a fountain of immortality protects the Indian culture and therefore it will continue to exist despite forbidding odds.

Apocryphal Narratives

Here is an example of a mythological narrative. For some reason, Ṛṣi Viśvāmitra said: "Go, turn into a river" and she turned into a river. That cursed river is Gaṇḍakī. This incident has been related to a river simply to keep it alive in our memories. Similarly, Dhruva, son of King Uttānapāda, has no link to the *dhruva* (Pole Star). Even then this narrative has been related to the Pole Star.

You may question the need for such creative stories. Why cannot these *tattvas* (fundamentals) be explained in plain and simple language? The reply is clear. Everyone is not equally intelligent or perceptive. Most of us are endowed with common intelligence and can only understand the truth through the medium of narratives – प्रजापतिर्वै स्वां दुहितरमभ्यध्यायत्-दिवं वा, उषसमित्यन्ये (*prajāpatirvai svāṁ duhitaramabhyadhyāyat-divaṁ vā, uṣasamityanye*). How easily this quotation explains the astronomical system is something which only the devotees of this science can realize.

While explaining this non-real medium of instruction, Bhagavān Bhartṛhari has said:

> उपायाः शिक्षमाणानां बालानामुपलालनाः ।
> असत्ये वर्त्मनि स्थित्वा ततः सत्यं समीहते ॥ – *वाक्यपदीय*
>
> *upāyāḥ śikṣamāṇānāṁ bālānāmūpalālanāḥ* ।
> *asatye vartmani sthitvā tataḥ satyam samīhate* ॥ – *Vākyapadīya* 2.238

Geographers and meteorologists use the medium of globes, maps and charts to explain geographical and astronomical realities, and if intelligent people like you were to use such methods, what offence has the Purāṇas committed? Try to comprehend the situation deeply.

Veda: The Scientific Meaning

While explaining the inflowing and outflowing motions in relation to the word *hṛdayam*, it was explained that such Vedic words contain their meaning within themselves. The same principle applies to the word *veda*.

According to the rules of grammar, the *dhātu* (root) *vid* means knowing, existence and *rasa* (vital essence). Knowledge is consciousness (*cit*), is bliss (*ānanda*) and existence is reality (*sat*). Put together they become *saccidānanda*: this is Veda, this is Vidyā, this is Brahmā. This is the meaning and definition of the word *veda*.

Now your attention is being drawn to the functional meaning which clearly explains the true meaning of "Veda". This *mantra* is from *Taittirīya Brāhmaṇa* 3.12.9.1:

ऋग्भ्यो जातां सर्वशो मूर्तिमाहुः-
सर्वा गतिर्याजुषी हैव शश्वत्।
सर्वं तेजः सामरूप्यं ह शश्वत्-
सर्वं हेदं ब्रह्मणा हैव सृष्टम्॥

ṛgbhyo jātāṁ sarvaśo mūrtimāhuḥ-
sarvā gatiryājuṣī haiva śasvat ।
sarvaṁ tejaḥ sāmarūpyaṁ ha śaśvat
sarvaṁ hedaṁ brahmaṇā haiva sṛṣṭam ॥

All that is *mūrti* (solid), all that has a form is born of *Ṛk-tattva*. Solidity, shape, substance and physical matter – these are the functional definitions of the word *mūrti*. In the *Praśnopaniṣad*, it is pointed out that *rayi* is *mūrti* (*tasmānmūrtireva raiyiḥ*). The contracting *soma* which pours itself into *prāṇāgni* (vital fire) by converting into solid shape is *Ṛk*. And on this basis, *śruti* has accepted *rayisoma* also as *mūrti*. Vedic science defines *rayisoma* as *asmāsoma*.

The matter is divided into three categories – *dhruvāsi*, *dhartramasi* and *dharuṇamasi* (*Yajur Saṁhitā* 1.18). Dhruva is solid, *dhartra* is liquid and *dharuṇa* is vapour. The two basic elements constituting the universe, *bhṛgu* and *aṅgirā*, turn themselves into *āpaḥ* (liquid), *vāyu* (air), *soma* and *agni*. The physical solid is constituted by the interaction of *dhruvasoma* and *dhruvāgni*. As we have forgotten the Vedic scientific tradition, a well-known course book of Sanskrit is committing the mistake of accepting the fluidity of water as a permanent property while water actually turns into snow when *dhruvāgni* enters it, and turns into liquid when *dhartrāgni* enters and becomes vapour when *dharuṇāgni* acts on it. In the Vaiśeṣika philosophy of Ṛṣi Kaṇāda, he has thrown light on some of the definitions of the science of matter. It has been pointed out in the *Vaiśeṣikasūtra*:

अपां संघातो विलयनं च तेजः संयोगात्।

apāṁ saṁghāto vilayanaṁ ca tejaḥ saṁyogāt ।

How did the Nyāya theory accept that the liquid property of water is permanent? It is these characteristics which make Sanskrit superior to other languages. But, alas! it remains neglected in present times.

The most serious allegation levelled against Sanskrit today is that it is a language which needs cramming and that it is non-scientific, and is almost a dead language. It is true that you have to memorize a lot in Sanskrit. But this question may be put impertinently, whether a language in which one has to cram letters also along with words is more difficult and terse than a language where only full words are required to be memorised. In other languages, you have to memorize even the letters. As far as the scientific content of the language is concerned, we have no right to say anything about it because we have forgotten the scientific definitions of our language due to our foolishness in the course of the last many centuries.

From the point of view of philology, perhaps there is no other language in the whole world which is so meaningful, lucid and clear. Without the knowledge of technical terms, Hindi is also no less difficult. If you are in an English town and ask for *lāla mircī* (red chilli), can anyone understand you? We have gone far away from Sanskrit and that is why the thoroughly scientific and easy language appears to be difficult.

तत्संस्कृतं किमपि जङ्गमधामशुद्धं-
यत्राधिदेव इव वेदपुमान् विभाति।

tatsaṁskṛtaṁ kimapi jaṅgamadhāmaśuddhaṁ-
yatrādhideva iva vedapumān vibhāti ।

This is a language which has been eulogized in these words; it contains the treasure of knowledge and science, the Vedaśāstra. To forget such a language is to forget one's own existence. Who will not be attracted towards a language which is the mother of all languages and which has been praised by *ṛṣi*s as Sarasvatī, which is really full of *rasa* from all sides?

Perhaps due to our love for Sanskrit, we have digressed a little. I was pointing out that all forms or solids in this universe are made from the *Ṛgveda*. The element of motion in every solid, which is composed of the inflow, is born of the *Yajurveda*. The solid itself has no independent existence of its own. As long as there is motion in the solid, it remains in that form. As soon as the motion is put at rest, the form of solid fritters away (सर्वा गतिर्याजुषी हैव शश्वत् – *sarvā gatiryājuṣī haiva śaśvat*). The *mantras* elucidate the concept of motion related to the *Yajurveda*.

The third sentence is सर्वं तेजः सामरूप्यं ह शश्वत् (*sarva tejaḥ samarūpyaṁ ha śaśvat*). A little intelligence is necessary to understand the literal meaning of this portion of the *mantra*. It is a common belief that it is the solid which we see in front of us. But in reality, it is not so. The *piṇḍa* (mass) can only be touched, it can never be seen. That which we see, we cannot touch. That which we are touching, we cannot see. We see the envelope which is the diffused projection of vital light around the mass.

In modern Indian philosophical discourse, there is a heated debate regarding the eyes. This debate is referred to as *prāpyakartva* vs *aprāpyakartva*. This debate is essentially childish or dogmatic. The question is – whether our eyes reach the object of sight or the objects "come to" our eyes? After raising this question, philosophers have reached the conclusion that while ears, nose and skin remain at their own places and subjects of hearing, smelling and speech reach these organs. In the case of eyes, the situation is the opposite. The objects do not approach the eyes, rather it is the sight which approaches the object.

It is obvious that from the point of view of Vedaśāstra, this philosophical proposition has no significance. Neither the eyes approach the object nor does the object approach the eyes. In reality, the envelope of beams around the sphere of a particular form enters the envelope of the eyes and results in the consciousness of the object. Therefore, the controversy regarding the eyes in the Vedic philosophy is irrelevant.

Why did this philosophical controversy start in this scientific country? The reason is obvious. The conceptions of the *Ṛk* and *Sāma* related to the touchable mass and visible envelope were forgotten completely in the philosophical age. Philosophers have considered the Vedas only as a means for worship.

The touchable mass is different from the visible envelope. Here is an instance to elaborate the point. The planet on which we live, move and exist is called *bhūpiṇḍa* (earth). Whenever the Purāṇaśāstra analyses the science of Creation, it is *pṛthvī*, not *bhūpiṇḍa*, which becomes the focal point. In the world of Vedic science, *bhūpiṇḍa* and *pṛthvī* are entirely different entities – *bhūpiṇḍa* is the planet on which we are sitting and moving, and *pṛthvī maṇḍala* (sphere) is that thousandfold *prāṇātmaka* (vital) envelope which emanates from this *bhūpiṇḍa* in all directions and is believed to have its sphere a little above the sun.

The sun is known as the chariot of *devatā*s. Since the envelope of the earth transcends this chariot of the sun, the outer limit of the sphere of earth's envelope is called *rathāntara-sāma* (that which exceeds the chariot). The Purāṇas say that the sun is situated in the Puṣkar island of the earth. Does it mean that the sun is situated on some island of this earth? Definitely not. It must be conceded, therefore, that *bhūpiṇḍa* is a different entity from *pṛthvī*. The *prāṇāgni*, which keeps this earth as the centre and remains attached to it and makes for itself an independent envelope of beams of *prāṇa*, is called *pṛthvī* due to its expanded sphere. This is also clear from the break-up of the word *pṛthvī* itself (यद्प्रथयत् तस्मात् पृथिवी – *yadaprathayat tasmāt pṛthivī*). This envelope of *pṛthvī-prāṇa* is *sāma* and the science related to it is called *sāma-vidyā*, which has also been called in various contexts as *punaḥpada-vidyā* and *artha-vidyā*.

The sharp and subtle envelope of *prāṇa*-beams emanating from every mass of matter is called the *Sāmaveda*. Or to express it differently, the *Sāmaveda* is the creation of this outer enveloping exterior. As the envelope goes on increasing, the appearance (to our sight) of the mass becomes gradually reduced because the distance of the two points on the two sides of the centre of the mass gets reduced. But this is a subtle process which cannot be explained in this general lecture.

The appearance of form (*mūrti-bhāva*) as a result of the *sāma maṇḍala* goes on becoming smaller as we recede away from a man and that is why the envelope around the man appears to us as smaller. Why does an object appear bigger from near and smaller from a distance? The only reason for this phenomenon is the *Ṛk* related to the mass and the *Sāma* related to the envelope thereof. Every mass of matter is *ṛk mūrti* and the vital envelope of the mass of matter is *prāṇātmaka*, is *sāma*. The sages have, therefore, said: सर्वं तेजः सामरूप्यं ह शश्वत् (*sarvaṁ tejaḥ sāmarūpyaṁ ha saśvat*).

The subject of sight is neither the *Ṛgveda*, which is mass, nor the *Yajurveda* which is motion, it is the *Sāmaveda* which is the subject of sight. That is why while narrating the divine qualities, Bhagavān Vāsudeva-Kṛṣṇa enunciated the following principle in the *Bhagavadgītā* – वेदानां सामवेदोऽस्मि (*vedānāṁ sāmavedo 'smi*). It does not mean that *Ṛk* and *Yaju* are inferior to *Sāma*.

Which is that factor which helps in the projection of the *Ṛgveda* (signifying mass), the *Yajurveda* (signifying motion) and the *Sāmaveda* (signifying envelope)? Only this question remains to be answered. Explaining this question, *ṛṣi*s have said: सर्वं ह्येदं ब्रह्मणा हैव सृष्टम् (*sarvaṁ hyedaṁ brahmaṇā haiva sṛṣṭam*). The technical and meaningful word *brahmā* here means the *Atharvaveda*. The *atharva-tattva* belongs to *parameṣṭhi-loka* and is considered to be the elder (son) of Svayambhū.

Brahmā, in *vijñāna* tradition, is *somātmaka* while the *Ṛgveda*, signifying form, is related to *agni*, the *Yajurveda*, signifying motion, is related to *vāyu* and the *Sāmaveda*, signifying envelope, is related to *āditya*. The term *āditya* can be freely translated as the sun. But it must be specially borne in mind that the *Sāma* is related to *āditya* and not *sūrya* (sun). In scientific terminology, *sūrya* and *āditya* are not synonymous; while *sūrya* is alone and single, the *āditya-prāṇa* is divided into twelve parts as is clear from the following *mantra*:

> इन्द्रो-धाता-भगः-पूषाः-मित्रोऽथ-वरुणोऽर्य्यमा ।
> अंशुर्विवस्वान्-त्वष्टा च, सविता-विष्णुरेव च ॥
>
> *indro-dhātā-bhagaḥ-pūṣāḥ-mitro 'tha-varuṇo 'ryyamā* ।
> *aṁśurvivasvān-tvaṣṭā ca, savitā-viṣṇureva ca* ॥

In this connection here is another quotation from *Manusmṛti* 1.23:

> अग्नि-वायु-रविभ्यस्तु त्रयं ब्रह्म सनातनम् ।
> दुदोह यज्ञसिद्ध्यर्थं ऋग्-यजुः-सामलक्षणम् ॥
>
> *agni-vāyu-ravibhyastu trayaṁ brahma sanātanam* ।
> *dudoha yajñasiddhyarthaṁ ṛg-yajuḥ-sāmalakṣaṇam* ॥

The literal meaning of this quotation is this:

> For the fulfilment of *yajña*, for giving *yajña* its shape, Prajāpati Brahmā has milched the *Ṛk*, *Yaju* and *Sāma* from *agni*, *vāyu* and *āditya* and has also milched Sanātana Brahmā or the *Atharva*.

The *Atharva* or *Brahmāveda* has been called Subrahmā in the *Gopatha Brāhmaṇa* and it is the *Sāmaveda*. When these are offered as oblation three times, the *Agniveda* or the *agni-somātmaka yajña* is completed. The *Ṛk* that is *agni*, the *Yajur* that is *vāyu* and the *Sāma* that is *āditya*, these three are called the triadic Vedas. How long can the three Vedas keep their own form intact? The answer is – as long as the oblation of Soma Brahmā continues in them. Please keep in mind that through the medium of these Vedas, we are approaching the *agni-soma vidyā*.

Are the Vedic books the Veda? Even now if you are not satisfied, here is another quotation which clearly points to the real meaning of the three Vedas. Explaining the subtle and mysterious science of *agni*, Bhagavān Yājñavalkya says:

> यदेतन्मण्डलं तपति। तन्महदुक्थं, ता ऋचः। स ऋचां लोकः। अथ यदेतदर्चिर्दीप्यते तन्महाव्रतं, तानि सामानि, स साम्नां लोकः। अथ य एष एतस्मिन्मण्डले पुरुषः-सोऽग्निः, तानि यजूंषि, स यजुषां लोकः। सैषा त्रय्येव विद्या तपति। तद्धैतदप्यविद्वाँस आहुः – 'त्रयी वा एषा विद्या तपति' – इति॥ – शत॰ब्रा॰ १०.५.२.१-२
>
> *yadetanmaṇḍalaṁ tapati । tanmahdukthaṁ, tā ṛcaḥ । sa ṛcāṁ lokaḥ । atha yadetadarcirdīpyate tanmahāvrataṁ tāni sāmāni, sa sāmnāṁ lokaḥ । atha ya eṣa etasminmaṇḍale puruṣaḥ-so 'gniḥ, tāni yajūṁṣi, sa yajuṣāṁ lokaḥ । saiṣā trayyeva vidyā tapati । taddhaitadapyavidvāṁsa āhuḥ – 'trayī vā eṣā vidyā tapati' – iti* ॥ – *ŚataBrā* 10.5.2.1-2
>
> This solar envelope which is afire is *mahaduktha*. They are *ṛcā*s, this is the place of *ṛcā*. This splendour of beams shining around this is *mahāvrata*. This is the *Sāma*, this is the abode of the *Sāma*. This *puruṣa* (in the form of motion), having abode in the form and envelope both, is *agni* and this is the *Yaju*, and this is the world of the *Yaju*. The learned know this mystery. Even ordinary uneducated villagers (of that age) knew that the sun was the conflux of the three *vidyā*s – the Veda.

This is the literal meaning of the *mantra*. It would, however, require another volume to explain the basic and essential meaning of this *mantra*.

If we were to keep in mind the part of the *śruti mantra* which says that even the ordinary people of that age knew this subtle mystery, we could see the lamentable state to which we have fallen. Even the common people knew, due to their traditions and their influence on their mind, that *sūrya* (sun) was three Vedas combined into one. Today even the scholars are unaware of this basic knowledge.

If *agnimīḷa purohitam* – letters, words and sentences – mean the *Sūryaveda*, does it mean that the Vedic books are afire in form, envelope and motion? Let us close our eyes and try to comprehend the proposition in our mind. This *tattvātmaka veda* has not been produced or made by any man, it is a divine *tattva* (phenomenon) and therefore there is no doubt that this is divine and eternal.

As far as the Vedic books are concerned, Bhagavān Kaṇāda's statement – बुद्धिपूर्वा वाक्यकृतिर्वेदे (*buddhipūrvā vākyakṛtirvede*) – should suffice. These Vedic books not only offer a rational explanation and elaboration of the basic Vedic phenomenon, as we have pointed out earlier, these Vedic books are also reflective creations of the Veda. The *tattva* and Veda have become inseparable. This inseparability is related to the faultless vision of the *ṛṣi*s who saw and realized the fundamental Veda themselves. This inseparable relationship is like that of a word and its meaning. Bhagavān Jaimini, creator of Pūrva-Mīmāṁsā Darśana, has equated the Vedic books with *veda-tattva*, which is clear from the following quotation:

> औत्पत्तिकस्तु शब्दस्यार्थेन सम्बन्धस्तस्य ज्ञानमुपदेशोऽव्यतिरेकश्चार्थेऽनुपलब्धे तत्प्रमाणं बादरायणस्य-अनपेक्षत्वात्। – पूर्व०मी०सू० १.१.५
>
> *autpattikastu śabdasyārthena sambandhastasya jñānamupadeśo 'vyatire-kaścārthe 'nupalabdhe tatpramāṇam bādarāyaṇasya-anapekṣatvāt* ।
> – *PūMīSū* 1.1.5

While saying on the one hand that *buddhipūrvā vākyakṛtir*, how does the Indian intellect believe the Vedaśāstra to be divine and superhuman. This question is connected with the intellect called *brāhmī-prajña* as enunciated in the following *mantra*s:

> अचिन्त्याः खलु ये भावा न तांस्तर्केण योजयेत्।
> प्रकृतिभ्यः परं यच्च तदचिन्त्यस्य लक्षणम्॥
>
> आविर्भूतप्रकाशानामनभिप्लुतचेतसाम्।
> ये भावा, वचनं तेषां नानुमानेन बाध्यते॥
>
> अतीन्द्रियानसंवेद्यान् पश्यन्त्यार्षेण चक्षुषा।
> अतीतानागतज्ञानं प्रत्यक्षान्न विशिष्यते॥ – महा०, भीष्म पर्व ५.१२.१-३
>
> *acintyāḥ khalu ye bhāvā na tāṁstarkeṇa yojayet* ।
> *pṛakṛtibhyaḥ paraṁ yacca tadacintyasya lakṣaṇam* ॥
>
> *āvirbhūtaprakāśānāmanabhiplutacetasām* ।
> *ye bhāvā, vacanaṁ teṣāṁ nānumānena bādhyate* ॥
>
> *atīndriyānasaṁvedyān paśyantārṣeṇa cakṣuṣa* ।
> *atītānāgatajñānaṁ pratyakṣānna viśiṣyate* ॥
> – *MBh*, Bhīṣma Parva 5.12.1-3

On the basis of the discussion we have had so far, we have reached the conclusion that the four Vedas, viz. the *Ṛk*, *Yaju*, *Sāma* and *Atharva*, are in essence *agni*, *vāyu*, *āditya* and *soma*. Amongst them the first *agni-vidyā* is *ṛg-vidyā* and the *śāstra* which explains this is the *Ṛgveda*. The *vāyu-vidyā* is *yajur-vidyā* and the *śāstra* propounding it is the *Yajurveda*. The third *āditya-vidyā* is *sāma-vidyā* and the *śāstra* propounding it is the *Sāmaveda*. The fourth *soma-vidyā* is *atharva-vidyā* and the *śāstra* propounding it is the *Atharvaveda*.

The science of *agni* is *ṛg-vidyā* and the text dealing with this branch of science is the *Ṛgveda*. The science dealing with *vāyu* is *yajur-vidyā* and the book explaining this branch of science is the *Yajurveda*. The science of *āditya* is *sāma-vidyā* and the book dealing with this particular branch of Vedic knowledge is the *Sāmaveda*. The fourth science of *soma* is *atharva-vidyā* and the book explaining this science is the *Atharvaveda*.

The mass or form is a product of *agni* and the Veda which explains its nature is the *Ṛgveda*, this is the earthly Veda (*pārthiva-veda*). The Veda which explains the nature of *vāyu*, which causes liquidity and hence motion, is the *Yajurveda*. This is the Veda of the mid-region. The Veda which explains the nature of envelope or sphere, which is based on gaseousness, is the *Sāmaveda*. The *Sāmaveda* which keeps this triple *agni* in its form is the *Atharvaveda* and this is the Veda of *parameṣṭhi* and thus four *loka*s have been conceived for the four Vedas.

Could we have, engrossed in the world of our own imagination, ever conceived of this? Here is what the *ṛṣi*s say about it:

त्रयो वा इमे त्रिवृतो लोकाः। अस्ति वै चतुर्थो देवलोक आपः। प्रजापतिस्तपोऽतप्यत। स तपस्तप्त्वा प्राणादेव इमं लोकं, अपानादन्तरिक्षलोकं, व्यानादमुं लोकं प्राबृहत्। सोऽग्निमेवास्माल्लोकात् – वायुमन्तरिक्षलोकात् – आदित्यं दिवः – असृजत्। सोऽग्नेरेवर्चः, वायोर्यजूंषि, आदित्यात् सामानि – असृजत्। – *शाङ्खायन ब्राह्मण* ३.१०

trayo vā ime trivṛto lokāḥ। asti vai caturtho devaloka āpaḥ। prajāpatistapo 'tapyata। sa tapastaptvā prāṇādeva imaṁ lokaṁ, apānādāntarikṣalokaṁ, vyānādamuṁ lokaṁ prābṛhat। so 'agnimevāsmāllokāt – vāyumantarikṣalokāt – ādityaṁ divaḥ – asṛjat। so 'gnerevarcaḥ, vāyoryajūṁṣi, ādityāt sāmāni – asṛjat।

– *Śāṅkhāyana Brāhmaṇa* 3.10

The three Agni Vedas – *Ṛk*, *Yaju* and *Sāma* – which are in the nature of *agni*, *vāyu* and *āditya*, swallow the fourth *Atharvaveda* which is the form of *soma* and hence in the nature of fuel. Thus the first three remain important. It is on this basis that the *trisatyavad* (principle of triple truth) based on the *tritattva* (triple elements) of the Veda is propounded.

The *ātmā* of man, inspired by the *prāṇātmaka* core of fire, conceives truth on the basis of this ternary (triadic) nature. According to *sakṛdiva vai pitaraḥ* (सकृदिव वै पितरः), *somya pitṛ* are conceivable in one effort only. The *āgneya deva* can be conceived only by threefold effort. The threefold *śāntipāṭha*, threefold *ācamana*, threefold *sandhyā*, all are based on these triadic *devatā*s. Even in courts, a man is called out thrice. That is why it is said: आत्मा उ एकः सन्नेतत् त्रयम्, त्रयं सदेकमयमात्मा (*ātmā u ekaḥ sannetat trayam,* *trayaṁ sadekamayamātmā* – These three – action, body and self – are all one – *Bṛhadāraṇyaka Upaniṣad* 1.4.3). It is on the basis of this divine truth that Mr President has planned this three-day programme.[4]

Please refresh your memory about the term *hṛdayam* referred to earlier, which is truthful and hence three-lettered.

The Ṛgvedic *agni* is earthly. The earth is just before you and near you. Only to point out this subtle mystery (of Ṛgvedic *agni*), the book conceiving this science commences with the *mantra* – अग्निमीळे पुरोहितं होतारं रत्नधातमम् (*agnimīḷe purohitaṁ hotāraṁ ratnadhātamam*)। *Purohitam* means "which is in front of you". By pointing out the word *purohitam, ṛṣis* are saying, "we are analysing the science of creation through the medium of earthly *ṛg-agni* in this *Ṛgveda*".

The inaugural *mantra* of the *Yajurveda* is as follows: इषे त्वोर्जे त्वा वायव स्थ देवो वः सविता प्रापयतु श्रेष्ठतमाय कर्म्मणे (*iṣe tvorje tvā vāyava stha devo vaḥ savitā prāpayatu śreṣṭhatamāya karmmaṇe*). It is clear that the word *vāyavastha* is directing our attention towards the basic element which is symbolized by the function of motion in the mid-region. The *āditya* is Sāmavedic, which is based in *dyauloka*, far from this earth. That is why the *Sāmaveda* starts with this *mantra*: अग्न आयाहि वीतये गृणानो हव्यदातये (*agna āyāhi vitaye gṛṇāno havyadātaye*). That which is far away is indicated by the word *āyāhi*.

Similarly, the 21-101-1000-9 branches of four Vedic books are parallel to branches of the basic *veda-tattva*. The *agni* has, by addition and subtraction, twenty-one spheres. According to the *prajāpatirekaśatavidha, vāyu* has 101 spheres. But, which *vāyu*? प्राणात्मक यजुः वायु (*prāṇātmaka yajuḥ vāyu*). Its original and actual form is *yajjū*, but in indirect language it is called *yaju*. I draw your attention towards this quotation from *śruti*:

> अयं वाव यजुः – योऽयं पवते। एष हि यन्नेवेदं सर्वं जनयति। एतं यन्तमिदमनु प्रजायते। तस्माद्वायुरेव यजुः। अयमेवाकाशो जूः – यदिदमन्तरिक्षम्। एतं ह्याकाशमनु जवते। तदेतत्-यजुर्वायुश्चान्तरिक्षञ्च। यच्च जूश्च। तस्माद्यजुः। तदेतत्-यजुर्ऋक्सामयोः प्रतिष्ठितम्। ऋक्सामे वहतः। – शत०ब्रा० १०.३.५.१-२
>
> *ayaṁ vāva yajuḥ – yo 'yaṁ pavate। eṣa hi yannevedaṁ sarvaṁ janayati। etaṁ yantamidamanu prajāyate। tasmādvāyureva yajuḥ। ayamevākāśo jūḥ – yadidamantarikṣam। etaṁ hyākāśamanu javate। tadetat-yajurvāyuścāntarikṣañca। yacca jūśca। tasmādyajuḥ। tadetat-yajurṛksāmayoḥ pratiṣṭhitam। ṛksāme vahataḥ।* – *ŚataBrā* 10.3.5.1-2

[4] The lectures were originally planned for three days but the President extended them by two more days.

It is clear that the Vedic books are not products of imagination, a belief widely held by the present-day Vedic scholars. Rather, the divisions of branches in the Vedic books are exactly in accordance with the division of branches in the basic phenomenon.

In the beginning, we have referred to the indirect approach and it was presented that the *devatā*s preferred the indirect approach and disliked the direct approach. Just a few words to explain this viewpoint.

The direct approach, which may also be termed blunt, is considered to be contrary to the Indian concept of etiquette. Be in daily life or in the spiritual world, a subtle and indirect approach has been preferred. Why? Because it is not only the lifeless matter which is worshipped here, along with matter, *prāṇa*s are also propitiated and worshipped. The *prāṇa-tattva* (vital element), which is the basis of the matter, is beyond concepts of form, taste, smell, touch and sound. Therefore, it is a very fine element and hence impossible to be realized by human physical organs. It exists, but does not occupy any space, and this *prāṇa-tattva* has been described in detail in the *Prāṇopaniṣad*, which is also called the *Praśnopaniṣad*.

For realizing and conceiving this *prāṇa-tattva*, which is the basis of all universe, the *ṛṣi*s have accorded prime importance to the indirect approach. That is why high-sounding external exclamations and craving for publicity has been given no place in the world of realization of this *tattva*. To remain engaged in studies alone, in private and with innermost conviction, has been the fundamental basis of life in our land.

The concepts of *agni*, *vāyu*, *āditya* and *soma* related to the *Ṛk*, *Yaju*, *Sāma* and *Atharva* are wholly *prāṇātmaka*. We have till now not referred to *bhūtāgni*, the fire with which we are well-conversant. The *bhūtāgni* or fire is that *agni* from which light comes after sunset and which has been called *vasvāgni*. This directly visible *bhūtāgni* has been referred to by the *ṛṣi*s in the following words:

अग्निं तं मन्ये तो वसुरस्तं यं यन्ति धेनवः ।
अस्तमर्वन्त आशवोऽस्तं नित्यासो वाजिन इषं स्तोतृभ्य आ भर ॥ – ऋ० ५.६.१

agnim̐ tam̐ manye to vasurastam̐ yam̐ yanti dhenavaḥ ।
astamarvanta āśāvo 'stam̐ nityāso vājin iṣam̐ stotṛbhya ā bhara ॥

– *ṚV* V.6.1

The *ṛṣi* says:

In our view, *bhūtāgni* is that which is Vāsu and which is related to the earthly material conception, and due to which the earthly sphere has been called *vasundharā* and from which rays emit after sunset. The *bhūtāgni*, which is visible to our eyes in the form of flames, is felt in the human body. It keeps the body warm and alive and is known as *vaiśvānarāgni*. Indians worship it daily.

It was customary among devout and cultured Indian women to offer some food to the flames, before the family ate – it symbolized *vaiśvānarāgni*. Nowadays, even the habit of taking food at home has become an exception. Wherever this tradition exists, the tradition of *vaiśvānarāgni* also continues.

What is the concept of this *vaiśvānarāgni*? Please pay attention.

In the Vedic definition, there are three *loka*s – *pr̥thvī*, *antarikṣa* (interspace) and *dyau*. In these three worlds, three *prāṇāgni*s, viz. *agni*, *vāyu* and *āditya*, related to the *R̥k*, *Yaju* and *Sāma*, are established. These three *prāṇāgni*s have been stated as the controllers, the foundation or the master of these three worlds, respectively. The technical Vedic word for this is *śavasonapāt*.

Bhū – this is the first world and this is the earth. *Bhuvaḥ* – this is the second world and this is interspace. *Svāhā* – this is the third world and this is *dyau*. The three vital *agni*s of the three worlds known as *agni*, *vāyu* and *āditya* interact, and these interactions are called the *tānunaptra* ritual. The act of taking mutual oath is called *tānunaptra* in the Vedas. It is on the strength of this that the *devatā*s defeated the *asura*s. Even in today's materialistic world, this method of taking oath is prevalent.

From the interaction of three *nara*s of three *loka*s emerges the *agni* which has the property of heat and is called Vaiśvānara. This has been analysed in detail in the science of Vaiśvānara. Of the Vedas: आ यो द्यां भात्यापृथिवीम् – वैश्वानरो यतते सूर्य्येण (*āyo dyāṁ bhātyāpr̥thivīm – vaiśvānaro yatate sūryyeṇa*) – this principle of *śruti* refers to the threefold characteristics of *vaiśvānarāgni* which pervades from the earth to the sun. There is a particular type of sound in the three worlds which is accepted as the latter stage of *nāda* and which is the mother of "word". It is that Vaiśvānara on the basis of which the principle of अग्निर्वाग् भूत्वा मुखं प्राविशत् (*agnirvāg bhūtvā mukhaṁ prāviśat* – Agni, representing speech, then entered the mouth – *Aitareya Upaniṣad* 1.2.4) is established and it is on this basis that Bhagavān Bhāṣyakāra has said: तस्माद् ध्वनिः शब्दः (*tasmād dhvaniḥ śabdaḥ* – therefore sound is speech).

In the physical bodily structure, the base is *bhū*, the stomach is *bhuvaḥ* and the chest is *svāhā*, and the fourth, head, is *parameṣṭhi-loka*. In the first three places, three vital forces – earthly *apāna*, mid-regional *vyāna* and the solar *prāṇa* – exist. They are respectively called *agni*, *vāyu* and *āditya*. Maharṣi Pippalāda said about them: प्राणाग्नय एवैतस्मिन्पुरे जाग्रति (*prāṇāgnaya evaitasminpure jāgrati* – *Praśnopaniṣad* 4.3). The material fire which emerges from the interaction of the three vital forces of the human body – *apāna*, *vyāna* and *prāṇa* – is the physical Vaiśvānara, which exists as a *uktha* (centre) in stomach, but as it beams it spreads through the whole body except in the short hairs and nail-ends. This *vaiśvānarāgni* can be felt by closing the nostrils and ears. A sound which is then heard inside the body is the sound of Vaiśvānara. And the heat which we feel wherever we touch is its manifestation in the form of touch. That is heard, this is seen,

अहं वैश्वानरो भूत्वा प्राणिनां देहमाश्रितः

ahaṁ vaiśvānaro bhūtvā prāṇināṁ dehamāśritaḥ ।

These words of *Bhagavadgītā* XV.14 explain the concepts of the *vaiśvānarāgni* of human body:

स यः स वैश्वानरः – इमे स लोकाः । इयमेव पृथिवी विश्वं, अग्निर्नरः । अन्तरिक्षमेव विश्वं, वायुर्नरः । द्यौरेव विश्वं, आदित्यो नरः । (विश्वेभ्यो नरेभ्यो जातः अग्निरेव यौगिको वैश्वानरः) । – शत०ब्रा० ९.३.१.३

sa yaḥ sa vaiśvānaraḥ – ime sa lokāḥ । *iyameva pṛthivī viśvaṁ, agnirnaraḥ* । *antarikṣameva viśvaṁ, vāyurnaraḥ* । *dyaureva viśvaṁ, ādityo naraḥ* । (*viśvebhyo narebhyo jātaḥ agnireva yaugiko vaiśvānaraḥ* । – *ŚataBrā* 9.3.1.3

स एष आधिदैविको वैश्वानराग्निः । अयमग्निर्वैश्वानरः – योऽयमन्तः पुरुषे (शरीरे प्रतिष्ठितः) । येनेदमन्नं पच्यते, यदिदमद्यते । तस्यैष घोषो भवति, यमेतत्कर्णावपिधाय शृणोति । स यदा –उत्क्रमिष्यन् भवति – नैतं घोषं शृणोति । – शत०ब्रा० १४.८.१०.१

sa eṣa ādhidaiviko vaiśvānarāgniḥ । *ayamagnirvaiśvānaraḥ – yo 'yamantaḥ puruṣe* (*śarīre pratiṣṭhitaḥ*) । *yenedamannaṁ pacyate, yadidamadhyate* । *tasyaiṣḥ ghoṣo bhavati, yametatkarṇāvapidhāya śṛṇoti* । *sa yadā – utkramiṣyan bhavati – naitaṁ ghoṣaṁ śṛṇoti* । – *ŚataBrā* 14.8.10.1

The first basis of *prāṇātmaka agni-soma* pair is *prāṇāgni* named *agni*, *vāyu* and *āditya* based on *ṛk*, *yaju* and *sāma*, and *sāma* and *atharva-soma*. Born of these *prāṇāgni* is *vaiśvānarāgni* and *bhūta-soma* in the form of earthly edibles which are of four types. This is the second pair of *agni–soma*.

The Vedic pair of *agni-soma* has been called the first *avatāra* (incarnation) of *agni-soma* and the pair of *vaiśvānarāgni* and *anna* (food) is called the second *avatāra* of *agni-soma* and the third *avatāra* based on the two is the *agni-soma* based on *saṁvatsara*, which is the crude physical third pair. This will be explained presently.

The *vaiśvānarāgni* born of the clashes of Vedic *prāṇāgni* – *agni*, *vāyu* and *āditya* – is further divided into three – *virāṭa*, *hiraṇyagarbha* and *sarvajña*. When *agni* is the fire and *vāyu* and *āditya* are the fuel, the threefold form is called Vaiśvānara. It is called *virāṭa* when *agni* dominates. When *vāyu* is the fire and *agni* and *āditya* the fuel, it is *hiraṇyagarbha*, and when *āditya* is the fire and *agni* and *vāyu* are the fuel, this Vaiśvānara is called *sarvajña*. The Virāṭa Vaiśvānara has 1,000 feet, Hiraṇyagarbha Vaiśvānara has 1,000 eyes and *sarvajña* has 1,000 heads.

त्रयो वा इमे त्रिवृतो लोकाः – त्रिवृदग्निः (*trayo vā ime trivṛto lokāḥ – trivṛdagniḥ*). *Śruti*s like these explain the threefold functioning of *agni*, *vāyu* and *āditya*. This has been further explained in the *Chāndogyopaniṣad* – तासां त्रिवृतं त्रिवृतामेकैकां करवाणि (*tāsāṁ trivṛtāṁ trivṛtāmekaikāṁ karavāṇi*). Each of the three is threefold. The only difference is this: in *virāṭa*, *agni* dominates; in *hiraṇyagarbha*, *vāyu* dominates and in *sarvajña*, *āditya* dominates. This can be explained further – *virāṭa* is the initiator of *artha* (matter of object), *hiraṇyagarbha* is the regulator of *kriyā* (activity or motion) and *sarvajña* is the centre of knowledge. Thus, based on the *vedāgni-soma* pair, the product of *agni*, *vāyu* and *āditya*, *vaiśvānarāgni* is the initiator of knowledge, activity and object (*jñāna*, *kriyā* and *artha*) and thus regulates the *adhyātma* and *ādhidaivata*. The residue of *agni*-dominated Vaiśvānara in the human body is Vaiśvānara; the residue of *vāyu*-dominated *hiraṇyagarbha* is called *tejas* and the residue of the *āditya*-dominated *sarvajña* is called Prajña. The vital truth in the form of the triadic *agni* – *virāṭa*, *hiraṇyagarbha* and *sarvajña* – is *Īśvara* of *jīva* and Vaiśvānara; *taijasa prajña* (vital truth) is the *jīva* of *Īśvara* which has been explained in तेन त्यक्तेन भुञ्जीथाः (*tena tyaktena bhuñjīthāḥ* – Having renounced all desires, have no desire for wealth. All belong to *ātman* (*ĪśaUp* 1)).

The natural vital truth in the form of triadic *agni* has been called Sākṣī Suparṇā and this has been called *Bhagavān* in the Vedic terminology and the *jaiva devasatya* in the form of the triadic *agni* is the Bhoktā Suparṇā and this is the *jīva* in the form of *bhagavad aṁśa* for which the ममैवांशो जीवलोके जीवभूतः सनातनः (*mamaivāṁśo jīvaloke jīvabhūtaḥ sanātanaḥ*) (*Bhagavadgītā* XV.7) principle has been established and this has been described in *śruti* in the following words:

द्वा सुपर्णा सयुजा सखाया समानं वृक्षं परि षस्वजाते।
तयोरन्यः पिप्पलं स्वाद्वत्त्यनश्नन्यो अभि चाकशीति॥ – ऋ० १.१६४.२०

dvā suparṇā sayujā sakhāyā samānaṁ vṛkṣaṁ pari ṣasvajāte ।
tayoranyaḥ pippalaṁ svādvattyanaśnanyo abhi cākaśīti ॥ –*ṚV* I.164.20

As far as the human intellect is concerned, perhaps nothing remains to be known by it except knowledge, action and essence related to intellect, mind and physical body. These in turn are related to *prajñā*, *tejas* and *vaiśvānara*. As all human efforts end in these functions of knowledge, action and object, man considers them to be the end point of his form.

The *Talavakāropaniṣad*, which is known as the *Kenopaniṣad*, also tries to remove this terribly mistaken notion of man. It has been related in this *Upaniṣad* that once upon a time, Agni, Vāyu and Indra (gods of knowledge, motion and object) became proud that this world was in their command – "We are absolute masters of all in this world". With the purpose of removing this sense of false pride, a *mahā-yakṣa* appears, which is actually *mahān*, a reflection of *cit*, the Avyaya Brahmā. He places a straw before them. *Agni* fails to burn it, *vāyu* fails to move it in the air and as soon as Indra arrives on the scene the straw disappears. The knowledgeable straw draws out Indra, which also has the same function in its sphere of envelope. At this stage a great power named Haimavatī Umā, who is full of *soma* and hails from *parameṣṭhi*, appears and tells the three: ब्रह्मणो वा विजये महीयध्वम् (*brahmaṇo vā vijaye mahīyadhvam*). This is not your victory, but it is due to the victory of Brahmā that you have become the conquerors of the world.

The basic and inherent meaning of this narrative is this: *agni-soma* is not supreme and the humanity of man does not end with the functions of knowledge, action and object. But the real man is expressed in his original form and fullness of *ātma-brahma*, which is beyond the intellect – Indra. Unless this *ātma-brahma* is there at the foundation, all the triple vital energies and all this physical world around us are of no use.

Those whom we call lifeless are predominated only by *vaiśvānarāgni* and are therefore called *ekātma jīva*, single functional bodies. Is there no knowledge or action in such beings? Without doubt, there is. According to ईशावास्यमिदं सर्वं यत् किञ्च जगत्यां जगत् (*īśāvāsyamidaṁ sarvaṁ yat kiñca jagatyāṁ jagat*), all are associated with the existence of Īśvara Brahma. Keeping in view this basic feeling, the *ṛṣi*s have used the words: "Oh, stones, please pay attention to our requests". Please keep this in view that it is not an ornamental or allegorical language, but a scientific language with inherent meaning. The allegories, ornamental and flowery expressions of language, came into vogue only during the Gupta Age. Do you know what the poetry of the Vedas is? Do you want to know the ornamental use of the language in it? Here it is:

विधुं दद्राणं समने बहूनां युवानं सन्तं पलितो जगार।
देवस्य पश्य काव्यं महित्वाद्या ममार स ह्यः समान॥ – ऋ० १०.५५.५

vidhuṁ dadrāṇaṁ samane bahūnāṁ yuvānaṁ santaṁ palito jagāra ।
devasya paśya kāvyaṁ mahitvādyā mamāra sa hyaḥ samāna ॥

– *ṚV* X.55.5

A new man, who had no trace in this world till now, is born in a happy and prosperous family with a new handsome artistic body. This child, in due course of time, becomes a stout and healthy young man with the help of the creator's artistic creations. This is the second era of prosperity. Just like a new poem of Prajāpati, this man, after some time, loses all his beauty and charm. His face becomes lifeless, mouth, teeth and skin become emaciated and dilapidated, and his backbone turns into an arch. One day, he disappears as if he was never on this stage of the world. And then he becomes ready for rebirth. This is the ever-flowing torrent of Prajāpati's poetry.

Could you create such astonishing, axiomatic, great and grand poetry? Bhṛgu is the poet who is the originator of this poetry of creation, which he does by combining *soma* with *agni* by the process of *yajña* and gathers them within his fold at the time of *sarga* (the process of creation). The main purpose of the great and grand Vedaśāstra of the *ṛṣi*s is to achieve victory over death, to achieve immortality on the basis of realization of this ever-changing, ever-beautiful poetry of life and death.

The superficial indulgence of mind and body, fashion, literature, music and art are in no way connected or related with that grand poetry. The language of the *ṛṣi*s, who defied death on the basis of the analysis of the great poetry of Prajāpati, is the *sāṁskṛtika-kavitā* (cultural ode) of this nation and not that poetry which is simply an artful use of words; it is an expression of emotions of one's own mind only. Those Vedic *ṛṣi*s, who gave the message of victory over death, should be accepted as *rāṣṭrīya* (national) poets of the land and not those poets who have been simply trying to gain name and fame by pleasing people. The Purāṇas, which depict the basic Indian culture integrating the *ātmā* (self), *buddhi* (intellect), *mana* (mind) and *śarīra* (body) will be respected in this country as real poetry, or the poetry of Vālmīki, who taught the Indian system of living based on Vedic concepts through the medium of Rāma, will be accepted as the poetry of the nation. That is why Vālmīki has been acclaimed as the first poet from the viewpoint of people's literature.

Mr President, pardon me for this reference to poetry; it may seem a digression. This speaker, who has become incoherent studying the Veda, is completely uninitiated in the latest methods of pleasing the audience in a conference. I have devoted myself completely to the study of the Vedas in isolation, as directed by the *ṛṣi*s and for such a person, harbouring any desire for name or fame is totally prohibited. The administrators of the institute have brought me face to face with Mr President, who is seated on the highest seat at the centre of our great nation. It is just to draw your attention towards this almost vanishing *ṛṣi* culture, which is scientific, systematic, non-communal and beneficial for mankind, that I have been audacious enough to express the feelings of my heart, although they might be a little irrelevant to the subject. The fact that the message of our culture is being delivered at such a place today, shows that it will definitely be possible to resurrect and rejuvenate this culture.

Coming back to our main subject, your attention was being focused on the sphere of the living articulated by *vaiśvānarāgni*.

Plants Have Life

Single functional lifeless beings were referred to by *śṛṇotu grāvāṇaḥ*. They are also known as *asaṁjña jīva*s. Herbs, vegetables and creepers have been defined as dual functional creatures and hence they have been termed as *antaḥsaṁjñā*.

> तस्माद् रुदन्ति पादपाः जिघ्रन्ति पादपाः, हसन्ति पादपाः, शृण्वन्ति पादपाः।
>
> *tasmād rudanti pādapāḥ, jighranti pādapāḥ, hasanti pādapāḥ, śṛṇvanti pādapāḥ* ।
>
> अन्तःसंज्ञा भवन्त्येते सुखदुःखसमन्विताः। – *मनु* 1.29
>
> *antaḥsaṁjñā bhavantyete sukhaduḥkhasamanvitāḥ* । – *Manu* 1.29

These quotations clearly illustrate that dual functional creatures like herbs continue to operate all functions of organs, as if in a dream, through their skin. It is due to the realization of this concept of consciousness in them that the Hindu culture reverentially says ओषधे त्रायस्व (*oṣadhe trāyasva* – Oh herbs! protect us).

On the basis of this understanding, unnecessary cutting of trees is also prohibited. According to the traditions of our culture, touching trees in the evening has been particularly prohibited. If an Indian, who says *śṛṇotu grāvāṇaḥ* or *oṣadhe trāyasva*, hits a tree with pieces of stones while walking or inflicts pain on trees and plants, he commits violence. His vital force trembles due to these activities. This cannot be observed by naked eyes. An Indian who keeps all living or lifeless matter at its proper place systematically is the true follower of the path of non-violence and it is on this basis that principle of मा कश्चिद् दुःखभाग्भवेत् (*mā kaścid duḥkhbhāg-bhavet*) has been enunciated; *ātmā* does not end at matter. Even a vain, purposeless action, purposeless walking, laughing, sleeping and talking, all purposeless, non-*śāstrīya* or imaginary activities, are included in this definition of non-violence, which is in no way related to imaginary non-violence. It is true that our people have been nearly-hypnotized by the use of words like non-violence and humanity but these terms are not used by their protagonists in their true sense.

Conduct against nature and *āśrama*s harms the order of vital force of nature and they in their turn cause disruptions in the *prāṇa* of nature and *aśrama*, and the conduct which harms the *prāṇa* of nature in turn disrupts the *prāṇa* of the individual. This concept of *prāṇa* is the concept of *ṛṣi* or the vital force and it is on this basis that elements like the sun, the moon, sky, air, sun's rays, herbs and vegetables are worshipped. The fact that the solar light removes coldness or that the lunar light soothes and cools a man and similar other material viewpoints are not reasons for such venerations, though some modern Indologists have let their imagination run riot on these lines. They have not understood the essence of the Indian outlook towards the worship of various gods.

In the *antaḥsaṁjñā* dual-functional herbs and vegetables, the property of motion based on *vāyu* is manifested along with the property of matter based on *agni*. The third group of the living is called *sasaṁjña*. The living being in which, along with *vaiśvānarāgni* and *tejas vāyu*, the *prajñā āditya* are also manifested and are known as *sasaṁjña jīva*. They are divided into five categories – worms, insects, birds, beasts and man. Does the sphere of the being end at these three groups – single functional (*asaṁjña*; consciousness, non-living), like clay stones; double-functional *antaḥsaṁjñā* (semi-consciousness), like herbs and *sasaṁjña* (conscious), like insects?

From the point of view of *agni*, the answer will be in the positive, but from the point of view of *soma*, the answer will be in the negative. These three groups are articulated by *agni*, *vāyu* and *āditya* in the form of *vaiśvānara*, *tejas* and *prajña*. The lunar *soma* is still to be considered.

The sphere of being related to *soma* is the fourth one, which has been subdivided into eight groups – *yakṣa, rākṣasa, piśāca, gandharva, aindra, prājāpatya, paitra* and *brāhma*. In the conscious earthly beings, eleven organs are dominant but in the lunar beings there are two organs, viz. eight *siddhi*s and nine *nidhi*s. Semi-conscious and unconscious beings have been grouped together because both of them are primarily dominated by *tamo-guṇa* and, therefore, this group has been called *tamo-viśāla* and the technical term used for this particular group is *stambhasarge*. The fivefold (*pārthiva*) earthly beings have been grouped together as all of them belong to the mid-region and their group is called *rajo-viśāla* and eightfold *sattva-viśāla*, the beings are divided into fourteen classes, as has been pointed out in the Sāṁkhyaśāstra – चतुर्दशविधोभूतसर्गः (*caturdaśavidhobhūtsargaḥ*). In these fourteen "physical" groupings, the unitary group, *tamo-viśāla*, is named Stambha of which there are two *asaṁjña* and *antaḥsaṁjñā* groups and five groups of worms, insects, beasts, birds and man are grouped together and are called *agni*-dominated beings and the eightfold lunar group is called *soma*. And thus in the second pair of *agni-soma* – *agni* – in the form of *agni, vāyu* and *āditya* and *soma* we find manifestation of fourteen kinds of *agni-somātmaka* beings.

End of the Material Sphere: Beginning of the Vital Sphere

Does the sphere of the beings end here? Undoubtedly the sphere of the beings and, therefore, the "material" world or the *bhūta* culminates at the fourteenfold being of triple *vaiśvānarāgni* and the lunar *soma*. The sphere which now commences is not that of the physical (*bhūta*), but of the *prāṇa*.[5] This is related to the solar *agni* and the *parameṣṭhi soma*, which is the base of the earthly *vaiśvānarāgni* and the lunar *soma*. According to त्रयस्त्रिंशद्वै सर्वे देवाः (*trayastriṁśadvai sarve devāḥ*), the *sūrya prāṇāgni* is divided into thirty-three categories. Beyond the sun, in *parameṣṭhi*, there are three *prāṇa*s – (1) *āpya-prāṇa*, (2) *vāyavya-prāṇa*, and (3) *saumya-prāṇa*. The *āpya-prāṇa* is demonic and is divided into 99 categories – thrice that of the *deva-prāṇa*s. The *vāyavya-prāṇa* is *gandharva*, which is also divided into many categories like *aṅghāri* and *bammāri*. *Saumya-prāṇa* are *pitṛ* which are divided into seven categories, like *ājyapā* and *somapā*. And here, the

[5] *prāṇa* – The word *prāṇa* has been incorrectly and unfortunately described as vital energy. It has a definite and different connotation. But for the purpose of this translation terms like "vital force" and "vital energy" have been used for convenience of readers.

sphere of *prāṇa* related to the first pair of *soma-agni* – *ṛk, yaju, sāma* and *atharva* – concludes.

Does the sphere of the *prāṇa* end at *parameṣṭhi*? No. One more sphere of *prāṇa* remains which is called the sphere of *svayambhū* from where the basic *vedātmaka* pair has originated.

The original basic *svayambhū-prāṇa* is *vāmapalita* and this is the basic sphere. This is called the sphere of *ṛṣi*s. We have heard the name of *ṛṣis*[6] like Vasiṣṭha, Viśvāmitra, Bharadvāja, Atri and Aṅgirā. They are actually *prāṇātmaka ṛṣi* elements. What is the form and concept of this *ṛṣi-tattva*? Explaining this difficult question, Mānava Maharṣi says:

विरूपास इद्दषयस्ता इद्गम्भीरवेपसः ।
ते अङ्गिरसः सूनवस्ते अग्नेः परि जज्ञिरे ॥ – ऋ० १०.६२.५

virūpāsa idṛṣayastā idgambhīravepasaḥ ।
te aṅgirasaḥ sūnavaste agneḥ pari jajñire ॥ – *ṚV* X.62.5

The Basic Question: What Was There, When There Was Nothing?

These *ṛṣi-prāṇa*s are divided into innumerable categories. In this connection, it is well known that a series of questions and answers had cropped up.

"What was there, when there was nothing?"

"What was there before this creation?"

Śruti answered, "Before this creation, there was *asat*" – *asat* means void. Then, does it mean that there was nothing before this creation. No, this *asat* does not denote void or absence of everything; rather it has a positive content and hence it is *tattvātmaka*.

The next question followed: "What was the form of that *asat*?" *Śruti* answered: "*Ṛṣi* was that element of *asat*". You may say this is like explaining one mystery by another and therefore naturally another question was put: "What was the form of *ṛṣi*?". Reply came forth: "*Prāṇa-tattva* was called *ṛṣi*". Now a glimpse into the meaning seems to be emerging. Things which have *prāṇa* are called *sat*. *Prāṇa* itself has no *prāṇa* and therefore it is called *asat*, which means pure *sat* itself. That is why at another place it is said: सदेवेदाग्रे सोम्य! असदासीत् कथमसतः सज्जायेत (*sadevedāgre somya*! *asadāsīt kathamasataḥ sajjāyeta* – "Oh! That *asat* was *sat* itself. Thus it is said").

Now only one question remains to be answered, "Why was the word

6 Incorrectly translated as sages.

ṛṣi used for this *prāṇa-tattva*?". Replying to this query, *śruti* says: "In view of the fact that this (*prāṇa-tattva*) vital force itself came into motion with the desire of creation, therefore, according to the derivation रिषति-गच्छति-गतिशीलो भवति (*riṣati-gacchati-gatiśīlo bhavati*), the *tattva* was called *ṛṣi*. Explaining the concept of this fundamentally basic *ṛṣi-prāṇa*, which is the initial cause of all causes of creation, *śruti* says:

> असद्वा इदमग्र आसीत्। तदाहुः – किं तदसदासीदिति? ऋषयो वाव तदग्रेऽसदासीत्। के ते ऋषयः? प्राणा वा ऋषयः। ते यत् पुरा-अस्मात् सर्वस्मात्-इदमिच्छन्तः श्रमेण-तपसा-अरिषन्-तस्मात्-ऋषयः। – शत०ब्रा० ६.१.१.१
>
> *asadvā idamagra āsīt* । *tadāhuḥ – kiṁ tadasadāsīditi? ṛṣayo vāva tadagresadāsīt* । *ke te ṛṣayaḥ? prāṇā vā ṛṣayaḥ* । *te yat purā-asmāt sarvasmāt-idamicchantaḥ śrameṇa-tapasā-ariṣan-tasmāt-ṛṣayaḥ* ।
> – *ŚataBrā* 6.1.1.1

This basic *ṛṣi-prāṇa* is divided into many categories like *ekarṣi* (one), *dvayarṣi* (two), *trayarṣi* (three) and *saptarṣi* (seven). These *ṛṣi-prāṇa*s have become the foundation of various aspects of creation – *ādhidaivata*, *ādhyātma* and *ādhibhūta* (vital, physical and material respectively).

For example, let us take a *saptarṣi-prāṇa* named *sākañja*. Two ears, two eyes, two nostrils and one mouth, there are seven "doors" in the portion of our body above the neck. Amongst them, eyes, ears and nose are twins, double; while the seventh – mouth is alone. The *indriya-prāṇa* which provides the basis of functions to these organs of body are called *saptarṣi-prāṇa* (seven *ṛṣi-prāṇa*s) as is obvious from the following Vedic *mantra*:

> साकञ्जानां सप्तथमाहुरेकजं षळिद्यमा ऋषयो देवजा इति।
> तेषामिष्टानि विहितानि धामशः स्थात्रे रेजन्ते विकृतानि रूपशः॥ – ऋ० १.१६४.१५
>
> *sākañjānāṁ saptathamāhurekajaṁ ṣaḷidyamā ṛṣayo devajā iti* ।
> *teṣāmiṣṭāni vihitāni dhāmaśaḥ sthātre rejante vikṛtāni rūpaśaḥ* ॥
> – *ṚV* I.164.15

What is this head? It seems as if a cup has been placed with its bottom upwards; eight *kapāla*s joined together have made this *mahā-kapāla*. It is lying upside down and the essence of the human body is filled in it. In the *yajña* language, this is called *puroḍāśa*. It is to free this from all ties and knots that in India the scientific system of *kapāla-kriyā* is performed after death. This *puroḍāśa* is called *sahasradala kamala* in Yogic language, *mastiṣka* in the language of medicine and *bhejā* in the colloquial dialect. It is from this *rasa* that all organs acquire their essence. On the sides of this "cup" named *camas*, lying upside down, the above-mentioned seven *ṛṣi-prāṇa*s are placed perfectly and it is this subtle mystery which has been explained in the following *mantra*:

अर्वाग्बिलश्चमस ऊर्ध्वबुध्नस्तस्मिन् यशो निहितं विश्वरूपम् ।
तस्यासत ऋषयः सप्त तीरे वागष्टमी ब्रह्मणा संविदाना ॥ – शत०ब्रा० १४.५.२.४

arvāgbilaścamasa ūrdhvabudhnastasmin yaśo nihitaṁ viśvarūpam ।
tasyāsata ṛṣayaḥ sapta tīre vāgaṣṭamī brahmaṇā saṁvidānā ॥
– *ŚataBrā* 14.5.2.4

Another reference in this connection will be relevant. This *rasātmaka* head which provides the basis for function of the organs is called *śrīḥ*. This is indirectly called *śiraḥ* (head). This *śriraḥ* has been well protected by Prajāpati and is covered from all sides. That is why in Indian culture, it is considered auspicious to cover one's head. The whole body, except the male organs, may be uncovered but the head must always remain covered. This is the auspicious tradition of our nation. Uncovered heads are considered inauspicious in our country. Writing *śrī* before commencing letters, *śrī* before reading or teaching; use of this *śrī* – a symbol of opulence and affluences – is a tradition of our country. But unfortunately this practice is being steadily given up by our people or they are being forced to drop it, due to repulsion from imaginary communalism.

We are at the moment discussing the concept of *prāṇa*. These *prāṇa*s are innumerable. *Prāṇa*, *udāna*, *vyāna*, *apāna* and *samāna* are five *prāṇa*s and the *prāṇa* located in the middle, viz. *vyāna*, has innumerable facets. This *vyāna* is divided into 72,000 *mudrā*s and is further expanded as is explained in the following:

शतं चैका हृदयस्य नाड्यस्तासां मूर्द्धानमभिनिःसृतैका ।
तयोर्ध्वमायन्नमृतत्वमेति विष्वङ्ङन्या उत्क्रमणे भवन्ति ॥ – छा०उप० ८.६.६

śataṁ caikā hṛdayasya nāḍyastāsāṁ mūrdhānamabhiniḥsṛtaikā ।
tayordhvamāyannamṛtatvameti viṣvaṅṅanyā utkramaṇe bhavanti ॥
ChāUp 8.6.6

There are 101 arteries connected with the heart. One of them goes up to the top of the head. A person who goes up following this artery attains immortality. The other arteries go in different directions and cause one to depart from the body in other ways.

हिता नाम नाड्यो द्वासप्ततिसहस्राणि हृदयात्पुरीततमभिप्रतिष्ठन्ते ताभिः प्रत्यवसृप्य पुरीतति शेते । – बृ०उप० २.१.१९

hitā nāma nāḍyo dvāsaptatisahasrāṇi hṛdayātpurītatamabhipratiṣṭha nte tābhiḥ pratyavasṛpya purītati śete । – *BṛUp* 2.1.19

हृदि ह्येष आत्मा। अत्रैतदेकशतं नाडीनां, तासां शतं शतमेकैकस्यां। द्वासप्ततिर्द्वासप्ततिः प्रतिशाखानाडीसहस्राणि भवन्त्यासु व्यानश्चरति। – प्र०उप० ३.६

hṛdi hyeṣa ātmā । *atraitadekaśataṁ nāḍīnāṁ, tāsāṁ śataṁ śatamekaikasyāṁ* । *dvāsaptatirdvāsaptatiḥ pratiśākhānāḍīsahasrāṇi bhavantyāsu vyānaścarati* । – *PraUp* 3.6

The *ātman* dwells in the heart where there are 101 arteries; for each of these there are 100 branches, and for each, again, there are 72,000 subsidiary vessels; *vyāna* moves in these.

The basic *prāṇa*, which originates in *svayambhū* and is the cause of all motions, is called *ṛṣi*. He who first experimented, visualized and observed a particular *prāṇa* by (*tapa* and) hard labour was bestowed the name of that *ṛṣi-prāṇa* and became known by that name. In fact, these *ṛṣi-prāṇa*s are innumerable and their limitlessness is indubitable. There is no basic element in creation which *ṛṣi*s did not recognize or observe by *agni-soma yajña-vidyā*.

Whatever was to be known has been known and that which is beyond the creation and therefore unknowable can never be known. That is why *ṛṣi*s in our country were given such titles as विदितवेदितव्याः अधिगतयाथातथ्याः (*viditaveditavyāḥ-adhigatayāthātathyāḥ*). One should not forget that this language is not of the *prāṇī* (being) but of the *prāṇa*. This is an infinitely subtle language of that infinite. We have turned away from that *prāṇa-bhāṣā* (language of vital forces); we are, therefore, not entitled even to utter it. Therefore, I am embarrassed to submit anything about the Vedic science. That is why I have always considered myself inept in the task of propaganda. I could not contain the attraction of being present here today because of the hope that due to the inspiration of our President, who respects Indian culture, this almost vanishing culture might be revived, a culture which was considered uplifting not only for people of this land but of other countries also (through the medium of Indian *dvijāti*s). There is no doubt that the *ṛṣi* culture, the Hindu culture, based on Vedic knowledge and science is not related to any narrow communalism. Who will refuse to accept the *saptarṣi-prāṇa* related to the head? Who will not accept the *agni-soma vidyā*, which is its foundation? Who will not be eager to learn from the planetary narratives? That is why Rājarṣi Manu, propounder of *mānava dharma* (humanism), expressed his conviction about the *dvijāti*s in the following unmistaken words:

> एतद्देशप्रसूतस्य सकाशादग्रजन्मनः ।
> स्वं स्वं चरित्रं शिक्षेरन् पृथिव्यां सर्वमानवाः ॥ – मनु० 2.20
>
> *etaddeśaprasūtasya sakāśādagrajanmanaḥ* ।
> *svaṁ svaṁ caritraṁ śikṣeran pṛthivyāṁ sarvamānavāḥ* ॥ – *Manu* 2.20

Modest beginnings are always good. This is our tradition. Today's lecture is therefore ending with reference to the *agni-soma vidyā* in a few words. Infinite sphere of *svayambhū-prāṇa* and on that is based the sphere of ninety-nine *asura-prāṇa*, sphere of twenty-seven *gandharva-prāṇa*, sphere of seven *pitṛ-prāṇa* and the sphere of thirty-three *deva-prāṇa* of *parameṣṭhi*. After the computation of these *ṛṣi–asura–gandharva–pitṛ* and *deva* sphere of *prāṇa* in *ṛk*, *yaju* and *sāma prāṇāgni* and *atharva-prāṇa soma*, based on this initial pair of *agni-soma* emerge *agni*, *vāyu*, *āditya* – earthly *agni* and lunar *soma*, the second pair of *agni-soma*. In their womb emerges *vaiśvānara*, *tejas* and *prajña* related to *agni*, *vāyu* and *āditya*, and by their interaction emerges the sphere of the being which is divided into fourteen categories as has been explained earlier. The *ādhidaivata* form of *vaiśvāṇarāgni* is *virāṭa*, *hiraṇyagarbha* and *sarvajña*, and their totality is *saṁvatsara* (year). We shall now try to point out the material *agni* and material *soma* related to *saṁvatsara*.

Three Sectors of Saṁvatsara

The *saṁvatsara* on which the *agni-soma vidyā* is based is divided into three sections – the sun, the moon and the earth. We shall consider all of them together and shall try to understand it only through the medium of *bhūtāgni* and *bhūtasoma*. The correct term is *sarvatsara* which, in indirect language, is called *saṁvatsara*. The earth is rotating in its orbit, around the sun. This rotation is not circular but elliptical. In the language of the Purāṇas, it is called *brahmāṇḍa* and in astrological terminology it is called *dīrgha vṛtta*. This orbit is elliptical, which is formed by placing three circles with different centres adjacent to each other. Just as the sun is pulling the earth towards itself by its gravitational force, the earth too is attracting the sun. This mutual gravitation has been called *prayutam saṁyogaḥ* in the Vedas. Due to this mutual attack and counter-attack of *prāṇa* and *apāna*, the earth continuously rotates on a definite path.

Bhagavān Yājñavalkya says:

देवाश्च वा असुराश्च उभये प्राजापत्याः पस्पृधिरे। तान्त्स्पर्द्धमानान् गायत्री अन्तरा तस्थौ। या वै सा गायत्री आसीत्, इयं वै सा पृथिवी। इयं हैव तदन्तरा तस्थौ। अग्निर्वै देवानां दूत आस। सा देवानुपावर्त्तत। – शत०ब्रा० १.४.१.३४

devāśca vā asurāśca ubhaye prājāpatyāḥ paspṛdhire । tāntsparddhamānān gāyatrī antarā tasthau । yā vai sā gāyatrī āsīt, iyaṁ vai sā pṛthivī । iyaṁ haiva tadantarā tasthau । agnirvai devānāṁ dūta āsa । sā devānupāvarttata । – *ŚataBrā* 1.4.1.34

This quotation analyses the twist and contortion of the movement of the earth on its orbit. A circle can be made only if every successive point has some twist. The earth proposes to move straight with its *prāṇa;* the sun attracts it towards itself on some particular point. From here the earth again tries to go straight. The sun again twists the path by a point. And by this continuous gravitational process and consequential contortion, every point becomes twisted. This twist, this contortion, creates the orbit.

स प्रजापतिः सर्वत्सरोऽभवत्। सर्वत्सरो ह वै नामैतत्-यत् सम्वत्सरः।
– शत०ब्रा० ११.१.६.१२

sa prajāpatiḥ sarvatsaro 'bhavat । sarvatsaro ha vai nāmaitat-yat saṁvatsaraḥ । – *ŚataBrā* 11.1.6.12

According to this explanation, this orbit is called *sarvatsara*, and it has become *saṁvatsara* in the indirect language of *ṛṣi*s.

An astronomical circle has 360° and the semi-circles around north and south poles have 180°. The circular strip in the centre is called *bṛhatīcchanda*, which is called *viśvadvṛtta* (equator) in astrology. Ninety degrees north of it is the North Pole and 90° south lies the South Pole. As the centre of earth's orbit is called Kadamba, the gravitational centre of the Equator is called Dhruva (pole). The strip of sphere between 24° north of the Equator and 24° south of the Equator is named *saṁvatsara*.

It has two forms – one is the limit and the other is the limited (one is the form, the other is the content). The former is the time – *kālātmaka saṁvatsara*; the latter is the "matter" (content) which is based on the former. This is *agnyātmaka saṁvatsara*, which is called Sattāsiddha.[7]

[7] All matter is divided into three categories: (1) Sattāsiddha, (2) Bhātisiddha, and (3) Ubhayasiddha. Matter that is perceived but has unreal existence is Bhātisiddha; that which has existence is Sattāsiddha; that which has existence and is perceivable is Ubhayasiddha.

The circle which is formed around 48° north and south of the Equator forms the orbit on which the earth is rotating. This is, in short, an outline of *saṁvatsara*. On this basis, we have to compute and understand the *agnyātmaka saṁvatsara* and have to understand this *agni-soma* concept.

There can be no creation from *satyāgni* and *satya-soma*, because these become the main articles of consumption for the creator. The sun and the earth are *satyāgni* masses. The moon and *vīrya* (semen), are *satya-soma* matter. That part of *agni* or *soma* which is the residue of the former is called *ṛta*. According to this principle, beings are created from the oblation of *ṛta-soma* in *ṛta-agni*. This process of oblation is called *saṁvatsara yajña*. This is the basic cause of creation of all earthly beings. That is why *saṁvatsara yajña* has also been called Prajāpati.

The *ṛta-agni* moves from south and that is why the crops in the field get grey from the south. And that is why Indian farmers always start cutting their crops from the south.

The unique feeling of communion, which is generated from the oblation of *soma* in *agni*, is called *ṛtu* (season).

Though popularly it is held that there are six seasons, according to scientific *yajña* principles there are only five seasons. The five organs, five *prāṇa*, five *bhūta*, five *jñāna* and five *karma* organs and five figures are inspired by the fivefold season of the fivefold *saṁvatsara yajña*.

> हेमन्तशिशिरयोः समासेन – *hemantaśiśirayoḥ samāsena* (Śiśira and Hemanta are incorporated in one).

According to this principle, Hemanta and Śiśira both are included in one winter season and hence the five seasons. Every season is divided into seventy-two days. In folk idioms of Rajasthan, it is said: पून्यूँ पड़वा टाले, तो दिन बहत्तर गाले (*pūnyūṅ paḍavā ṭāle, to dina bahattara gāle*). Every season of seventy-two days is divided into three parts. The morning or the childhood, the noon or the youth and the evening or the old age. The first and the last laps of the season are sixteen days and the middle one is forty days. The middle period of forty (*cālīsa*) days in Rajasthan is called *cillā*.

What is the meaning of the various seasons which define the *saṁvatsara yajña*? We can understand the meanings of various names of seasons also by applying the same principle, which clearly states that the construction of Vedic words is such that the meaning is inherent in it.

Assume it is winter now. *Saṁvatsara* is devoid of *agni* and is born after the extreme development of *somātmaka* (coldness). Newly-born particles of *agni* start settling down on the *soma* leaves. This is the first season of spring (*vasanta*), which is derived thus:

> यस्मिन् काले अग्निकणाः पदार्थेषु वसन्तो-निवसन्तो भवन्ति, स कालः – वसन्तः ।
>
> *yasmin kāle agnikaṇāḥ padārtheṣu vasanto-nivasanto bhavanti, sa kālaḥ – vasantaḥ* ।

After some time, particles of *agni* gather matter with more strength.

> यस्मिन् काले अग्निकणाः पदार्थान् गृह्णन्ति, स कालः – ग्रीष्मः ।
>
> *yasmin kāle agnikaṇāḥ padārthān gṛhṇanti, sa kālaḥ – grīṣmaḥ* ।

According to this derivation, this (summer) season is called *grīṣma agni* that now becomes more powerful and becomes uncontrollable. It appears, as if, it will burn all the matter. This is called *nidāgha*. According to this derivation, नितरां दहत्यग्निः पदार्थान् (*nitarāṁ dahatyagniḥ padārthān*). After the supreme state of summer is reached, the development of *agni* is halted and its contraction starts. The state of contraction is called rainy (*varṣā*) season. According to the derivation, अतिशयेन उरु-अग्निः-यस्मिन् काले (*atiśayena uru-agniḥ-yasmin kāle*). The *uru* (earth) contracting state of *agni* is converted into *varṣā* (rain). Thus, *agni* by its expansion and contraction is converted into spring, summer and rain. Spring becomes the period of commencement, summer the middle period and rain its concluding period. It is on this basis that for brāhmaṇa, kṣatriya and vaiśya, spring, summer and rainy season have been accepted as the period of lighting fire as is clear from:

> वसन्ते ब्राह्मणः-ग्रीष्मे राजन्यः-शरदि वैश्यः-अग्नीनादधीत ।
>
> *vasante brāhmaṇaḥ-grīṣme rājanyaḥ-śaradi vaiśyaḥ-agnīnādadhīta* ।

Why is the third season (stage) of *agni* called *varṣā*, denoting the whole year (*saṁvatsara*)? In response, *śruti* answers: When the north wind blows, the rainy season is associated with a glimpse of spring, after the rain a glimpse of autumn; before this, a glimpse of winter. This season is, of course, *varṣā* itself. And thus, वर्षा त्वेव सर्वेऋतवः (*varṣā tveva sarveṛtavaḥ*), because in the rainy season, one finds glimpses of all seasons. The Indian masters of music have considered it appropriate to sing all *rāgas* in this season. The reference to *agni* now concludes. Let us now draw our attention towards *soma*.

Since spring, the *agni* particles have been expanding and from now on (i.e. since rain) they start contracting in the same proportion –

यस्मिन् काले अग्निकणाः शीर्णा भवन्ति – सः कालः शरत्।

yasmin kāle agnikanāḥ śīrṇāḥ bhavanti – sa kālaḥ śarat ।

The *agni* particles contract further and coldness increases. Therefore,

यस्मिन् काले अग्निकणाः हीनतां गता भवन्ति – सः कालः हेमन्त।

yasmin kāle agnikaṇāḥ hīnatāṁ gatā bhavanti – sa kālaḥ hemanta ।

Ultimately, the particles of *agni* become totally devoid of strength and this is reflected in the following words:

पुनः पुनरतिशयेन शीर्णाः-अग्निकणाः – स कालः शिशिर।

punaḥ punaratiśayena śīrṇāḥ-agnikaṇāḥ – sa kalaḥ śiśira ।

Here the contraction, the downward trend of *agni* ends. In short, the commencement of *agni* takes place from Vasanta and of *soma* from Śarat (autumn). The culmination of *agni* takes place in Varṣā and that of *soma* in Śiśira (winter). The supreme expression of *agni* converting itself into *soma* and the contraction of *soma* converting itself into *agni* is thus demonstrated. This interchange of *agni* and *soma* results in the emergence of seasons. The seasons form from अग्नीषोमात्मकं जगत् (*agnīṣomātmakaṁ jagat*) which is controlling and directing the whole world.

In Our Conjugal Life

Let us observe this *agni-soma* in our conjugal life also. If you stand with your face towards the sun, the north will be on your left and the south on your right. Right side will be dominated by *ṛta-agni* moving from south to north. Therefore in the same manner there is *agni* as well as *soma*. The *agni* is man and manliness; *soma* is woman and womanliness. Therefore, your right side being primarily dominated by *agni* is considered to be dominated by manliness and the left being primarily dominated by *soma* will be considered being womanly. On this basis, in the scientific tradition of India, the worship of Ardhanārīśvara, the worship of Śiva and Śakti as one, is based.

Man is dominated by *agni-prāṇa* and therefore is considered *āgneya*; woman is dominated by *soma-prāṇa* and therefore she has been considered *saumyā*. Both are semicircular half of that *agni-somātmaka saṁvatsara*. The sphere and the conjunction of both complete the physical *saṁvatsara* circle. It is in this conjugal unification from the oblation of *saumya*, semen of man in the *agni* of woman's blood, that this *yajña* is completed, resulting in the birth of a child and the influence of this *yajña* extends up to seven generations.

This is the reflective similarity we came across in the *viśvadvṛtta*. In this physical *saṁvatsara*, it is the "backbone". The sphere of 48° in that *ādhidhaivat saṁvatsara* actually means 24° on each side (of the Equator). These 24° are reflected in the twenty-four ribs each of man and woman. In the *saṁvatsara yajña*, the *soma* is the sacrificial post and in this physical *saṁvatsara* the head is that *yūpa* (sacrificial post) in which are tied and controlled the lower physical or the animal portions of man and woman. In conclusion, whatever we find in the *ādhidaivata saṁvatsara* we find in the conjugal *saṁvatsara* also. It is on this basis that the following principle was established:

पुरुषो वै यज्ञः – यज्ञो वै पुरुषः ।

puruṣo vai yajñaḥ – yajño vai puruṣaḥ ।

The *agni* and *soma*, based on *saṁvatsara*, are twins. In other words, the expanding *agni* on reaching the highest peak of expansion converts itself into *soma* and the contracting *soma* on reaching the point of maximum contraction turns itself into *agni*.

The relationship between *agni* and *soma* is that of fire and fuel. At one stage, this *agni* is fire and at a later stage on being converted as *soma* it becomes fuel. This fuel, when converted into *agni*, becomes fire. And due to this process of *agni-soma*, everyone in this world is "fire" as well as "fuel". This mysterious phenomenon has been explained in the following words:

अहमस्मि प्रथमजा ऋता३स्य । पूर्वं देवेभ्योऽमृतस्य ना ३ भायि । यो मा ददाति स इदेव मा३ वाः । अहमन्नमन्नमदन्तमा३द्मि । – तै०उप० ३.६.१०

ahamasmi prathamajā ṛta3sya । *pūrvaṁ devebhyo 'mṛtasya nā 3 bhāyi* । *yo mā dadāti sa edeva mā3 vāḥ* । *ahamannamannamadantamā3dmi* ।
– *TaiUp* 3.6.10

I have been created before the creation of *devatā*s and nobody can survive without consuming me. Those who donate me in *yajña*, etc. I protect them and bestow them with the result of pious deeds.

It is to be borne in mind carefully that the form of the above-mentioned *agni-soma* pair is located in that *saṁvatsara* which is fundamentally *saṁvatsara*. The *krāntivṛtta*, which has a continuous twist in its motions, is the circular wheel of *saṁvatsara* and the form of *agni* and *soma* is protected in its womb. Spontaneity and candour are the characteristics of self and not of the universe. The universe is based on and consists of, *agni-soma* and has a fire–fuel relationship. The projection of the outer or external universe depends on *saṁvatsara* having twists and contortions. Due to our good fortune, the *agni* of this nation, which is called Bhārata, due to its association with *agni* called Bhārata, has blazened today. The *agni* of this nation is fully independent. For the protection of its form or in other words for the protection of newly-won freedom, this nation should adopt the *saṁvatsara* system based *agni-somātmaka jagat* of our basic culture, the Vedaśāstra, which is *saṁvatsara* due to its twisted and contorted motion. Recalling this *saṁvatsara*, the inaugural lecture of today is presented to Mr President with the following uplifting reference:

> अग्निर्जागार तमृचः कामयन्ते-अग्निर्जागार-तमु सामानि यन्ति ।
> अग्निर्जागार-तमयं सोम आह-तवाहमस्मि सख्ये न्योकाः ॥
>
> *agnirjāgāra tamṛcaḥ kāmayante-agnirjāgāra-tamu sāmāni yanti* ।
> *agnirjāgāra-tamayaṁ soma āha-tavāhamasmi sakhye nyokāḥ* ॥

॥ ओमित्येतत् ॥
॥ *omityetat* ॥

The first lecture on the Science of Agni-Soma is concluded.

Second Discourse

The Science of Five-Divisional Universe

IN THE PREVIOUS lecture some fundamental scientific subjects connected with the principle of अग्निषोमात्मक जगत् (*agni-somātmaka jagat*) were explained. Elaborating the basic Vedic *tattva* it was submitted that form, motion and envelope or sphere, *ṛk, yaju* and *sāma* respectively, are related with three *prāṇāgni*s, viz. *agni, vāyu* and *āditya*. This triple *agni*, in conjunction with *atharva-soma*, is functioning as the base of this universe. Second pair of this *agni-soma*, foundation of the universe, is *vaiśvānarāgni* and *anna* (fuel) which functions within the *saṁvatsara maṇḍala* and this second pair inspires the six seasons, viz. spring, summer, rain, autumn, cold and winter. While explaining the third pair of *agni-soma* it was submitted that the collective unit of the six seasons, Saṁvatsara Prajāpati is that Yajña Prajāpati which has divided itself into five seasons and has become fivefold. What is the outline or concept of this fivefold universe? In other words, what is meant by the fivefold universe? In today's lecture, which is the second in this series, an attempt will be made to answer this question.

The subject is exceedingly intricate. And in view of the fact that these are pure and simple (*tattva*) fundamentals, there is absolutely no scope in it for entertaining and interesting references and anecdotes, and therefore it is likely to prove very dry, drab and uninteresting. I beg, therefore, to be excused in the beginning for making a special request that you should listen to this *puṇḍīra vidyā* with all the attention at your command.

Universe and Its Divisions

The science dealing with the fivefold universe is called, in the symbolic language, as *puṇḍīra-vidyā*, which means the science of the divisions of this universe. This universe is one and its divisions are five. This science is therefore called पञ्चपुण्डीरा-प्राजापत्यबल्शा-विद्या (*pañca-puṇḍīrā-prājāpatyabalśā-vidyā*). The science of universe related to this Vedic science of creation and the *veda-vidyā*, which is the basis on which all of them operate, is really very comprehensive and difficult, and the extent of its comprehensive scope can be understood by the following narrative which is related to the mysterious and meaningful "conversational" language between Maharṣi Aṅgiras Bharadvāja and Devendra. It is said:

> To satisfy his desire of knowing and reading the Vedas, renowned Vedic teacher Maharṣi Bharadvāja propitiated the solar Indra-*tattva*, which increases the span of a person's life. Devendra was pleased with him and bestowed him a lifespan of 300 years. During the 300 years of his life, which Maharṣi Bharadvāja had obtained in boon, the sage submerged himself completely in the study and realization of the Vedic *tattva*. After this time was over, the body of Maharṣi Bharadvāja became completely emaciated; he was overcome by old age and completely deprived of any physical strength and became bedridden. Thus caught in the grip of old age, Bharadvāja was waiting for his last moment when suddenly one day Devendra appeared and asked Bharadvāja, "Bharadvāja! if I bestow upon you another 100 years of life, how will you spend these hundred years?"

From Maharṣi Bharadvāja, who was devoted to the Vedas, the following reply came forth spontaneously:

> Oh my Lord! I shall spend those years also in meditating on the Vedas, because my knowledge of the Vedas is still incomplete.

Devendra was overwhelmed by the devotion of Bharadvāja towards the Vedas. With the intention of enlightening him with the true character of the Vedas through the medium of Savitra-Agni, Devendra placed before him three huge mountainous piles of Vedas; which were invisible to Bharadvāja till then. Devendra took one handful of Vedas from each of the three piles and, inviting the attention of Maharṣi Bharadvāja towards them, said:

> Oh *ṛṣi*! Do you see these huge, mountainous piles? These are the Vedas. In the 300 years of life which you have spent so far, you have been able to gather one handful from each of the three. Uptil now, this limitless mountainous Vedic knowledge is unknown to you. The Vedas are limitless. Who has ever been able to fathom them? Therefore you should leave the hope that even if another 100 years were available, you will fulfil your desire of knowing the Vedas. If you really want to

know that Infinite you should propitiate the Savitra-Agni. I am placing before you today its concept.

Devendra put before him the analysis of the character of Savitra-Agni.

Illustrating this mysterious incident, which deals with basic scientific fundamentals, Bhagavān Tittiri says:

> भरद्वाजो ह वै त्रिभिरायुर्भिर्ब्रह्मचर्य्यमुवास। तं ह जीर्णिं, स्थविरं, शयानं – इन्द्र उपव्रज्य उवाच। भरद्वाज! यत्ते चतुर्थमायुर्दद्यां, किमनेन कुर्य्या इति? ब्रह्मचर्य्यमेवैनेन चरेयमिति होवाच। तं ह त्रीन् गिरिरूपानविज्ञातानिव दर्शयाञ्चकार। तेषां हैकैकस्मान् मुष्टिमाददे। स होवाच – भरद्वाजेत्यामन्त्र्य – वेदा वा एते। अनन्ता वै वेदाः। एतद्वा एतैस्त्रिभरायुर्भिरन्ववोचथाः। अथ त इतरदनूक्तमेव। एहि! इमं विद्धि! अयं वै सर्वविद्या इति। तस्मै हैतमग्निं सावित्रमुवाच। एषो एव त्रयी विद्या। तं विदित्वा (भरद्वाजः) अमृतो भूत्वा स्वर्गं लोकेमियाय आदित्यस्य सायुज्यम् इति।
>
> – तै०ब्रा०३.१०.११.२-५
>
> *bharadvājo ha vai tribhirāyurbhirbrahmacaryyamuvāsa* । *taṁ ha jīrṇiṁ, sthaviraṁ, śayānaṁ* । *indra upavrajya uvāca* । *bharadvāja! yatte caturthamāyurdadyāṁ, kimanena kuryyā iti? brahmacaryyamevainena careyamiti hovāca* । *taṁ ha trīn girirūpānavijñātāniva darśayāñcakāra* । *teṣāṁ haikaikasmān muṣṭimādade* । *sa hovāca – bharadvājetyāmantrya – vedā vā ete* । *anantā vai vedāḥ* । *etadvā etaistribharāyurbhiranvavocathāḥ* । *atha ta itaradanūktameva* । *ehi! imaṁ viddhi! ayaṁ vai sarvavidyā iti* । *tasmai haitamagniṁ sāvitramuvāca* । *eṣo eva trayī vidyā* । *taṁ viditvā (bharadvājaḥ) amṛto bhūtvā svargaṁ lokemiyāya ādityasya sāyujyam iti* ।
>
> – *TaiBrā* 3.10.11.2-5

Infinitive Vedas and Infinitive Parameśvara are inseparable in Indian culture. We are placing before you some aspects of *savitrāgni* which are related to the Vedas and from these aspects you will be in a position to appreciate this inseparable characteristic. While illustrating the six seasons, it was submitted that *soma* is flowing from north to south and *agni* from south to north. Which *agni* and *soma* flow like this? The answer is *ṛta-agni* and *ṛta-soma*. What are these *ṛta-agni* and *ṛta-soma*? This question has been answered in that *mantra* which the Indian *dvijāti*s recite everyday in their *sandhyā karma* (daily meditations).

> ऋतं च सत्यं चाभीद्धात्तपसोऽध्यजायत।
> ततो रात्र्यजायत ततः समुद्रो अर्णवः॥
>
> समुद्रादर्णवादधि संवत्सरो अजायत।
> अहोरात्राणि विदधद्विश्वस्य मिषतो वशी॥

> सूर्याचन्द्रमसौ धाता यथापूर्वमकल्पयत्।
> दिवं च पृथिवीं चान्तरिक्षमथो स्वः ॥ – ऋ० १०.१९०.१-३
>
> *ṛtaṁ ca satyam cābhīddhāttapaso 'dhyajāyata* ।
> *tato rātryajāyata tataḥ samudro arṇavaḥ* ॥
>
> *samudrādarṇavādadhi saṁvatsarao ajāyata* ।
> *ahorātrāṇi vidadhadviśavasya miṣato vaśī* ॥
>
> *sūryācandramasau dhātā yathāpūravamakalpayat* ।
> *divaṁ ca pṛthivīṁ cāntarikṣamatho svaḥ* ॥ – *ṚV* X.190.1-3

The tenth *maṇḍala* of the *Ṛk Saṁhitā*, which deals with the subtle analysis of science of creation, has 191 *sūkta*s. The last *sūkta* explains the science of creation in an easy manner. In this 190th *sūkta* which has three *mantra*s, the entire science of creation is incorporated. It is the conclusion of the whole Ṛgvedic science of creation. In other words, this one *mantra* contains the whole science of creation in a subtle manner. Through this *mantra*, the *ṛṣi*s have desired from the *dvijāti*s to recall *jñāna* and *vijñāna* while meditating on Gāyatrī everyday and to awaken the nation by these *tattva*s, fundamentals of creation, which are based on science and knowledge. He must strictly follow this scientific path of pursuing duties of life.

The literal meaning of the *mantra* is clear:

> At first *ṛta* and *satya* or the Brahma-Subrahmā *tattva* originated from the burning efforts of *prāṇa* and the incessant action of mind, inspired by the vocal efforts of Prajāpati, who is a collective unit of the seven *ṛṣi-prāṇa*s. The triple Brahmā was called Brahmā and it became *satya*. The fourth Atharva Brahmā was called Subrahmā, it became *ṛta*. At first, *satya-svayambhū* and *ṛta-parameṣṭhi* are manifested by the inflaming efforts of Prajāpati. The *satya* was incorporated by *ṛta* in its womb. And that is why *ṛta-parameṣṭhi* became dominant subsequently. The watery night emerged out of this *ṛta-parameṣṭhi* which had in its womb the *svayambhū* which is *satya*.
>
> The principle of *ambhovad* is based on this phenomenon of nature and on this is based the principle सर्वमापोमयं जगत् (*sarvamāpomayaṁ jagat*). This *ṛta-tattva*, which was watery, emerged later as an earthly ocean and was called Arṇava Samudra. The *satya* ocean of *svayambhū* is called Nabhasvān; the ocean of *parameṣṭhi*, which is in the form of night, is called Sarasvān; the ocean of triple worlds of the sun, moon and earth is called Arṇava, which later on converts itself in the twilight of *saṁvatsara*. In the womb of this Arṇava ocean there was a *prerṇātmaka agni* called *aṅgirā*.

> Due to the interaction of this *aṅgirā* in the Arṇava ocean, the sphere of *agni* emerged, which is called *saṁvatsara*. The Arṇava night was divided here into two – day (*agni*) and night (*soma*). The compact integrated mass of the day (*agni*) converted itself into the sun and the compact integrated mass of night (*soma*) converted itself into the moon. Thus the original *ṛta* and *satya* elements in due course found expression in the sun and the moon. This sphere of *saṁvatsara*, based on the sun and the moon, later on developed as *pṛthvī*, mid-region, the sun and the fourth watery world named Svaḥ, and thus the creation of Prajāpati was completed.

This is the literal meaning of the *mantras* and we shall deal here only with two words *ṛta* and *satya* which are technically very important.

Purāṇas: Elaboration of the Vedas

It should always be borne in mind that the Purāṇas are explanations and elaboration of the Vedas. These aspects of creation, which have been indicated in the Vedas in a subtle and indirect language, have been explained and expressed in the Purāṇas in direct language, using terms which are in vogue, as is obvious from this quotation:

> इतिहासपुराणाभ्यां वेदं समुपबृंहयेत्।
>
> *itihāsapurāṇābhyāṁ vedaṁ samupabṛṁhayet* । – *MBh* 1.1.267
>
> Study of Vedas should be supplemented with Itihāsa and Purāṇa.

It is not only my belief but conviction that without making the Purāṇas as our medium, it is not possible to understand the *veda-tattva*. This is why my *guru* gave the Purāṇas the name of *ārya sarvasva*. Traditional narratives and history containing mysteries of creation form the core contents of the Purāṇas which, though being old, explain the creation and are thus ever-new. पुरा-नव-भवति (*purā-nava-bhavati*), this is the derivation of the word *purāṇa*. It was on the basis of these ever-old but ever-new narratives that the compiler of Veda Saṁhitās, Bhagavān Vyāsa, compiled the Purāṇa Saṁhitās earlier than the Vedas, which was later on elaborated by Mahābhāga Sūta in eighteen Purāṇas. It is on this basis that it is said:

> प्रथमं सर्वशास्त्राणां पुराणं ब्रह्मणा स्मृतम्।
> अनन्तरञ्च वक्त्रेभ्यो वेदास्तस्य विनिःसृताः ॥ – *वायुपुराण* १.६०-६१
>
> *prathamaṁ sarvaśāstrāṇāṁ purāṇaṁ brahmaṇā smṛtam* ।
> *anantarañca vaktrebhyo vedāstasya viniḥsṛtāḥ* ॥ – *Vāyu Purāṇa* 1.60-61

Due to the continuous neglect of Purāṇaśāstra, which explains all aspects of mysteries of creation and philosophy, the flow of scientific knowledge of the Vedas has been blocked and if we wish to make it flow again then we have to return to the Purāṇas. It was most unfortunate that a devotee of the Vedas, in his imaginary devotion, called the Purāṇas as "imaginary". What a shame? Oh, what a shame! Modern archaeologists, musicians and connoisseurs of art, who display their anxiety towards research in national culture, organize functions based on old relics, debris and stones which merely satisfied the mind and body, that too momentarily. Or they organize functions of music, art and craft which only have entertainment value. These activities simply satisfy the emotion of the people fleetingly. To call such functions as "cultural" is to insult the culture of the Indian nation; it is to throw it down into the depths of neglect. The subtle and refined realisation of Indian culture is possible only in the Vedas which have been expressed differently and elaborately in the Purāṇaśāstra and Āgamaśāstra.

And thus from the popular point of view, the Purāṇas are the proud symbol of our culture. Renowned national leader of our country, late Shri Madan Mohan Malviyaji, kept this point partly in view, as was proved in his call: "Let there be reading of the Purāṇas at various places". But the country forgot this cultural viewpoint of the great national leader. Truly speaking, where can we see the Indian culture except in the Purāṇas, where apart from innumerable worldly and other-worldly cultural topics, the following eighteen basic scientific subjects have been dealt in detail: 1. Sarga, 2. Pratisarga, 3. Vaṁśa, 4. Vaṁśānucarita, 5. Manvantara, 6. Gāthā, 7. Kalpaśuddhi, 8. Ḍāmara, 9. Jāmal, 10. Tantra, 11. Saṁhitā, 12. Aṣṭavidha Ākhyāna, 13. Upākhyāna, 14. Khagola-Vidyā, 15. Bhuvanakośa, 16. Udakārgalavidyā, 17. Āyatī, and 18. Yāmala.

This is clear from the following *mantra*:

सर्गश्च-प्रतिसर्गश्च-वंशो-मन्वन्तरस्तथा।
आख्यानश्चाप्युपाख्यानैर्गाथाभिः कल्पशुद्धिभिः।
पुराणसंहिताञ्चक्रे भगवान् बादरायणः॥

sargaśca-pratisargaśca-vaṁśo-manvantarastathā ।
ākhyānaścāpyupākhyānairgāthābhiḥ kalpaśuddhibhiḥ ।
purāṇasaṁhitāñcakre bhagavān bādarāyaṇaḥ ॥

It is the tragic misfortune of the Indian nation that it treated the great Purāṇas, which carried the message of Indian culture, as mythology, and as a result entirely forgot its cultural treasure.

Basic Definitions of Purāṇas

Just like the Vedas, the Purāṇas also have their own basic definitions. As naive people do not know these basic definitions, they commit the blunder of treating them as figments of imagination. For example, take *āyu* (age). According to the Jaimini principles of अहर्वा विसंख्यानात् (*aharvā visaṁkhyānāt*), one day on this earth has been called, in Paurāṇic definitions, as a year (*varṣa*) from the point of view of the rotation of the earth. Keeping this in view, when it is said that a particular *ṛṣi* was engaged in meditation for 36,000 years, it meant 36,000 days, which in turn meant 100 years. This means that he meditated for his whole life, a meaning which is fully corroborated by the Vedic principle शतं जीवेम शरदः (*śataṁ jīvema śaradaḥ*) (you may have a full life, i.e. 100 years).

Subjects which have been dealt with in the Vedas have been explained in the Purāṇas in its own unique terminology. The difference lies only in the fact that being ignorant of the Vedic language named *chandobhyastā*, the critics could not criticize the Vedas as they found it difficult even to translate the meaning literally. But as the Purāṇas were written in the popular Sanskrit language, for those whose intelligence ended only at the literal meaning of words, criticized the technical subjects dealt with in the Purāṇas. There is no doubt that in course of time, the meaning of the Purāṇas will also become clear through the basic definition of the Vedas. For the present, let this be all regarding the Purāṇas which were relevant in this context.

Two Keywords: Ṛta and Satya

We have to keep in mind two words, *ṛta* and *satya* of the *mantra*: ऋतं च सत्यं चाभीद्धात्तपसोऽध्यजायत (*ṛtaṁ ca satyam cābhīddhāttapaso 'dhyajāyat*), which deals with the science of creation. What is the meaning of these words from the scientific point of view? The *ṛṣi* answers this question thus: सहृदयं सशरीरं सत्यम्, अहृदयं अशरीरं ऋतम्, अहृदयं सशरीरं ऋतसत्यम् (*sahṛdayaṁ saśarīraṁ satyam, ahṛdayaṁ aśarīraṁ ṛtam, ahṛdayaṁ saśarīraṁ ṛtasatyam*), i.e. while a matter which has both form and centre is called *satya*, a matter, which has neither an independent centre of its own nor an independent form of its own, is called *ṛta*. Those which have no centre but have a form are called *ṛta-satya*. Thus all matters of this world can be divided into three categories – *satya*, *ṛta* and *ṛta-satya*. Stones, clay, the sun, the moon and plants have their own independent centres as well as form. Therefore, such matters, which have a centre as well as form, will be called *satya*. Air, water, *prāṇa* and *soma* have neither a centre of their own nor a form of their own. They are converted into the form of the base on which they are based (or in which they are kept). Their form is dependent on the form of their base:

यद्यत्स्वरूपमादत्ते तेन तेन स युज्येत ।

yadyatsvarūpamādatte tena tena so yujyate ।

Since they have no independent centre of their own, if one portion of this material is held or collected, it will not mean that the other portion will follow. But as far as those which have a centre as well as form are concerned, if any portion is held or collected it will mean that the whole body has been held or collected. Camphor, mercury, sulphur, mica and cloud have no independent centre of their own, but they have a shape and a form. As they have no centre, they possess the property of flying or moving in parts and getting scattered hither-thither. As they have no centre, they are *ṛta*; as they have form, they are *satya*. Such matter having no centre but having form is called *ṛta-satya*, i.e. having qualities of both. We have to commence the science of divisions of the universe by keeping in view these two terms.

From the scientific point of view, the mass of matter with a centre is called *satya*. It is obvious that if one portion of such matter is seized, it means that the whole form of matter has been seized. The science of attraction has been called *garbha-vidyā* and has been explained by the following *mantra*:

प्रजापतिश्चरति गर्भे अन्तरजायमानो बहुधा विजायते ।
तस्य योनिं परिपश्यन्ति धीरास्तस्मिन्ह तस्थुर्भुवनानि विश्वा ॥ – *यजुःसंहिता* ३१.१९

prajāpatiścarati garbhe antarajāyamāno bahudhā vijāyate ।
tasya yonim paripaśyanti dhīrāstasminha tasthurbhuvanāni viśvā ॥
– *Yajuḥsaṁhitā* 31.19

Prajāpati exists in the womb, i.e. centre of all matter; he does not take birth and therefore is unborn. But everything is born from him. The concept of the centre of this Prajāpati can be realized only by a patient, intelligent scientist. On the basis of this centre, the seven, or say five, sectors of every form of matter exist.

This is the literal meaning of the *mantra*. The central force which operates in every form of matter in the form of inflow–outflow and regulation of both is *hṛdayam* and it is called Prajāpati about which it is well known that हृदि-अयं हृदयम् (*hṛdi-ayaṁ hṛdayam*) – *hṛdaya* exists on *hṛdaya*. This means that Prajāpati, which is an embodiment of incoming force, outgoing force and the force which regulates both, exists in the centre.

What is the concept of *hṛdaya* in which this *hṛ-da-ya* exists? Answering this question, the *ṛṣi*s have used the term – *antaḥ*. *Hṛdaya* is not a physical matter, the shape of which can be outlined or can be held and pointed out. Even in the most subtle and sharp point, there is a centre and therefore *hṛdaya* cannot be pointed out by the sharpest amongst the sharpest points. And, therefore, if this *prāṇātmaka hṛdaya* is expressed, it is only by the word *antaḥ*. It is absolutely impossible to express the shape of the shapeless *prāṇātmaka* centre by physical forms and shapes. *Antaḥ* means inside of the inside, the last point to which your imagination can go. This only can be a definition independent of the word *hṛdaya*.

Change and Creation

Physical forms continually change. This change is creation, this is "taking birth". The non-physical *hṛdaya*, which has no shape, never changes. Therefore, it has been called *ajāyamāna* – that which is never created. This *hṛdaya-tattva* is unchangeable.

Due to this central force *hṛdaya*, all forms and physical matter, having form, have the property of change, that is of creation. This *hṛdaya* is the creation of physical matter. How can this central force be understood? The *ṛṣi*s have answered: तस्य योनिं परिपश्यन्ति धीराः *(tasya yonim paripaśyanti dhīrāḥ* – He is born in sundry form. Only the discerning sages see the source of his birth (*Yajurveda* 31.19)). Patient and intelligent persons realize and see this centre with their intelligence. This means that *hṛdaya* cannot be seized in a physical way, but can be seized upon with the help of scientific outlook. Is there no concrete way of understanding this *hṛdaya*? Explaining this, the *ṛṣi*s say in the end: तस्मिन्ह तस्थुर्भुवनानि विश्वा (*tasminha tasthurbhuvanāni viśvā* – All these worlds lie in him only).

Location of Centre

By balancing matter, it is possible to realize the centre. The weight of all matter is balanced on its centre. You can take a stick in your hand. Try to balance it. When your finger connects with the centre, the weight of both parts of the stick becomes balanced – it will not shake, it becomes motionless. The seven or five sectors of cane or of all matter are balanced on this centre. In the wide universe, there are seven or five sectors or divisions. There are similar divisions in all forms of matter, which are part of that wide universe. As it is there, so it is here. That is also full, a whole; this is also full, a complete whole. Please concentrate on the following *mantra*:

ॐ पूर्णमदः पूर्णमिदं पूर्णात्पूर्णमुदच्यते ।
पूर्णस्य पूर्णमादाय पूर्णमेवावशिष्यते ॥ – ईश०उप०

oṁ pūrṇamadaḥ pūrṇamidaṁ pūrṇātpūrṇamudacyate ।
pūrṇasya pūrṇamādāya pūrṇamevāvaśiṣyate ॥ – *ĪśaUp*

That is the complete whole. Therefore, this is also a complete whole. This whole has come out of that whole. As it is made from the remains of that, this is also like that, because the result always has the properties of the components. If you fully understand the wholeness or fullness of this whole, then the concept of that whole is also before you completely. In a powerful and living language, the *ṛṣi*s have put forth the concept of *pūrṇa*. The properties, which are there in water of a particular kind, will also be found in every drop of it. Similarly, in the matter born of that *mahān*, we shall find all those "properties" which that *mahān* has. It is on this basis that the following principles have been established:

एकेन विज्ञातेन सर्वमिदं विज्ञातं भवति ।

ekena vijñātena sarvamidaṁ vijñātam bhavati ।

यदेवेह तदमुत्र, यदमुत्र-तवन्विह ॥

yadeveha tadamutra, yadamutra-tavanviha ॥ – *Kaṭha Upaniṣad* 2.1.10

What indeed is here, is there. Likewise, what is there, is here.

This is the viewpoint of the *ṛṣi*s: The emotional people, who were unable to understand its meaning properly, have indulged in a misconceived imagination of Śūnyavāda. By explaining the *mantra*, it is submitted here that the *prāṇa-tattva* existing in the centre of each form of matter is the definition of the concept of *satya*.

Universe and Reality

Does it mean that the form of matter is not truth, is *asatya*, or all this universe which is an extension of physical matter is untrue and unreal? No, never. This physical world which has name, form and functions is definitely real, as it is correlated with the central basic truth. On the one hand, the basic truth or the *hṛdaya* is immortal *jñānātmaka* face of that Saccidānanda Brahma; on the other, the form is mortal, *vijñānātmaka* facet of that immortal Brahma: अमृतं चैव मृत्युश्च सदसच्चाहमर्जुन (*amṛtaṁ caiva mṛtyuśca sadasaccāhamarjuna* – The Lord is immortality as well as death – *Bhagavadgītā* IX.19).

This unity of the immortal *prāṇa* and the mortal form is *aham*, i.e. Brahmā; which has been clearly defined in the principle अहं ब्रह्मास्मि (*ahaṁ brahmāsmi*). While on the one hand, the *mantra* सत्यं ज्ञानमनन्तं ब्रह्म (*satyam jñānamanantaṁ brahma* – Brahmā is supreme, ultimate truth and infinite – *Taittirīya Upaniṣad* 2.1.1) propounds the *prāṇa-hṛdaya* as the central truth, on the other hand, नित्यं विज्ञानमानन्दं ब्रह्म (*nityaṁ vijñānamānandaṁ brahma*) *mantra* propounds the reality of matter, form and universe. The central *prāṇa* reality has been called *amṛta*. The Vedānta scholars, who missed this Vedic viewpoint due to their contacts with imaginary unrealism, like Śūnyavāda, committed the blunder of defining this universe which is the projection of that truth as unreal. It is proper in this context to know what the Vedas say about the universe which has name, form and function:

> तदेतत् – त्रयं सदेकमयमात्मा । आत्मा उ एकः सन्नेतत् त्रयम् । तदमृतं सत्येन छन्नम् । प्राणो वा अमृतम् । नामरूपे सत्यम् । ताभ्यामयं प्राणश्छन्नः । – श॰ब्रा॰ १४.४.४.३
>
> *tadetat – trayaṁ sadekamayamātmā । ātmā u ekaḥ sannetat trayam । tadamṛtaṁ satyena channam । prāṇo vā amṛtam । nāmarūpe satyam । tābhyāmayaṁ prāṇaśchannaḥ ।* – *ŚataBrā* 14.4.4.3

The form, which has a name and a form, is real and the centre of the form is also real. As this central truth is the base on which the formal truth is established, it has been called truth of the truth (*satyasya satyam*). As the basic *jñānajyoti*, on which the physical light of the sun, the moon, electricity, fire and stars depends, is called *jyotiṣāṁ jyotiḥ* (light of lights), similarly the central truth, *hṛdaya* of the formal truths, can also be called truth of the truth, reality of the reality. The whole manifestation of the universe is the manifestation of that Īśvara Prajāpati and in that case, He is definitely the manifestation of all these manifestations and it is from this basic manifestation that the whole universe is manifested.

No Form: No Centre-Ṛta

Now, we are to consider the word *ṛta*. That which has no form of its own nor any independent centre is called *ṛta* and when it makes *satya* as its base, it converts itself into *satya*. When there is an oblation of *ṛta*, this *satya* converts this *ṛta* also into *satya*. The *balātmaka* universe is basically *ṛta*, but on being derived from *rasātmaka satya*, it is converted into *satya*.[1]

---

[1] *Rasa* and *bala* are two very subtle, but scientific terms; understanding of these words only can make it possible to understand the beginning of creation. They have been explained in the fourth lecture.

Subtle and intricate is the definition of *ṛta* and *satya*, which is the subject of an independent study. *Ṛta* and *satya* are the keywords of the Vedic viewpoint and they have been expounded and discussed in the *mantra*: ऋतञ्च सत्यं चाभीद्धात्तपसोऽध्यजायत (*ṛtañca satyam cābhīddhāttapaso 'dhyajāyata* – The eternal law and truth are born of arduous penance).

What has the Purāṇa said in this connection? Those who commit the terrible sin of separating the Purāṇaśāstra from the Vedaśāstra should keep before them the following quotations from *Bhāgavata Purāṇa* 10.2.26:

सत्यव्रतं सत्यपरं त्रिसत्यं सत्यस्य योनिं निहितं च सत्ये।
सत्यस्य सत्यं ऋतसत्यनेत्रं सत्यात्मकं त्वां शरणं प्रपन्नाः ॥

satyavrataṁ satyaparaṁ trisatyam satyasya yoniṁ nihitaṁ ca satye ।
satyasya satyam ṛtasatyanetraṁ satyātmakaṁ tvāṁ śaraṇaṁ prapannāḥ ॥

Oh Lord! You never deviate from Your vow, which is always perfect because whatever You decide is perfectly correct and cannot be stopped by anyone. Being present in the three phases of cosmic manifestation – creation, maintenance and annihilation – You are the Supreme Truth. Indeed, unless one is completely truthful, one cannot achieve Your favour, which therefore cannot be achieved by hypocrites. You are the active principle, the real truth, in all the ingredients of creation, and therefore You are known as *antaryāmī* (inner force). You are equal to everyone, and Your instructions apply for everyone, for all time. You are the beginning of all truth. Therefore, offering our obeisances, we surrender unto You. Kindly give us protection.

Satya-Agni-Soma Pair

Following the natural meaning of the words, *ṛta* and *satya*, *agni* and *soma*, which divide the universe into five sectors, are also divided into two divisions each. *Satya-agni* and *satya-soma* is one pair of these *tattva* while *ṛta-soma* and *ṛta-agni* is another pair. Of these two pairs, the second is related to *saṁvatsara*, which is a total of six seasons as explained in yesterday's lecture.

Today, we are to keep in view, in connection with the science of the five divisions of the universe, the first pair of *satyāgni-soma*, which is related to सूर्य्याचन्द्रमसौ धाता यथापूर्वमकल्पयत् (*sūryyācandramasau dhātā yathāpūrvamakalpayat* – Creator in the beginning created the sun and moved the heaven, the earth, the firmament, and the happy (sky) – *ṚV* X.19). The sun having a centre as well as a form is *satyāgni* and similarly the moon is *satya-soma*, about which it is said thus: एष वै सोमो राजा देवानामन्नं, यच्चन्द्रमाः (*eṣa vai somo rājā devānāmannaṁ yaccandramāḥ*). *Satya-soma* has magnitude, while *ṛta-soma* has none. *Satyāgni* has magnitude, while *ṛtāgni* is just opposite. According to this definition, the sun which has a place in the astronomical sphere is *satyāgni* and the moon is *satya-soma*. Creation takes place from *ṛta-agni-soma*, but the fundamental basis of these creations is *satyāgni-soma*. By what process this *satyāgni-soma* gets converted into *ṛtāgni-soma*? Answers to this question are related with the rotation of various parts of the universe (like planets) which is called the *darśapūrṇamāsa* process in *yajña* terminology. To understand this process, please keep in view the two planets, the sun and the moon.

The moon, having a form and a centre, is rotating round the earth on its orbit called *dakṣavṛtta* in the same way as the *bhūpiṇḍa*. The earth is rotating on its orbit called *krāntivṛtta* around the sun. It is true that the Indian astrologers of the present day, followers of the Mayāsura sect and disciples of Śrī Varāhamihira, accept the sun as moving and the earth as stationary, while the Western modern science says that the earth is rotating and the sun is stationary. Are we committing the blunder of blindly following this Western material science and are submitting falsely in the name of the Vedas that the earth is rotating. Never, never in a dream can such a thing happen. In this context, it becomes imperative to refer to three independent branches of science because their ignorance might create many mistaken beliefs.

Three Branches of Science

The *ṛṣis* have divided the science of creation into three branches on the basis of head, heart and foot. These branches have also been called *sṛṣṭimūlā*, *sthitimūlā* and *dṛṣṭimūlā*.[2] The science which deals with creation from the "head" has been called *sahasraśīrṣa-vidyā*. The science which deals with creation from the point of view of "heart" has been called *sahasrākṣa-vidyā* and the branches of science which deal with the universe from the point of view of "foot" is called *sahasrapāt-vidyā*. The fundamental bases of these three branches of science of creation are *svayambhū*, *sūrya* (sun), *bhūpiṇḍa* (earth) sectors of this wide five-divisional universe, as will be explained herein.

To explain the creation with the earth as the focal starting point is

[2] These three branches of Vedic science have been so long ignored, as it was difficult to understand these technical terms. Explained generally, the *sṛṣṭimūlā* branch deals with the universe as it was created; the *sthitimūlā* deals with the universe as it is; the *dṛṣṭimūlā* deals with the universe as it appears to the eyes.

one branch, with the sun as the focal starting point is the second branch and with *svayambhū* as the starting point is the third branch. This five-divisional universe is Prajāpati. The first division of this universe is *svayambhū* and is the head of Prajāpati, the sun which is the centre of the universe is its heart and the earth which is the culminating point of the universe is its foot. That is why the branch of science which deals with the universe with *svayambhū* as the starting point is called the science of head and that which has earth as the initiating point is called the science of foot. To explain again, *svayambhū* is the head, the sun is the heart and the earth is the feet of this wide universe called Prajāpati.

Appearance, Existence and Creation

Svayambhū is the starting point of creation; the creation commenced with *svayambhū*. That is why this first branch of science of creation has been called the *sṛṣṭimūlā sṛṣṭi-vidyā*. The sun is the centre of the universe as it exists. Existence of this wide five-divisional universe which has emerged from *svayambhū* is entirely dependent on the sun. As long as there is sun, there is also the universe. When there will be no sun, the whole form of this universe will be dissolved. Therefore, this second branch of science of creation is called the *sthitimūlā sṛṣṭi-vidyā*.

The first object of our sight is the earth. Therefore, the third branch of the science of creation will be called *dṛṣṭimūlā sṛṣṭi-vidyā*. And thus the creation is explained from these three entirely separate viewpoints – creation, existence and appearance. From the point of view of creation, the starting point will be *svayambhū*; from the point of view of appearance, the earth will be the starting point. Let us consider the latter as the first viewpoint and follow the three branches.

When we start understanding the science of creation as it is seen, it appears as if the earth is stationary and the sun is rotating, and it is on this basis perhaps that Indian astrology has accepted the earth as stationary and the sun as rotating. It is not only accepting a thing, but from the point of view of appearance it is real. It is from this viewpoint that the earth has been called *dharā, dharitrī, dharaṇī* and other similar names, which denote its stationary character. It is on this basis that the Vedas have themselves said, "Sitting on a Golden Chariot, God[3] (Bhagavān) sun is coming, seeing the three worlds"; it means that the

[3] The word "God" has been used for Īśvara, Parameśvara, Devatā, Bhagavān, etc. It is incorrect. All these words have widely different technical meanings.

sun is moving. The rising and setting of the sun are dependent on this, as the *śruti* has pointed out:

आ कृष्णेन रजसा वर्तमानो निवेशयन्नमृतं मर्त्यं च ।
हिरण्येन सविता रथेना देवो याति भुवनानि पश्यन् ॥ – *यजुःसंहिता* ३३.४३

ā kṛṣṇena rajasā vartamāno niveśayannamṛtaṁ martyaṁ ca ।
hiraṇyena savitā rathenā devo yāti bhuvanāni paśyan ॥
– *Yajuḥsaṁhitā* 33.43

Now consider the creation from the second viewpoint of existence. From this point of view, the earth is rotating around the sun. Only then the *darśapūrṇamāsa yajña* is completed and therefore the existence of the universe is protected. The same Veda, which from the point of view of appearance, says:भुवनानि पश्यन्नायाति सविता (*bhuvanāni paśyannāyāti savitā*) (the sun has come out to see the world), states the following from the point of view of existence:

अथ तत ऊर्ध्व उदेत्य नैवोदेता नास्तमेतैकल एव मध्ये स्थाता तदेष श्लोकः । न वै तत्र न निम्लोच नोदियाय कदाचन । देवास्तेनाहँ सत्येन मा विराधिषि ब्रह्मणेति । न ह वा अस्मा उदेति न निम्लोचति सकृद्दिवा हैवास्मै भवति । – *छा०उप०* ३.११.१-३

atha tata ūrdhva udetya naivodetā nāstametaikala eva madhye sthātā tadeṣa ślokaḥ । *na vai tatra na nimloca nodiyāya kadācana* । *devāstenāhaṁ satyena mā virādhiṣi brahmaṇeti* । *na ha vā asmā udeti na nimlocati sakṛddivā haivāsmai bhavati* । – *ChāUp* 3.11.1-3

सूर्यो बृहतीमध्यूढ़स्तपति । बृहद्ध तस्थौ भुवनेष्वन्तः ।

sūryo bṛhatīmadhyūḍhastapati । *bṛhaddha tasthau bhuvaneṣvantaḥ* ।

The sun neither rises nor sets. Rather, it is completely stationary in the centre of the universe alone, in the centre of the equatorial circle which is called *bṛhatīcchanda*. This is the literal meaning of this *mantra*. Translating this *śruti*[4] principle literally, the *Vāyu Purāṇa* 2.15.15 has said thus:

नैवास्तमनमर्कस्य नोदयः सर्वदा सतः ।
उदयास्तमनं दर्शनादर्शनं रवेः ॥

naivāstamanarkasya nodayaḥ sarvadā sataḥ ।
udayāstamanaṁ darśanādarśanaṁ raveḥ ॥

There is, in truth, neither rising nor setting for the sun, for it is always there, and these terms (of rising and setting) merely imply his presence and disappearance.

[4] That which has been said by *śruti*.

You might say that the devotees of the Veda have somehow proved the stationary character of the sun, but it has not yet been proved that the earth rotates. Please listen to what the Vedas say in this context:

सोमः पूषा च चेततुर्विश्वासां सुक्षितीनाम्।
देवत्रा रथ्योर्हिता। – *सामसंहिता* २.२.६.१०

somaḥ pūṣā ca cetaturviśvāsāṁ sukṣitīnām।
devatrā rathyorhitā। – *Sāmasaṁhitā* 2.2.6.10

The literal meaning of this *mantra* is that the "moon is rotating on its circle called *dakṣavr̥tta* and the earth is rotating on its orbit called *krāntivr̥tta*". These *dakṣa* and *krānti* circles are vital. This means that the chariot referred to is no material or physical chariot. They are Bhātisiddha[5] *prāṇātmaka* spherical chariots. Why are the moon and the earth rotating? For the "livelihood" of their "subjects". (The meaning is obvious.) It is from the rotation of the moon and the earth that seasons occur; seasons give birth to agricultural products, crops and herbs. They are the means of life.

The words *soma* and *pūṣā* mentioned in the *mantra* सोमो राजा चन्द्रमाः (*somo rājā candramāḥ*) and इयं वै पृथिवी पूषा (*iyaṁ vai pr̥thivī pūṣā*) are indicative of the earth and the moon. Modern science has, on the basis of the second viewpoint, accepted the sun as stationary and the earth as rotating and is ignorant of the first point of view. It has not yet been able to answer why are they rotating? But the *r̥ṣis* have answered this "why" – विश्वासां सुक्षितीनाम् (*viśvāsāṁ sukṣitīnām*).

In this context, we put another question before the modern material scientists: Who caused the earth to rotate and how did he cause the earth to rotate around the sun? Can they solve this question in accordance with the science of creation? What have those *r̥ṣis*, who according to the modern material scientists were engaged in unknowable self-realization, said in this connection? Will modern physical material scientists want to know it? Let them be kind enough to hear it.

यज्ञ इन्द्रमवर्धयद्यद्भूमिं व्यवर्तयत्।
चक्राण ओपशं दिवि । – ऋ० ८.१४.५

yajña indramavardhayadyadbhūmiṁ vyavartayat।
cakrāṇa opaśaṁ divi। – *R̥V* VIII.14.5

Yajña gave strength to Indra. Being strengthened by this *yajñabala* (strength of *yajña*), the solar Indra hit the earth with his foot and thus the

[5] Bhātisiddha is that which does not exist in reality but appears to exist.

earth moved in the same way as a football moves by the kick of a football player. To understand the real meaning of terms like *yajña* and Indra, scientists will have to come to the shelter of the Vedas and its study.

Now your attention is invited towards the third viewpoint based on creation, a viewpoint which modern material science has not even imagined in dreams. Does the creation or the form of the universe end in the sun? This third viewpoint is the *sṛṣṭimūlā sṛṣṭi-vidyā* which we have also called *svayambhuva-vidyā*. According to this third point of view, even the sun is not stationary. The sun is rotating around a planet which is innumerable times greater than it on the circle called *ayanavṛtta* and this complete circular movement is completed in 25,000 years. The equatorial pole rotates on *ayanavṛtta* around the नाकस्थ पारमेष्ठ्य विष्णु (*nākastha pārameṣṭhya viṣṇu*). It is in fact the solar rotation of *krāntivṛttīya kadamba*. This is a subtle and scientific subject and this is not the occasion to deal with it. Explaining this polar rotation, which is actually related to the solar rotation, venerable *guruvara*[6] has said:

नाकस्थविष्णोः परितस्तु वेदद्दग्
व्यासार्द्धजे सञ्चरति ध्रुवं ध्रुवः ।
वृत्ते ध्रुवस्तत्र तदा पुरा युगे
प्राग्मेरुखस्वस्तिकगोऽभिजित्यभूत् ॥
– इन्द्रविजय, त्रैलोक्य प्रसंग, ३२

nākasthaviṣṇoḥ paritastu vedadṛg
vyāsārddhaje sañcarati dhruvaṁ dhruvaḥ ।
vṛtte dhruvastatra tadā purā yuge
prāgmerukhasvastikago 'bhijityabhut ॥
– *Indravijaya*, Trailokya Prasaṅga, 32

The pole star moves in the radius of 24° latitude, around the firmament-point on which *viṣṇupada* (feet of Viṣṇu) is situated. For this reason, in ancient days, the pole star occupied a position in the Abhijita *nakṣatra* (one of the lunar asterisms) on *kha-svastika* formed by the movement of 24° in all four directions around the firmament point. When reversed or inverted, it formed a 24° circumference around the *svastika* of Pāmīr mountains.

Does the process of rotation culminate in the sun? The *parameṣṭhi* which is watery and is in the form of Sarasvān ocean around which the sun is rotating on its circuit, that *parameṣṭhi* itself is rotating on the *aṇḍa* circuit around *svayambhū* which is the greatest amongst the greatest planets

[6] Paṇḍit Madhusūdan Ojhā.

and is vital-ocean, that is in the form of widest sky. And it is here that the *darśapūrṇamāsa* process of rotation ends, which is, as has been said before, the cause of the creation of the earth.

On the basis of this science of creation, which is divided into three branches, we can say that when we take Svayambhū Prajāpati as the central point, all other parts of the universe are rotating and moving. Is Svayambhū not moving? The answer to this question will be that *Svayambhū* does not move. It is pure motion itself. Pure motion is that element[7] which is absolutely devoid of rest at all. And according to scientific principles, the motion from which all duration and permanence is taken out becomes absolutely permanent and durable, *manaso javīyaḥ*. It is this property of pure motion of *svayambhū* which the *śruti* has in mind when it says:

अनेजदेकं मनसो जवीयो नैनद्देवा आप्नुवन् पूर्वमर्शत्।
तद्धावतोऽन्यानत्येति तिष्ठत्तस्मिन्नपो मातरिश्वा दधाति॥

तदेजति, तन्नैजति, तद्दूरे तद्वन्तिके।
तदन्तरस्य सर्वस्य, तदु सर्वस्यास्य बाह्यतः॥ – *यजुःसंहिता* ४०.४-५

anejadekaṁ manaso javīyo nainaddevā āpnuvan pūrvamarśat।
taddhāvato 'nyānatyeti tiṣṭhattasminnapo mātariśvā dadhāti॥

tadejati, tannaijati, taddūre tadvantike।
tadantarasya sarvasya, tadu sarvasyāsya bāhyataḥ॥

– *Yajuḥsaṁhitā* 40.4-5

Let us correlate the cosmic scene thus:

The moon along with its envelope of moonlight is rotating on its *dakṣavṛtta* around the earth. Keeping this moon with an envelope in the womb of its (earth's) envelope called *rathāntara-sāma*, the earth is rotating on its *krāntivṛtta* around the sun. Keeping the moon and the earth along with their respective envelopes in its own envelope called *bṛhatsāma*, the sun is rotating on its *ayanavṛtta* around *parameṣṭhi*. The *parameṣṭhi* keeps the earth, the moon and the sun along with their respective envelopes in its envelope called *sarasvān*, as the ocean keeps a bubble and is rotating along with its envelope on a circuit around *svayambhū* which is *prāṇātmaka* and therefore pure motion and therefore pure (absolute) *parajyotiḥ* (motionlessness of motion).

The *rūpaiḥjyotpiṇḍa* of the earth, *svajyotiḥpiṇḍa* of the sun and *ṛta-piṇḍa* of *parameṣṭhi* are sectors of the universe which are rotating on the

---

[7] *tattva* (basic natural essential).

basis of *svayambhū*, which is the light of lights and truth of truths and they have thus become the participating natural elements in *sarvahūta yajña* which is related to *svayambhū*. This is a short outline of the five-divisional universe, in other words, a universe of *svayambhū*, *parameṣṭhi*, the sun, the moon and the earth divisions of Prajāpati. Seven sectors have also been accepted of these five divisions due to Gāyatrī which has seven aspects. The earth is *bhū* and the sun is *svāhā*. The mid-region of the two where the moon exists is *bhuvaḥ*, *parameṣṭhi* is *janaḥ* and the mid-region between the sun and *parameṣṭhi* is called *mahaḥ*. *Svayambhū* is *satya* and the mid-region between *svayambhū* and *parameṣṭhi* is *tapaḥ*. Thus, the five divisions are converted into seven. Of them, the first six – *bhū*, *bhuvaḥ*, *svaḥ*, *mahaḥ*, *janaḥ* and *tapaḥ* – are moving and these have been called *rajorūpaloka* as is clear from इमे वै लोका रजांसि (*ime vai lokā rajāṁsi*).

The seventh *satya-svayambhū* is pure motion and thus absolute permanence and is separated from *rajobhāva* or *lokabhāva* and is *aja* (that which is not born), is Brahmā and is the fundamental base of the universe in which all the six *rajo-loka*s culminate. Expressing the form of this seven-sectional universe, the *śruti* says:

अचिकित्वाञ्चिकितुषश्चिदत्र कवीन्पृच्छामि विद्मने न विद्वान्।
वि यस्तस्तम्भ षळिमा रजांस्यजस्य रूपे किमपि स्विदेकम्॥ – ऋ० १.१६४.६

acikitvāñcikituṣaścidatra kavīnpr̥cchāmi vidmane na vidvān ।
vi yastastambha ṣaḷimā rajāṁsyajasya rūpe kimapi svidekam ॥
– *R̥V* I.164.6

The *r̥ṣi* says:

> I am unable to analyse this mysterious *tattva*. Those who know this and are able to see this *tattva*, I am asking them (with humility). I am asking because I wish to know it and I do not know it myself. I wish to know only that which has controlled these six *rajas* with strength. Which is that element which exists on its own and is unchangeable?

This is to be borne in mind that the *r̥ṣi*, who has said (seen) the above *mantra* is Dīrghatamā, who has analysed the most intricate, the most subtle and the most mysterious science of creation in his अस्य वामीय सूक्त (*asya vāmiya sūkta*). Is Maharṣi Dīrghatamā, who knew everything, ignorant? Is he not a learned person? Try to understand this method of erudite warning of a *maharṣi*.

He, who is proud of his "intelligence" and "reason", and is overwhelmed by his sense of individual and personal prestige, will never be able to penetrate deep into the interior of this Vedic mystery of creation as long as he does not completely assimilate his pride and concentrate on studying this science with devotion and veneration in his heart. Those who cannot assimilate their sense of personal position, prestige and power, which gave them fame and name, those who consider themselves as great intellectuals, thinkers and logicians are intoxicated with this pride. Those who, due to this intoxication, consider it beneath their dignity to express their queries before learned persons and are devoid of veneration and faith do not even deserve to hear the subtle exposition of Vedic science, as is obvious from the *mantra-śruti*s: विद्या ह वै ब्राह्मण-माषपाम (*vidyā ha vai brāhmaṇamāṣapāma*). It was for this relevant education, with the intention of telling the way of understanding the mysteries of Vedas that such learned and great *maharṣi* said: अचिकित्वान्-विद्मने-न-विद्वान् (*acikitvān-vidmane-na-vidvān* – Ignorant, I inquire of the sages who know (the truth); not as one knowing, for the sake of (gaining) knowledge; what is that one alone, who has upheld these six spheres in the form of the unborn? – *Ṛ̥V* I.164.6).

That which is called *nāma* (name) in popular language is called *vyāhṛti* in Vedic language. The name of *satya-prāṇa* of *svayambhū* (due to its property of pure motion) is *ṛṣi*, as has been explained yesterday while dealing with the derivation of terms like *ṛṣi-prāṇa*. *Svayambhū*, which is in the form of *ṛṣi-prāṇa* and *sarvahūta yajña*, is the master (*pati*) of all subjects (*prajā*). Of its many names, one is Prajāpati *ṛṣi*. The seven masters, *bhū*, *bhuvaḥ* and *svaḥ* are the seven names of Prajāpati. They are the seven *vyāhṛti* of *svayambhū Īśvara*, which are explained by the well-known *gāyatrī-vidyā*. The *gāyatrī-tattva* has been called eight-lettered (having eight *akṣara*), *akṣara* is another name for *prāṇa*. From the viewpoint of *chanda*, the size of *prāṇa* is *pradeśa*. The measure of a *pradeśa* is ten and half-finger breadth. Therefore, by eight *akṣara*s the whole *gāyatrī chanda* becomes eighty-four-fingers wide. This is the measure of *Īśvara*. That is why the *Chāndogya* (*Upaniṣad*) has analysed the science of division of this universe from the viewpoint of Gāyatrī.

Every human being, in which *gāyatrī-tattva* is the predominating base, should definitely measure eighty-four fingers according to his own fingers' breadth. Even a six-month old child is eighty-four fingers' wide when measured from his own finger's breadth. If somewhere there is a difference of one or two fingers, it will not be considered a violation of *chanda*: न वै एकेनाक्षरेण छन्दांसि वियन्ति, न द्वाभ्याम् (*na vai ekenākṣareṇa chandāṁsi viyanti, na dvābhyām*).

But if the difference is of five or seven fingers breadth, it will be considered a defect. It is due to faulty physical *yajña* of conjugal life, as has been explained clearly in *gāyatrī-vidyā*. This *gāyatrī* measure exactly applies to the seven-sectoral Viśva Prajāpati. Like *mana*, *Īśvara*, which is in inseparable form, is also eighty-four fingers from his own finger. There is a slight difference in the method of measurement; while the measure of man is taken by *pradeśa* which is ten-and-a-half fingers wide, the measure of *Īśvara* is taken from *pradeśa* which is twelve-fingers wide – *bhū*, *bhuvaḥ*, *svaḥ*, *mahaḥ*, *janaḥ*, *tapaḥ* and *satyam*. These seven *loka*s are seven *vitasti*s[8] of *Īśvara* Prajāpati which is twelve fingers wide. Therefore, in the language of Purāṇas, it is called *sapta-vitastikāya* (that which measures seven *vitasti*s, which means eighty-four fingers wide). See what *Bhāgavata Purāṇa* 10.14.11 says in this context:

क्वाहं तमोमहदहंखचराग्निवार्भूसंवेष्टिताण्डघटसप्तवितस्तिकायः। क्वेदृग्विधाविगणिताण्डपराणु चर्य्यावाताध्वरोमविवरस्य च ते महित्त्वम्॥

kvāhaṁ tamo-mahadahaṁ-khacarāgnivārbhūsaṁveṣṭitāṇḍa-ghaṭasaptavitastikāyaḥ। kvedṛgvīdhāviganịtāṇḍaparāṇucaryyāvātād hvaromaviavarasya ca te mahittvam॥

What am I, a small creature measuring seven spans of my own hand? I am enclosed in a potlike universe composed of material nature, the total material energy, false ego, ether, air, water and earth. And what is Your glory? Unlimited universes pass through the pores of Your body just as particles of dust pass through the openings of a screened window.

The five divisions or seven divisions of creation, which is divided into three branches and is related to the viewpoints of head, heart and foot has also been called *virāḍ-vidyā*. The following *Yaju-mantra* is its basis:

सहस्रशीर्षा पुरुषः सहस्राक्षः सहस्रपात्।
स भूमिं सर्वतः स्पृत्वात्यतिष्ठद्दशाङ्गुलम्॥ – *यजुःसंहिता* ३१.१

sahasraśīrṣā puruṣaḥ sahasrākṣaḥ sahasrapāt।
sa bhūmiṁ sarvataḥ spṛtvātyatiṣṭhaddaśāṅgulam॥ – *Yajuḥsaṁhitā* 31.1

Due to its universal aptitude, Svayambhū Prajāpati has been called Viśvakarmā (creator of the universe) and this five-divisional science of creation has also been called *tridhāma-vidyā* (science of three worlds). The aggregate totality of *parameṣṭhi* and *svayambhū* has been called *parama dhāma*. The sun has been called *madhyama dhāma* and the aggregate of moon and earth has been called *avama dhāma*. The science of creation,

---

[8] An ancient Indian unit of length, approximately 21 cm.

correlating the five divisions and three *dhāmas*, has also been accepted as the *mahimā-vidyā* of Viśvakarmā Prajāpati, the science of manifestation of the creator of the universe:

प्रकृतिषद्विकृतिः कर्त्तव्या – यद्वै देवा अकुर्यस्तत् करवाणि ।

prakṛtiṣadvikṛtiḥ karttavyā – yadvai devā akuryastat karavāṇi ।

Following this natural principle to its every letter, cultured Indians, who understood *tattva*, have accepted three *dhāmas* on the basis of their arrangement in nature. They did it for their worship and it has been elaborately explained in the Purāṇas. We are quoting here some *mantras* of the Veda which deal with five-divisional science of creation related to the three Paurāṇic *dhāmas*, to show the interrelation between the Vedas and Purāṇas.

य इमा विश्वा भुवनानि जुह्वदृषिर्होता न्यसीदत्पिता नः ।
स आशिषा द्रविणमिच्छमानः प्रथमच्छदवराँ आ विवेश ॥ १॥

विश्वतश्चक्षुरुत विश्वतोमुखो विश्वतोबाहुरुत विश्वतस्पात् ।
सं बाहुभ्यां धमति सं पतत्रैर्द्यावाभूमी जनयन्देव एकः ॥ ३॥

या ते धामानि परमाणि यावमा, या मध्यमा विश्वकर्मन्नुतेमा ।
शिक्षा सखिभ्यो हविषि स्वधावः स्वयं यजस्व तन्वं वृधानः ॥५॥ – ऋ० १०.८१

ya imā viśvā bhuvanāni juhvadṛṣirhotā nyasīdatpitā naḥ ।
sa āśiṣā draviṇamicchamānaḥ prathamacchadvarām̐ ā viveśa ॥1 ॥

viśvataścakṣuruta viśvatomukho viśvatobāhuruta viśvataspāt ।
saṁ bāhubhyāṁ dhamati saṁ patatrairdyāvābhūmī janyandeva ekaḥ ॥3 ॥

yā te dhāmāni paramāṇi yāvamā, yā madhyamā viśvakarmannutemā ।
śikṣā sakhibhyo haviṣi svadhāvaḥ svayaṁ yajasva tanvaṁ vṛdhānaḥ ॥5 ॥
– *ṚV* X.81

The beginning of the divisional universe *svayambhū* has been called Viṣṇu; the third sun has been called Indra; fourth *pṛthvī* as *agni* and the fifth the moon as *soma*. These are five *akṣaras* from where the five *kṣaras* (material) would emerge. This is in short the outline of the five-divisional universe.

At the culmination of this universe, the moon, born from the *agni-prāṇa* of *pṛthvī*, is situated. This moon being the culminating point (end) of the universe has also been called *nidhana*. The foundation of the divisions – *svayambhū*, *parameṣṭhi* and others – inspired the five *akṣaras*, which in turn are the base of the five *kṣaras*, is that *puruṣa* which is called *avyaya*. This *avyaya-puruṣa* has been explained as Aśvattha, in the famous *aśvattha-vidyā* of the Vedas. The five-divisional universe is only one twig of that *avyayāśvatha-brahma* tree. There are thousands and thousands of such twigs in that *aśvattha* tree. Infinite is the universal expansion of that *aśvattha-brahma*.

Of the thousands of such branches, only one branch is being explained (in today's lecture). The technical word for that twig is *balśā* (branch). There are five knots or divisions in this one branch of the Avyayeśvara Prajāpati. Just as one sugar cane has many knots, similarly this *prājāpatya balśā* has five knots. That is why it has been called the five-divisional *prājāpatya balśā*. Its fundamental base is *avyaya-puruṣa*.

The *avyaya-puruṣa* along with *svayambhū*, *parameṣṭhi*, the sun, the moon and the earth based on the former, the aggregate of the six is the short framework of the five-divisional science of creation which follows the *puruṣa*.

Exactly a similar state of things is reproduced in man himself. The difference is only in names (used for the five divisions). The name *puruṣa-vyaya* is common to both. The difference is only in the name of the five universal divisions. The *svayambhū*, *parameṣṭhi*, the sun, the moon, and the earth of the *ādhidaivata*, or the vital sphere, are known in man as *avyakta-mahān-buddhi* (intelligence), *mana* (mind) and *śarīra* (body). The following *śruti* of *Kaṭha Upaniṣad* (1.3.10-11) correlates the five-divisional science of creation which follows *puruṣa*:

इन्द्रियेभ्यः परा ह्यर्थाः अर्थेभ्यश्च परं मनः ।
मनसस्तु परा बुद्धिर्बुद्धेरात्मा महान्परः ॥

महतः परमव्यक्तम्-अव्यक्तात्पुरुषः परः ।
पुरुषान्न परं किञ्चित् सा काष्ठा सा परा गतिः ॥

indriyebhayaḥ parā hyarthāḥ arthebhyaśca paraṁ manaḥ ।
manasastu parā buddhirbuddherātmā mahānparaḥ ॥

mahataḥ paramavyaktam avyaktātpuruṣaḥ paraḥ ।
puruṣānna paraṁ kiñcit sā kāṣṭhā sā parā gatiḥ ॥

The outer sense organs are gross. The sense objects of sound, touch, form, taste and smell are subtler than the sense organs. The mind that processes these sense objects is subtler than the sense objects. The intellect is subtler than the mind. The *ātman*, referred here as *mahān* (great *ātman*) is subtler than the intellect. In verse 3.11, this chain of thought is expounded further as follows: The Unmanifest is beyond (subtler than) the great *ātman*, the *Puruṣa* is beyond the Unmanifest. *Puruṣa* is the supreme goal and there is nothing beyond Him.

> Beyond the senses are the objects; beyond the objects is the mind; beyond the mind intellect; beyond the intellect the great *ātman*, the Unmanifest; beyond the Unmanifest, the *Puruṣa*; beyond *Puruṣa*, there is nothing. This is the end, the supreme goal (*Kaṭha Upaniṣad* 3.10-11).

This is the structure of the fivefold universe which has been expanded by the essential *manotā-tattva*[9] divided into fifteen parts. The mysterious scientific explanation of this *manotā-tattva* is the subject of an entirely independent article. It will be sufficient here to know the names of the fifteenfold projections of *manotā*.

An idiom common among the masses is तीन-पाँच मत करो (*tīna-pāñca mata karo* – do not be clever). It appears that the origin of this idiom seems to be in the belief that the authority vests only in the universal Prajāpati. It is impossible for man to do such a thing. The three *manotā*s of *svayambhū* are *veda, sūtra* and *niyati*. The *manotā*s of *parameṣṭhi* are Bhr̥gu, Aṅgirā and Atri. The *manotā*s of the sun are *jyotiḥ, gauḥ* and *āyuḥ*. The *manotā*s of the moon are *retaḥ, śraddhā* and *yaśaḥ*. And the three *manotā*s of the earth are *vāk, gauḥ* and *dyau*. Understanding scientifically the concept of the five-divisional universe, of which each division is expanded by these three *manotā*s, is to understand the five-divisional science of creation. In the words of the Vedas, he who understands this arrangement of three in five sectors understands the Vedas:

> यानि पञ्चधा त्रीणि त्रीणि तेभ्यो न ज्यायः परमन्यदस्ति।
> यस्तद्वेद स वेद सर्वँ सर्वा दिशो बलिमस्मै हरन्ति। – छा०उप० २.२१.३-४
>
> *yāni pañcadhā trīṇi trīṇi tebhyo na jyāyaḥ paramanyadasti* ।
> *yastadveda sa veda sarvaṁ sarvā diśo balimasmai haranti* ॥
> – *ChāUp* 2.21.3-4

> There are five parts of *Sāma*, and each of these is divided into three parts. There is nothing higher than these [fifteen forms of *Sāma*]. He who knows *Sāma* knows everything, and gifts come to him from all quarters. His vow will be to constantly say to himself, "I am one with all".

Prajāpati, which is the image of *sarahuta yajña*, becomes the propounder of the *adhyātma yajña* (process of life) of man in the shape of *saṁvatsara* by keeping it in the form of *agni* and *soma*, which are properties of the earth and the moon, the culminating points of universal Prajāpati. From the universal *agni-soma yajña*, which is a portion of the wide universe, how

---

[9] *Manotā* in Vedic *vijñāna* relates to the process of creation. It is an attribute of existence.

is the physical *yajña* in man matched? This subject is connected with the real behaviour pattern in a man's life and inspired by the fundamental scientific deliberations which have taken place just now. It is also being explained in a few words. The definition of the physical *yajña* in man is expressed by three words – *anna, ūrka* and *prāṇa* – which are known as the bodily *yajña* in man. Try to understand this definition of *yajña* by the following example.

Bodily Yajña of Man: An Example

At a particular fixed time, one feels hungry. To pacify this hunger, we offer the oblation of food in the fire burning fiercely in the entire body except the short hairs on the body and nail ends and is known as *vaiśvānarāgni*. For this act of oblation, we say in popular language, we have taken our food to our satisfaction. The natural property of fire is to break, to separate and this food which is given in oblation in *vaiśvānarāgni* is also "broken" by the fire first in two parts. The first part is *rasa* (essence) and the part which is separated is called *mala* (the excreted or impure portion). Thus, the food is divided in *rasa* and *mala* portions. Again the process of breaking up continues. Again the essence is separated from the impure or excreted portion. The essence of *rasa* is called blood and the excreted portion remains *rasa*. Again the process and the essence of the blood portion becomes flesh and the excreted portion remains blood. The same process of breaking up by the *vaiśvānarāgni* continues and the core portion of the flesh becomes fat and the excreted portion flesh. From fat, the excreted essence which comes out makes bones and the portion that remains becomes fat. Again the same breaking up happens and the excreted portion becomes bone and the essence is called *majjā* (pulp) and the excreted portion which remains becomes bones. The process of breaking up continues further and the essence which now comes out is called *śukra* (semen). Thus starting from food up to the formation of semen, the process of breaking up continues and *rasa*, blood, flesh, fat, bones, pulp, semen are formed and all of them are connected with the earthly solid element.

Does the process of breaking associated with the process of churning end at semen virile? No. Why? Because uptil now only a solid portion of the food has been churned. The mid-regional liquid and the lunar property of sparseness (gaseousness) still remain. In the formation of food, the earthly, the mid-regional and lunar properties of all the three *loka*s, viz. solidness, liquidity and gaseousness, are incorporated. The above-mentioned seven ingredients are earthly ingredients. Even now the churning of two liquid and gaseous ingredients remain. In the last earthly ingredient, semen virile, the process of churning starts. The essence which is now separated is not material but vital essence of mid-regional character (*vāyavya-prāṇa*) and it is called *oja* (freely translated as vigour). In view of the fact that semen is the starting point of production of vigour, therefore vigourness depends on the protection of semen. This *oja* is called *ūrka* in the technical and scientific Vedic language and *ūrka* was given second place in the previously mentioned definition of *yajña*. All the seven ingredients starting from food and ending at semen, being earthly, are grouped together under the head *anna* (food) and then the mid-regional *oja* finds its place.

Vigour, i.e. *ūrka*, is considered as essence related to semen, which is considered excreted in relation to former. In *oja*, there is still a lunar essence. It is the excreted lunar *saumya* essence which is excreted from *parameṣṭhi* and which has been explained by यो वै शिवतमो रसः (*yo vai śivatamo rasaḥ* – Sweet love of affectionate mothers (*ṚV* X.9.2)). In the continuous churning process, *oja* is also churned and the lunar *śivatama rasa* is called *rasa* and its excreted portion became *oja*. This lunar vital *śivātmā* essence is called *prajñāna* mind (as different from the organic *janaja* mind we are well aware of). *Śruti* चन्द्रमा मनसो जातः – मनश्चद्रेण लीयते (*candramā manasojātaḥ – manaścandreṇa līyate*) points out to the formation of mind from the moon, from which it has said: अन्नमयं हि सोम्य मनः (*annamayaṁ hi somya manaḥ* – Mind is nourished by food (*Chāndogya Upaniṣad* 6.5.4)). That mind is this fine lunar essence and the purity of this *śivatama rasa* symbolized by the *prajñāna* mind depends on the purity of food. In India, where scientific truths have become part and parcel of life, men and women, young and old, learned and unlettered all know this idiom. As will be your food, so will be your mind. Whichever type of food one takes, *sāttvika*, *rajas* or *tamas*, one's mind is formed accordingly at the end of the process of churning. The lunar essence which is formed by *sāttvika* food is considered to be the foundation of *sāttvika* character, which is a resultant of *śivatama rasa*. Only such a mind will bear noble feelings and thoughts. Referring to this noble mind, *ṛṣi*s have said:

यत्प्रज्ञानमुत चेतो धृतिश्च यज्ज्योतिरन्तरमृतं प्रजासु।
यस्मान्न ऋते किञ्च न कर्म्म क्रियते तन्मे मनः शिवसंकल्पमस्तु॥ – *यजुःसंहिता* ३४.३

yatprajñānamuta ceto dhṛtiśca yajjyotirantaramṛtam prajāsu ।
yasmānna ṛte kiñca na karmma kriyate tanme manaḥ śivasaṅkalpamastu ॥
– *Yajuḥsaṁhitā* 34.3

That is why in comparison to other rules of behaviour and conduct, the *ṛṣi*s have been most careful about food. Rājarṣi Manu has also emphasized that faulty food, more than anything else, proves to be the prime reason of the death (destruction) of brāhmaṇa:

अनभ्यासेन वेदानां आचारस्य च वर्जनात्।
आलस्यादन्नदोषाच्च मृत्युर्विप्राञ्चिघांसति ॥ – मनु॰
anabhyāsena vedānāṁ ācārasya ca varjanāt ।
ālasyādannadoṣācca mṛtyurviprāñcighāṁsati ॥ – *Manu*

To what extent is the purity of food important for Indians? The answer to this question is clearly given by the process of churning explained above. It is a matter of immense misfortune for this wise Indian nation that Indians have forgotten the basic and ancient scientific tradition and have become indisciplined and unbridled in their eating habits. The Indians do not rest at this, but are in the frontline of those who ridicule the system of eating which was systemized by the *ṛṣi*s and has been proved scientifically and traditionally. To what further extent can people of this nation degrade?

Physical Yajña: The Next Stage

The context now is of the physical or bodily (*ādhyātmika*) *yajña*. The churning of the seven earthly ingredients gave the man bodily healthiness; *oja* gave vigour; and the *śiva saṅkalpātmaka mana* gave him nobility of mind. The *yajña* of physically strong, vigorous and noble-minded man is continuously processed by *anna*, *ūrka*, *prāṇa* or the seven ingredients, vigour and mind. This is the definition of the bodily *yajña* and this is the fundamental correlation of the process.

Let us try to state this in an easier way. The act of taking food is completed. Eaten food is converted into *rasa*. This essence of the food strengthens the physical vital energy which is almost defunct and unconscious before taking food. By oblation of essence, the almost-dead *prāṇa* is awakened, just as fire starts blazing when fuel is added. The meaning is clear. The eaten food after being changed into the form of essence is ultimately converted into *prāṇa* in course of time. This blazing vital energy, a resultant of food, has been called the life-force. This vital energy converted into the form of life-force becomes, for the purpose of the functioning of various bodily organs, the promoter-inspiration which inspires willful thought and deliberately guarded action. By this inspiration of vital energy, we proceed to work, in which we engage ourselves and we spend this vital energy. As this process of spending continues, the vital energy becomes devoid of strength and gradually our aptitude towards work also becomes weak. With this weakness, the vital energy starts becoming, as if, unconscious and defunct. This state of "unconsciousness" is called *aśanāyā* which literally means "desire to take food" or, in other words, to feel hungry. Again this hunger and its satisfaction by taking food, oblation of eaten food in the bodily fire, conversion of food into vital energy by becoming *rasa*, aptitude for action due to strengthened vital energy and weakening of vital energy due to activity and desire to take food again, and again taking food ... in this way the circular motion of *anna*, *ūrka* and *prāṇa* flows continuously and this is in short the definition of physical (bodily) *yajña*.

According to the science of *cayana*, the shape of a baby is formed for nine months continuously in the womb by the coating of *agni*. This act of laying seven coatings of *agni* is completed in nine months. At this stage, *agni* becomes a complete unit. And by the push of a particular wind called *avayāmarut*, the baby leaves the womb and is thrown outside, on the ground.

His first act is *rūdana* (weeping). The baby which is an aggregation of *agni* is *rūdana*-personified, *agnirvā rudra*. The *prāṇa-devatā*s (vital energy) of various bodily organs are shaken due to this *rudrāgni*. Immediately, the oblation of *guḍa* (treacle – first thickening of cane juice after boiling) and honey is offered. Thus Rudradeva is pacified and the weeping baby who is the personification of the coating of *agni* becomes silent. Rudradeva is pacified by "water" in the form of *anna*. This is why in Indian culture, it is a general practice to offer water to a guest, who is Rudra in a different form, to pacify the *rudrāgni* which is activated due to the exertions of the way (he must have travelled). The Śrāvaṇa (month corresponding to July–August) month has therefore been called the month for propitiating Sāmba Sadāśiva: when the earthly *agni*, i.e. Rudra, proceeds towards the ocean and is thus converted into soggy Sāmba Sadāśiva. This *soma*, which pacifies the *rudrāgni*, has been called *śāntarudriya* which in direct language has been called *śatarudriya* (see *Śatapatha Brāhmaṇa* 9.1.1.1). The blazing fire (*agni*) is pacified by the associated natural, essential *soma*, as the *ṛṣi* has said:

अग्निर्जागार तमृचः कामयन्तेऽग्निर्जागार तमु सामानि यन्ति।
अग्निर्जागार तमयं सोम आह तवाहमस्मि सख्ये न्योकाः ॥ – ऋ० ५.४४.१५

agnirjāgāra tamṛcaḥ kāmayante 'gnirjāgāra tamu sāmāni yanti ।
agnirjāgāra tamayaṁ soma āha tavāhamasmi sakhye nyokāḥ ॥

– *ṚV* V.44.15

The form of man is being protected by this *yajña* of *agni-soma*. The *soma anna* which is offered in oblation has been divided by the *ṛṣis* into four groups – *dadhi* (curd), *ghṛta* (ghee), *madhu* (honey) and *amṛta* (nectar). Only that food is considered appropriate for physical *rudrāgni* in which all the four are developed and are in satisfactory proportion; unripened food is inedible for human beings. Only when the corn is ripened in the field, or say when the milk is converted into curd, that ripe paddy (or any other corn) becomes his food; because in it all the four properties are present. The solid portion is the *dadhi* (curd); this is helpful for flesh and bones, etc. the solid portion of the human body. When water is mixed with flour, a property of lubricating unctuousness is manifested, this is the *ghṛta* portion. The *dadhi* portion is earthly property while the *ghṛta* portion is the mid-regional property.

According to *śruti*, when Prajāpati was forming "subjects", he poured a large pot full of *ghṛta* at the time of making the boar by way of oblation. As a result, the proportion of fat is more in boar than in other animals. The mid-region is that pot in which *ghṛta* in the form of *ājya* is filled. In a fatty boar, this is found in abundance; *ghṛta* has this characteristic. That is why a boar is a brilliant and strong beast. It is for this reason that a strong man is called *śūra* for his strength and a kṣatriya who performs the Rājasūya *yajña* (a royal ritual) is asked to wear shoes made of boar's skin.

The *rasa* of the third *dyauloka* is *madhu*, which is poured down in Bharaṇī *nakṣatra* by the *candra* (lunar) *nāḍī*. That is why Bharaṇī *nakṣatra* has been called a parasole of honey. When the sun passes through star Bharaṇī, the Pūrṇamās *yajña* of *madhu* commences. This means, vital honey pours on earth in abundance. That is why the month of Caitra, which is considered to be the period of pouring of *madhu*, has been called Madhumāsa. During this month, everywhere in the conscious and semi-conscious beings (tree etc.), a period of festivity begins.

There is sweetness all-round. During this period of spring, which is called the king of seasons, vegetables, crops and fruits become sweet and fresh. This sweetness in food articles or corn is the element of *madhu*. The mid-regional *ghṛta* portion supplements and strengthens the liquid portion in the body essence (blood), etc. and the solar honey (*madhu*) portion strengthens the semen virile in a man's body. That is why *śukra* (semen virile) has been called *madhu* also and the disease connected with it is called *madhumeha*.

Now we arrive at the fourth stage of *amṛta*. It is that rare and singular vital essence which comes from the fourth *parameṣṭhi-loka* situated above the sun. It is that *śivatama rasa* which nourishes the mind. In every victual (vegetable, herb, etc.), *somarasa* is also present. But the Indra *prāṇa* which permeates in the air drinks this *somarasa*. Therefore, all corn is deprived of this *rasa*. Only in rice (paddy), Indra cannot enter because it is cultivated in fields where Varuṇa mostly predominates. And due to this water, Indra cannot penetrate rice. The enmity between Indra and Varuṇa is well known. Due to this unimpaired presence of *soma* in rice, it is called *akṣat* which is specially used in the Indian traditional festivities. In the scientific प्रेतपितृश्राद्धकर्म्म (*preta-pitṛ-śrāddha-karmma*), which is related to the satisfaction of the dead forefathers – who have predominantly *soma* vital energy – rice is used. Rice is *parameṣṭhi-tattva* and the presiding God of *parameṣṭhi* is Viṣṇu. Therefore, on the *vaiṣṇavī ekādaśī*, eating rice is prohibited. This *amṛta soma* nourishes the human mind. If this *amṛta rasa* goes out of a particular food, it cannot be relished by the human mind. In such a case, men say, "I have taken food but unwillingly". Old food, or food kept for some days, is devoid of this *soma* property. Indra, who is placed in Vāyu, drinks (soaks) it. That is why the amount of *soma* which is present in fresh milk after milching is not found in the milk which is kept in the open for some time. Just for convenience, this *amṛta rasa* is what makes our food delicious.

Of all edible things, *soma* is placed in its own form only in cow's milk. This is clear from the following principle of Āyurveda:

> स्वादु-पाकरसं-स्निग्धं-ओजस्य-धातुवर्द्धनम् ।
> प्रायः पयोऽत्र गव्यं तु जीवनीयं रसायनम् ॥ – *अष्टाङ्गहृदय* ५.२१-२२
>
> *svādu-pākarasaṁ-snigdhaṁ-ojasya-dhātuvardhanam* ।
> *prāyaḥ payo 'tra gavyaṁ tu jīvanīyaṁ rasāyanam* ॥
> – *Aṣṭāṅgahṛdaya* 5.21-22

Ignorant of the basics of Indian culture, but self-styled masters and authority on it, modern material scientists say:

> These Indians consider animals as their mother, they have started worshipping cows. Really they are merely blind devotees of tradition.

The Hindus of this country will welcome such traditionalism, because everything in this tradition is based on subtle and mysterious science of nature. Any one, who understands the basic truths of these viewpoints, will become a devotee of these traditions. You talk of cows. The Hindu worships even the dog in *bali karma* and offers *bali* to the crow. Why only this, worshipping ass is a religious rite for him. The ass is worshipped as the carrier of mother Śītalā, which is worshipped in the form of a special "power". Is he worshipping the physical object before him? No. Through physical objects, vital energy is propitiated.

He knows that a cow is also an animal just like any other animal. But he also knows that the basic fundamental base of the cow is that of *prāṇa* (vital energy), which is associated with other *prāṇa-śakti* (vital energies) like Rudra and Vasu. He knows that cow's milk is not ordinary milk, it is a milk in which life-giving *amṛta soma* of *parameṣṭhi* exists in abundance. This *gau* (cow) *tattva* is called Aditi in the language of *ṛṣi*s. Troubling a cow in any manner will invite harm to one's life-giving vital *rasa*. Cow is definitely an object of worship by the whole of mankind. If it is not so, it should be. The Hindu has understood its basic truth. Does it therefore become his sectarianism? I feel that many are misguided in this respect because scientific principles underlying them have been forgotten. Here is what *ṛṣi*s say about this animal which has the *gau-prāṇa*:

माता रुद्राणां दुहिता वसूनां स्वसादित्यानाममृतस्य नाभिः ।
प्र नु वोचं चिकितुषे जनाय मा गामनागामदितिं वधिष्ट ॥ – ऋ० ८.१०१.१५

mātā rudrāṇāṁ duhitā vasūnāṁ svasādityānāmamṛtasya nābhiḥ ।
pra nu vocaṁ cikituṣe janāya mā gāmanāgāmaditiṁ vadhiṣṭa ॥
– *ṚV* VIII.101.15

The cow is the mother of Rudras, daughter of Vasus, sister of Ādityas. I have told (so) wise persons that they should never hurt the unoffending cow.

Cow is another form of Aditi; because it is the centre of *amṛta soma*. The shape of man is self and body. The self is the form of *jñāna-brahma* and the body is vital energy associated with activity. Knowledge and action – these two words explain the form of man. The fountainhead of knowledge (*jñāna-brahma*) of a nation is Brahmā and that of action is the animal cow. The *ātmā* of the nation becomes lifeless and unconscious if Brāhmaṇas, who are devotees of knowledge and science, fall from grace. The body of that nation weakens, power of vitality and action also weakens seriously where the cow, which is a symbol of life-giving vital energy, is endangered. The decline of brāhmaṇa and cow denotes the fall of the soul and body of a nation. It means as if the whole nature has shaken and this is the meaning of endangering *dharma*. It is in a situation like this that *Parameśvara*, who is inseparable from nature, takes incarnation. The saying गो-ब्राह्मणहिताय च (*go-brāhmaṇahitāya ca*) (for the welfare of cow and brāhmaṇa) means for the welfare of the power of knowledge and power of action of a nation which has in brāhmaṇa and cow its living symbols.

In the context of cow, which is full of *soma amṛta*, this additional but no less relevant issue is being placed before the wise listeners today because it is intimately connected with life-giving vital energy of man. In human victuals, the four divisions of the universe – earth, mid-region, the sun and *parameṣṭhi* – are represented by *dadhi*, *ghṛta*, *madhu* and *amṛta*. By oblation of such victuals, the *yajña*, associated with *anna*, *ūrka* and *prāṇa* goes on, and it is by keeping in view the scientific principle behind it that man justifies his title of *mānava*.

The central truth of his existence is the fourth *amṛta soma*, which is *śivatama rasa*, because the purity of the human mind is dependent on it. What are the characteristics of this *parameṣṭhīya śivatama rasa* of the human mind which has the properties of *amṛta*? Here is the answer:

पवित्रं ते विततं ब्रह्मणस्पते प्रभुर्गात्राणि पर्येषि विश्वतः ।
अतप्तनूर्न तदामो अश्नुते शृतास इद्वहन्तस्तत्समाशत् ॥ – ऋ० ९.८३.१

pavitraṁ te vitataṁ brahmaṇaspate prabhurgātrāṇi paryeṣi viśvataḥ ।
ataptanūrna tadāmo aśnute śṛtāsa idvahantastatsamāśat ॥

–*ṚV* IX.83.1

It is quite possible that your minds have become tired of this dry technical talk. To save myself from this accusation, I am narrating a story which is relevant to the context:

> Once upon a time some problems cropped up before the three gods who were lords of three *lokas*. It was decided that *Bhagavān* should go to Vaikuṇṭha Dhāma and should place those problems before Bhagavān Viṣṇu, who is the Lord of innumerable unlimited triple worlds and lives in Goloka. It was also decided that arrangements should be made according to instructions received from him. Accordingly, Bhagavān Śaṅkara arrived in Goloka Dhāma along with his divine musical instrument *ekatārā*. After waiting for a long time, Bhagavān Śaṅkara was able to see Nārāyaṇa who lived on the Śeṣanāga. Śrī Śaṅkara placed all the problems with humility before him and solutions to them were obtained. In that vast ocean, in the *japa* of Bhagavān Viṣṇu, Lord of the whole universe, was the mother of the world, Mahā-Lakṣmī. She made this request to Bhagavān Śaṅkara: "You are the greatest and first master of divine music. It has been long since I heard your music. You will have to fulfil my wish today."

Śaṅkara hesitated a little and did not show much enthusiasm, Nārāyaṇa, then himself, said, "Bholenātha! when Mahādevī is requesting, you must". Forced thus, Bhagavān Śaṅkara began playing his divine music from *ekatārā*. All the *devatā*s of all the worlds assembled there to hear this music, which is rare even for gods. As the rhythm and rhyme of music proceeded upward, the eyes of *devatā*s began to close. Later on, all *devetā*s were overwhelmed by this music, forgot themselves and went back, as if in a trance. And thus the grand divine music of Bhagavān Śaṅkara concluded after a long period of time.

After the music was over, all *devatā*s woke up slowly. But an unimaginable surprise was there. At the exact place on the bed of Nāga where Lord Viṣṇu was lying, there was no trace of Viṣṇu. Bright water was flowing there. There was an outcry in the whole universe at this most astonishing incident. When the whole universe trembled in the absence of Nārāyaṇa, an unheard of sound emanated from the wide sky (*paramākāśa*): "Oh *devatā*s! There is no cause of anxiety. I have melted due to the divine music of Lord Śaṅkara which you can see in the form of water in my bed. This sacred water will pierce down the solar universe and travel in the locks of hairs of Lord Śiva for some time. Later, only with the *tapa* of Bhagīratha, it will find release in the north and from there by the *tapa* of Maharṣi Jahnu it will cause the salvation of the sons of King Sagara and of all Indians having veneration and devotion in their hearts.

Really, Goddess Bhāgīrathī is not water, but is the melted Viṣṇu and those lucky ones who bathe in it say:

काकैर्निष्कुषितं-श्वभिः कवलितं गोमायुभिर्लुण्ठितम्
स्रोतोभिश्चलितं तटाम्बुलुलितं वीचीभिरान्दोलितम्।
दिव्यस्त्रीकरचारुचामरमरुत्संवीज्यमानः कदा
द्रक्ष्येऽहं परमेश्वरि त्रिपथगे भागीरथि स्वं वपुः॥

kākairniṣkuṣitaṁ-śvabiḥ kavalitaṁ gomāyubhirluṇṭhitam ।
srotobhiścalitaṁ taṭāmbululitaṁ vīcībhirāndolitam ।
divyastrīkaracārucāmaramarutsaṁvījyamānaḥ kadā
drakṣye 'haṁ parameśvarī-tripathage bhāgīrathi svaṁ vapuḥ ॥

This Paurāṇic narrative is mysterious and meaningful, which is interrelated with *adhyātma* (physical), *ādhidaivata* (vital), *ādhibhūta* (material) and *adhinakṣatra* (astronomical) points of view. On *amṛta* and with reference to this fourth *amṛta-tattva* – the most sacred Gāṅgeya known as Brahmaṇaspati Soma – definition of the fourfold victuals is concluding.

अन्नमयं हि सोम्य मनः (*annamayaṁ hi somya manaḥ*) – according to this principle, the pure mind made from food is the cause of salvation and bondage. The form of *yajña* becomes defective due to defect in food. Due to the defect in the form of *yajña*, the *avyakta mahān* portion of man is deprived from the elevating influence of *svayambhū* and *parameṣṭhi* divisions of the universe. And as a result, man violates the natural laws incorporated in *dharma* and indulges in self-destruction. In this context, a Vedic narrative is narrated here in few words.

It is heard Prajāpati gave birth to five subjects – *asura*s (demons), *devatā*s, *pitṛ*s (forefathers), *manuṣya* (man) and *paśu* (animal). All the five expressed before Prajāpati the desire that he should be kind enough to make arrangement of food and light for them, so that they could exist and they may live. First of all, *asura*s came before Prajāpati impertinently. Prajāpati rebuked them and said: "you are my eldest ones, let me first arrange for the younger ones. Wait aside till then." Then came *devatā*s very humbly. Prajāpati arranged that *yajña anna* (food) and sunlight will be available to them and, once in a year, the *uttarāyaṇa* day was fixed as their main day. The *devatā*s went away satisfied. Then *pitṛ*s came forward with traditional mellowness and humility. They were instructed that *svadhā* will be their food and they will take food once a month on the *amāvasyā* day and moon will be their light. Then came forward men, bowing their head in respect. They were directed that *namaḥ* will be their food and they will take food twice in twenty-four hours, in the morning and in the evening, and *agni* will be their light. And then came in their entirely natural free mood, the animals. Prajāpati told them:

यथाकाम वोऽशनम्। यदैव यूयं कदा च सम्भाव्यै – यदि काले यद्यनाकालिवैवाश्नायेति।

yathākāma vo 'śanam । *yadaiva yūyaṁ kadā ca sambhāvyai – yadi kāle yadyanākālivaivāśnāyeti* ।

In other words, there will neither be any bondage of time for them, nor any regulation on edibles. Whenever they desire, walking, sitting, sleeping and standing, in the morning, evening, night and midnight, and whatever is available, they can eat. Intelligent human beings will act as light for you. Animals also went away satisfied and then in the end came *asura*s, oldest and strongest among them, sheer materialists and concerned only with their bodies and presented themselves before Prajāpati in a manner which expressed, as if they wished to say, "you see, we have kept patience for a long time, therefore we should be given the best, the bulkiest food and light". Prajāpati, as if keeping in view this desire, said: "Fraud, deceit, bluff, trickery, falsehood, jealousy, quarrel, etc. will be your food and deep darkness will be your light." The *asura*s were perhaps happy beyond expectations at this.

Concluding this meaningful, but hidden narrative, Bhagavān Yājñavalkya says:

> न वै देवा अतिक्रामन्ति, न पितरः, न पशवः, नासुराः। मनुष्या एवैकेऽतिक्रामन्ति।
>
> *na vai devā atikrāmanti, na pitaraḥ, na paśavaḥ, nāsurāḥ । manuṣyā evaike 'tikrāmanti ।*

It means that the rules which Prajāpati had formed at the beginning of creation are not violated by *devatā* or *pitṛ* nor by *asura*. But it must be stated with regret that it is only man who violates the rule formed by Prajāpati. Why is it so? Answer to this question is the subject of an independent lecture.

Respectable intelligent friends! Concluding the five-divisional science of creation, we have to submit humbly that the Vedas, the foundation of Indian culture, are not communal or sectarian literature. This is a vast treasure of divine knowledge and science and intelligent persons of no age can have any difference with or objection to it. It is the misfortune of the Indian nation that during the last 3,000 years, due to passing fallacies of the human mind, there was no opportunity to reach the roots of its national treasure. And, therefore, this *ṛṣi* culture is also looked upon as sectarian and communal viewpoints. You all ought to submit this to the President of the Indian nation that the Vedas are immune from all communal sectarianism.

Sir! Inspired by a great man like you, who has faith in the *mānava* culture, the Vedic culture, which is the basic foundation of national life, should be resurrected and rejuvenated from the basic scientific viewpoint in this fortunate era of Independence, so that our cultural greatness might enhance everyday.

With this noble hope this lecture on five-divisional science of creation is being concluded with the following meaningful extract related to the five-divisional goddess of nature:

> पञ्चस्रोतोम्बुं पञ्चयोन्युग्रवक्त्रां
> पञ्चप्राणोर्मिं पञ्चबुद्ध्यादिमूलाम्।
> पञ्चावर्तां पञ्चदुःखौघवेगां
> पञ्चाशद्भेदां पञ्चपर्वामधीमः॥ – श्वेत०उप० १.५

pañcasrotombuṁ pañcayonyugravaktrāṁ
pañcaprāṇormiṁ pañcabuddhyādimūlām ।
pañcavartāṁ pañcaduḥkhaughavegāṁ
pañcāśadbhedāṁ pañcaparvāmadhīmaḥ ॥ – *ŚvetaUp* 1.5

We know the river with five currents, made turbulent and tortuous by the five sources, has waves in the form of the five organs of action, which has its origin that which is the root of the five cognitions (mind); which has five whirlpools (river), the rush of its water is constituted by the five sorrows and which has fifty branches and five stages.

Third Discourse

Vedic Concept of Man
An Exposition

WHILE concluding the lecture on the five-divisional science of creation, your attention was invited to a Vedic narrative, which states:

> न वै देवा अतिक्रामन्ति, न पितरः, न पशवः, नासुराः। मनुष्या एवैके अतिक्रामन्ति।
>
> *na vai devā atikrāmanti, na pitaraḥ, na paśavaḥ, nāsurāḥ। manuṣyā evaike atikrāmanti।*
>
> Neither gods nor ancestral forefathers, neither the animals nor the demons violate the natural laws of living, only man alone violates them.

I have been asked to submit something about the Vedic concept of man. Why does man violate the rules of creation determined by Prajāpati? In other words, why does he violate the divine laws as manifested by nature and how does he do it? While answering this question, I am placing before you, first, a narrative related to Bhagavān Bādarāyaṇa Vyāsa who was an unparalleled protector of Indian culture.

In the famous Naimiṣāraṇya forest, in the peaceful meadows covered with beautiful trees and at a place where the valley of hills met the flow of rivers, a place eminently suited for intellectual development, one day a question cropped up spontaneously before the assembly of *ṛṣi*s: Who is the greatest in this divisional universe?

From one of the learned *maharṣi*s, who was an authority on the concept of universe and an ardent devotee of intellectual pursuits, this answer came forth:

> The Supreme Lord of the universe, Lord of all, absolute, permanent, that which cannot be limited in shape or form or functions: the creator of all religions, known as Śāśvata (eternal) Brahmā is the greatest in this five-divisional universe.

All the learned *ṛṣi*s gathered in the assembly looked silently at each other and expressed their feelings without speaking it and it was obvious that they were not satisfied with the answer: वातो देवेभ्य आचष्टे यथा पुरुष ते मनः (*vāto devebhya ācaṣṭe yathā puruṣa te manaḥ* – the silent external atmosphere indicates the mind of man). According to the *śrauta* (Vedic) principle, the *ṛṣi* who had answered immediately understood the dissatisfaction of the assembly of *ṛṣi*s. And immediately, the following alternative answer came from him:

> Lord of *dyauloka*, *sarvajña* Indra, Lord of mid-region, the image of Hiraṇyagarbha Vāyu and earthly *agni* which is the image of *virāṭ* should be considered greatest as they are the manifestation of Parātpara Brahma, who is the Lord of all.

Again the same indifference and lack of enthusiasm was felt. And then the learned *maharṣi* gave the following answer:

> Bhagavān Brahmā, who is the image of Vedas and creator of *Gāyatrī-Mātṛkāveda* is supreme, or Bhagavān Viṣṇu, image of *sarvahūta yajña* and who "resides" in Goloka and is the benefactor of the whole universe is greatest, or Bhagavān Rudra, who annihilates everything and is also the protector of everything, is greatest among all (*mahāmaharṣi*), or who knows the mysteries of creation and the laws is most superior or the learned men of India who end various human infatuations by putting the science of *yajña* based on the science vital force into practice are greatest amongst all in this universe.

Man and Other Beings

While giving these answers one after another, the learned *maharṣi*, became aware in his mind that not one of the assembled *ṛṣi*s is satisfied by any one of the answers put forward by him. The same thing was obvious externally also. Everyone felt that these answers were only an excuse for a real answer as these were based on personal imagination. No one, therefore, expressed his acceptance, support or satisfaction. Purāṇapuruṣa Bhagavān Bādarāyaṇa Vyāsa was overwhelmed with happiness at this indifference of the *ṛṣi*s because in this assembly of *ṛṣi*s he had found real explorers of truth and those who were discussing the basic fundamentals were able and competent. Therefore, ultimately, the following answer came forth from Maharṣi Bhagavān Vyāsa:

> गुह्यं ब्रह्म तदिदं ब्रवीमि – न हि मानुषात् श्रेष्ठतरं हि किञ्चित्।
>
> *guhyaṁ brahma tadidaṁ bravīmi – na hi mānuṣāt śreṣṭhataraṁ hi kiñcit* ।
>
> – *MBh* 22.299.20

There is nothing higher than man in this world. God transcendent is beyond us. Every human being must be regarded as sustaining the possibility of rising to the divine state.

The Purāṇapuruṣa said, "oh *ṛṣi*s! I am placing before you that secret fundamental; on hearing which you will be suddenly astonished. You should positively place this fact firmly in your hearts that man is superior amongst all beings, according to the Vedic principles: पुरुषो वै प्रजापतेर्नेदिष्ठम्, अहं मनुरभवम्, अहं सूर्य्य इवाजनि, योऽहं-सोऽसौ योऽसौ-सोऽहम्, पूर्णमदः-पूर्णमिदम् (*puruṣo vai prajāpaternediṣṭham, ahaṁ manurabhavam, ahaṁ sūryya evājani, yo 'haṁ-so 'sau, yo 'sau-so 'ham, pūrṇamadaḥ-pūrṇamidam*). According to these principles, the *puruṣa*, who fully symbolizes the *sarvajña*, *hiraṇyagarbha* and *virāṭa* facets of that Prajāpati, who is the basic foundation of universe, or man who has in him completeness and fullness and is known as *mānava* due to his relation with Manu is supreme and greatest amongst all. Really nothing is superior in this universe to man, because by developed intellectual faculty, he has brought *devatā*, *pitṛ* and Brahmā also within the bounds of his knowledge and has thus earned the sole right of saying this:

ब्रह्मविद्यया ह वै सर्वं भविष्यन्तो मन्यन्ते मनुष्याः ।

brahmavidyayā ha vai sarvaṁ bhaviṣyanto manyante manuṣyāḥ ।

– *Bṛhadāraṇyaka Upaniṣad* 1.4.9

Men say, when they learn *brahma-vidyā*, they will learn all.

Man's Supremacy over Other Beings

How, why and what this man was in ancient times? What has become of the man, who is supreme, rather greatest amongst all due to his natural faculties of body, mind and intellect. This has become a complicated question today. How and why the superior man of the past has been reduced today to this horrible state?

In reply to this timely question, this emotional self (the speaker) is indulging in the impertinence of suggesting that though trying to respect the sentiments of the people, they should proceed to explore such basic realities about man, which modern man, especially those in modern India, is forgetting, so that it may be placed before him again and he might be awakened by his devotion and strength of culture and might say again to the enemies of *mānava dharma*, the following words:

न हि मानुषात् श्रेष्ठतरं हि किञ्चित् ।

na hi mānuṣāt śreṣṭhataraṁ hi kiñcit ।

Through the medium of the above narrative, we arrive at this conclusion that if there is any being in this universe who can achieve the same-sphereness, proximity, resemblance or identification with *Parameśvara*, it is man alone. Inspired by all the energies of *Īśvara*, Prajāpati, always associated with the fundamental *manu-tattva*, which is the projection of Prajāpati in the form of Śāśvata Brahmā and known as *mānava*, who is based on the central *manu-tattva*, is supreme among all beings. Why should such an abundant and accomplished man violate the bounds of universal propriety? This question is really intricate and we are to analyse it carefully in today's lecture.

Man's Violation of Natural Principles

Why does man violate the natural principles? The answer to this question will begin with the statement that man possesses all qualities that are there in *Īśvara*. But in addition to them, he possesses such qualities which *Īśvara* does not have.

> क्लेशकर्म्मविपाकाशयैरपरामृष्टः पुरुषविशेष ईश्वरः ।
>
> *kleśakarmmavipākāśayairaparāmr̥ṣṭaḥ puruṣaviśeṣa iśvaraḥ* ।

According to this *yoga* principle of Patañjali, while *Īśvara* is fully dissociated with afflictions and bad qualities like ignorance, egoism, attachments, dogmatism and demonic qualities of lie, malice, arrogance, hypocrisy and distrust, man misuses his independent strength of action, errs in these qualities and assumes himself to be something greater than *Īśvara*. And it is definite that this eagerness to become something greater than *Īśvara* leads him to the violation of natural vital disciplines. To express more clearly, man creates imaginary rules and regulations which are opposite to the natural, absolute, permanent and truthful rules. Caught in the trap of attachment towards his own imaginary rules, man forgets his own self and violates the natural disciplines. Afflicted with hypocrisy, self-praise, dogmatism, attachment, egoism and ignorance, man becomes proud of his intelligence and becomes intellectually blind and thus forgets himself. This has also been called narcissism, blind love of oneself. Influenced by what he calls the "obvious", influenced by what others say of him, man becomes emotional and is ruled by his mind (not by his intellect) and progressively follows blindly a path which is absolutely contrary to his own form. Thus, when he becomes eager to do more than what *Īśvara* has done, in other words, when he slights the *īśvarīya* rules and engages in framing imaginary rules and laws of life based on his own mental imagination and feelings, then he falls (from the high pedestal indicated above) and this is his violation. The devastating results of this violation which he has to bear might not be expressed by him due to the false sense of position, prestige and personality. But in course of time, man is never able to save himself from the doom that follows.

Manu: The Absolute Central Truth

The meaning of the word *mānava* is "the son of Manu". Therefore, it has been explained as मनोरपत्यं मानवः (*manorapatyaṁ mānavaḥ*). By this Manu, do we mean the saintly king who has been referred to and described in the Itihāsa and Purāṇas? No. Manu is a name for that imperishable (*tattva*), fundamental natural essential which has been accepted as the basic foundation of the universe and the essential *śraddhā* has been described as "wife" or partner of *manu-tattva*. In the previous discourse about the divisions of the universe, I had pointed out the central truth, the truth of all truth. Manu is another name of that central truth. The *manu-tattva* exists in all living and lifeless matters of the universe and thus from this point of view all of them should have been called *mānava*. But in view of the fact that in all, except man, this Manu is in a diffused state, like beams and rays, and not as an independent central entity, therefore they are not directly "benefited" by Manu. In man, the *manu-tattva* exists in the form of an independent entity. This is why man is superior, great.

In various contexts of creation, this *manu-tattva* has been described variously as *satyāgni*, Indra, *prāṇa*, Śāśvata Brahmā, which have been referred to thus:

आत्मैव देवताः सर्वाः सर्वमात्मन्यवस्थितम्।
आत्मा हि जनयत्येषां कर्म्मयोगं शरीरिणाम्॥

प्रशासितारं सर्वेषामणीयांसमणोरपि।
रुक्माभं स्वप्नधीगम्यं तं विद्यात्तं पुरुषं परम्॥

एतमेके वदन्त्यग्निं मनुमन्ये प्रजापतिम्।
इन्द्रमेके, परे प्राणमपरे ब्रह्म शाश्वतम्॥

एष सर्वाणि भूतानि पञ्चभिर्व्याप्य तिष्ठति।
जन्म-वृद्धि-क्षयैर्नित्यं संसारयति चक्रवत्॥ – मनु॰ १२.११९.१२२-२४

ātmaiva devatāḥ sarvāḥ sarvamātmanyavasthitam ।
ātmā hi janayatyeṣāṁ karmmayogaṁ śarīriṇām ॥

praśāsitāraṁ sarveṣāmaṇīyāṁsamaṇorapi ।
rukmābhaṁ svapnadhīgamyaṁ taṁ vidyāttaṁ puruṣaṁ param ॥

etamake vadantyagniṁ manumanye prajāpatim ।
indrameke pare prāṇamapare brahma śāśvatam ॥
eṣa sarvāṇi bhūtāni pañcabhirvyāpya tiṣṭhati ।
janma-vṛddhi-kṣyairnityaṁ saṁsārayati cakravat ॥
– *Manu* 12.119.122-24

Manifestation of Manu in Man

Following is a substance of this exposition. The name of the central truth is Manu. The being in which it has found expression in its own form is *mānava* (man). This means that he in whom his true self has been fully expressed can be called *mānava*. At this stage, we must understand something about the form of man. In the five-divisional universe, the earth, the moon and the sun are evident and the fourth fundamental is invisible, unmanifested or latent. Thus, the universe can be divided into one invisible and three visible or manifest divisions. Man has also been formed by these four divisions. Therefore, a balanced and coordinated state of the four will be called *mānava*. The property of the earth which man inherits constitutes his body. The property of the moon in man is called his mind. The property of the sun in him is called his intellect and the fourth invisible property is called the human soul (the self). This unmanifest *ātmā* is the *manu-tattva* and man has been called *mānava* due to its fullest expression and manifestation in him. Thus, the structure of man is the invisible *ātmā*, solar intellect, lunar mind and earthly body, and on this basis, it can be said that body alone is not man, mind alone is also not man, intellect alone is also not man and only the soul or the self is also not man. Rather, an integrated state of the four – body, mind, intellect and self – is *mān*(*ava*) and this is the initial outline of the concept of man on the basis of which we are to understand the full form of man. In this context, we should first pay attention towards the four classifications of earthly beings.

Living and Lifeless Beings: The Differentiating Factor

Divide all that you see, first in two categories – living and lifeless. It must be borne in mind that these two classifications are not at all relevant from the point of view of that all-pervading *ātmā*. Whether it is living or lifeless, *ātmā* exists in latent form in all and everything, as is clear from the principle ईशावास्यमिदं सर्वं यत् किञ्च जगत्यां जगत् (*īśāvāsyamidaṁ sarvaṁ yat kiñca jagatyāṁ jagat* – All this is enveloped by the Supreme Being – *Īśa Upaniṣad* 1); it is on this basis that सर्वं खल्विदं ब्रह्म (*sarvaṁ khalvidaṁ brahma*) principle has been enunciated. Generally people think that those who have soul have life and those who have no soul are lifeless. But from this scientific and essential viewpoint this idea is baseless and misguided. Existence and otherwise of *ātmā* is not the dividing factor between the living and the lifeless, because *ātmā* pervades and exists in everything. The dividng factor is the property of the organism as is clear from the principle सेन्द्रियं चेतनं द्रव्यं निरिन्द्रियमचेतनम् (*sendriyaṁ cetanaṁ dravyaṁ nirindriyamacetanam* – Matter having sense organs is conscious while matter without sense organs is unconscious – *Caraka Saṁhitā*). Those beings in which bodily organs are manifest and developed are called the living, and those in whom they are not manifest are called lifeless. Please study the following *mantra*:

> पराञ्चि खानि व्यतृणत्स्वयंभूस्तस्मात् पराङ् पश्यति नान्तरात्मन्।
> कश्चिद्धीरः प्रत्यगात्मानमैक्षदावृत्तचक्षुरमृतत्वमिच्छन्॥ – क०उप० २.१.१
>
> *parāñci khāni vyatṛṇat-svayaṁbhūstasmāt parāṅ paśyati nāntarātman* ।
> *kaściddhīraḥ pratyagātmānamaikṣadāvṛttacakṣuramṛtatvamicchan* ॥
> – *KaUp* 2.1.1

Prajāpati has made the bodily organs with their face outward. Our eyes are always diverted towards the outside physical world, therefore, we remain incapable of self-realization of seeing ourselves. Knowledge of organisms is the knowledge of exterior and intoxicated with this knowledge, we exclaim "we shall see, then shall we believe". It is being enraptured in this material vision that those who depend on their organs, and on the obvious, are deprived of the knowledge of the internal world of the invisible vital energy just like animals who can see only outwards. Nowadays, qualities like truthfulness and non-violence draw much respect and this should be considered good luck for the nation. This virtuous conduct should be welcomed. But we should be careful, lest we commit the mistake of accepting the truth perceived by bodily organs as truth or imagined, or apparent non-violence based on imaginary feelings as real non-violence. If it be so, in that case we shall definitely overwhelm our natural human form in the excitement and dogmatism of imaginary conception of truth, non-violence, etc. and consequence of such a situation could only bring tragedy to this world. As a result, faith in self and reality of the world is impaired. It is therefore essential that we should not be emotionally excited by words like truth and non-violence related only with mental or bodily perceptions. Instead, we should try to understand their inherent and fundamental concepts. It is clear that man in his excitement commits a mistake and in realizing the mistake repents throughout his life. Therefore, there should never be a mistake in seeing a mistake.

Truth: Ostensible and Real

For example, let us take the word *satya* in the eyes of common people; speaking truth is considered to be very important. But according to *ṛṣis*, "truth is essentially a characteristic of the *ātmā*, which cannot be enacted or expressed by an organ of speech". Speaking practical truth may be considered as speaking the truth, but the essential truth can never be a subject of speech. As a matter of fact, even in practice, the human bodily faculties can only "touch" the fringe of truth and not capture it in entirety. The clock is before you. You are asked: what is the exact time at this moment. Your eyes reach the clock's dial and you say "it is exactly eight now". But is your "exact" really "exact"? No. It is not exact, because you cannot speak exactly and simultaneously at the moment when your eyes reach and read the clock. By the time you speak, some time has already elapsed. Therefore, it is obvious that even practical truth cannot be expressed by organs (of speech). What then is the significance of speaking truth? It is on this basis that the Vedas themselves have raised the question and have solved it from a practical point of view. When the *yajamāna* in *yajña* is directed (स वै सत्यमेव वदेत् – *sa vai satyameva vadet*) that he should speak the truth till the *yajña* is over, the *ṛṣi* immediately raises the question (कोऽर्हति मनुष्येषु सत्यं वदितुम् – *ko 'rhati manuṣyeṣu satyam vaditum*): when truth cannot be enacted by organs, then on what basis this direction concerning speaking truth should be put into practice?

Śruti solves the problem thus, चक्षुर्वै सत्यम् (*cakṣurvai satyam*), whatever is perceived by *cakṣu* (eyes) is truth. "Does it mean that our bodily organs of sight are called *cakṣu*?" No. This is basically a false viewpoint, which is based on seeing the obvious and is unrelated to truth. प्रत्यक्षमेदेति चार्वाकाः (*pratyakṣamedeti cārvākāḥ*) – *cakṣu* here means the scientific fundamental sight which has been clearly explained in the words तद्विज्ञानेन परिपश्यन्ति धीराः (*tadvijñānena paripaśyanti dhīrāḥ* – Brahmā is perceived by scientific sight). This scientific "sight" is the real "sight" and through its medium the intellect of man is gradually able to follow the core truth. In this connection, there occurs in the Veda a narrative, which is being put forth before you. Once a feeling of rivalry grew between mind and speech. The mind claimed that he was superior to speech because "if I do not conceive, you (speech) cannot express anything". Contrary to this, the speech argued, "if I am not there, your ideas and resolutions will remain as such and will never be put into practice and, therefore, I am superior". Thus, this rivalry and claim of superiority continued.

When they were not able to decide, they went to Prajāpati for a decision. Prajāpati said, "mind is superior to speech". The speech became angry with Prajāpati and turned away saying that "now in future I shall not bear *havi* (offerings) for you". That is why oblation for Prajāpati is given silently without reciting any *mantra*.

The inherent meaning of this narrative is clear. Mind is closer to the central truth, Prajāpati and then speech. Ideas and resolutions of those persons bear fruit even without speech whose mind is integrated with the central truth. Those whose resolutions are contrary to this central truth fail to get them fulfilled even by speech. It has to be accepted that the self truth is the real truth and it is not shouted from house tops.

Non-violence: Illusion and Reality

The same is the case with the word "non-violence". Non-violence can never be defined as an act of "never causing pain to anybody", because non-violence is also like truth related to subtle and fine *prāṇa-tattva*. There are certain acts which are "violent" but which are beneficial to man. Such acts will be considered non-violent. There are certain non-violent acts which cause immense harm to man. Such acts, though outwardly non-violent, will be considered violent. It is never possible to decide about violence or non-violence by looking at the obvious or the ostensible. *Mahinsyat sarva bhūtāni* (never commit violence on anyone) culminates in the definition of *prāṇa*. It is not possible to decide about violence and non-violence from the "obvious" viewpoint. In this universe, which is changing every moment, fire–fuel (related to *agni-soma*) relationship operates amongst all "matters" according to जीवो जीवस्य भक्षकः (*jīvo jīvasya bhakṣakaḥ*). All are being eaten (fuel) and all are eating (fire); सर्वमिदमन्नादः, सर्वमिदमन्नम् (*sarvam idam annādaḥ, sarvam idam annam*). No believer in non-violence can oppose the scientific principle यो ना ददाति, स इदेव भावत्। अहमन्नमन्नमदन्तद्मि (*yo nā dadāti, sa ideva bhāvat । ahmannamannamadantadmi*). This principle is well known – he who creates me, ultimately he "eats" me. I am his victual, and (I am also eating him, who is eating me)". What is then the significance of always shouting about non-violence related only to obvious perception of bodily organs, "protection of the other, while protecting yourself is the root of non-violence, but it can be understood only when the meaning of 'self' and 'other' is clear". This is not the subject of today's lecture. Concluding this complementary issue, your attention is again drawn towards classifications which were referred to above.

It has been submitted that the beings in which bodily organs are developed are considered "living" or sentient and those in which there are no bodily organs and therefore in whom the central *ātmajyoti* has no opportunity of outward expression are "lifeless" matter. Thus in the beginning, we can divide all matter into two categories – sentient and lifeless, those having organs and those which do not have them.

Which is superior of the two? Answer is भूतानां प्राणिनः श्रेष्ठाः (*bhūtānāṁ prāṇinaḥ śreṣṭhāḥ*). Those material objects which have bodily organs and sentients are superior to those which do not have them. Those who have motion are sentient, those who have no motion are inanimate. "Inanimate" means outward material body, and sentient means bodily organs along with mind. Vital-force Indra is the foundation of bodily organs. The lunar mind *prajñā* is based on vital force *prajñā*. This vital force has been called Indra. When integrated with this *prajñā*, the bodily organs become capable of performing their functions. Without mind, organs cannot function. Therefore, those beings, who have organs, necessarily have a mind also. Those, who do not have organs, signify absence of mind and it means these are inanimate matter. In other words, those beings in which earthly properties are predominant, viz. clay and stones, having no mind and organs are inanimate matter. Those beings in which along with properties of the earth, property of the moon is also expressed, are called sentient, having organs and minds.

This latter class of beings has been divided into four – worms, insects, birds and animals. On minute analysis, some differences might be found in earthly and lunar properties in these four classes of beings having mind. But all these culminate in the sphere of mind and therefore they have been classified together.

Sphere of Sentient Beings

In these four types of beings, in which facts of mind is predominant, certain types of worms, birds like *cakravāka*, cuckoo, and parrot, and animals like elephant have some speciality as compared to other ordinary worms, insects, birds or animals. This speciality, this difference, this additional faculty has been called intelligence. There are certain categories in this group of sentient beings which have even more intelligence than man. From this point of view, the sentient beings (divided into four classes) can be grouped into two groups – those with mind as predominant characteristics and those having intellect. The sentient beings, which have solar vital force along with the lunar, are called "intelligent" (having the characteristic of intellect or *buddhi*). According to ज्ञानमस्ति समस्तस्य जन्तोर्विषयगोचरे (*jñānamasti samastasya jantorviṣayagocare* – All living beings have knowledge through senses – *Durgā Saptaśatī* 1.47), while mental faculty is common in all sentient beings, the faculty of intellect is considered to be a special quality of some chosen birds and beasts, who are considered superior to the general and common sentient beings. It has therefore been said that प्राणिनां बुद्धिजीविनः श्रेष्ठाः (*prāṇinām buddhijīvinaḥ śreṣṭhāḥ* – among the sentients, intelligent beings are superior).

Thus, in the world of beings, we have made three clear classifications in accordance with predominance. Those who are dominated by body are inanimate; those with mind are sentient beings, viz. common birds, animals, etc.; those having intellect are special birds and animals. Here the three manifest aspects of the universe, the earth, the moon and the sun end. The inanimate beings on earth have only their body, ordinary animals have mind as their main characteristic and special animals have intellect as well. The three are inspired by the earth, the moon and the sun, and are divided into lower, medium and superior classes.

The Unmanifest Sector

The lunar beings themselves are divided into thirty-three divisions, which have been explained in the first lecture. All these spheres of the beings and *jīva* culminate in the sun. Now remains the Unmanifest, the "property" of soul or the self. The beings in which this Unmanifest is expressed in its fullness is considered the superior most. Those beings will be considered higher and having "self-faith" due to this important quality and will be considered superior to the triple earthly groups, eightfold lunar classifications and thirty-threefold solar groups. This fourth group will be that of man about whom it has been said: बुद्धिमत्सु नराः श्रेष्ठाः (*buddhimatsu narāḥ śreṣṭhāḥ*) – among those with intellect, man is superior. Keeping in mind these four classes of being, having body as their dominant base and having self-faith, Bhagavān Manu has said:

> भूतानां प्राणिनः श्रेष्ठाः प्राणिनां बुद्धिजीविनः ।
> बुद्धिमत्सु नराः श्रेष्ठाः नरेषु ब्राह्मणाः स्मृताः ॥ – *मनु०* १.९६
>
> *bhūtānāṁ prāṇinaḥ śreṣṭhāḥ prāṇināṁ buddhijīvinaḥ* ।
> *buddhimatsu narāḥ śreṣṭhāḥ nareṣu brāhmaṇāḥ smṛtāḥ* ॥ –*Manu* 1.96

Is there no *ātmā* in insects, worms and animals? *Ātmā*'s domain extends everywhere. Why then man alone has been called *ātmaniṣṭha*? This question is very serious and related to high scientific thought. The two words *jīva* and *ātmā* have become synonymous due to mistaken notions born out of the belief that philosophical ways of thinking are different from scientific ways of thinking. That is why the word *jīvātmā* is prevalent amongst common people. As a matter of fact *jīva* is related to *akṣara prakṛti* (nature) as is clear from

जीवभूतां महाबाहो! ययेदं धार्य्यते जगत् ॥ – *गीता* ७.५

jīvabhūtāṁ mahābāho! yayedaṁ dhāryyate jagat ॥ – *Gītā* VII.5

While *ātmā* is independent and above the *akṣara* and *kṣara* classifications of *prakṛti* and is related to the unchangeable, imperishable, unmanifest *puruṣa* and though it is the base of all, it exists in them in a diffused relationship (*vibhūti sambandha*); in man alone, it is expressed in its fullness. That is why man keeps nature in "his" limits and is *ātmaniṣṭha puruṣa*. This is his "proximity" with Prajāpati. While all other beings are directed and controlled by nature's rules, man is bestowed with his own faculty of action and is thus fully independent from all rules. This is, for long, an accepted idea. In animals, there is *jīva*, but there is no *ātmā*; the *ātmā* in them is in a diffused manner. The full expression of *ātmā*, which is dependent and related to the independent centre, is found only in man.

Four Aspects of Man

As far as the body is concerned, man is placed in the category of inanimate matter. As far as mind is concerned, he is placed in the category of sentient animals who have organs as well as mind. And as far as intelligence is concerned, man is placed in the category of those special animals who have organs, mind and along with that have intellect also. And thus, as far as body, mind and intellect are concerned, which are properties of the earth, the moon and the sun respectively, man is placed in one of the categories. From this point of view, man need not be called *mānava* but may have the right to be called sentient animal. It is only when he is associated and integrated with the fourth characteristic of full expression of *ātmā* that he becomes an appropriate claimant of the title "man". It means that a healthy, strong and tall body is not a barometer of the "man"-ness of man, because in this arena of universe there are many animals who are healthier and stronger than man (lions for example, whose terrible roar is sufficient to crush the pride of man).

Similarly, the lunar mind submerged in art, music, crafts, etc. is also not the measure of man because ordinary birds and animals having minds are also bestowed with such talents. Where does the voice of man stand in comparison to the sweet voice of the cuckoo? Similarly, only intelligence cannot be accepted as the required measure, because in many aspects some animals like elephants and horses are ahead of man in intelligence.

It is therefore proper to say that if you have a handsome body, by that right alone you cannot claim to be a man. If your mind has beautiful imaginations, can pursue music, art, etc.; by these qualities alone, you cannot claim to be man. If you are intelligent and by your intelligence you are capable of producing astonishing inventions in the material world, you can impose your personality on others by the art of speechmaking, if you can lead the fools by your intelligence, you cannot claim to be man by these rights alone. Because, according to *yo parastāt saḥ* (*Bhagavadgītā*), the only foundation of *mānavatā*, the unmanifest *ātmā* is even beyond the bounds of intellect, the Vedas cannot and should not call you as man as long as you do not associate your *jīva* with *ātmā* – in other words, as long as your body, mind and intellect do not become integrated with the self. This is the real form of man. This realization has been considered from the point of view of *ṛṣis* as the supreme achievement and purpose of man, which is absolutely unconnected with the so-called learning. See, what the *śruti* says:

नायमात्मा प्रवचनेन लभ्यो न मेधया न बहुना श्रुतेन।
यमेवैष वृणुते तेन लभ्यस्तस्यैष आत्मा विवृणुते तनूँ स्वाम्॥ – क०उप० १.२.२३

nāyamātmā pravacanena labhyo na medhayā na bahunā śrutena ।
yamevaiṣa vṛṇute tena labhyastasyaiṣa ātmā vivṛṇute tanūm̐ svām ॥
– *KaUp* 1.2.23

The basic seed of *mānavatā* (humanism) is *ātmā*. Humanism is that subtle system of the self which can never be enacted by speech. *Mānavatā* can only be practised in true natural varied form. And here I may say, the manness of man is the natural systematization of the functions of his body, mind and intellect integrated with self. This concept of man's form is definitely astonishing, but failure to realize this has led to many problems.

On the basis of this definition of man, it can now be said that some men are engrossed today only with their body and activities related to it and they have no time to recall the necessity for the development of their mind, intellect and self. The second category of persons is submerged in mental entertainment and is ignoring the body, intellect and self. The third category consists of those who continuously indulge in dry intellectual pursuits and travel in the valleys of deep thoughts, completely turned away from body, mind and self. And, there is that fourth category of people, wearing coloured clothes and claiming to be pure spiritualists and who are entirely deprived of mental pleasure or physical development and are thus proving to be a burden for the nation. Thus man today is divided into four sections and is therefore physically fatigued, mentally worried, intellectually bored and restless from the point of view of self.

In a natural way, this situation can be expressed thus – the wearers of the coloured clothes, claiming to be pure spiritualists, have separated themselves from the entire stream of national life and are eager to prove themselves to be supernatural and superhuman beings. Such spiritualists, deprived from national intellectual pursuits, mental meditation and physical satisfaction, and those who follow them, turn the nation away from the healthy and natural systematic life (*āśrama jīvana*) and indulge in shouting unreal cries of truth, non-violence and world brotherhood and mislead the people who do not understand themselves. Many "intellectuals", having no faith and devotion, are submerged in their imaginary philosophical pursuits; they neither relish entertainment, nor their body is healthy. These dry people have no connection with spontaneously satisfying literature dealing with divine bliss. There is no dearth of such pitiable dry intellectuals even today. Then, there are others who are deeply attached only to the world of mind. They can think of no other cultural activity except the roars and acrobatics of songs, music, dance and similar pursuits, which are related only to the body and mind, and are passing symbols of civilizations and are in no way related to a culture which is based on intellect and self. The last category is those who are engrossed in physical feats and development of the body; they are not even aware of the fact that in the mind too some delicate emotions exist.

In conclusion, the four aspects of man – self, intellect, mind and body – are devoid of integration and as a result of this disintegration, (our) nation's "man" is today bodily unhealthy, mentally dissatisfied, intellectually insatiate and restless as self. Perhaps, we should ask one another this question: "Why is man, despite all accessories and resources, not happy today?". Man will have to find the correct answer to this question himself by realizing and understanding these divided and split facts of man. Ignorance of directions given by Bhagavān Vyāsa – *tattu samanvayāt* (integrate all the aspects of man) is the real cause of this unhappiness.

The *ṛṣis* have suggested and decided upon four objects and paths of pursuit for an integrated and all-side development for health, satisfaction, station and peace. Man has upset all of them today. *Artha* (acquisition of wealth) is related to the body, *kāma* (satisfying desires) is related to the mind, *dharma* (fulfilling one's duties as fixed by the *dharma*) is related to intellect and *mokṣa* (liberation from the cycle of life and death) is related to self. Of these four pursuits, man placed *dharma* and *mokṣa*, related to intellect and self, in a secondary position and gave prime importance to *artha* and *karma*. *Artha* swallowed *dharma*. Frantic pursuit of sensual and physical, and money is eating into man's vitals. Should such a purposeless man even be honoured with the title of "man"?

Leave aside these fundamental issues of integration, today man has become indifferent to those *svastyayana*[1] acts which protect man indirectly. Certain acts were decided upon by the *ṛṣis* which resulted in the well-being (*svasti*) of the common people and therefore they were called *svastya* (well-being). Those who follow these actions properly proceed on the path of prosperity. In popular dialect, they are called auspicious acts and the opposite of them is called inauspicious acts. *Svastyayana* acts are really a great boon from *ṛṣis* to us and we have really ourselves to blame for forgetting them in the glamour of material pursuit. It is said that the well-known thirteen inauspicious acts deprive even independent and sovereign nations of their prosperity. Material wealth is called *lakṣmī* and the vital force which is the essence (*rasa*) and on which *lakṣmī* is based is called *śrī*. According to श्रीश्च ते लक्ष्मीश्च पत्न्यौ (*śrīśca te lakṣmīśca patnyau* – Beauty and wealth are your two wives – *Yajurveda* 31.22), both of them spring from Parameṣṭhi Viṣṇu and therefore they are called Viṣṇu-*patnī* (wife of Viṣṇu). It is true that by our material strength we can gather *lakṣmī* (wealth) and can be successful in the economic *śrī*. But without the foundation of that vital-force (*śrī*), we cannot achieve *aiśvarya* (natural prosperity). Wealth, which does not have prosperity at its base, is bound to slip away by certain inauspicious acts. Wealth coupled with prosperity has been considered real greatness

[1] These are small rules of conduct and action which protect the inner strength of man and give him prosperity, peace and bliss.

and glory of a nation but which can become static and decay by certain acts. Listen to the following:

नित्यं छेदस्तृणानां, भुवि नखलिखनं पादयोरल्पपूजा-
दन्तानामल्पशौचं, वसनमलिनता ग्रासहासातिरेकः ।
द्वे सन्ध्ये चापि निद्रा, विवसनशयनं, रूक्षता मूर्द्धजानाम्
स्वाङ्गे पीठे च वाद्यं हरति धनपतेः केशवस्यापि लक्ष्मीः ॥

nityaṁ chedastṛṇānāṁ, bhuvi nakhalikhanaṁ pādayoralpapūjā-
dantānāmalpaśaucaṁ, vasanamalinatā grāsahāsātirekaḥ ।
dve sandhye cāpi nidrā, vivasanaśayanaṁ, rūkṣatā mūrddhajānām
svāṅge pīṭhe ca vādyaṁ harati dhanapateḥ keśavasyāpi lakṣmīḥ ॥

– *Aṣṭaratnam* 3

That is:

तृण तोरे, नख लिखे, भूमि-निज अङ्ग बजावे ।
कौर काट के खाय, भोग कबहू नहिं लावे ॥

शीघ्र मुखारी करे, पाँव-कर सूक्षम धोवे ।
नगन वसन तन, खाट प्रात सन्ध्या को सोवे ॥

रूख शिखा, मैला वसन्, दिन मैथुन जे करहिं नर ।
इन तेरह अवगुननतें रहे न विद्या, लक्ष्मी-राजघर ॥

tṛṇa tore, nakha likhe, bhūmi-nija aṅga bajāve ।
kaura kāṭa ke khāya, bhoga kabahū nahiṅ lāve ॥

śīghra mukhārī kare, pāṅva-kara sūkṣama dhove ।
nagana vasana tana, khāṭa prāta sandhyā ko sove ॥

rūkha śikhā, mailā vasan, dina maithuna je karahiṅ nara ।
ina teraha avagunanateṅ rahe na vidyā, lakṣmī-rājaghara ॥

To whistle unnecessarily, to sit with both legs drawn out, to chew one's nail-ends, indulging in unrestrained laughter and laughing while eating are some of the inauspicious acts which have been dealt with in full detail in the Śāstras. How the system of vital forces inside a *mantra* is upset by these inauspicious acts and how the auspicious ones regulate them? This is really a remarkable and subtle technical subject which is called the Indian Svastiśāstra. Today's man has become a believer in the "actual" and the "obvious" to such an extent that unless he gets a hard slap on his cheeks on wrong things, he thinks that nothing has happened. The materialist man can never understand the minute changes connected with vital forces. The reason is obvious. The action related to the vital force does not yield results immediately. We do not know by our eyes, which cannot observe minute things, how particular actions effect, how and when the effect saturates and how that becomes (what we call in our ignorance) "luck". It is due to this ignorance that believers commit the audacity of saying: "Oh what happens! if we do like this. All this is simply a blind faith of old people, which has no significance in the present scientific age."

It is true that these inauspicious acts do not result in the devastation of the whole world. If nature would also become similarly impatient and revengeful, as is the materialist man of the present age, then not a single man would survive. It is better not to recall (प्रकृतिस्त्वां नियोक्ष्यति – *prakṛtistvāṁ niyokṣyati*) the punishment she inflicts when the time ripens. Perhaps time itself will awaken these misguided people.

Why does man violate? The definition of man has been narrated here in the context of this question. To understand this violation by man, please keep in view two facets of his four-facet form, i.e. intellect and mind. From these two words, *buddhimānī* (acting intelligently) and *manamānī* (acting according to whim) have emerged. Solar intellect is *āgneya* and lunar mind is *saumya*. Confidence is an expanding *āgneya* substance and is therefore, a "companion" of man who is *āgneya*, while devotional faith (*śraddhā*) is contracting *saumya* substance and is therefore inspired by woman who is also *saumya*. *Śraddhā* is womanhood, it is *śakti*. *Āgneya* confidence is Rudra substance, Śiva substance. The couple, man and woman, can save their natural relationship if these two "substances", *śraddhā* and *viśvāsa*, devotion and confidence, Bhavānī and Śaṅkara are integrated, and are in a union. When both become diversified, both follow the path of violation.

To understand properly what *rati* means, it will be necessary to understand the five branches of mental love. Imagine a mind as a pot in which liquid *somarasa* is filled in the same way as water is filled in a pot. As water in a pot moves, so is the case with the mind filled with *somarasa*. The *rasa* which flows is called "love" as this flow is possible only in five ways, therefore love also has five definite aspects. When *rasa* of the younger one flows onwards to that of the older, it is called respectful devotion. Love of a son towards his father, of a disciple towards his *guru*, of a devotee towards his devoted is *śraddhā*. Here the place of lover is lower and that of the beloved is higher. This set of positions is natural. Now completely reverse the order of positions. Flowing of mental *rasa* of the older towards the younger is called *vātsalya* (affection). It is difficult to have respectful devotion in the younger towards the elder because the spontaneous flow of liquid mental *rasa* is downward. Therefore, some difficulty is experienced in the flow of liquid towards a plane higher than where it is placed. It must always be borne in mind regarding this characteristic of respectful devotion that if the fountain of this respectful devotion is dried up, it is almost impossible to acquire it again. He, whose *śraddhā rasa* is dried up, is deprived of the blessings of *ātma-puruṣa* and thus almost loses his form. Therefore, this property of *śraddhā* should be protected at all costs. A man devoid of *śraddhā* is like a lonely dry tree in a graveyard, which generates sorrow and nothing else. Affection is a *rasa* which flows spontaneously. A son may not have a sense of respectful devotion towards his parents but it is impossible that parents may not have love towards their son because it is difficult to block the flow of this *rasa* which flows downward. Especially a mother, who is mind (*mana*) predominant, can never turn her mind away from her offspring. A son, who turns away from such parents, especially from mother, can never find rest and quietitude. It is well known: कुपुत्रो जायेत-क्वचिदपि कुमाता न भवति (*kuputro jāyeta kvacidapi kumātā na bhavati* – a son may be wicked, but mother can never be so).

A popular tale is well known – once a grown up son was flying a kite in scorching heat on the roof of his house. His father forbade him many a time. But the son continued to ignore his father's advice, saying, "it has become your habit to always interfere in all matters". But the affectionate father was not satisfied. He thought of a plan immediately. He took his grandson to his bosom and started walking in the sun. The attention of the son was suddenly drawn towards his son and he asked his father, "Why have you brought the boy in the sun. He might fall ill due to this scorching heat." Immediately, the father said excitedly, "oh fool! Just as you have a feeling of affection towards this boy, so do I feel about you, which you have realized now".

Third Category of Love: Attachment

Leave aside this aspect of "high" and "low". At a level where the mental *rasa* of two equal (having same qualities and habits) persons flows towards each other on an even level, it is called *sneha* (attachment). This type of love is predominant between two friends. Where there is no equality and still one bears a pretense of friendship, it is definite that there is some cunningness somewhere in such a friendship. Fortunate are those who get even one such "equal" friend in this life. It is impossible to get many friends these days.

Love of Inanimate Beings, Kāma

In devotion, affection and attachment, the beloved is sentient. These three types of love are possible only amongst living beings. There is another type of love where the object of love is inanimate. Books, clothes, ornaments, gardens, etc. are not aware of the emotion of love which their owner may have for them, but the mental *rasa* flows towards them also. Such one sided "love" towards inanimate things is called *kāma* (desire or longing).

Where all these four currents of love intermingle and integrate, it is called *rati*. And, there are only two occasions of *rati* in the whole universe – one is "God" to whom one is devoted and the other is conjugal life. Divided into two categories, *ātma-rati* and *dāmpatya-rati*, love protects the man's form. Man and woman can never violate the natural rules of the universe if they tread on these two paths and have faith in *dharma*.

Yogīs striving for emancipation have restful devotion towards him, whom they worship and his form will be deemed to be related to the super worldly Vāsudeva form of *Bhagavān* which is related to self and intellect, and about which it is well known वासुदेवः सर्वमिति स महात्मा सुदुर्लभः (*vāsudevaḥ sarvamiti sa mahātmā sudurlabhaḥ*). For emotional devotees, there is an inspiration of affection also and it is related to that *nandanandanātmaka* form of *Bhagavān*, which is related to the two facets of body and mind. He is also worshipped in the form of friendly attachment in which the devotee is actively attached and devoted in relationship of *sākṣī* devoted and *bhakta* devotee and a glorious example of this type of devotion is the friendship between Kṛṣṇa–Sudāmā and Kṛṣṇa–Arjuna friendship and this has been supported by the following *mantra*:

> द्वा सुपर्णा सयुजा सखाया समानं वृक्षं परि षस्वजाते ।
> तयोरन्यः पिप्पलं स्वाद्वत्त्यनश्नन्नन्यो अभि चाकशीति ॥ – ऋ० १.१६४.२०
>
> *dvā suparṇā sayujā sakhāyā samānaṁ vṛkṣaṁ pari ṣasvajāte* ।
> *tayoranyaḥ pippalaṁ svādvattyanaśnannanyo abhi cākaśīti* ॥
> – *Ṛ̥V* I.164.20

And

> अचिन्त्यस्याप्रमेयस्य निर्गुणस्य गुणात्मनः ।
> उपासकानां सिद्ध्यर्थं ब्रह्मणो रूपकल्पना ॥
>
> *acintyasyāprameyasya nirguṇasya guṇātmanaḥ* ।
> *upāsakānāṁ siddhyarthaṁ brahmaṇo rūpakalpanā* ॥

According to these principles, self *rati* is divided into many classifications, viz. *anurūpa*, *pratirūpa*, *pratīka* and *nidāna* and is explained and manifested clearly by the *śruti*:

> ... आत्मैवेदं सर्वमिति। स वा एष एवं पश्यन्नेवं मन्वान एवं विजानन्नात्मरतिरात्मक्रीड़ा आत्ममिथुन आत्मानन्दः स स्वराड् भवति ... – छा०उप० ७.२५.२
>
> *... ātmaivedaṁ sarvam iti । sa vā eṣa evaṁ paśyannevaṁ manvāna evaṁ vijānannātmaratirātmakrīḍā ātmamithuna ātmānandaḥ sa svarāḍ bhavati...* – *ChāUp* 7.25.2

The second sector is that of conjugal *rati*, which is based on self *rati*. That is why Indian marriage is not merely a social relationship but an axiomatic integration of two semicircular halves (two *bhūtama*s of one *saṁvatsarai ātmā*). Even in popular language, conjugal love has been called a meeting of two selfs (*ātmā*s). The husband is an object of devotional respect for the wife (पतिरेव गुरुः स्त्रीणाम् – *patireva guruḥ strīṇām*). The wife also has a feeling of affection towards her husband. This is a matter of self-experience. Attachment is also clearly manifested, as is expressed by सहधर्म्म चरताम् (*sahadharmma caratām*), the sensual love towards the physical body of her husband is also natural. Thus the wife gives company to her husband with *rati*, an integration of all aspects of love.

Similarly, a husband also has a respectful devotion towards his wife. The यत्र नार्य्यस्तु पूज्यन्ते (*yatra nāryyastu pūjyante* – *Devatā*s reside where women are worshipped – *Manusmṛti* 3.56) principle is well known. It must be borne in mind that this principle has become today a verbal expression of idealism. It has become today only a demagogy, meant for deception of women by men. Due to this hateful deception of women by men in our country, the internal and external lives of Indian women have become completely disorganized and anarchic, and it has, therefore, become a cause of deep anxiety. Women are worshipped only in words and in loud pronouncements. But in actual practice, it is just the opposite. As a result, the Indian woman is following the path of reaction. That is why in due course of time all that we understand by Indian womanhood will be completely subdued and along with it the form of man and his *mān*(*ava*) will be completely submerged. Whatever woman does today in excitement of reaction, born from the intellectual fault of man himself, is understandable. The Indians who praise women, especially those who claim themselves to be religious, say with such pride, these ladies of our families are images of patience. They bear everything silently and thus literally protect the prestige of the position of a mother. The womanly qualities cannot be saved by such pleasing and praising (but deceptive) utterances the religious Indian who has thrown all burdens of the family on women can never remain happy and peaceful by this indifference (to responsibility). The Indians have forgotten the ideal of सहधर्म्म चरताम् (*sahadharmma caratām* – doing everything religiously and together) today and therefore they have to bear its evil consequences. If he does not awaken today, no one knows what lies in store for him in the future. The situation cannot be restored only by idealist pronouncements. In actual conduct, he will have to offer respectful devotion towards women. Only then can the anguish in a woman be pacified. I have to submit here that like a wife, a husband should also have respectful devotion towards his wife. There is affection, as well as attachment and of course there is that sensual love according to हरन्ति सन्तो मणिनूपुरा इव (*haranti santo maṇinūpurā iva*). Thus, by the integration of the four types of love, man is also offering *rati* to woman. What is the result of this *rati* on both sides? It is an understanding of this question that can possibly solve the problem (मनुष्या एवै अतिक्रामन्ति *manuṣyā evai atikrāmanti*) of violation of natural principles by man. This problem, posed yesterday, has also become the starting point today. Please try to understand the solution to this question carefully.

The fullness, the superiority of man has been clearly elaborated earlier. A man, who has this fullness, never violates the natural rules of discipline. Only he, who does not have this fullness, violates them. In other words, an incomplete man violates. At this stage, we shall have to analyse the fullness of man based on *yajña*, which is related to astronomical *yajña*. In the first day's lecture, I dealt with क्रान्तिवृत्तीय संवत्सर (*krāntivṛttīya saṁvatsara*) related to seasons based on *agni-soma*. Your attention is being drawn again towards the same today. *Krāntivṛtta*, spread over a continuous area of 48°, is *saṁvatsara*. We shall call it *yajñākāśa* and the sun and the moon are situated in this *yajñākāśa*. The sun is the master of day and the moon is the master of night. The sun is the master of half of *saṁvatsarīya ākāśa* and the moon is the master of the other half. Man's form is made by the solar *āgneya ākāśātmaka* (related to day) semi *saṁvatsara* of 24° and the form of woman is made by the other 24° which is nocturnal and related to the lunar *saumya* sky. In the astronomical *sāṁvatsarika* eclipse, half of the sky, related to the sun, is husband and the other half related to the moon is wife. By the integration of these two halves, by the conjugal unification of two semicircular skies, the *yajña-puruṣa* in the form of *saṁvatsara* becomes complete. Thus, the same *saṁvatsara* Prajāpati is converted into the form of husband and wife by these two solar and lunar halves and gives "birth" to this wide three-worldly offsprings and this eternal order of nature has been expressed by Rājarṣi Manu in the following words:

> द्विधा कृत्वात्मनो देहमर्द्धेन पुरुषोऽभवत्।
> अर्द्धेन नारी तस्यां स विराजमसृजत् प्रभुः॥ – मनु० १.३२
>
> *dvidhā kr̥tvātmano dehamarddhena puruṣo 'bhavat* ।
> *arddhena nārī tasyāṁ sa virājamasr̥jat prabhuḥ* ॥ – *Manu* 1.32

The semicircular half of the solar *saṁvatsara* is the Manu of the vital world of natural order and the semicircular half of the lunar *saṁvatsara* is Śraddhā, wife of Manu. This is full *ākāśa* which is *saṁvatsara* and an integration of Manu and Śraddhā. Both are complementary to each other in the same way as positive and negative are mutually complementary. Neither man is complete nor is woman complete. The husband–wife relationship, denoting conjugal life, is the fullness of individuals. It is their completeness. The form of this physical *saṁvatsara yajña* is exactly similar to that of *saṁvatsara yajña*. This is confirmed by संवत्सरो वै यज्ञः (*saṁvatsaro vai yajñaḥ*). The central circle of *saṁvatsara*, the Equator, is represented by the backbone in the physical *yajña*. When husband and wife stand facing each other, the backbones form a full circle. The 24° of *krāntivr̥tta* are twenty-four ribs in man and the other twenty-four ribs in woman. By the integration of these two, the form of *krāntivr̥tta*, having 48°, is completed. In conclusion, the full *saṁvatsara* is exactly reproduced here in the conjugal relationship. All offspring have been created by *saṁvatsara yajña*, therefore, it has been called *iṣṭakāmadhuk*, as is clear from following extract of *Bhagavadgītā* III.10:

> सहयज्ञाः प्रजाः सृष्ट्वा पुरोवाच प्रजापतिः।
> अनेन प्रसविष्यध्वमेव वोऽस्त्विष्टकामधुक्॥
>
> *sahayajñāḥ prajāḥ sr̥ṣṭvā purovāca prajāpatiḥ* ।
> *anena prasaviṣyadhvameva vo 'stviṣṭakāmadhuk* ॥
>
> In the beginning, the creator, having created human beings along with *yajña*, said "By this *yajña* you shall multiply". May this *yajña* be a wish fulfilling cow for you.

All specialities are born from this *yajña*. In ancient India, scientific deliberations used to take place on the basis (and through the medium) of *yajña*. Today, due to our childishness, we indulge in mutual recriminations and quarrel on issues of image worship (*avatāra śraddhā*), etc. which are proved by the Vedas. It is not necessary to answer such childish questions because such questions are resolved automatically in due course. The learned persons of India should never indulge in discussions on such childish issues. How did the intellectuals of this country engage themselves in discussion and exchange of ideas? A historical incident is being placed before you in this connection.

Once Uddālaka, son of Aruṇa, a well-known authority of his time on *yajña*, arrived in Punjab to become Brahmā in some *yajña*, where gold was placed before him as *niṣṭhā* (a token of respect). The well-known master of fundamental aspects of mystery of creation, Maharṣi Svaidāyana put the question in this form, "oh, Uddālaka, son of Gautama! only he should have the courage of going outside on invitations to become Brahmā if he can answer the following questions. You should therefore answer these questions." "There is oblation of semen, which has no solidness, in blood and yet offspring has bones. Why? Tell me, why does a baby have no teeth when he is born? Why does the tooth grow later on? Why do they fall? Why do they grow again and then fall? Why do they not grow again? Why are there only five fingers? Why the colour of hairs change according to age?" Unable to answer these questions, Uddālaka offered the gold given to him as a token of respect to Svaidāyana with respectful humbleness and stood up before him with *samidhā* (offerings) in his hand, indicating his preparedness to become his disciple. Svaidāyana himself answered those questions through the medium of mysteries of *saṁvatsara yajña*. This uplifting narrative has been analysed in detail in the commentary on the *Śatapatha Brāhmaṇa*:

स वै गौतमस्य पुत्र वृत्तो जनं धावयेत् ...

sa vai gautamasya putra vṛtto janamdhāvayet ...

As is clear from the above-mentioned narrative, all these "mysteries" can be solved by an eagerness to know, accompanied with devotion and respect. The great *tattvajña* of Kurupāñcāladeśa, a learned man of the stature of Maharṣi Uddālaka, did not hesitate in standing before Maharṣi Svaidāyana as a disciple. On the other hand, today those who have not even come in contact with any scientific subject, ask questions about the Indian fundamental thoughts in such an impertinent manner as if they knew much and were asking this question only to confirm their intelligence, learning and views. They are deprived of understanding the subtle and inner meaning of these subjects due to the absence of eagerness to know. This science of *yajña* of the Vedas is very mysterious and meaningful and within it lies answers to all questions.

One aspect related to *anna*, *ūrka* and *prāṇa* was referred to yesterday.

Nābhānediṣṭha, Bālakhilya, Marut, Vṛṣākapi, etc. are various vital energies which conduct the womb, and man and woman are images of *saṁvatsara*. By exactly reproducing the same, *ṛṣi*s invented the *yajña-vidyā* which is a great science based on the Indian *brahmavijñāna dhārā*. It is a tragic misfortune of our country that such subtle, meaningful and scientific *yajña* has been explained, understood and accepted by the devotees of the Vedas, in their imaginary ignorance, as a process of purifying air. What a tragedy? Less said about it the better. Man born from semi-*saṁvatsara* becomes complete only when wife, born of the lunar semi-*saṁvatsara*, is placed in the half of his celestial sphere: सोऽयमाकाशः पत्न्याऽपूर्य्यते (*so 'yamākāśaḥ patnyā 'pūryyate*). According to this principle, a wife alone can fill the empty half of the man's form (*ākāśa*). That is why the wife has been called *ardhāṅginī* (half part of man) स एकाकी न रमते। तद् द्वितीयमैच्छत् पतिश्च-पत्नी च। (*sa ekākī na ramate*। *tad dvitīyamaicchat patiśca-patnī ca*। – He was not happy alone. He wanted a mate. He parted this body into two – from that came husband and wife – *Bṛhadāraṇyaka Upaniṣad* 1.4.3). According to these *śrauta* principles, one *bhūtātmā* divides itself by *saṁvatsara yajña* in husband and wife and is thus associated as one *pūrṇa* (full) *ātmā* in conjugal unification and this is the fullness of man in which husband and wife are integrated by conjugal bonds as one unit.

By associating with Pūrṇa Prajāpati, man becomes *pūrṇa* (complete) by "self" love in *Pūrṇeśvara* man becomes a claimant of that fullness. In other words, first of all, he will have to spend his conjugal life entering the *gṛhasthāśrama*. It is *gṛhasthadharma* which gives fullness to the conjugal *saṁvatsara* and neither man nor woman can violate (the natural disciplines) when they base their life on it. Only the *āśrama* system of life related to *gṛhasthadharma* can save man and woman from violating the natural bond and discipline as has been eulogized by poet Kālidāsa:

शैशवेऽभ्यस्तविद्यानां, यौवने विषयैषिणाम्।
वार्द्धक्ये मुनिवृत्तीनां, योगेनान्ते तनुत्यजाम्॥ – रघुवंश, प्रथम सर्ग

śaiśave 'bhyastavidyānāṁ, yauvane viṣayaiṣiṇām।
vārddhakye munivṛttināṁ, yogenānte tanutyajām॥
– *Raghuvaṁśa*, 1st sarga

Study in the first period by leading a life of *brahmacarya*, attainment of *sāṁvatsarika*, attain wholeness in youth by *gṛhastha dharma*, and realize self by following pure *ātmaniṣṭha* in the end. This is the *āśrama* system of our life; a man who follows this system with conviction makes his worldly life worthwhile. A man who spends his life according to the above-mentioned *āśrama* system saves his body and mind from violation by hard labour and keeps his intellect organized and sharpened by intellectual pursuits.

By integrating physical, mental and intellectual efforts, he makes his "self" full and complete by the integrated *āśrama* life. Thus, by integrating the *āśrama*-system related to *ātmā*, *pariśrama* related to intellect and *śrama* related to mind and body, man is able to regulate all the four facets of his form by dutiful regulations and thus saves himself from violation of natural duties and disciplines.

Such a man does not violate (*nātirmanti*). It is obvious that basis of this *āśrama* system of life, in which *śrama*, *pariśrama* and *āśrama* are interwoven, and in which self, intellect, mind and body are integrated is *gṛhasthāśrama* and on its foundation, the other three *āśrama*s of man – *brahmacarya*, *vānaprastha* and *saṁnyāsa* – function. Eulogizing this *gṛhasthāśrama*, which is the base of all other *āśrama*s and superior-most amongst all, Bhagavān Manu, who has analysed the concept of *āśrama* life, has said:

वेदानधीत्य वेदौ वा वेदं वापि यथाक्रमम् ।
अविप्लुतब्रह्मचर्य्यो गृहस्थाश्रममावसेत् ॥

यथा वायुं समाश्रित्य वर्तन्ते सर्वजन्तवः ।
तथा गृहस्थमाश्रित्य वर्तन्ते सर्व आश्रमाः ॥

यस्मात्त्रयोऽप्याश्रमिणो ज्ञानेनान्नेन चान्वहम् ।
गृहस्थेनैव धार्यन्ते तस्माज्ज्येष्ठाश्रमो गृही ॥ – मनु॰ ३.२.७७-७९

vedānadhītya vedau vā vedaṁ vāpi yathākramam ।
aviplutabrahmacaryyo gṛhasthāśramamāvaset ॥

yathā vāyuṁ samāśritya vartante sarvajantavaḥ ।
tathā gṛhasthamāśritya vartante sarva āśramāḥ ॥

yasmāttrayo 'pyāśramiṇo jñānenānnena cānvaham ।
gṛhasthenaiva dhāryante tasmājjyeṣṭhāśramo gṛhī ॥ – *Manu* 3.2.77-79

A student who has studied in due order of the three Vedas, or two, or even one only, without breaking the rules of studentship, he shall enter the order of householder.

An oblation duly thrown into fire, reaches the sun; from the sun comes rain, from rain comes food, therefrom the living creatures.

As men of three orders are duly supported by the householder with gifts of sacred knowledge and food, therefore the order of the householder is most excellent.

The fullness of man lies in spending *gṛhasthāśrama* with self-regulations and self-control through the medium of study of basic thoughts. All other *āśrama*s rest on this *gṛhasthāśrama*. And this is that highway, provided by the great Indian *ṛṣi*, which leads the Indian man, who follows it, to all-round personal, family, social and national prosperity, and makes him a messenger of universal brotherhood and humanism based on यथा वः सुसहासति (*yathā vaḥ susahāsati* – Let us be united – *ṚV* X.191.4) and *sahāstitva* (co-existence).

It is obvious that in course of last 3,000 years, whenever man has ignored this *gṛhasthāśrama*, which is the basis of conjugal life and which leads to fullness, and whenever he has indulged in imaginary ideas of uselessness and unreality of this world, and whenever he has, as a result, indulged in cries of imaginary non-violence and truth, it has resulted in progressive all-round deterioration of man. We shall continue to fall till we do not organise the conjugal life, which is the base of the *āśrama* system of life.

It is axiomatic that men who think that the world is unreal and who believe that there is nothing in this world, are those for whom the principle of violation of natural principles is applicable (मनुष्या एवैके अतिक्रामन्ति *manuṣyā evaike atikrāmanti*). Undoubtedly, for realizing his absolute fullness, man will have to make himself full and complete. To achieve this end, he will have to be initiated into the conjugal life in a dhārmic manner in the presence of *saṁvatsarāgni*. It is only then that man along with woman will be able to attain the fullness of *saṁvatsara yajña*. Only then can man be properly placed in the systems and disciplines of *yajña*, which are of universal discipline, along with his other half. Indian history, which contains incidents related to such disciplines, is witness to this fact that Bhagavān Rāma had to use the golden image of Sītā as a medium for completion of his *yajña*. According to the principle, पत्युर्नो यज्ञसंयोगे (*patyurno yajñasaṁyoge*), relationship of woman as a wife in this *yajña* includes a disciplined, regulated and conjugal life.

How does this conjugal life, spent according to the principle of *sahadharmma caratām*, makes the worldly journey of man life successful? How does it free the lunar *mahān-ātmā* from entanglement (knots) by सपिण्ड्यसम्बन्धानुगत (*sapiṇḍya sambandhānugata*)? How worldly prosperity and other-worldly bliss are attained by conjugal life? We should take the shelter of Prājāpatya Vedaśāstra. For meaningful and subtle solutions of all these questions, there is no other way at all. The centre of all personal and national desires is conjugal life and the basic centre of this conjugal life is woman, who is placed at the high position of mother. Those old persons, who have denounced women as the door to hell (*narakasya dvāram*), have thrown mud on themselves. The *purandhiryoṣā* woman, who brings up her children affectionately, is a supreme object of desire of *ṛṣi*s for conjugal life. It is on the fulfilment and attainment of this desire that all other desires of knowledge like wealth and strength are fulfilled.

What is the outline of this aspiration of the Indian nation? In other words, what are the aspirations of the Indian nation? Try to understand this aspiration and follow them and bless yourself, and make the nation great by these aspirations.

आ ब्रह्मन् ब्राह्मणो ब्रह्मवर्चसी जायताम्!
आ राष्ट्रे राजन्यः शूर इषव्योऽतिव्याधी महारथो जायताम्!
दोग्ध्री धेनुः, वोढानड्वान्, आशुः सप्तिः!
पुरन्धिर्योषा!
जिष्णू रथेष्ठा!
सभेयो युवास्य यजमानस्य वीरो जायताम्!
निकामे निकामे नः पर्जन्यो वर्षतु!
फलवत्यो न औषधयः पच्यन्ताम्!
योगक्षेमो नः कल्पताम्! – *यजुःसंहिता* २२.२२

ā brahman brāhmaṇo brahmavarcasī jāyatām!
ā rāṣṭre rājanyaḥ śūra iṣavyo 'tivyādhī mahāratho jāyatām!
dogdhrī dhenuḥ, voḍhānaḍvān, āśuḥ saptiḥ!
purandhiryoṣā!
jiṣṇū ratheṣṭhā!
sabheyo yuvāsya yajamānasya vīro jāyatām!
nikāme nikāme naḥ parjanyo varṣatu!
phalavatyo na auṣadhayaḥ pacyantām!
yogakṣemo naḥ kalpatām! – *Yajuḥsaṁhitā* 22.22

Oh Prajāpati! In our nation, such brāhmaṇas should be born who may have command over knowledge and science. Those who represent the strength of the nation, should possess fast-moving conveyance. Cows should be of abundant milk. Bulls should be capable of carrying heavy loads. Women should be protectors of the *prajā* (offsprings), the charioteer should be victorious, the young son of *yajamāna* should have interest in meetings and societies and should be strong. *Parjanya devatā* should cause timely rainfall in our country and thereby nation should grow rich in vegetable and crops and thus livelihood of nation should continue.

There is no doubt that aspiration for satisfactory availability of shelter has prime importance from the point of view of common people and our sovereign and independent nation is engaged in solving that problem. It is also true that unless the problem of food and shelter is solved and unless this anxiety is overcome, our nation cannot think of anything else. This national desire, related to mind and body, should be welcomed. But the question which arises in this context is, "Why is man unsuccessful in solving this problem despite continuous efforts?" The Vedas have offered the following solution. Please be kind enough to hear it.

The nation, whose intellectual strength, the treasure of knowledge, becomes dormant or is overcome due to political conspiracy of determined imperialists, fails to solve the problem of livelihood despite all efforts and resources available. It is well known that intelligent persons use the wealth which belongs to the fools. Its implications are clear. The main strength of a nation is the strength of *jñāna* (knowledge), which has been called *brahmavarcas* (light of knowledge) by *ṛṣis*, and includes *jñāna* and *vijñāna* (science) *brahmavarcas*. This has been the first aspiration or the desire of our nation and even today it should be the first goal. If this aspiration is fulfilled, then all other aims are achieved automatically. It is on this basis that *ṛṣis* have expressed the attainment of knowledge as the first object of the nation. Our nation has forgotten this object due to its attractions towards useless materialism. It is absolutely true that unless and until *jñāna* is not made the foundation of our nation's aspirations, no amount of national plans will solve the problem of livelihood, food and shelter.

The question of livelihood is entirely negligible for a nation with people having *brahmavarca*. A question arises: Why was the birth of such strong and *jñāna-niṣṭha* offsprings blocked in our country? This question is related to the sublime aspiration, expressed by the words, *pūrandhiryoṣā*. Woman has become simply a medium of pleasure and entertainment today. The carnal man has abandoned the basic duty of affectionate upbringing of children which is an inherent quality in a woman. Man has turned away from the faith of *dharma* and has given up the ideal of *dharmma caratām*. Instead, he has made a woman, who is a partner in *dharma* and an associate in intellect and self, a medium of bodily pleasure and entertainment. Is it a surprise therefore if strong and intelligent children are not born from such a relationship which has only a sensual base and has no connection to reverent faith, attachment and affection? And should it cause surprise if such a man and a woman, who have only sensual relationships, violate natural disciplines.

Basic Quality of Womanhood

As long as the womanhood of this land is not associated with the quality of *pūrandhir* (affectionate upbringing of children), the conjugal life of man will never be organized on the basis of the *āśrama* system. Man will remain merely sensual without following the *āśrama* system of conjugal life. In that case there will be no place for conjugal *rati* which has been considered as the beginning of self-bliss according to तद्यथा प्रियया स्त्रिया सम्परिष्वक्तः (*tadyathā priyayā striyā sampariṣvaktaḥ* – As a man embraced by his beloved wife is unaware of his surroundings, self embraced by Supreme Self is oblivious to all – *Bṛhadāraṇyaka Upaniṣad* 4.3.21) *śruti*. Only children born from such conjugal pleasure, which has self-*rati* in its roots, can have the qualities of respectful faith, affection and attachment. Only by integrating these qualities, the human children can attain fullness.

By this well-integrated and well-developed form, men and women of a nation can attain personal and social prosperity and also feel reverence, affection, attachment and longing for the nation. Only then, they can have the quality of national love (*rati*). These days, when sensualism prevails, it is meaningless to recall this concept of national love. It is true that we have a sense of *kāma* (sensual attachment) towards the nation. This is also true that we have a sense of attachment towards it, but it is also a fact that our sense of respectful devotion and affection towards the nation have been completely subdued. And, therefore, we are unable to love the nation entirely and completely. Individual desires, which have *kāma* in their roots, have deprived us from full and complete love towards the nation even in this age of independence.

Pardon me. Mr President, whatever I am going to submit, might be within the limits of the Constitution, but it is definitely unpalatable to hear. While respecting the constitutional limits, I have to analyse and point out some harsh truths regarding conjugal life while explaining the concept of man. In our nation today, does anybody have a sense of respectful devotion towards anybody, or a sense of affection or attachment? Definitely, people have and they shout about it from house-tops. But at the root of all pretensions of devotion, affection or attachment, you will find everywhere the lifeless sensualism based on some hidden desire for popularity or some other gain. Nobody has respectful devotion itself. Nobody has affection for the sake of affection only. This is visible everywhere. The doors of attachment for the sake of attachment are firmly bolted. Rather, all these are displayed only with lifeless "sensual" objects.

Turn your eyes towards the present-day Indian *bābā*s – the whole situation will become clear. The way in which these *bābā*s say "oh my son!" towards their simple "devotees" in a pious manner, in low voice and with display of affection such that their devotees had not received even at the hands of their parents during their childhood. For the fulfilment of our sensual and material desire we do not hesitate to pretend respect and devotion towards them. With the object of getting wealth, knowledge of God without effort, we run after these *bābā*s with devotion like the emotional *pañca-kauṇḍinya*s. Both are clever actors. This is not the proper occasion to analyse the results. It is sufficient to state what the *śruti* has said in this connection:

> अविद्यायामन्तरे वर्तमानाः स्वयं धीराः पण्डितंमन्यमानाः ।
> जङ्घन्यमाना परियन्ति मूढा अन्धेनैव नीयमाना यथान्धाः ॥ – मु०उप० १.२.८
>
> *avidyāyāmantare vartamānāḥ svayaṁ dhīrāḥ paṇḍitaṁ-manyamānāḥ* ।
> *jaṅghanyamānā pariyanti mūḍhā andhenaiva nīyamānā yathāndhāḥ* ॥
> – *MuUp* 1.2.8
>
> Living in the midst of ignorance and considering themselves intelligent and enlightened, the senseless people go round and round, following crooked course, just like the blind led by the blind.

For the fulfilment of hateful, selfish desires, we do not hesitate even for a moment to praise mean and dirty people with epithets like venerable, most respectable and honourable, despite the fact that we know in our hearts the "dishonourable" history of these "honourables". If our selfish ends are met by showing affection towards youngsters we are not ashamed to demonstrate abounding affection towards them. A similar situation obtains in relation to display of "artificial" attachment. Most of the people are engaged in various development plans of our nation due to their "sensual" feeling born out of desire for popularity. They are not all inspired by a feeling of devotion. That is why even in the smallest amongst the smallest plans of the nation, din and bustle of publicity is tumultuous. But when actual success is assessed, a uniform reply comes forth, "we had to face many problems and therefore desired progress could not be achieved".

It is obvious that the human mind attains fullness only by *rati*, which is an integration of devotion, affection, attachment and longing. A full mind alone leads to development of intellect. When a well-developed and determined intellect is integrated with the self, it is known as "self-determined intellect" (*ātmaniṣṭha buddhi*). Such an *ātmaniṣṭha* man is intelligent, such an intelligent man has fullness of mind and such a man can never violate the natural laws. In conclusion, "self-determination" (*ātmaniṣṭha*) integrated with mind controlled by intellect is the basis of protection of man's form. The *rati* of the mind is its stability, which is attained by man in the *āśrama* system, following conjugal relations. That is why mind has been called the cause of enslavement and liberation of man:

न देहो न जीवात्मा नेन्द्रियाणि परन्तप! ।
मन एव मनुष्याणां कारणं बन्ध-मोक्षयोः ॥

na deho na jīvātmā nendriyāṇi parantapa! ।
mana eva manuṣyāṇāṁ kāraṇaṁ bandha-mokṣayoḥ ॥

Man led by his desires violates. Material characteristics (frigidity, stupidity, etc.) are not to be hated or discarded. There is no doubt that all lifeless manifestations of the universe are the manifest and developed form of *caitanya puruṣātmā*. It is on this basis that *śruti*s have said:

इह चेदवेदीदथ सत्यमस्ति न चेदिहावेदीन्महती विनष्टिः ।
भूतेषु भूतेषु विचित्य धीराः प्रेत्यास्माल्लोकादमृता भवन्ति ॥ – के०उप० २.५

iha cedavedīdatha satyamasti na cedihāvedīnmahatī vinaṣṭiḥ ।
bhūteṣu bhūteṣu vicitya dhīrāḥ pretyāsmāllokādamṛtā bhavanti ॥
– *KeUp* 2.5

If a man knows *ātman* here, he then attains the true goal of life. If he does not know it here, a great destruction awaits him. Having realized the Self in every being, the wise relinquish the world and become immortal.

But unless the inanimate matter is based on *cidbrahma*, it can never result in propriety. Only sensual longing of man, which has no devotion in it, covers up the *cidbhāva* of man. In that case, there does not remain any appreciable difference between man and beast, having no expression of the self. In this condition, man unduly attached to various objects in an inanimate way commits intellectual default. What should man do to control this intellectual default? In reply to this question, many methods have been explained in the Śāstras and this is an independent subject of study. At the root of all those methods is the intellectual mind of man.

It has been submitted earlier that the intellect born from solar vital-force is *āgneyī* and the mind made of lunar *soma* is *saumya*. There is much difference in the form of the two intellect and mind. For example, while intellect "goes" towards the subject, subjects "come" to mind. Subjects which come to mind are called feelings, desires and deep-rooted habits (*saṁskāra*). Mind wanders in this world. Intellect has a dominant quality of original imagination; mind has the dominant quality of reproduction or copying. Intellect decides the dos and don'ts on the basis of an assessment of gains and losses, mind decides on the basis of imitation of others. While intellect likes well-thought out action, mind likes imitation. While intellect arrives at a conclusion after assimilating and analysing a situation, the mind is influenced by the obvious and decides on its course of action immediately. Thus, various functions of mind and intellect can be contrasted and understood.

It has been stated above that subjects come to mind. It is clear therefore that the dreams in which the mind indulges in are reproductions of imprints made earlier during the awakened state. A man sees in a dream that he is dead. The reason thereof is that the imprint of the dead is also there on the mind and the imprint "I" is there. This "imprint" of "I" establishes a relationship with the imprint of the dead. Thus, by interrelations of these deep-rooted imprints, oddity is reproduced in dreams.

Two Classifications of Desire

The desire of the mind with imprint is called *utthāpyākāṅkṣā* – spontaneous desire; natural desire and artificial desires are two desires expressed differently. Spontaneous desire is associated intellect and is the manifestation of *Īśvara*'s will. It never allows man to violate and this is called wisdom.

Artificial desire following the mind is *jīva*'s will, which always leads man to violate. This functions according to the unrestrained dictates of mind. There is rivalry and clash between the two in the being. The mind says, "let me drink (wine) today". The intellect says, "This is bad, you should never do so". The mind again says, "what harm is there in drinking only once". Just at this stage, if intellect is successful in controlling the mind, man is saved from violation and if the mind ignores intellect, then man indulges in drink and finally leads himself to destruction.

Familiar defects of ignorance, lack of confidence, attachment and dogmatism inspire the mind to become unrestrained and thus lead to violation. On the other hand, knowledge, self-prosperity, non-attachment and *dharma* give strength to intellect and regulate and control the mind. Knowledge of the Śāstras is knowledge. Not to know it is ignorance; development of the self is prosperity, and its opposite is lack of confidence. Man has richness in him, due to this fault of *asmitā*, man always considers himself to be poor, pitiable and devoid of everything. This is a terrible fault of man. A man who always uses negative terms and always worships the feelings of sorrow, ultimately finds himself really in that situation. See:

> असन्नेव स भवति। असद्ब्रह्मेति वेद चेत्। अस्ति ब्रह्मेति चेद्वेद। सन्तमेनं ततो विदुरिति।
> – तै०उप० २.६
>
> *asnneva sa bhavati* । *asadbrahmeti veda cet* । *asti brahmeti cedveda* ।
> *santamenaṁ tato viduriti* । – *TaiUp* 2.6
>
> If a person knows *Brahman* as non-existent, he himself becomes non-existent. If he knows *Brahman* as existent, then (knowers of *Brahman*) know him as existent.

That is why according to Indian etiquette, even when two people meet in a state of tragedy, they always exchange greetings with these words – it is all pleasant by the grace of God. Acting without any attachment or animosity is *vairāgya*. Being tied up in various entanglements due to animosity is *āsakti* (attachment). The natural state and fulfilment of natural duties is *dharma*. Bigotry leads to forgetting this natural state. *Dharma*-knowledge, non-attachment and self-prosperity strengthen the intellect; bigotry, ignorance, lack of confidence and attachment weaken the intellect and makes the mind indisciplined. An undisciplined mind causes violations and a disciplined mind checks it. The main factor in controlling it is *āśrama* life. The main foundation of *āśrama* life is conjugal love (*rati*) and within it the form of man and woman is protected.

This conjugal pair of objects of *karma*, which are images of *karmāśvattha*, remains well placed in the *āśrama* way of life and keeps *īśvarīya brahmāśvattha*, denoting self *rati* as its central foundation. In such a situation, one need not fear a fall or violation. May man realize his basic foundation, may he keep *mānavāśrama* (with *śrama*, *pariśrama* and integration of body, mind, intellect and self inherent in it) in view and may fulfil the title *mānava* bestowed on him and prove thereby that none else is superior to man. With this hope, today's lecture concludes.

Fourth Discourse

Science of Aśvattha
An Outline

IN the last lecture, explaining the form of man, it was submitted that while man is *karmāśvattha*, the basic foundation is *paramāśvattha*. In today's lecture this intricate Vedic science of *aśvattha* will be explained. In local newspapers, these lectures were described as "Vedic science". Before today's subject is dealt with, it will not be out of context to submit that word "science" (*vijñāna*), which is used by the common people nowadays, actually means science of matter or material science and this connotation has nothing to do with the Vedic word *vijñāna*. Rather, from the Vedic point of view, the word *vijñāna* has its own independent meaning and technical definition. In the modern age, the word science is an object of attraction for everyone. Many Indians are overwhelmed by the novel inventions of material science and are turning away from their *śāstrīya* determination; they have been completely swayed away by this word. Due to the evil result of this harmful influence, there may be some misguided speculations about the use of the word *vijñāna*, which is not at all desirable. Therefore, it is necessary to explain in a few words the technical meaning of the word *vijñāna* from the Indian Vedic point of view as has been done in a separate article on the subject.

Respectable listeners might remember that in the first day's lecture, I had submitted that the technical meaning of a term is incorporated in the construction of the word itself. The basic essentials, which *ṛṣis* want to express, are placed by the use of symbolic letters in the word itself. To explain this ancient method, an example of *hṛdayam* was placed before you. On the next day, some gentlemen had said that while the meaning of the letters *hṛ* and *da* was clear, the meaning of the letter *yam* could not be understood fully. It was my desire that there should be no talk about *yam* in Rashtrapati Bhawan. But when a query has been made, an uplifting (*śivātmaka*) explanation of the third letter becomes necessary. The force which takes in is *hṛ* and the force which throws out is *da*. Popularly speaking, giving is *da* and taking is *hṛ*. Taking is *hṛ* and giving is *da*. If we try to find some simple word in Sanskrit for giving and taking it will be *agati* (inflow) and *gati* (outflow). What is the meaning of inflow and outflow? Going from the centre towards circumference will be called outflow and coming from circumference towards the centre is called inflow. *Agati* will be considered to be related to the intaking *hṛ* letter, while *gati* will be considered to be related to the outstanding *da* letter. Coming and going – this is the form of motion. It is an essential characteristic of action till it gets a neutral base or it becomes entirely inoperative of motion or all motions. Such a neutral, motionless base is necessary. The earth is a neutral base; that is why we can walk on it. We can execute the action of swallowing, because there is the neutral base of the mouth. The action of visibility and non-visibility takes place on a neutral base of the eyes, similarly for all actions (motion), it is necessary that there should be some neutral base.

The base on which the actions or motions of inflow and outflow operate, and is regulated and controlled, is called *niyaman*, which means "regulated intermission". The essential on the neutral basis of which the inflowing and outflowing motion operates, that third essential which regulates motion or action, is expressed by the word *yam* (God of death). नियमयति यत् सर्वान् गत्यागतिभावान् (*niyamayati yat sarvān gatyāgatibhāvān*) – meaning thereby that which regulates the inflowing and outflowing motion is the third *yam* letter. For this third essential also we had to search for a word in popular language and the word is *sthiti* (rest or motionlessness). The regulated or controlling essential has been called rest or motionlessness in popular language. Thus, through the medium of the three words *hṛ*, *da* and *yam* – inflow, outflow and rest – these three essentials are expressed before us.

Vedic Terms for Inflow, Outflow and Rest

The symbolic technical Vedic names for these three essentials are Brahmā, Viṣṇu and Indra. The essential rest is, according to ब्रह्म वै सर्वस्य प्रतिष्ठा (*brahma vai sarvasya pratiṣṭhā*), Brahmā which is the base of all operations. The outflowing motion is due to *balavṛtti indra* (या च का च बलकृतिरिन्द्रकर्म्मेव तत् – *yā ca kā ca balakṛtirindrakarmmeva tat*). And the inflowing motion due to its intaking, appetizing property of intaking foods, is called Viṣṇu. The basis is the motionless of the neutral base of Brahmā. The mutual rivalry between Indra and Viṣṇu, the incoming and outgoing energies, goes on, which can be easily understood by the physical *yajña*. In the first twenty-five years of man's age, the inflowing energy is on the increase and outflowing energy is on the decline. What comes in is more than what goes out. Therefore, in this first period of man's life his form grows. In the competition between inflowing Viṣṇu and outflowing Indra – Viṣṇu wins and Indra loses. Between 25 to 50 years, both inflow and outflow are equal. What comes in is equal to what goes out. And therefore in connection with this middle age, it can be said that neither Viṣṇu is scoring over Indra, nor Indra is losing to Viṣṇu. From the age of 50 to 75, inflowing energy becomes weak and due to various types of frictions resulting from increase in bodily hairs, etc., outflowing energy is strengthened. Income is less and expenditure is more. As a result, it is said about this age that Indra is winning and Viṣṇu is losing. And in the fourth and the last period of a man's life, 75 to 100, the incoming of Viṣṇu grows increasingly weak and the outgoing Indra becomes increasingly stronger, when the intake of food eases altogether, Indra in company with *agni* converts itself in the form of pure Rudra and shatters the structure bearing the name of man. Of these periods, referring to the third period between 25 to 50 years when Indra and Viṣṇu, outflowing and inflowing force, are equally strong, the *śruti* has said, "all other *devatā*s want to defeat Indra and Viṣṇu (inflowing forces)". But they were not defeated by any (*prāṇa-devatā*) vital forces. At the same time, neither of them is meant to defeat the other. On the basis of *āpya pārameṣṭhya mahān* watery physical body, this combat, which is continuous, gives birth to three *sāhasrīs*,[1] *vāk–veda–loka* and the analysis of this *sāhasrī-vidyā* related to these three *sāhasrī*s is a subject of an independent lecture. Explaining this "combative" relationship on inflowing and outflowing forces, *śruti* says:

उभा जिग्यथुर्न परा जयेथे न परा जिग्ये कतरश्चनैनोः ।
इन्द्रश्च विष्णो यदपस्पृधेथां त्रेधा सहस्रं वि तदैरयेथाम् ॥ – ऋ० ६.६९.८

ubhā jigyathurna parā jayethe na parā jigye kataraścanainoḥ ।
indraśca viṣṇo yadapaspṛdhethāṁ tredhā sahasraṁ vi tadairayethām ॥
– *Ṛ̥V* VI.69.8

किं तत् सहस्रमिति? – इमे लोकाः, इमे वेदाः, अथो वागितिब्रूयात् । – ऐत०ब्रा० २८.७
kiṁ tat sahasramiti? – ime lokāḥ, ime vedāḥ, atho vāgitibrūyāt ।
– *AitaBrā* 28.7

---

[1] *Sāhasrī-vidyā* is a particular branch of Vedic science divided into three branches.

Relationship of Viṣṇu and Indra

Synonyms for "Viṣṇu" in the *Amarakośa* are "Upendra" and "Indravaraja" (उपेन्द्रइन्द्रावरजश्चक्रपाणिश्चतुर्भुजः – *upendraindrāvarajaścakrapāṇiścaturbhujaḥ*). The inflowing Viṣṇu is in proximity with the outflowing Indra, that is why he has been called Upendra. The inflow, outflow and rest are various forms of motion itself. Outflow or motion is the principal motion. Indra, signifying outflow, has therefore been considered to be elder, stronger, superior to other vital forces as is clear from the principle इन्द्रो वै देवानामोजिष्ठो बलिष्ठः श्रेष्ठो ज्येष्ठः (*indro vai devānāmojiṣṭho baliṣṭhaḥ śreṣtho jyeṣṭhaḥ*). Due to the predominance of motion (outflow), Viṣṇu is considered to be younger. That is why he has also been called Indravaraja, which means younger brother of Indra. This must always be borne in mind that Brahmā, Indra and Viṣṇu of *upāsanā-kāṇḍa* (the sphere of worship) are entirely different from these vital forces (*devatā*) related to *yajñātmā* of *karma-kāṇḍa* (sphere of *yajña*) and the Brahmā and other *devatā*s related to the *vijñāna-kāṇḍa* (sphere of science) are different.

Original and basic *śāstra*, explanatory Brāhmaṇaśāstra and further elaboration of these Vedas and Brāhmaṇas, the Purāṇas the Indian basic thought is thus divided into three sectors – *vijñāna-kāṇḍa*, *karma-kāṇḍa* and *upāsanā-kāṇḍa*. Brahmā and other *devatā*s of *mantra* Vedas are products of nature, the Brahmā, brāhmaṇa, etc. of Brāhmaṇa are various vital forces (*prāṇavidha* and *abhimānīvidha*). And the Brahmā and other *devatā*s of the Purāṇas are physical objects of worship. Historical *devatā*s are also included in this category.

The Indian science of vital forces (*devatāvāda*) is very subtle and meaningful. Being unable to understand it, people have indulged in many misguided speculations in this respect. These three branches of Indian thought merge into one at a particular point. *Ṛṣi*s have explained the essential *devatā*s in various ways only from the viewpoint of eligibility of those who try to understand them. The methods of language, derivation and analysis of the three are entirely different. Keeping this point in view, we shall engage ourselves in understanding the Indian science of vital forces from different points of view. At present, we have the school of *vijñāna* in view, according to which Brahmā and others are explained as articles of matter.

Classify the situation a little more. Three *devatā*s which are referred to here as inflow, outflow and rest are related to the sphere of *vijñāna*, which deals with the science of matter and its essentials. When *karma-kāṇḍa* (sphere of actual practice) will be analysed it will be entirely different and explained differently and in the Purāṇic *upāsanā*s (sphere of worship) their forms will be expressed differently and in that context statements saying that Viṣṇu is the younger brother of Indra, Brahmā is the essential rest and Indra is the essential outflowing motion, will be totally incorrect. All theists are aware of the forms of *devatā*s as related to the sphere of worship – Brahmā with four faces, Viṣṇu with four arms and Śiva with three eyes, and Indra, the lord of heaven, are worshipped by all. The Indian thinkers also know the forms of *yajñīya devatā*s (vital forces of the sphere as they appear in *brāhmaṇe svāhā, indrāya svāhā, viṣṇave svāhā, āgnaye svāhā, somāya svāhā*). But the forms of the *vaijñānika* (scientific) *devatā*s have been totally forgotten nowadays. And due to this, the Indian science of vital forces has been an intricate riddle. That is why scientific and entirely rational (based on essentials) Indians have been denounced with the use of epithets like slaves of *devatā*s by misguided persons. In this connection, this should also be believed that there is no contradiction between *devatā*s related *upāsanā* because at a particular point they are all correlated. This triple branch of Indian *devatā*s is later on divided into eight branches:

1. Conscious, earthly *devatā*s,
2. Conscious non-absolute lunar *devatā*s,
3. Inanimate, unmanifest, non-absolute solar vital *devatā*s,
4. Formless inanimate material *devatā*s,
5. *Abhimānī devatā*s,
6. *Pratyakṣa mantra devatā*s,
7. *Karma devatā*s, and
8. *Ātmā devatā*s, which can be realized by the self only.

These forms of *devatā*s have been explained and elaborated in the commentary on the *Śatapatha Brāhmaṇa*.[2]

Terms in Indian Science

In the language of the science of matter, rest and inflow are named Brahmā, Viṣṇu and Indra. Are these three different essentials? No. The एका मूर्तिस्त्रयो देवा ब्रह्म-विष्णु-महेश्वराः (*ekā mūrtistrayo devā brahma-viṣṇu-maheśvarāḥ*) principle is well known. These three *devatā*s are three stages

[2] Shastriji has written a comprehensive commentary on the *Śatapatha Brāhmaṇa*. It can be accessed through www.shankarshikshayatan.org.

of one continuous essential. Or three facets of one object. What is the meaning of this manifestation or stages? Rest is the aggregation of two motions of inflow and outflow. An aggregate of two motions in two opposite directions or many motions in mutually opposite directions is rest. Try to understand rest as follows. The motion going from the centre towards circumference is outflow and the same motion coming from circumference towards the centre is inflow and when both mutually opposite motions meet at one point it is called the rest. Thus, the same motion is converted into three forms: centrifugal motion, centripetal motion and integrated motion. These are popularly called inflow, outflow and rest respectively. The same motion, the same vital force, thus follows three paths and converts in three forms. The word *hṛdayam* is one, of which *hṛ*, *da* and *yam* are three letters.

Contraction and Expansion

Later, from this essential motion, from the triple motions of *hṛdayam*, two more motions develop. When inflowing motion is regulated in the envelope of rest, contraction or shrinkage emerges.

When outflowing motion is engulfed in the envelope of rest, an expanding motion develops. These contracting and expanding motions are also known as *snehagati* and *tejogati*. Motion towards the centre is pure inflow, motion away from the centre towards circumference is pure outflow; regulating motion is rest, inflow embodied in the rest is contraction, outflow embodied in the rest is expansion. Thus, the same vital motion (which is called *akṣara* and which is the basic nature of the universe) is converted into five vital motions or five *akṣaras*. *Hṛdayam* where inflow, outflow and rest are integrated is an independent essential which has also been called *antaryāmī*. An expanding and contracting motion form an independent essential and they are called *sūtrātmā*. These five motions, or five states of one vital force *akṣara*, have been called *pañcākṣara*. These are well known by the names of Brahmā, Viṣṇu, Indra, Agni and Soma. Motionlessness or of motions is Brahmā, inflowing motion is Viṣṇu, outflowing motion is Indra. *Hṛ*, *da* and *yam akṣaras* constitute *antaryāmī* which is placed in the centre of all units of matter. Expanding motion is *agni* and contracting motion is *soma*. Both are *akṣaras* of external form. This is *sūtrātmā* from which the form of matter is composed. Referring to these five *akṣaras* or five stages of one *akṣara*, the *śruti* says:

यदक्षरं पञ्चविधं समेति, युजो युक्ता अभियत्संवहन्ति।
सत्यस्य सत्यमनु यत्र युज्यते तत्र देवाः सर्व एकं भवन्ति॥ – ऐत०आ० २.३.८.२०

yadakṣaraṁ pañcavidhaṁ sameti, yujo yuktā abhiyatsaṁvahanti ।
satyasya satyamanu yatra yujyate tatra devāḥ sarva ekaṁ bhavanti ॥

– *AitaĀr* 2.3.8.20

Interdependence of Motion and Rest

According to the scientific principle:

न हि ध्वान्तमीदृङ् न यत्र प्रकाशः, प्रकाशो न तादृक् – न यत्रान्धकारः

na hi dhvāntamīdr̥ṅ na yatra prakāśaḥ, prakāśo na tādr̥k – na yatrāndhakāraḥ

Darkness cannot remain in its form unless it has light in its composition and light cannot exist without darkness in it.

Similarly, there is no motion which does not incorporate rest or motionlessness. In the same way, there is no rest which does not incorporate motion in it. The property of motion is protected because there is rest in it. If this element of rest is taken out from motion, in that case motion itself gets converted into rest. Exactly in the same way, property of rest exists on the incorporation of motion in it. If this motion is taken out from the rest, it will be converted into motion. Try to correct this amazing principle by the following example.

Four persons of equal strength, from among you, leave their residence for their office exactly at 9 a.m. which is two miles away. All the four leave at the same time but they arrive at different times. Suppose the respective time taken by the four is one hour, half an hour, twenty minutes and five minutes. Why these differences in time taken by them? A simple answer would be that those who walked fast reached earlier and those who walked slowly reached late. What does it mean? Those in whose motion there was less "rest" reached fast and those in whose motion there was more "rest" reached late. In popular dialect, those who moved their feet fast reached early and those who moved their feet slowly reached later. It means that those who reduced the element of rest from their motion appreciably reached sufficiently early and those who reduced the element of rest from motion ordinarily reached late; it can be said about the gentleman who reached in five minutes that he walked very fast. In other words, the element of motion in his rest was very little. It was difficult to know when he raised his feet and when he put them forward. He was moving without stopping at all. Take your imagination a little further. He who walks faster than this person will reach in three minutes. It is possible that you may find those who will reach you even in one minute. Let us imagine that it is reduced to one second. This "in a second" will mean that in motion there is one second measure of rest. Now imagine the last point and take out this one second rest from the sphere of his motion. What will be the result? The answer is obvious. Just at the same moment you will be at home, you will also be present in the office. Thus, when the essential "rest", which protects the property of in motion, is taken out of your motion, motion is converted to motionlessness or rest. And it is on this basis that the following scientific principle has been enunciated. If the rest is taken out of motion, then motion is converted into rest. We (the earthly beings) cannot become an example of this last stage because *kṣara* matter rest can never be taken out completely from its motion. Therefore, in earthly sentient and inanimate matter, motion, with rest in its ambit and rest with motion in it, relative rest and relative motion will be available. *Sarveśvara prāṇa brahma*, who is the regulator of the material universe, will be accepted as an example of the state of absolute rest. He is pure or absolute motion and therefore pure or absolute rest. He moves in the whole universe in the same moment and exists (rest) in the entire universe at the same moment. He can only be Viśveśvara Brahmā and referring to his motion and rest, the *maharṣi* has said:

अनेजदेकं मनसो जवीयो नैनद्देवा आप्नुवन्पूर्वमर्षत्।
तद्धावतोऽन्यानत्येति तिष्ठत्तस्मिन्नपो मातरिश्वा दधाति॥ – ईश०उप० ४

anejadekaṁ manaso javīyo nainaddevā āpnuvanpūrvamarṣat ।
taddhāvato 'nyānatyeti tiṣṭhattasminnapo mātariśvā dadhāti ॥
– *ĪśaUp* 4

He is devoid of any shaking, trembling, is devoid of any motion, but is faster than mind, possessing the characteristic of motion. In other words, he is pure motion by this characteristic of *bala* and is pure rest or motionlessness by this characteristic of "rest". These characteristics, *rasa* and *bala*, are likely to be defined later. And the (*devatā*) vital forces operating within the limits of the universe, which leave earlier than him, are never able to overtake this Brahmā. He is always found ahead of these *devatā*s, who are actually one and the same place. In such astonishing essential which is motionless, a vital force named *mātariśvā* (bear) offers oblation of *āpaḥ śukra* which is *śabdabrahmātmaka*. "On the basis of this motionless Brahmā by the oblation of this *śukra*, this universe is created by the interaction of relative rest and motion."

This is the literal meaning of the *mantra* quoted above to explain the science.

Interrelationship of Rest and Motion

The purpose of today's discourse is to explain the science of *aśvattha*. The second example is therefore left for some other occasion. It is sufficient to know in this context that all such matter which is at rest is, as a matter of fact, in all-round motion. The matter is at rest by incorporating motion within their ambit. By the conjunction of a minimum of two opposite motions or when motion from "all" sides becomes centripetal, a state of rest emerges. They get into motion, or move from one place to another when motion from the opposite direction is removed. It is on this basis that science has established the following principle that "rest maintains its restness by keeping motion in itself converted into motion". The same principle is applicable to the relationship between light and darkness. If light is taken out of darkness, then darkness itself is converted into light. And if darkness is completely removed from light, then light is converted into darkness. This subtle theory is related to the science of *agni-soma*, of which only one fact related to seasons, *saṁvatsara*, was explained in the first lecture.

Now, therefore, it can be stated that Prāṇa-Brahmā and the form of pure motion and pure rest cannot be defined by human intelligence only with the aid of material science, while it is abundantly clear from the scientific viewpoint. It was to show this difference of (scientific viewpoint from) the material viewpoint that *ṛṣis* used such descriptions for it as "that which is beyond thought, that which is beyond discussion, that which is beyond knowing". Due to their failure in understanding this point of view, many modern material scientists have indulged in misguided comments.

What a shame? Oh! What a shame! The subtle essential self, which the material science of today has not been able to touch even, was seen and realized by *ṛṣis*. Despite Herculean efforts, modern material science has been unable to remove the obstacles of space and direction, while *ṛṣis* were successful in removing these obstacles by regulating vital forces. Due to this direct realization of vital forces, they were called *ṛṣis* and less said the better about those ignorant Indians who, in their attachment towards English, are ignoring the path shown by the fundamental outlook of *ṛṣis* in their basic literature consisting of Veda-Purāṇas.

In connection with the word *hṛdayam*, the definition of *pañcākṣara* or totality of five forms of motions was placed before you because later this essential *hṛdayam* is going to be the base of *aśvattha-vidyā* as has been indicated by ऊर्ध्वमूलोऽवाक्शाख एषोऽश्वत्थः सनातनः (*ūrdhvamūlo 'vākśākha eṣo 'śvatthaḥ sanātanaḥ*). Science of five *akṣara* is the science of motion in the ambit of which the sciences of *kṣara* and universe are included. It is to symbolize this auspicious fact in actual practice that in the beginning of the fifth year of age, an Indian child is taught five auspicious letters, these five letters are indicative of the five essential *akṣara* indicated above. Thus, in the beginning of life, initial imprints of these essential sciences are made on the intellect of Indian children through the medium of five letters. Just as the whole basic science of *Para-Brahman* is based on these five *akṣaras*, viz. Brahmā, Viṣṇu, Indra, Agni and Soma, the whole science of vocal words (sound) is based on five letters – *a, i, ū, ṛ, lṛ*. It was to indicate this subtle mystery that the great master (*ācārya*) of the science of words, Bhagavān Pāṇini covered the entire science of words in two opening *sūtras* of his fourteen *māheśvara sūtras*.

It has been pointed out that Brahmā, Viṣṇu and Indra, which are in the form of *hṛdayam* or *antaryāmī*, form an independent separate unit. It is to show this separation that *a*, *i* and *ū*, these three letters have been grouped separately in the *sūtra*. And for *agni* and *soma*, which provide the form and background and are associated with *kṣara* matter, have been grouped separately. In basic natural essential called *akṣara*, *agni* and *soma*, matter (*kṣara*) are also associated. The same is the case with letters and they are not pure vowels like *ā, ī, ū*. Inanimate consonants *ra* and *la* are also associated with vowels. Brahmā is *akāra*, it is rest, Viṣṇu is *lakāra*, it is inflow. Indra (which has been called Śiva in the Purāṇa) is *ukāra*, this is motion. According to grammatical rules, the sound *u* is converted into *ba* and its symbolic reproduction is the word *bam*, which in its basic form is indicative of Śiva, which is represented by the letter *u*. All devotees of Śiva are aware of the devotional cries of "Bam Śaṅkara". This is a short definition concept of inseparable relationship between word and matter; which follows the Śabdārtha Brahmā and this has been referred by *śruti* in the following *mantra*:

द्वे विद्ये वेदितव्ये तु शब्दब्रह्म परं च यत्।
शब्दब्रह्मणि निष्णातः परं ब्रह्माधिगच्छति॥ – ब्रह्मबिन्दु उप० १७

dve vidye veditavye tu śabdabrahma paraṁ ca yat ।
śabdabrahmaṇi niṣṇātaḥ paraṁ brahmādhigacchati ॥
– *BrahmabinduUp* 17

Interrelationship of Word and Its Material Meaning

Śabda-Brahman and *Para-Brahman*, or to express differently, word and the material content conveyed by that word are two facets of the same

Brahmā. He who understands the definition and form of *Śabda-Brahman* fully understands the *Para-Brahman*.

This is the literal meaning of the *mantra*, while it is related to a very subtle and meaningful topic. In the second day's lecture explaining the five-divisional universe, it was stated that there was a sphere of Soma (*somaloka*) which is above the sun. To correlate the relationship between word (*śabda*) and its meaning (*artha*), you should keep in view this sphere of Parameṣṭhi. In the great ocean of Parameṣṭhi named Sarasvān, contracting Bhṛgu essential and expanding Aṅgirā essential exist. The Bhṛgu stream which is full of *soma* is called Āmbhṛṇīvāk. This has been explained scientifically in the Āmbhṛṇī Sūkta of the *Ṛgveda*. The Aṅgirā stream which is full of *agni* has been called Sarasvatīvāk. From the Āmbhṛṇī Bhṛgu stream all matter emerges which is considered to be the sphere of Lakṣmī (goddess of wealth) and words from Sarasvatī Aṅgirā stream, which is the sphere of Sarasvatī. Both essentials come into existence together and are manifested in our *triloka* in the form of the sun and the earth. The *āpomayī-bhṛgumayī* earth is primarily dominated by matter and the *aṅgirāmaya* sun is primarily dominated by *śabda* (sound) as is clear from त्रिधा बद्धो वृषभो रौरवीति महो देवो मर्त्या आविवेश (*tridhā baddho vṛṣabho rauravīti maho devo martyā āviveśa* – Tethered in three points, the bull roars loudly; the mighty God hath entered in to mortals – *ṚV* IV.58.3). The sun is the sphere of Sarasvatī and the earth is the sphere of Lakṣmī. The earth is lotus, it is the abode of Lakṣmī. The sun is the abode of *devatās*. Sarasvatī is primary, Lakṣmī is secondary. *Śabda-tanmātra*[3] has been stated as the basic essential giving birth to matter. Lakṣmī exists on the basis of Sarasvatī. The basic seeds of both of them are held in *parameṣṭhi* in the form of Aṅgirā and Bhṛgu. Both are companions. Therefore, according to the principle अत्रा सखायः सख्यानि जानते-भद्रैषां निहिता वाचि लक्ष्मीः (*atrā sakhāyaḥ sakhyāni jānate-bhadraiṣāṁ nihitā vāci lakṣmīḥ* – Where, like men cleansing corn-flour in a cribble, the wise in spirit have created language. Friends see and recognize the marks of friendship: their speech retains the blessed sign imprinted – *ṚV* X.71.2), this companionship is clearly proved. It is a misfortune of this country that as a result of unscientific imagination even learned persons of the day have come to believe in animosity between Sarasvatī and Lakṣmī. Poverty has turned away the learned scholar from basic thinking. Without making Sarasvatī its basic foundation, Lakṣmī cannot exist.

3 The basic sound which is the "mother" (creator) of words has been referred to by the form *śabda-tanmātra*.

Sarasvatī is Śrī, which means prosperity, on the basis of which material wealth and property exist. The nation, where prosperity is subdued, also loses its Lakṣmī (wealthiness). As was submitted in yesterday's lecture, Āgneyī Sarasvatī and Saumyā Lakṣmī, both combined together form the basic foundation of the universe. The season of Āgneyī Sarasvatī is spring, when worship of Śāradā takes place and that of Lakṣmī is the rainy season, at the end of which worship of Goddess Kamalā takes place. Spring is Śrīḥ and rain is Lakṣmī. Both are wives of Pārameṣṭhya Viṣṇu. Integrated association of the two is for the upliftment of the nation, which in its attachment towards sheer wealth ignores Sarasvatī (learning). A nation devoid of such intellect, definitely loses its accumulated wealth after a little time. The sum and substance of our submission is that creation of words emerges from the Aṅgirā stream and that of *artha* (matter) emerges from the Bhṛgu stream. Therefore, words and their meanings are interrelated by origin and are identical. It is on this basis that Bhagavān Bhartṛhari has said:

न सोऽस्ति प्रत्ययो लोके यः शब्दानुगमादृते।
अनुविद्धमिव ज्ञानं सर्वं शब्देन भाषते॥ – *वाक्यपदीय* 131

na so 'sti pratyayo loke yaḥ śabdānugamādṛte ।
anuviddhamiva jñānaṁ sarvaṁ śabdena bhāṣate ॥ – *Vākyapadīya* 131

It is the word, which is the basis of all the sciences, crafts and arts. Whatever is created due to it, can be analysed (and communicated).

वागर्थाविव सम्पृक्तौ वागर्थप्रतिपत्तये।
जगतः पितरौ वन्दे पार्वती-परमेश्वरौ॥ – *रघुवंश* १.१

vagarthāviva sampṛktau vāgarthapratipattaye ।
jagataḥ pitarau vande pārvatī-parameśvarau ॥ – *Raghuvaṁśa* 1.1

In *Artha-Brahman*, there are three facets – *avyaya*, *akṣara* and *kṣara*; similarly in *Śabda-Brahman* (words) there are three facets – *sphoṭa*, vowels and consonants. In *Artha-Brahman* all matter emerges on the basis of *avyaya*, from *kṣara*; similarly in *Śabda-Brahman* all words are born from one *akṣara* on the basis of *sphoṭa* and from here the 288 alphabets develop. Perhaps no other language has such alphabets.

अकारो वै सर्वा वाक्। सैषा स्पर्शोष्मभिर्व्यज्यमाना बह्वी नानारूपा भवति। – ऐत०आ०

akāro vai sarvā vāk । *saiṣā sparśoṣmabhirvyajyamānā bahvī nānārūpā bhavati* ।
– *AitaĀr*

According to this principle, one *akāra* is pronounced in 288 alphabets due to changes in proportion of heat and touch of various places in the mouth. Touch conveys contraction, heat conveys expansion. Contraction is the function of *soma* and expansion is the function of *agni*. According to the principle *agni-somātmaka jagat*, all matter emerges from the interaction of *agni* and *soma*. All letters and vowels emerge by the combination of *soma* in the form of touch and *agni* in the form of heat. Whatever takes place in the *Para-Brahman* sphere is exactly reproduced in the sphere of words. Both the facts are divided into equal streams and basic mystery and cause of the *upāsanā* of words, based on *praṇava* (*oṁ*) of *mantra japa* and the reading of sacred books is based on this principle. Advantages of the knowledge of essential science are also accrued by the *upāsanā* of the *mantra*s relating to that particular essential science. Propriety of various paths is dependable on the quality of the individual concerned.

According to the principle, अहरहर्देवाः सूर्य्यः (*aharahardevāḥ sūryyaḥ*), vowels *a*, *āi* and *ī*, etc. have been stated to have emerged from the sun and consonants *ka*, *ca*, *ṭa*, *ta*, etc. have emerged from the earth. Just as the earth cannot exist for a single moment without solar gravitation, similarly consonants, emerging from the earth, cannot be uttered without the vowels emerging from the sun.

Vowels are the base of the consonants. Vowels are *bṛhatīvāk*.[4] This is a solar *vāk*. Consonants are *anuṣṭupvāk*. This is speech. Just as a cock crushed and chewed one grain of paddy, tearing it and assimilating it, *bṛhatīvāk* chews and crushes the consonants. *Bṛhatī* is *aindrī* (emerging from Indra) *vāk*, *anuṣṭup* is *āgneyī vāk*. The former is the base of the latter, which has developed only in man among all sentient beings. Keeping in view this meaningful, but mysterious relationship between *bṛhatī* and *anuṣṭup*, *ṛṣi* has said:

बीभत्सूनां सयुजं हंसमाहुरपां दिव्यानां सख्ये चरन्तम्।
अनुष्टुभमनु चर्चूर्यमाणमिन्द्रं नि चिक्युः कवयो मनीषा॥ – ऋ० १०.१२४.९

bībhatsūnāṁ sayujaṁ haṁsamāhurapāṁ divyānāṁ sakhye carantam ।
anuṣṭubhamanu carcūryamāṇamindraṁ ni cikyuḥ kavayo manīṣā ॥
– *ṚV* X.124.9

The sage called the sun the ally of those who are frightened, abiding in the friendship of the waters of heaven; the wise have honoured with their praise Indra, who ceaselessly moves after the Anuṣṭup.

Aindrī bṛhatī vowels are related to the sun, that is why *bṛhatī* speech has been accepted as having nine letters, which means *vāk* having nine

---

4 A metre of thirty-six syllables.

points. At this stage you will have to understand a little more. The circle in the centre of which the sun is situated is called *bṛhatīcchanda* and it is known as *viśva-vṛtta* (Equator) in astrology. This *bṛhatīcchanda* has nine letters and has four *caraṇas*[5] and thus the total number of vowels reaches thirty-six. With each *akṣara* 1,000 rays of the sun are related. Thus from thirty-six *bṛhatī akṣara* emerges 36,000 *sāhasrīs*; in other words, the division of the solar age which has three *manotās* – *jyoti*, *gau* and *āyu* – in 36,000 numbers. Every day, man gets one unit of vital solar force through *suṣumṇā-nāḍī* situated at *brahmarandhra*, a point in head where the hairs of the head end. This treasure of vital force is spent in 36,000 days, which means 100 years of man's life (शतायुर्वै पुरुषः – *śatāyurvai puruṣaḥ*). This *bṛhatī prāṇa*, which initiates the vowels, has nine points. Of these nine points, the central fifth and the associated six points become the central base of vowel, consonants cannot be placed here, 1, 2, 3, 4 points earlier to these and 7, 8, 9 points afterwards are empty. In these points before and afterwards, vital force of the centrally situated vowels has its area of influence and on them maximum of seven consonants can be placed. Prātiśākhyaśāstra[6] has given the example *stryarkaṭ* – *s-t-r-y* ... these four consonants find place in the four points before vowels and *r-k-ṭ* ... these three consonants are placed afterwards. In the central *a* no one can place a consonant. For that, another vowel will be needed to write *upanyāsa* or *saṁnyāsī*, but pronounce it as *upanyāsa* or *saṁnyāsī*. Why is it so? Answers to this question are also based on the science of speech of vowels. Four points before the vowel and three points after the vowel are "hungry" for swallowing fuel, viz. consonants, in *upanyāsa*. The *a* associated with *p* wants to swallow the *u* and *a* of *yā* and also wants to swallow it thus conferred from both sides in pronunciation, it becomes inclined both ways. This is the grandeur of vowels on which the Vedaśāstra is based.

The Veda is not some speech which may have emerged in the imagination of man. Rather, it is *Brahman* speech which is eternal and proven by science and that is why it is described as superhuman. Just like the meaning of the *mantra*, words of the *mantra* themselves draw strength from scientifically supported principles on which the *mantra japa siddhi* is based. Failure in understanding its subtle basis led to Saṅkīrtanavāda. By one family consonant vowel or *mantra* the same *mantra* can be as disastrous as Vṛtrāsura's war with Indra:

---

[5] *Suṣumṇā-nāḍī* is related to the moon.

[6] Grammar of the Vedas.

दुष्टः शब्दः-स्वरतो वर्णतो वा मिथ्याप्रयुक्तो न तमर्थमाह।
स वाग्वज्रो यजमानं हिनस्ति यथेन्द्रशत्रुः स्वरतोऽपराधात्॥ – *महाभाष्य* १.१.१

duṣṭaḥ śabdaḥ-svarato varṇato vā mithyāprayukto na tamarthamāha ।
sa vāgvajro yajamānaṁ hinasti yathendraśatruḥ svarato 'parādhāt ॥
– *Mahābhāṣya* 1.1.1

Based on the principle अचिन्त्यो हि मणिमन्त्रौषधीनां प्रभावः (*acintyo hi maṇimantrauṣadhīnāṁ prabhāvaḥ*), the sacred tale of the inseparability of word – *Śabda-Brahman* and *Para-Brahman* – was explained in context with five Vedic *devatā*s, which are reflected by five motions. The Vedic principle five *devatā*s has been narrated in the Purāṇas as the principle of three *devatā*s when *agni* and *soma* are unregarded with Indra, then with solar Indra light, lunar *soma* light and earthly fiery light, the three-eyed Śiva is formed. The Veda defined these five separately according to the science of motion, then the Purāṇas express sun, *agni* and *soma* by one Śiva and in the form of "Brahmā, Viṣṇu and Maheśa" the essential *devatā* is explained through the medium of worship.

While the Veda is Vijñānaśāstra, the Purāṇas is Kathāśāstra and the basis of this *kathā* is the science of *nidāna* (diagnosis). The *nidāna* of science of medicine (Āyurveda) is entirely different. The meaning of *nidāna* in the Purāṇas has a different connotation. The science which, for the purposes of explaining the basic vital forces, uses a material object as a medium having similar vital forces and thus explains the functions of vital forces through matter is called the science of *nidāna*. Because of this branch of Indian science, many allegations are levelled against the sphere of Indian *upāsanā* (method of worship). Strange *devatā*s in strange form, their strange means of carriages, strange arms and their strange worship – all these are related to this (*nidāna*) symbolic science. For example, the mouse is symbolic of that earthly vital force Gaṇeśa on which another vital force (Gaṇapati) is based. Lotus is the symbolic form for the earth, vine is the symbolic form of attachment. *Triśūla*[7] is the symbolic form of the power of destruction, etc. It is on this basis that the forms of vital-force (*prāṇa-devatā*) are conceived and explained. We are blessing our imagination by the following symbolic reflection of Śiva:

व्याख्यामुद्राक्षमाला-कलशसुलिखिते बाहुभिर्वामपादं-
बिभ्राणो जानुमूर्ध्ना पदतलनिहितापस्मृतिर्द्युद्रुमाघः।

[7] A special type of arms having three formed knicks on the top and on the handle.

सौवर्णे योगपीठे लिपिमयकमले सूपविष्टस्त्रिनेत्रः-
क्षीराभश्चन्द्रमौलिर्वितरतु विबुधां शुद्धबुद्धिं शिवो नः ॥

vyākhyāmudrākṣamālā-kalaśasulikhite bāhūbhirvāmapādaṁ-
bibhrāṇo jānumūrdhnā padatalanihitāpasmṛtirdyurdrumāghaḥ ।
sauvarṇe yogapīṭhe lipimayakamale sūpaviṣṭastrinetraḥ-
kṣīrābhaścandramaulirvitaratu vibudhāṁ śuddhabuddhiṁ śivo naḥ ॥

Lotus has been described as a symbol for the earth because according to the *śruti*, आपो वै पुष्करपर्णम् (*āpo vai puṣkaraparṇam*), the first solidified stage of water (*āpaḥ*) is reflected by lotus. It is on this basis that earthly Brahmā has been described as Padmabhū; it is also explained as the native of Puṣkar island. The first lotus stage of water becomes the cause of the formation of Bhūpura. That which caused this *pura* is the Purāṇas. In the whole of India, the grand fortune of symbolically representing Bhagavān Padmabhū, Brahmā – the creator of the Vedas, has fallen on the part of Puṣkar, a city in Rajasthan, a state which has always shown its faithful devotion to the Vedas. It is true that due to some reason, Rajasthan was deprived of this Puṣkar area for some time but now again it has become a part of Rajasthan. And it should be hoped that, now after including this auspicious area, Rajasthan will become a centre, not only of India, but of the whole world by its eternal devotion to the Vedas. Such actions of nature cannot be speculated upon. These are beyond the pale of discussion. Immediately after the inclusion of Puṣkar in Rajasthan, this cultural Vedic message is now being delivered at the centre of inspiration of that creator of the Veda, resident of Puṣkar, Bhagavān Brahmā and thus the future of basic Vedic culture seems to be bright.

Process of the Formation of Earth

Please keep in view the abode of Bhagavān Brahmā called *bhūpadma* (lotus) or the earth. When the earth had not been formed, there was only a wide ocean named Arṇava. Air entered this watery ocean and water bubbles formed. Before the bubbles could burst another coating of water, air and solar vital-force covered the bubble. Thus water, air and solar vital became "solidified" by this continuous coating and turned into foam. The covering, by the continuous coating, turned into ashes, ash in the form of clay, clay in the form of sand, the sacred treasure of Rajasthan and was converted into stones and later on stone turned into raw iron and ultimately this solid material was converted into metals like gold, copper, silver and lead, and thus the process of formation of earth was completed. The form of earth has been made by water, foam ash, clay, sand, stone, iron and metal. That is why this earth which has been called *bhū* is eight-lettered, Gāyatrī has eight facets and in the Purāṇas it has been described as the wife of Brahmā, and in her conjugal association Brahmā is conducting the earthly *yajña*. After the formation of these eight materials, Prajāpati became content and took recourse to music as a pastime. That is why according to the derivation *yā gāyat* the earth has been called Gāyatrī.

स प्रजापतिः-आपः, फेनं, मृदं, सिकतं शर्करां, अश्मानं-अयः-हिरण्यं-असृजत्। अभूद्वा इयं प्रतिष्ठेति-तद्भूमिरभवत्। यदप्रथयत्-सा पृथिव्यभवत्। सेयं सर्वा कृत्स्ना मन्यमाना अगायत्। यदगायत्-तस्माद् गायत्री। तस्मादु है तद्यः सर्वः कृत्स्नो मन्यते, गायति, वैव गीते वा, रमते। – शत०ब्रा० ६.१.१.१२-१५

sa prajāpatiḥ-āpaḥ, phenaṁ, mṛdaṁ, sikataṁ śarkarāṁ, aśmānaṁ-ayaḥ-hiraṇyaṁ-asṛjat । *abhūdvā iyaṁ pratiṣṭheti-tadbhūmirabhavat* । *yadaprathayat-sā pṛthivyabhavat* । *seyaṁ sarvā kṛtsnā manyamānā agāyat* । *yadgāyat- tasmād-gāyatrī* । *tasmādu hai tadyaḥ sarvaḥ kṛtsno manyate, gāyati, vaiva gīte vā, ramate* । – *ŚatBrā* 6.1.1.12-15

Time for Rest

The last portion of this *śruti* conveys a lesson for the people of our nation. When should the nation take to music, dance, art, crafts and other mediums of entertainment? These should be organized only when its power of knowledge, action and material wealth has acquired a firm root. After his form had been fully developed, Prajāpati took to music and other mediums of mental satisfaction and entertainment. A nation has no right to celebrate functions of music, entertainment, dance, etc. until it develops its power of knowledge, wealth and strength.

तस्मात् – यः सर्वः कृत्स्नो मन्यते गायति दैव गीते वा रमते वा

tasmāt – yaḥ sarvaḥ kṛtsno manyate gāyati daiva gīte vā ramate vā

Bowing down to this direction of *śruti*, the nation should take to entertaining recreations accordingly (after the fulfilment of the objectives noted above).

Meaning of Vijñāna

The narration of science of symbols, relevant in this context, is now over. Again, I bring before you the word *hṛdayam* which is presented here as an example for understanding the word *vijñāna* (science). The three-lettered central *akṣara* is *hṛdayam*; this is *antaryāmī*. And the (two-lettered) *agni-soma* is the external form of matter. It is *sūtrātmā*. This is divided into the science of the centre and the science of form (*pṛṣṭha*). The science of the centre is the pure science of *akṣara*, the science of form is the pure science of *kṣara*. The science of form is the science of *kṣara*, with *akṣara* in its ambit. The central science of the self is *akṣara-vidyā*. This is *para-vidyā*. The science of the universe, placed in the former is *akṣara-vidyā*, this is *aparā-vidyā*. Explaining the concepts of these two sciences, *ṛṣi* has said:

> द्वे विद्ये वेदितव्ये इति ह स्मयद्ब्रह्मविदो वदन्ति परा चैवापरा च। तत्रापरा ऋग्वेदो यजुर्वेदः सामवेदोऽथर्ववेदः, शिक्षा कल्पो व्याकरणं निरुक्तं छन्दो ज्योतिषमिति। अथ परा यया तदक्षरमधिगम्यते॥ – मु॰उप॰ १.१.४-५
>
> *dve vidye veditavye iti ha smayadbrahmavido vadanti parā caivāparā ca*। *tatrāparā ṛgvedo yajurvedaḥ sāmavedo 'tharavedaḥ, śikṣā kalpo vyākaraṇaṁ niruktaṁ chando jyotiṣamiti*। *atha parā yayā tadakṣaramadhigamyate*॥ – *MuUp* 1.1.4-5
>
> To him, he said, two kinds of knowledge must be known – that is what the knowers of *Brahman* tell us. They are higher knowledge and lower knowledge.

One Element, Three Forms

One element converted itself into the form of *hṛ*, *da* and *ya* in the beginning. These three became converted into five facets and by permutation and combination of these five facts, *kṣara* and *akṣara* have converted themselves into hundred, hundred thousand, million, billion and infinite forms. *Jñāna* converts itself in the manifold *vijñāna*. One Brahmā, which is *jñāna* and *satya*, develops into internal bliss and *vijñāna* pervades all around. To know the science of the multifaceted universe is *vijñāna* and to have the knowledge of one self is *jñāna*. Brahmā is सत्यं ज्ञानमनन्तं ब्रह्म (*satyaṁ jñānamanantaṁ brahma*) – this *śruti* has propounded self-realization (*jñāna*) of *akṣara-vidyā* (*parā-vidyā*), while नित्यं विज्ञानमानन्दं ब्रह्म (*nityaṁ vijñānamānandaṁ brahma*) – this *śruti* has explained the scientific understanding of the universe by *kṣara-vidyā* (*aparā-vidyā*). Thus the Indian Vedaśāstra has propounded science integrated with knowledge and has proved that it is the treasure of all knowledge, सर्वविद्यानिधानत्व (*sarvavidyānidhānatva*). This has been analysed by Bhagavān Kṛṣṇa in these words:

> ज्ञानं तेऽहं सविज्ञानमिदं वक्ष्याम्यशेषतः।
> यज्ज्ञात्वा नेह भूयोऽन्यज्ज्ञातव्यमवशिष्यते॥ – *गीता* ७.२

jñānaṁ te 'haṁ savijñānamidaṁ vakṣyāmyaśeṣataḥ ।
yajjñātvā neha bhūyo 'nyajjñātavyamavaśiṣyate ॥ – *Gītā* VII.2

I shall now reveal unto you fully this knowledge and wisdom, knowing which nothing else remains to be known in this world.

Creation and Dissolution

The prefix *vi* (in *vijñāna*) means contrary, special and many, and thus the meaning of the word *vijñāna* can be derived in three ways – "contrary" knowledge is science (विरुद्धं ज्ञानं विज्ञानं – *viruddhaṁ jñānaṁ vijñānaṁ*), special knowledge is science (विशेषं ज्ञानं विज्ञानं – *viśeṣaṁ jñānaṁ vijñānaṁ*) and multiple or manifold knowledge is science (विविधं ज्ञानं विज्ञानं –*vividhaṁ jñānaṁ vijñānaṁ*). Of these three, special is covered by multipleness and we have two definitions before us. The Indian Vedic word *vijñāna* denotes multiple knowledge which includes special knowledge and it is science. Explaining the "multiple" on the basis of the "unit" is science. In other words, keeping "self" as the base while explaining the universe is science. To know the development of *kṣara* through the medium of *akṣara* is science. How Brahmā converted himself into so many facets? Analysing and understanding this question and its answer is science and how all this multiple variety is converted ultimately into the basic unit is *jñāna*. In the language of Purāṇas, knowledge of creation is science and knowledge of dissolution is *jñāna*. Creation is science, dissolution is knowledge. It must be borne in mind that according to this viewpoint, nothing is ever destroyed. It only changes. Conversion of Unmanifest into Manifest is creation and conversion of Manifest back into Unmanifest is dissolution. According to *ṛṣi*s, there is appearance and disappearance. Fullness of this viewpoint is completely protected.

अव्यक्ताद्व्यक्तयः सर्वाः प्रभवन्त्यहरागमे ।
रात्र्यागमे प्रलीयन्ते तत्रैवाव्यक्तसञ्ज्ञके ॥ – *गीता* ८.१८

avyaktādvyaktayaḥ sarvāḥ prabhavantyaharāgame ।
rātryāgame pralīyante tatraivāvyaktasaṁjñake ॥ – *Gītā* VIII.18

At the advent of Brahmā's day, all living beings emanate from the unmanifest source. And at the fall of his night, all embodied beings again merge into their unmanifest source.

अव्यक्तादीनि भूतानि व्यक्तमध्यानि भारत! ।
अव्यक्तनिधनान्येव तत्र का परिदेवना ॥ – *गीता* २.२८

avyaktādīni bhūtāni vyaktamadhyāni bhārata ।
avyaktanidhanānyeva tatra kā paridevanā ॥ – *Gītā* II.28

Oh scion of Bharat! all created beings are unmanifest before birth, manifest in life, and again unmanifest on death. So why grieve?

यदा स देवो जागर्त्ति तदेदं चेष्टते जगत्।
यदा स्वपिति शान्तात्मा तदा सर्वं निमीलति ॥ – मनु॰ १.५२

yadā sa devo jāgartti tadedaṁ ceṣṭate jagat ।
yadā svapiti śāntātmā tadā sarvaṁ nimīlati ॥ – *Manu* 1.52

When that divine being is awake, then this world is active; when he slumbers, with his mind in calm repose, then all vanishes.

Perishable and Imperishable

This verse embodies the Vedic principle of imperishableness or permanence. The perishable universe is definitely passing or mortal. But when it is established on the base of the immortal imperishable (*amṛta*), how can it be destroyed? It is heard that he who drinks *amṛta* even once achieves immortality and becomes free from emaciation and death. It is unnecessary, therefore, to discuss the immortality of that mortal *kṣara* which always keeps at its base the *rasātmaka* (immortal) *akṣara*. Mortality is well placed in the ambit of immortality. Thus, death itself has become immortal. It is only a change of state. We have everywhere the kingdom of that Pūrṇa Brahmā which is always in a constant and unchangeable state. According to the principle *pūrṇamadaḥ pūrṇamidam*, when that is full and complete, then manifestation of that must always be full. Fullness is bliss. Therefore, bliss prevails all around. Incompleteness, hollowness, suffering, etc. are misguided imaginations of misguided persons. Misguided sentimentalists who are turned away from the existence of the fullness of the self Brahmā says "all this is unreal". For their awakening, the *ṛṣis* have always described the whole as eternal and permanent. For removing emotional expression of unreality of this universe and incompleteness, the principle of fullness and completeness has been enunciated. For the wail of "suffering and sorrow" by non-believers (in the self) the victorious cries of "Bliss!" have been raised, such as:

आनन्दाद्ध्येव खल्विमानि भूतानि जायन्ते। आनन्देन जातानि जीवन्ति। आनन्दं प्रयन्त्यभिसंविशन्तीति। – तै॰उप॰ ३.६

ānandāddhyeva khalvimāni bhūtāni jāyante । *ānandena jātāni jīvanti* । *ānandaṁ prayantyabhisaṁviśantīti* । – *TaiUp* 3.6

Bhṛgu understood that *ānanda* (bliss) is *Brahman*; from *ānanda*, all things are born and all things live by *ānanda*.

The Indian (*vijñāna-kāṇḍa*) scientific sector has worshipped and mediated this manifestation of absolute permanent fullness and bliss. By forgetting the scientific sector, the "complete" man of the past has become a follower of the *śūnya* (non-substantiality) and of the unreality of the world under the influence of emotionalism and as consequence is distressed by (the principle of) suffering everywhere. The same grief pervades the minds of those material scientists who have similar characteristics and who are also influenced by the manifest.

These followers of unreality (Śūnyavādīs) should not forget that the concept and form of man is complete. Bliss permeates the entire pattern and stream of his life. The basic root of all attitudes and actions is the permanent blissful *vijñāna ātmā*. If a man is proceeding towards the gallows, it will be concluded that this act of his is also based on a desire of bliss. This man, proceeding towards the gallows, knows that if he does not step forward, more suffering or punishment will be inflicted upon him. For giving himself the (bliss) pleasure of safety from this suffering, he proceeds forward towards the gallows. It is clear that fullness, completeness and bliss is the natural form of man and not non-substantialism (*śūnyatā*), incompleteness and suffering. Misconceptions born of intellectual defects create such emotional confusion, which can be shed off by inculcating practices based on the Vedic science, which itself is based on scientific essential thoughts.

Evil Influence of Sectarianism

When basic scientific thoughts of a nation are submerged in layers of sectarianism, then man's intellect is dislocated from its centre. During such a state of (intellectual) confusion and dislocation such sectarian philosophies emerge, which influence persons, who, though integrated with traditional devotion and faith, are deprived of the correct concept of their own culture. Such sects invade the people's mind like a swarm of locusts and try to fulfil their selfish ends with cheap popularity. It becomes an essential duty to awaken such emotional people by their non-sectarian basic culture, based on knowledge and science.

Intellectual Defects and Emotionalism

Due to intellectual defects, in other words due to mental emotionalism inspired by tendency to be influenced by the obvious, many persons, though devoted and faithful towards their culture, are sometimes attracted by charming sects and forget the blissful and complete form. They commit the mistake of thinking that imaginary sectarian principles of "unsubstantiality and suffering" are great achievements of man. But as soon as these people become aware of their central form, they reject and throw away these sectarian principles in a moment. It is to strengthen this idea of completeness and fullness, that an easy elaboration of the science of *aśvattha* is being placed before him (such persons). This is a science which differentiates *amṛta* and *mṛtyu* on a scientific basis.

What is *amṛta*? That which never dies. What is *mṛtyu*? That which is always dead. Unitariness is *amṛta* and multipleness is *mṛtyu* as the *śruti* has said:

यदेवेह तदमुत्र यदमुत्र तदन्विह।
मृत्योः स मृत्युमाप्नोति य इह नानेव पश्यति॥ – क॰उप॰ २.१.१०

yadeveha tadamutra yadamutra tadanviha ।
mṛtyoḥ sa mṛtyumāpnoti ya iha nāneva paśyati ॥ – *KaUp* 2.1.10

Unit and Multiple

All sense of differentiation, separateness, multipleness is *mṛtyu*. According to this principle, यदुवरमन्तरं कुरुते अथ भयं भवति, द्वितीयाद्वै भयं भवति (*yaduvaramantaraṁ kurute atha bhayaṁ bhavati, dvitīyādvai bhayaṁ bhavati*), separate characteristics of name, form and function convert one *ākāśa* into innumerable, turn that natural essential, which has no parts, into parts. Whenever there is some void in unitariness, there occurs instability. From unitariness emerges *amṛta*, instability emerges from multipleness. Should we destroy this variety? Have we taken shelter behind the bliss of the Vedic science for this sole "achievement" (!)? No.

Relationship of Amṛta and Mṛtyu

Many people would really have been pleased at this definition of multipleness and unitariness. As if, the main purpose of this propagation of Vedic essential thoughts is abolition of the multiplicity of classes and divisions. Therefore, we shall have to explain in a few words the concepts of unitariness and multipleness, which are related to *amṛta* and *mṛtyu*. There is no doubt that multipleness (variety and separateness) is dangerous. But it is so only till unitariness is not made the basis of multipleness. If this is done, then the same multipleness or variety based on unitariness becomes protection of the universe and a cause of its popularity, satisfaction and provides strength. If multipleness is separated from unitariness, it causes destruction of the universe. If we remove the unitary concept of *jñāna* from the din and bustle of *vijñāna*, then science will cause our destruction, because it will then only encourage attainment of cheap popular influence.

Knowledge and Science

Knowledge, devoid of science or variety, is not useful. Similarly, science has no meaning if it does not have knowledge as its base. What is desirable for the Indian intellect in such a cause? Correct answer to this question will be – science coupled with knowledge. According to Vedic definition, it is inseparableness which tolerates separation and, according to the definition of Sāṁkhya, it is the unimpaired consequentialism. Vision will be one and equal, action will be various and different. समदर्शिनः भारतीयाः न तु समवर्तिनः (*samadarśinaḥ bhāratīyāḥ, na tu samavartinaḥ*). This is a natural definition of the form of the Indian concept of science coupled with knowledge. We have to initiate the science of *aśvattha* with this concept as our base. The following meaningful and subtle principles about the science of creation should be kept in view in this context:

यदस्ति किञ्चित्तदिदं प्रतीमोऽविचालि शश्वत्स्थमनाद्यनन्तम् ।
प्रतिक्षणान्यान्य-विकार-सृष्टि-प्रवाह-तद्वत् विरुद्धभावम् ॥ १॥

विरुद्धभावद्वयसन्निवेशात् सम्भाव्यते विश्वमिदं द्विमूलम् ।
आभ्वभ्वसंज्ञे स्त इमे च मूले द्रष्टाभु, दृश्यं तु मतं तदभ्वम् ॥ २॥
– *संशयतदुच्छेदवाद-मूलोषनिषत्*, प्रथम पर्व

yadasti kiñcittadidaṁ pratīmo 'vicāli śaśvatsthamanādyanantam ।
pratikṣaṇānyānya-vikāra-sṛṣṭi-pravāha-tadvat viruddhabhāvam ॥

viruddhabhāvadvayasanniveśāt sambhāvyate viśvamidaṁ dvimūlam ।
ābhvabhvasaṁjñe sta ime ca mūle draṣṭābhu, dṛśyaṁ tu mataṁ tadbhvam ॥
– *Saṁśyataducchedavāda-mūlopaniṣat*[8], first *sarga*

Foundation of the Universe

What is the root or foundation of the universe? Before answering this question, we should know what is the universe according to the principle कारणगुणा एव कार्य्यगुणानारभन्ते (*kāraṇaguṇā eva kāryyaguṇānārabhante*), the properties of the cause are transmitted in the effect also. If we were to know the properties of the effect of the universe, we would automatically know the properties of its roots. Every object or matter which has an effect can be seen by us in two ways. This creation was there, millions and millions (innumerable) years ago. It is there today and will be there in future also. The oceans, mountains, the Gaṅgā and the Yamunā,

---

[8] By Guru Paṇḍit Madhusūdan Ojhā.

all these are the same. About every object that exists (*sa evāyaṁ*) we can say it is the same. This characteristic and property of immortality and permanence is applicable in a natural way. And this is one way of looking at the universe.

Constant Change: Constant Permanence

According to the second viewpoint, every object or matter changes constantly. The *Śrīmad Bhagavadgītā* has stated that there are three stages of a matter: unmanifest–manifest–unmanifest, and has described the middle manifest stage as existence. It is essentially temporary and changeable and this amazing process of constant change takes place every moment and is clearly perceptible. The actual form of motion is unsubstantial. Those who cannot understand the Ātma-Brahma, which integrates everything into a unit, gave birth to the principle of Śūnyavāda. The Indian intellect also succumbed to this viewpoint through the system of philosophy. Though Indian philosophy emerged from this Śūnyavāda, it culminated in the end at indivisible-permanent Brahmā. Devadatta (Mr X) is changing every moment. That is why the changes of childhood, youth, old age, etc. occur in him. But we also say "he is the same Devadatta which I had seen in childhood", thus there are some unchangeable facts also in everyone. The streams of River Gaṅgā (Bhagavatī Gaṅgā) change every moment, but everyone describes it as the same Gaṅgā which liberated the sons of Sagar and which emancipated our ancestors. This unchangeable fact is also permanent. In lukewarm milk, something is added to coagulate in the evening. The same milk is found converted into the form of curd in the morning. There is no one particular moment when milk is converted into curd. Rather, the process of change starts when buttermilk is added to it for coagulation and we call a particular stage of its change as curd. On festivals like Dīpāvalī, the walls of almost all buildings are whitewashed. Believe it, that along with this whitewashing, a process of decay also commences. Both creation and dissolution are based on one central point. This central point is the unchangeable essential as the *śruti* has said:

संभूतिं च विनाशं च यस्तद्वेदोभयँ सह।
विनाशेन मृत्युं तीर्त्वा संभूत्याऽमृतमश्नुते॥ – ईश॰उप॰ १४

saṁbhūtiṁ ca vināśaṁ ca yastadvedobhayam̐ saha ।
vināśena mṛtyuṁ tīrtvā saṁbhūtyā 'mṛtamaśnute ॥ – *ĪśaUp* 14

He, who understands at the same time both the Unmanifest and the

Manifest crosses death through knowledge of the world and attains immortality.

To believe that creation and dissolution are different and separate is (non-Aryan) incorrect and defective point of view. This gives birth to the principle of unsubstantiality. Both are integrated at one point. As long as man tries to explain this universe by his intellectual arrogance, he cannot associate himself with the central point. The *śruti* has, therefore, said: पाण्डित्यं निर्विद्यबाल्येन तिष्ठासेत् (*pāṇḍityam nirvidyabālyena tiṣṭhāset* – A learned man will live by the strength of knowledge alone – *Bṛhadāraṇyaka Upaniṣad* 3.5.1)). Arrogance of learning is the main obstacle in the way of understanding reality. Arrogant pride makes us run after cheap popularity. To influence others becomes our main aim. In an extrovert mentality, there is no opportunity and occasion of seeing the self-centre. *Bālyena tiṣṭhāset* – this statement is very important and meaningful. Children in Rajasthan collect clay during the rainy season and build castles, palaces, sweets, etc. and remain engrossed in the play. At a proper time, they say with the same enthusiasm, "we constructed these and we are now destroying them". Thereafter they destroy these with their feet and at the same time extend an invitation for building them again the next day. "We created and we destroyed." In this childlike play, "creation and destruction" are based on one and the same point. These children find equal pleasure in both, while man is dislocated from his central point, because he is pleased at creation and laments at destruction. There is equality of vision neither in creation nor in destruction. Inequality pervades at both places and its only cause is arrogant pride of learning, attachment towards popularity and dogmatic pride of intellectualism. Equality is the *brāhmī* state and when man attains it, one never gets the occasion of succumbing to the notion of illusions of pride.

एषा ब्राह्मी स्थितिः पार्थ नैनां प्राप्य विमुह्यति। – *गीता* २.७२

eṣā brāhmī sthitiḥ pārtha naināṁ prāpya vimuhyati । – *Gītā* II.72

Thus in effect – in this universe – both changeable and permanent essentials are perceivable by all. Both are integrated at one point and this is the amazing phenomenon of *brahma vibhūti*. Unchangeable essential of *amṛta* and changeable essential of *mṛtyu*, both are facets of the self known as *aham*, as is enunciated in अमृतञ्चैव मृत्युश्च सदसच्चाहमर्जुन (*amṛtañcaiva mṛtyuśca sadasaccāhamarjuna* – (I am the immortality and mortality, and I am the being and the non-being – *Bhagavadgītā* IX.19), both have the relationship of identical unification and not that of the base and the based. Whether motion is in the finger or the finger is in motion? Correct solution of this question may be expressed as follows – to the extent the finger exists, to that extent motion in the form of movement exists. Keeping in view this strange relationship of integrated identical unification, *śruti* has said:

तदेजति तन्नैजति तद्दूरे तद्वन्तिके।
तदन्तरस्य सर्वस्य तदु सर्वस्यास्य बाह्यतः॥ – ईश०उप० ५

tadejati tannaijati taddūre tadvantike ।
tadantarasya sarvasya tadu sarvasyāsya bāhyataḥ ॥ – *ĪśaUp* 5

It moves, it is motionless. It is distant, it is near. It is within all, it is without all this.

अन्तरं मृत्योरमृतं मृत्यावमृतमाहितम्॥ – शत०ब्रा० १०.५.२.४

antaraṁ mṛtyoramṛtaṁ mṛtyāvamṛtamāhitam ॥ – *ŚataBrā* 10.5.2.4

In the relationship between the base and the based, there is a duality of existence. Here it is identical and does not have the relationship of the base and the based. Therefore, in spite of apparently dual existences, the principle of *ekmevadvitīyam brahma* (In the beginning, there was only non-existence and from this non-existence, emerged existence – *Chāndogya Upaniṣad* 6.2.1) is conclusively proved. Thus, if the effect – the universe – is double functional, then in the cause, the root *brahma*, there should be two functions, two facets. The cause of the changeable effect is called *abhva* and which in effect becomes the changing vision of the universe and the root of the unchangeable effect is *abhu*, which is the visionary in the universe. These two essentials have been described as *rasa* and *bala*. The *rasa* essential is one in number, is permanently at rest, is not limited by time, space and direction, is absolute, having no properties, and is *nirañjana* (spotless). The *bala* essential is innumerable in number, is permanently restless, limited by time, place and direction, having properties (*sāñjana*) changing and it is limited. These are the two fundamental essentials on which Vedic science is based. The essential *rasa* is converted into sixteen facets by processes of creation. These might be elaborated later on. The essential *bala* also has sixteen facets, which are called *balakośa* and are known as *māyā, hṛdayam, jāyā, dhārā, āpaḥ, bhūtiḥ, yajñaḥ, sūtraṁ, satyam, yakṣaṁ, abhvam, vayaḥ, vāyonādhaḥ, vayunam, mohaḥ* and *vidyā*. Independent study is necessary for knowing forms and definitions of these branches of the basic essential *balakośa*. The *mahābalakośa*, which is the beginning of all and is the base of all other *balakośa*, is called *mahāmāyā* and we have to keep that in view, because it is within the bounds of *mahāmāyā* that the *aśvattha* tree emerges. The *bala* which converts infinite, all-pervasive unlimited into finite, pervasive and limited is called *māyā-bala*. Thanks to the Vedāntic philosophy, the word *māyā* has received enough publicity. In the eyes of the common people, its meaning is understood or is being made to be understood as falsehood or imaginary. It is due to the total lack of knowledge of the essential form of *māyā-bala*, which is a fundamental phenomenon of nature, that for centuries Indians consider themselves absolved of all responsibilities simply by uttering the word *māyā*. This imaginary "ism" of *māyā* has blocked the flow of Vedic scientific streams. All material beauty, all prosperity, all qualities of knowledge and science have been subdued by Māyāvāda. Decadence of this nation commenced on the day when the ideal of this nation became confined to shaving off heads and becoming *saṁnyāsī*. Leave this undesirable reference and let us come back to *aśvattha* through the medium of *balakośa*.

A particular stage of *māyā-bala* is called *abhva*, which is the eleventh *balakośa* in the series. We shall place it before you to explain a particular viewpoint. The meaning of the word *abhva* is *abhvan bhavati*. That which is not an actual object but is only a conceptual object is called *abhva*, which is popularly called *abhu*. ते हैते ब्रह्मणो महती अभ्वे, महती यक्षे (*te haite brahmaṇo mahatī abhve, mahatī yakṣe*), in this way *śruti* itself has accepted *abhva* as great.

All matter are divided in three categories: *sattāsiddha* (actual), *bhātisiddha* (conceptual) and *ubhayasiddha* (dual). Matter which exists, but cannot be perceived or seen by bodily organs is called *sattāsiddha*. Vital forces like *Īśvara*, *ātmā*, *ṛṣi*, *pitṛ*, *deva*, *gandharva* and *asura* are included in this category. Such things which exist as well as can be seen or touched and can be perceived by bodily organs are called *ubhayasiddha* and are dual, e.g. the sun–moon–earth–plants–air–water, etc. There is a third category of "things" which have no existence, but their concepts have become the base of understanding or practice. This particular *bala* is called *abhva*, this is the third category of *bhātisiddha* objects. North, south, east, west, etc. and nearness, heaviness, lightness, liquidity, solidness, etc. are not independent objects having actual existence. But these relative concepts related to actual practice have become the medium of their perception. Has anybody touched (or seen) east or west, like a house, building, jars, clay, etc.? No, even then these conceptual "things" are being accepted and believed everywhere. Sixteen *ānnā*s in a rupee, forty *seers* in a *mauṇḍa*, all numbers except the unit one and similar other innumerable things are included in this conceptual (*abhva*) category.

Therefore, to those who argue in connection with pure actualities like *Īśvara*, *ātmā* and *prāṇa* that "shall we believe in these only when you show me before our eyes?". We wish to ask if they could show us east and west, which they continue to believe everyday and night? Believe it, it is only in following the *ātma-sattā* that our uplift lies. Within the ambit of *māyā* appears a particular conceptual (force) *bala* named *abhva*, which is like other *bala*, viz. *jāyā*, *dhārā*, etc. अमितस्य मितकरणी माया (*amitasya mitakaraṇī māyā*). This is the definition of *māyā*. माङ्-माने-शब्दे च (*māṅ-māne-śabde ca*) is the basic root of the word *māyā*. The *bala* which creates the basic sound (*śabda-tanmātra*) and limits the unlimited is called *māyā-bala*. In the Parātpara Brahmā (सर्वबलविशिष्ट रसैकघन – *sarvabalaviśiṣṭa rasaikaghana*), which keeps all *bala* in its ambit and is the image of *rasa* in a spontaneous way, *māyā-bala*, which creates various properties, emerges; unmanifest *māyā-bala* becomes manifest. This *māyā-bala* limits an insignificant portion of that infinite. It must be borne in mind that in its *rasa* form, that infinite is neither limited by anything nor is bound by anything. *Bala* itself, in its *bala* aspect, reflects the finite and infinite facets. It is never possible that *māyā* might limit the *māyī* (that which holds *māyā* in its ambit) or that *bala* might bind the *rasa*. Of course, this is a main function of *māyā* that, witnessed by *rasa*, it should convert itself in the form of the universe by the process of integrating itself in spontaneous bounds. It is only in respect of its aspect as a "witness" that one might say that *māyā* limits the infinite. The Advaita (non-dual) characteristic becomes obvious by this subtle analysis.

The initial base of the limited or finite universe is a bubble limited by *māyā-bala* (in that vast expanse of *rasa*). Until the emergence of fully independent *māyāpura*, *parātpara* was out of universal bonds. Immediately on the emergence of *māyāpura* the covered area became limited and it has been described as *purīśaya* due to this characteristic of *pura*. This word has become, in popular language, *puruṣa*. From now on, we have to understand the science of creation through the medium of the term *puruṣa*, which is related to the science of creation as is obvious from पुरुष एवेदं सर्व-यद्भूतं-यच्च भाव्यम् (*puruṣa evedaṁ sarva-yadbhūtaṁ-yacca bhāvyam* – Whatever all this is, whatever has been in the past, and whatever will it be in future, all that is in fact the cosmic man itself – *Yajurveda* 31.2). We must bear it in mind that while timing the span of these lectures we have to take care of the health of Mr President. It is alright. Why only tomorrow, it is a subject for the entire life of a person; rather of many lives. Who has ever been able to fathom the unlimited *vibhūti* (manifestation) of infinite? अनेकजन्मसंसिद्धा ततो याति परां गतिम् (*anekajanmasaṁsiddhā tato yāti parāṁ gatim*) (*Gītā*).

Due to the emergence of *māyā-bala*, an amazing phenomenon happens in this *māyāpura*. Until this stage there was no independent centre in *parātpara*. Rather, every point of it was a centre or it was the centre itself. It was in the form of *mahimā*. How is a particular centre possible in the infinite? Today at this stage in *māyāpura*, an independent particular regulated centre *bala* emerges. While many centres release various *bala*s from entanglements of knots and convert it in dissolution (*laya*), one centre integrates *bala*s in ties of knots and converts it in the form of creation. For systematization of the form of universe there should be one centre and all boundaries and limits of this *māyāpura* universe should be delegated and subservient to the centre with deep faith (should be integrated with and towards the centre). Only then the process of creation can continue and can remain systematized. In infinite *parātpara* also there was *bala*. But due to the fact that *māyā-bala* was Unmanifest, there was no independent centre and therefore *bala* could not be tied down together. Therefore, those innumerable *bala*s in *parātpara* were unrelated to the aptitude of creation and they are still unrelated from the point of view of *parātpara*.

न सती सा नासती सा नोभयात्मा विरोधतः ।
काचिद्विलक्षणा माया वस्तुभूता सनातनी ॥

na satī sā nāsatī sā nobhayātmā virodhataḥ ।
kācidvilakṣaṇā māyā vastubhūtā sanātanī ॥

According to this principle, the *rasa balātmaka* essential (in the form of *hṛdaya*) of Mahāmāyī Maheśvara Puruṣa, which emerged in the lap of *mahāmāyā*, which is many functional, by *sadarasa* and *asad bala*, has been called *māna*. It is due to this relationship that this *puruṣeśvara* has been called *manomaya*, e.g. मनोमयः पुरुषो कामनयः रसः सत्यसंकल्पः (*manomayaḥ puruṣo kāmanayaḥ rasaḥ satyasaṅkalpaḥ*). From the centre, *puruṣa* beams (*arka*s) continuously emit. These beams are desires (*kāma*). These beams of *kāma* become the seeds of creation as explained in *eko 'ham bahusyām*. This has been explained in the following *mantra* also.

कामस्तदग्रे समवर्तताधि मनसो रेतः प्रथमं यदासीत् ।
सतो बन्धुमसति निरविन्दन् हृदि प्रतीष्या कवयो मनीषा ॥ – ऋ० १०.१२९.४

kāmastadagre samavartatādhi manaso retaḥ prathamaṁ yadāsīt ।
sato bandhumasati niravindan hṛdi pratīṣyā kavayo manīṣā ॥

– *ṚV* X.129.4

In this *puruṣātmā*, desire (*kāmanā*) emerged. This *puruṣātmā* was operating within the limit of *mahāmāyā*, an aggregate unit of *rasa* and *bala*. This emergence of desire was for the attainment of fullness, completeness and manifestation of prosperity. What is the form of this (*manomaya kāmanā*'s) desire emerging in the centre? *Rasa* and *bala* constitute the form of this integrated or diffused form of desire. *Rasa*, which is *sad* and *bala*, which is *asad*, is desire. The two essentials *rasa* and *bala* function in the centre as well as in the circumference. These essentials constitute the form of *mana*, which resides in *hṛdaya*. Thus, as a result thereof, in desire of *kāmanā* emerging in and enwrapped in *mana*, there is absence of any third essential except *rasa* and *bala*; *rasa-bala* is the real form of *kāmanā*. Therefore, this desire (*manomayī kāmanā*) which follows the *avyaya-ātmā* can be given three names – *rasa-kāmanā*, *bala-kāmanā* and *rasa-bala-kāmanā*. The *mana* situated in *hṛdaya* can have desire of *rasa*, of *bala*, or of both. This is the actual form of *kāmanā*. The basic form of *uktha* becomes the foundation of desire. Desires, therefore, are in consonance with the centre from which they emerge, just as beams in consonance with the basic centre from where they are emitted. In actual existence, *rasa* and *bala* are available independently. Therefore in those contexts where *rasa* is referred, *bala* is automatically assumed to have *rasa* in it and wherever *bala* is referred in all such contexts, *rasa* is assumed to contain *bala* in its ambit. In other words, *bala* communicates *bala* having *rasa* in it and *rasa* means *rasa* having *bala* in it. Through the medium of this natural definition related to *rasa* and *bala* and their intermingled functions, we shall try to understand the science of *aśvattha*.

According to the above-mentioned natural definition, desire for *rasa* will mean *rasa-kāmanā* having *bala* in its ambit and it will be called *mumukṣu* and *bala-kāmanā* will mean desire for *bala* with *rasa* in its ambit. The *rasa-kāmanā* which liberates and frees entanglements of *bala* related to the form of creation will be called *mumukṣu* and the *bala-kāmanā*, which strengthens these relationships and knots of universe, is called *sisṛkṣā*.

Desire for destruction will be known as *mumukṣu* and desire for construction will be known as *sisṛkṣā*. Formation will be known as *sisṛkṣā* and dissolution will be known as *mumukṣu*. Both these entirely contradictory desires are integrated at one point, just like *rasa* and *bala*, as is clear from this *śruti*:

संभूतिं च विनाशं च यस्तद्वेदोभयँ सह।
विनाशेन मृत्युं तीर्त्वा संभूत्याऽमृतमश्नुते ॥ – ईश०उप० १४

saṁbhūtiṁ ca vināśaṁ ca yastadvedobhayaṁ̐ saha ।
vināśena mṛtyuṁ tīrtvā saṁbhūtyā 'mṛtamaśnute ॥ – *ĪśaUp* 14

The *rasa-kāmanā* having *bala* in its ambit emerges from the centrally situated *avyaya-mana*. There was a coating of layers of *bala* having *rasa* in its ambit, in the store of *rasa* and *bala* extending from centre to circumference, due to the emergence of desire in the surface of indivisible *puraṣa vyaya*. This *puruṣa-vyaya* is a total image of *rasa* and *bala*. This is called the first coating of *rasa*, with which *bala* was associated in an absolutely weak and loose relationship. Thus, in spite of the presence of this companionable *bala*, scientists describe this first coating of *rasa* which was inclined towards dissolution as a "coating of *rasa*". Therefore, in the field of knowledge, it is described as a coating of pure *rasa*. The first coating, the loose companionate pure coating, of *rasa* is called the first *ānandakalā* (facet of *ānanda*) of *avyaya-puruṣa* which has been explained by रसो ह्येव सः (*raso hyeva saḥ*), रसं ह्येवायं लब्ध्वाऽऽनन्दी भवति (*rasaṁ hyevāyaṁ labdhvā "nandī bhavati*). It must be borne in mind that *rasātmaka ānanda* or *ānandātmaka rasa* are different from the worldly pleasure of organs. While pleasure, due to its dependence on other subjects, has a beginning and an end and is thus momentary, passing and temporary, it is destructible and is tragic in the end. It is an essence of sorrow communicating favourable pains due to its relationship with the bodily organs, technically described as *kha* (sky). On the other hand, *ānandātmaka rasa* is firmly based on the central *bala* located in its own place of *avyaya* self. It expands and develops continually due to its relationship with centrally located *mana* named *śvovasīyas;* it is permanent and absolute, being a protector of the infiniteness it is indestructible. It can never be uprooted and is entirely free and unrelated to the bodily organs in the form of *kha* and is the initiator of absolute peace. It is just another form of permanent peace. आनन्दमयोऽभ्यासात् (*ānandamayo 'bhyāsāt*) – with these words Bhagavān Vyāsa has eulogized this first *avyaya-kala*, which is in the form of *ānanda* and is *rasa* itself.

By layers of *rasa-kāmanā* having *bala* in its ambit there was another coating of *rasa* (having *bala* in it) on the coating of *ānanda*. In this second coating both *rasa* and *bala* will be powerful or both will be balanced. But as *bala* will be deprived of the spontaneous and real state of exuberance and power due to the absence of internal integrated relationship (*yāga*), it will be considered weak and *rasa* will be described as dominant or awakened. Due to this predominance, this second coating will be considered to be the "coating of *rasa*".

As in this second coating of *rasa*, *bala* becomes more awakened and expressed as compared to the first coating of *rasa* (*ānanda*), therefore, the natural *mṛtya* characteristic of variety or multipleness of *bala* is also expressed. Due to the multipleness of *bala*, unitary *rasa* in the form of *jñāna* also becomes multiple. Due to this basis, only this second coating of *rasa* is described as the coating of *vijñāna*.

> विविध-ज्ञान-नानाभावापन्नं ज्ञानं-नानाभावानुगतो रस एव वा विज्ञानं। तस्यैषा चितिः-विज्ञान-चितिः
>
> *vividha-jñāna-nānābhāvāpannaṁ jñānaṁ-nānābhāvānugato rasa eva vā vijñānaṁ* । *tasyaiṣā citiḥ-vijñāna-citiḥ* ।

Due to this derivation, it will be called the coating of *vijñāna*; the integrated state of these two coatings of *rasa* is called *antaściti* (internal coating).

Now the *bala* portion becomes excited on the *kāma avyaya-mana*. Of this coating of *bala* also, there are two divisions, the coating of *prāṇa* and the coating of *vāk*, and both of them put together are called *bahiściti* (external coating). The coating of *prāṇa* is balanced by the coating of *ānanda* and the coating of *vāk* is balanced by the coating of *vijñāna*. The base of this external coating is defined as *sisṛkṣā*, which we have already explained as *bala-kāmanā*, having *rasa* in its ambit. Thus, due to the coating of *rasa* and *bala*, the centrally situated *niṣkala* (indivisible) *avyaya-puruṣa* is called *cidātmā*. As he becomes integrated with the four coatings of *ānanda*, *vijñāna*, *prāṇa* and *vāk*, by his *rasa-kāmanā* named *mumukṣu* and *bala-kāmanā* named *sisṛkṣā*, he is thus called *pañcakala* (having five facets). This must be borne in mind that these five coatings are related to *bala*. From the point of view of pure *rasa*, that *puruṣa* is always *niṣkala* (indivisible) fully, is independent and free of multipleness. That is why *Gopatha śruti* has described it as *avyaya*:

> सदृशं त्रिषु लिङ्गेषु सर्वासु च विभक्तिषु।
> वचनेषु च सर्वेषु यन्न व्येति तदव्ययम्॥ – *गोपथब्राह्मण*, पूर्व० १.२६
>
> *sadṛśaṁ triṣu liṅgeṣu sarvāsu ca vibhaktiṣu* ।
> *vacaneṣu ca sarveṣu yanna vyeti tadavyayam* ॥
> – *Gopatha Brāhmaṇa*, Pūrva, 1.26

Puruṣa is a totality of *ānanda*, *vijñāna*, *mana*, *prāṇa* and *vāk*, and it is the base of creation. This has been described in the principle किं स्विदासीदधिष्ठानम् (*kiṁ svidāsīdadhiṣṭhānam* – What was the place, material and the process which the creator achieved this creation – *Yajurveda Saṁhitā* 17.18).

Fivefold *akṣara*, which is described as the basic nature (*parā-prakṛti*) is inseparable from this five-functional *avyaya-puruṣa*. The fivefold basic nature has been explained earlier through the medium of science of motion as Brahmā, Viṣṇu, Indra, Agni and Soma. The five-functional *akṣara* in the form of basic nature is the incidental cause of creation. Five facets of *kṣara* are known as *prāṇa*, *āpaḥ*, *vāk*, *ānanda* and *aham*, and they emerge from five facets of *Akṣara-Brahma*. The five-functional *kṣara* is the material, inherent, cause of creation. This is the *aparā* (structural characteristic) of *avyaya-puruṣa*. Five-functional *kṣara puruṣa* is related to *aparā-vidyā*, five-functional *akṣara puruṣa* is related to *parā-vidyā* and their regulator is the five-functional *avyaya-puruṣa*. These three are the foundation, the incidental cause and inherent material cause of the creation of the universe. The basic foundation of all these three is the *parātpara*, which is out of the bounds of the universe and thus which is beyond *māyā*. That is accepted as the supplementary sixteenth essential. Thus, the totality of indivisible *parātpara* having sixteen characteristics itself, which is out of bounds of *māyā*, five-functional *avyaya* limited by *māyā*, five-functional *akṣara* having basic properties, five-functional *savikāra kṣara* is the *ṣoḍaśī prajāpati* (sixteen-facet Prajāpati). Therefore, like the sixteen *balakośa*, the Viśvātmā Prajāpati, related to *rasa*, also has sixteen facets or characteristics. Eulogizing the sixteen-functional (*ṣoḍaśī*) Prajāpati (lord of the universe), *śruti* has said:

> यस्मात्परं नापरमस्ति किञ्चिद्यस्मान्नाणीयो न ज्यायोऽस्ति कश्चित्।
> वृक्ष इव स्तब्धो दिवि तिष्ठत्येकस्तेनेदं पूर्णं पुरुषेण सर्वम्। – श्वेत०उप० ३.९
>
> *yasmātparaṁ nāparamasti kiñcidyasmānnāṇīyo na jyāyo 'sti kaścit* ।
> *vṛkṣa iva stabdho divi tiṣṭhatyekastenedaṁ pūrṇaṁ puruṣeṇa sarvam* ।
> – *ŚvetaUp* 3.9
>
> The whole universe is filled by the *Puruṣa*, to whom there is nothing superior, from whom there is nothing different, than whom there is nothing either smaller or greater; who stands alone, motionless as a tree, established in His own glory.
>
> यस्मान्न जातः परो अन्यो अस्तिय आविवेश भुवनानि विश्वा।
> प्रजापतिः प्रजया संरराणस्त्रीणि ज्योतींषि सचते स षोडशी॥ – *यजुसंहिता* ८.३६
>
> *yasmānna jātaḥ paro anyo astiya āviveśa bhuvanāni viśvā* ।
> *prajāpatiḥ prajayā saṁrarāṇastrīṇi jyotīṁṣi sacate sa ṣoḍaśī* ॥
> – *Yajuḥsaṁhitā* 8.36
>
> द्वाविमौ पुरुषौ लोके क्षरश्चाक्षर एव च।
> क्षरः सर्वाणि भूतानि कूटस्थोऽक्षर उच्यते॥

उत्तमः पुरुषस्त्वन्यः परमात्मेत्युदाहृतः ।
यो लोकत्रयमाविश्य बिभर्त्यव्यय ईश्वरः ॥ – *गीता* १५.१६-१७

dvāvimau puruṣau loke kṣaraścākṣara eva ca ।
kṣaraḥ sarvāṇi bhūtāni kūṭastho 'kṣara ucyate ॥

uttamaḥ puruṣastvanyaḥ paramātmetyudāhṛtaḥ ।
yo lokatrayamāviśya bibhartyavyaya īśvaraḥ ॥ – *Gītā* XV.16-17

Stationary like a tree, this sixteen-functional Prajāpati has been symbolically described and elaborated as *aśvattha* tree in Veda-Purāṇa-śāstra. This is a portion of that Mahāmāyī Ṣoḍaśī Prajāpati as is clear from the principle – एकांशेन जगत् सर्वम् (*ekāṁśena jagat sarvam*). It is stated that Prajāpati has four feet – *parātpara, avyaya, akṣara* and *kṣara*. Of these four feet, the first three feet are dominated by *rasa* and are therefore unshakable and stationary, and are entirely unconnected with the process, rules and methods of creation. The fourth foot, i.e. the *kṣara* portion is the material cause of the universe and converts itself into creation. Three feet form a separate group. Only one foot is related to the universe. We can, in other words, say that of these four feet, three feet are steady and stable, only the fourth *kṣara* foot is in motion in context of the changing material universe. It has movement. Expressing this mystery, *ṛṣi*s have said:

त्रिपादूर्ध्वं उदैतपुरुषः पादोऽस्येहाभवत्पुनः ।
ततो विश्वङ् व्यक्रामत्साशनानशने अभि ॥ – *यजुःसंहिता* ३१.४

tripādūrdhvaṁ udaitapuruṣaḥ, pādo 'syehābhavatpunaḥ ।
tato viśvaṅ vyakrāmatsāśanānaśane abhi ॥ – *Yajuḥsaṁhitā* 31.4

You must have seen a horse standing in its stable. Three feet of a horse rest on the ground. The fourth foot, as it hangs, shakes. Just as a potter and his process of making pots has been accepted as a symbol or an example to explain the method of creation of Prajāpati, similarly an example of a well-known animal, horse, has been put forward to explain the actual form of Brahmā having four feet. The position of Prajāpati is exactly the same as that of the horse. He is stable from three feet and is in motion by one foot; that is stable by its three feet – *parātpara, avyaya, akṣara* – but is in motion by its fourth foot, *kṣara*. Keeping in view this example, Ṣoḍaśi Prajāpati has been described as *aśvattha* (derivation, *aśvavat tiṣṭhati*, that which stands like a horse). The second derivation is related to that well-known *aśvattha* tree, which Indians, having faith in their culture, worship everyday. The third derivation is related to these changing motions. All these derivations are inspired by the subtle and meaningful branches of science of creation. It is not possible to deal with them even briefly here.

A technical name for the five-functional *avyaya*, which is inseparable from that *niṣkala parātpara* and is thus essentially indivisible itself, is *amṛta*. The fivefold *akṣara* (basic nature) is inseparable from this *amṛta vyaya* and has a technical name Brahmā. The technical name for the five-functional *kṣara* (structural nature), which is inseparable from Brahma Akṣara, is Śukra.

That *parātpara*, when integrated with *rasa* and *bala*, becomes *amṛta* in the *avyaya* form, when correlated with *māyā-bala*, it becomes Brahmā, i.e. *akṣara*, when correlated with basic properties, it becomes *kṣara*. That is why the ऐतदात्म्यमिदं सर्वम् (*aitadātmyamidaṁ sarvam*) principle is well known. He is *amṛta*, He is Brahmā and He is Śukra. That Lord of the universe, which is an aggregate image of Amṛta, Brahmā, Śukra and *rasa-bala* is the creator and cause of the universe and is Ṣoḍaśī Prajāpati named Aśvattha Brahmā, whose roots are above and branches are downward. The meaning of up and down in the scientific terminology is centre and circumference. From every point of the boundary of circumference, the point of centre is upward, while points of circumference are downward in relation to the point of centre. As submitted earlier, the whole universe has expanded and developed by the central desires of *mana* by *sisṛkṣā* and *mumukṣu*.

It is situated in the centre of *māyāpura*. Therefore, this *aśvattha* tree, consisting of *amṛta*, Brahmā and Śukra can definitely be stated to have roots at a higher point and branches downward. This is the primary outline of the science of *aśvattha*. On its basis, 1,000 branches have emerged. The science of *aśvattha* with centre and the branches is the main Indian Vedic science. All sciences are incorporated in this science of *aśvattha*. He who knows this science of *aśvattha* is described as "one who knows the Veda". He who worships daily the *aśvattha* tree, which is the symbolic representation of that Aśvattha Brahmā, is the real Indian sceptic devoted to culture. Recalling the auspicious and uplifting form of that Aśvattha Brahmā and by purifying the internal mind of ours by doing so today's lecture is concluded:

> ऊर्ध्वमूलोऽवाक्शाख एषोऽश्वत्थः सनातनः। तदेव शुक्रं तद्ब्रह्म तदेवामृतमुच्यते। तस्मिँल्लोकाः श्रिताः सर्वे तदु नात्येति कश्चन, एतद्वै तत्। – क॰उप॰ २.३.१
>
> *ūrdhvamūlo 'vākśākha eṣo 'śvatthaḥ sanātanaḥ। tadeva śukraṁ*

tad-brahma tadevāmṛtamucyate। *tasmiṁllokāḥ śritāḥ sarve tadu nātyeti kaścan, etadvai tat*। – *KaUp* 2.3.1

This is that eternal *aśvattha* tree with its roots above and branches below. That root is the *Brahman*, the Immortal. In that all worlds are contained. This is that.

ऊर्ध्वमूलमधःशाखमश्वत्थं प्राहुरव्ययम्।
छन्दांसि यस्य पर्णानि यस्तं वेद स वेदवित्॥ – *गीता* १५.१

ūrdhvamūlamadhaḥ-śākham-aśvatthaṁ prāhuravyayam।
chandāṁsi yasya parṇāni yastaṁ veda sa vedavit॥
– *Gītā* XV.1

They speak of the indestructible *aśvattha* tree as having its roots above and branches below whose leaves are the Vedas; he alone who knows these is a *veda* knower.

Fifth Discourse

Integrated Relationship of Vedaśāstra and Purāṇaśāstra

IN THE Vedic books, which are inseparable from the essential divine Vedic phenomena, many sciences have been explained. The basis of *vijñāna* are the Vedas which are infinite; the basis of the Veda is the वेदैकमेव सर्वेश्वर अश्वत्थब्रह्म (*vedaikameva sarveśvara aśvatthabrahma*), which shines in splendour and attains its greatness from the splendour and greatness of *Parameśvara* which is (*sarvabalaviśiṣṭa* and *rasaikaghana*) the intermingled image of all *bala*s and is permeated with *rasa*. On the vast infinite oceanic surface of that limitless *parātpara*, innumerable *māyā-bala* appear and subside continuously. Each of the *māyā-bala* is unlimited due to the *mahimā* (sphere) of Brahmā. Each *māyā-bala* has in its orbit one Aśvattha Brahmā, which was explained yesterday as the Ṣoḍaśī Prajāpati. In that ocean of *parātpara*, there are such innumerable and unlimited Aśvattha Brahmā and from the point of view of *parātpara* they have the same importance as one bubble in a vast ocean. In this Aśvattha Brahmā, which is *māyī maheśvara* and is like a bubble in that vast *parātpara* ocean, 1,000 branches emerge. In each branch there are *svayambhū* – manifestation of *ākāśa*; *parameṣṭhi* – manifestation of *vāyu*; *sūrya* – manifestation of *teja*; *candramā* – manifestation of *jala*; and *pṛthvī* – manifestation of *agni*. Totality of the five is described as the divisional *prājāpatya* tree which was explained in the second day's lecture under the title "The Science of Five-Divisional Universe".

The five divisions of *svayambhū* and *parameṣṭhi* are related only to a single branch of the Aśvattha Brahmā and have limitless manifestations. The moon, which is very large from our point of view, is like a bubble when compared to the *rathāntara-sāma* of the earth. The earth, along with its *rathāntara-sāma*, is like a bubble compared to the solar *bṛhatsāma*. Compared to the great unlimited *parameṣṭhi*, which is the image of *krandasi samudra*, the whole solar system along with its sphere (*mahimā*) has no more importance than that of a bubble in a vast ocean. This illimitable, great *parameṣṭhi* is also like a bubble in proportion to *svayambhū*, which is the image of that *paramākāśa*. Thus correlated in its finest and biggest forms, this infinite is playing with its infinite universes and is proving literally the saying of Bhagavān Vyāsa:

> लोकवत्तु लीलाकैवल्यम्। न विश्वमूर्तेरवधार्य्यते वपुः। सं विदन्ति न यं वेदाः अतद्व्यावृत्या यं चकितमभिधत्ते श्रुतिरपि। यतो वाचो निवर्तन्ते अप्राप्य मनसा सह।
>
> *lokavattu līlākaivalyam। na viśvamūrteravadhāryate vapuḥ। saṁ vidanti na yaṁ vedāḥ atadvyāvṛtyā yaṁ cakitamabhidhatte śrutirapi। yato vāco nivartante aprāpya manasā saha।*
>
> Creation is a mere sport for *Brahman*. There is no inequality and cruelty on the part of *Brahman*. The name, form, attributes and paraphernalia of the Lord cannot be ascertained through material means.

This infinite splendour is narrated and eulogised through the medium of infinite *aśvattha* since yesterday. In this connection, I am committing the audacity of submitting something from an entirely different angle today. Please listen, intently and attentively.

In the Vedic Saṁhitās, the science of creation and its base, the Aśvattha Brahmā, has been described and explained in many ways. All these ways may be deemed to be included in the following five *mantras*. I would urge upon intellectual friends present here, who might be devoted to the basic essential, that if they want to know the science of *aśvattha*, they should concentrate on the following five *mantras* in which answers to all questions concerning the foundation of the universe are subtly incorporated:

> किंस्विद्वनं क उ स वृक्ष आस यतो द्यावापृथिवी निष्टतक्षुः।
> मनीषिणो मनसा पृच्छतेदु तद्यदध्यतिष्ठद्भुवनानि धारयन्॥ – ऋ० १०.८१.४
>
> *kiṁsvidvanaṁ ka u sa vṛkṣa āsa*
> *yato dyāvāpṛthivī niṣṭatakṣuḥ।*
> *manīṣiṇo manasā pṛcchatedu tadya-*
> *dadhyatiṣṭhadbhuvanāni dhārayan॥* – *ṚV* X.81.4

Which was that vast forest? In that vast forest which was that vast tree, after cutting and mending, from which this seven sectoral great universe was made? Oh intellectual and learned men! ask this question in your own mind – He who created this universe from that vast tree; He who is bearing the seven sectors and is its foundation, He who is standing erect like a tree, who is He and how He is?

ब्रह्म वनं ब्रह्म स वृक्ष आसीत्।
यतो द्यावापृथिवी निष्ठतक्षुः॥

मनीषिणो मनसा विब्रवीमि वः।
ब्रह्माध्यतिष्ठद् भुवनानि धारयन्॥ – तै॰ब्रा॰ २.८.९.६-७

brahma vanaṁ brahma sa vṛkṣa āsīt ।
yato dyāvāpṛthivī niṣṭhatakṣuḥ ॥

manīṣino manasā vibravīmi vaḥ ।
brahmādhyatiṣṭhad bhuvanāni dhārayan ॥ – *TaiBrā* 2.8.9.6-7

The query in the form of question was made in the *Ṛk Saṁhitā* and the answer is given in the above-quoted extract from the *Taittirīya Brāhmaṇa*. The answer is also mysterious like the question. How does an ordinary man like me understand this answer? This problem is also not less intricate. Please concentrate only on the literal meaning of the *mantra*:

> There was a huge tree in the form of Brahmā and after cutting and mending somebody has made this universe that is *dyāvāpṛthivī*. Oh learned intellectuals! I have deliberated on this answer sufficiently in my mind.

We have to make this as a basis of our understanding in our own mind that Brahmā has made this universe, which is Brahmā, from Brahmā. Brahmā is the basis of this universe, Brahmā is made from Brahmā.

किं स्विदासीदधिष्ठानमारम्भणं कतमत्स्वित्कथासीत्।
यतो भूमिं जनयन्विश्वकर्मा वि द्यामौर्णोन्महिना विश्वचक्षाः॥ – ऋ॰ १०.८१.२

kiṁ svidāsīdadhiṣṭhānamārambhaṇaṁ
katamatsvitkathāsīt ।
yato bhūmiṁ janayanviśvakarmā
vi dyāmaurṇaunmahinā viśvacakṣāḥ ॥ – *ṚV* X.81.2

What was the foundation, the base and cause of this vast universe? How was it? What was the initial cause, the material cause of this universe? By what process, on what basis and by what material, who created the universe or rather the creator of this universe? Who expanded this *dyauloka* in the form of vast sky by this grandeur? What was the form of that creator of the universe? What is the base on which the universe is created? What is the material from which it is created? Who is the creator of this universe?

को अद्धा वेद क इह प्र वोचत्कुत आजाता कुत इयं विसृष्टिः ।
अर्वाग्देवा विसर्जनेनाथा अस्य को वेद यत आबभूव ॥

इयं विसृष्टिर्यत आबभूव यदि वा दधे, यदि वा न ।
यो अस्याध्यक्षः परमे व्योमन्त्सो अङ्ग वेद यदि वा न वेद ॥ – ऋ० १०.१२९.६-७

ko addhā veda ka iha pra vocatkuta ājātā kuta iyaṁ visṛṣṭiḥ ।
arvāgdevā visarjanenāthā asya ko veda yata ābabhūva ॥

iyaṁ visṛṣṭiryata ābabhūva yadi vā dadhe yadi vā na ।
yo asyādhyakṣaḥ parame vyomantso aṅga veda yadi vā no veda ॥
– *ṚV* X.129.6-7

Who clearly knows what is the basic mystery of the universe? In other words, no one has acquired that knowledge uptil now. He who might have known it, whatever that might be, has it been ever expressed clearly? That is, no one has done so. From where and on what base, by what material, by whom and when did this creation come about or emerge? What is the connection between creation and vital forces like *indra*, *vāyu*, *candramā* and *agni-soma*? Your answers will be completely irrelevant and therefore unacceptable because these *devatā*s themselves are correlated with *arvāk*. It means that they have taken form long after creation, from the womb of the creation; they are themselves created and they are creation themselves. How can they be accepted as the base, as the master and as the cause of creation? Thus, we essentially reach this conclusion – Can anyone know by what material the creation took place? The questions dealing with the basis of creation are innumerable and are, therefore, *anatipraśna*.

Perhaps he, from whom the creation emerged, is bearing it on himself; perhaps he is not bearing it or perhaps this creation was created in its form by itself. Thus, no decisive answer can be given in this context. If really there is some basic foundation, some master of creation, who being situated in *paramākāśa* is called by the name *paramovyoman*, then we, no doubt, can say this today that perhaps that creator may himself give or perhaps may not give the answer to the basic question of creation – viz. when, how and why and on what was it created. Such intricate questions concerning the basis of creation have been solved by the questioner *maharṣi* himself in these *mantra*s through the medium of science of *aśvattha* in an indirect language. Efforts should be made to understand it by self-study and self-meditation.

Embodying permanently restful *bala*, the image of permanently restful *rasa* having permanent restlessness in its ambit, but reflecting permanent rest, out of the bounds of *māyā* and universe, illimitably limitless, *parātpara Parmeśvara* is that Brahmā forest, which has no limit and no measured existence. In this vast forest, innumerable, illimitable *māyā-bala*s become unmanifest, manifest and unmanifest again like bubbles in the waves of an ocean. Limited by every *māyā-bala* of the limited *māyī parātpara* is called *puruṣa-vyaya*. Just as in a vast jungle there are innumerable trees, similarly in that illimitable *parātpara*, which is out of bounds of the universe, there are innumerable *māyī-avyaya puruṣa*s, which are correlated with innumerable *māyā-bala*s. Of these innumerable *aśvattha* trees, only one *aśvattha* tree is being referred to. The centrally situated *prāṇa* of this *aśvattha* tree is that essential Veda, the Vedic phenomenon which was explained in the first day's lecture.

From the essential vital *agni-somātmaka* Veda in the form of *Ṛk*, *Yaju*, *Sāma* and *Atharva*, this basic tree in the shape of *avyaya* tree derives its leaves, branches, fruits and flowers. One branch of this *avyaya* in the form of *aśvattha* tree is that *kṣara prakṛti* named *aparā*. From this *vikāra kṣara* the five-divisional and seven-sectoral universes have been created. *Avyaya* Brahmā is the base on which the creation took place. Its *parā-prakṛti* is the incidental unrelated cause of the creation and the *kṣara* in the form of the *aparā-prakṛti* is the material cause from which the universe is created. Thus, from the *avyaya* of the forest named *parātpara*, by the action of *akṣara* resulting in the mending and chiselling of the *kṣara* branch, this universe has emerged. There is not one branch but innumerable branches which have been expressed by the word "thousand" by *ṛṣi*s. Every branch is a five-divisional seven-sectoral universe. And the centre of all these facets is the *kāmamaya avyaya* mana. The a*vyaya-puruṣa* has become "all this" from this *kāmamaya avyaya* mana. It is on this basis that the पुरुषान्न परं किञ्चित् सा काष्ठा सा परा गतिः (*puruṣānna paraṁ kiñcit sā kāṣṭhā sā parā gatiḥ* – There is nothing higher than the *Puruṣa*. He is the culmination; he is the ultimate goal – *Kaṭha Upaniṣad* 1.3.11) principle has been established. It is on this basis that Bhagavān Kṛṣṇa, who was *avyaya* incarnate, has said of the *avyyeśvara*:

गतिर्भर्ता प्रभुः साक्षी निवासः शरणं सुहृत् ।
प्रभवः प्रलयः स्थानं निधानं बीजमव्ययम् ॥ – *गीता* ९.१८

gatirbhartā prabhuḥ sākṣī nivāsaḥ śaraṇaṁ suhṛt ।
prabhavaḥ pralayaḥ sthānaṁ nidhānaṁ bījamavyayam ॥ – *Gītā* IX.18

I am the Supreme Goal of all living beings, and I am also their Sustainer, Master, Witness, Abode, Shelter and Friend. I am the Origin, End and Resting Place of creation; I am the Repository and Eternal Seed.

उपद्रष्टानुमन्ता च भर्ता भोक्ता महेश्वरः।
परमात्मेति चाप्युक्तो देहेऽस्मिन्पुरुषः परः॥ – *गीता* १३.२२

upadraṣṭānumantā ca bhartā bhoktā maheśvaraḥ ।
paramātmeti cāpyukto dehe 'sminpuruṣaḥ paraḥ ॥ – *Gītā* XIII.22

Within the body also resides the Supreme Lord. He is said to be the Witness, the Supporter, Transcendental Enjoyer, the ultimate Controller, and the *Paramātmā* (Supreme Soul).

The *avyaya-puruṣa* becomes the base of all functions by his *kāma-bīja* which is *manomaya*. Due to the disappearance of technical definition, the term *mana* (mind) has become misleading nowadays. Here, we are not referring to that *mana* which the people in general have come to believe as mind. To understand this different viewpoint, it is important to know the outlines or the system known as mind. The *rasa-bala* which resides in the centre (*hṛdaya*) in conjunction with *māyā*, rather *hṛdaya puruṣa*, has been called Śvovasyas Brahma (श्वोवस्यस् ब्रह्म) in Veda *vijñāna*, which has also been referred to at other places as *śvovasyas*. This is the first *avyaya* mind which can also be called *ātma-mana*. This has been explained in the following words:

असतोऽधि मनोऽसृज्यत। मनः प्रजापतिमसृजत। प्रजापतिः प्रजा असृजत। तद्वा इदं मनस्येव परमं प्रतिष्ठितम्। यदिदं किञ्च। तदेतत्-श्वोवस्यसं नाम ब्रह्म।– तै०ब्रा० २.२.९.१०

asato 'dhi mano 'sṛjyat । *manaḥ prajāpatimasṛjata* । *prajāpatiḥ prajā asṛjata* । *tadvā idaṁ manasyeva paramaṁ pratiṣṭhitam* । *yadidaṁ kiñca* । *tadetat-śvovasyasaṁ nāma brahma* । – *TaiBrā* 2.2.9.10

In the absence of the universe, the essential which was beyond *asat* was no-existence; it was pure existence. From that *māyā-bala*, the first to emerge was the *mana*, symbolizing *rasa-bala*. This *mana* is converted into *ṣoḍaśī prajāpati aśvattha* symbolized by the coating of *rasa-bala* based on self-desire. From the *kṣara* portion of this Aśvattha Prajāpati, from the branch of the tree, the matter, the subject, i.e. the universe, emerges. With this matter, i.e. universe (subject) that Prajāpati is always correlated according to the principle, प्रजापतिः प्रजया संरराणस्त्रीणि ज्योतींषि सचते स षोडशी। (*prajāpatiḥ prajayā saṁrarāṇastrīṇi jyotīṁśi sacate sa ṣoḍaśī*).

Both *prajā* (subject, i.e. matter) and Prajāpati (master of subjects), all are based on that *avyaya-mana* which in view of being *śvaḥ śvaḥ vaseyaḥ* – being inclined towards fullness, it is called *śvovasyas* or *śvovasīyas* in *Taittirīya śruti*. This is the literal meaning of the *mantra*.

The mind which performs functions of acceptance, rejection,

decision and alternation is called *indriya-mana* (mind interrelated with bodily organs). According to this definition, *indriya* नियत-विषयत्वमिन्द्रियत्वम् (*niyat viṣayatvamindriyatvam – Atharva Saṁhitā*), *mana* is *indriya-mana*; it is clarified so in the *Atharvaveda* – पञ्चेन्द्रियाणि मनःषष्ठानि मे हृदि (*pañcendriyāṇi manaḥṣaṣṭhāni me hṛdi*). Sensual mind has been made from the earthly *bhāsvara soma* which pervades in the twenty-seventh *stoma* of the *mahā pṛthivī* which has nine, fifteen, seventeen, twenty-one, twenty-seven and thirty-three *stomas*. This fact is also balanced by other organs.

In every organ, two patterns of behaviour are apparent. One is convenience which is a reflection of pleasure, which is actually convenient pain and the other is inconvenience, reflection of sorrow which is actually inconvenient pain. Various functions of every organ are predetermined, i.e. seeing, smelling and tasting. But this feeling of convenient and inconvenient pain, convenient and repulsive functions, is common in all organs. This third *mana* which inspires this common characteristic, which is the base of all organs, is called *sarvendriya* or *anindriya* (non-organ mind). According to the principle सर्वाणीन्द्रियाणि अतीन्द्रियाणि (*sarvāṇīndriyāṇi atīndriyāṇi*), the *aninidriya* mind has also been described as *atīndriya* mind. In the state of slumber, this *sarvendriya-mana* in conjunction with vital forces of organs enters in the *purītati nāḍī* through intellect. In that state of sleep, all functions of bodily organs cease. The lunar *soma* becomes the material component of this third *sarvendriya-mana* through the process of gradual churning and splitting as has been explained in previous lectures. Sensual mind is inspired by the earthly *bhāsvara soma* and *sarvendriya-mana* is inspired by the lunar *soma* which has been referred to by the Upaniṣad as *prajñāna brahma*, described as continually related to intellect. The properties of emotions and desire are based on this mind. Original *śruti* has eulogized this in the form of *prajñāna*:

यत् प्रज्ञानमुत चेतो धृतिश्च यज्ज्योतिरन्तरमृतं प्रजासु।
यस्मान्न ऋते किञ्च न कर्म्म क्रियते तन्मे मनः शिवसंकल्पमस्तु ॥ – *यजुःसंहिता* ३४.३

yat prajñānamuta ceto dhṛtiśca yajjyotirantaramṛtaṁ prajāsu ।
yasmānna ṛte kiñca na karmma kriyate tanme manaḥ śivasaṅkalpamastu ॥
– *Yajuḥsaṁhitā* 34.3

The mind which is the knowledge supreme, the awakening as well as resolution, and which is the immortal light embedded within all creatures, without which no action whatsoever is performed, may that mind of mine be always guided by the best of intentions.

During this state of slumber when all these functions of organs stop, when functions of mind coupled with intellect also cease, even in that stage, this feeling of *aham* (ego) does not cease to function. It remains awake, "I am" this first person feeling remains awakened in all states. In other words, the functions of *mahātmā*, in the form of *parameṣṭhi ahaṁkṛti*, continue incessantly during sleep also. We get proof of this fact in the continuance of breathing and flow of blood. This "mind", which performs these functions even during slumber is called *sattva mana*, which has been described as *mahanmana* also. A person in which there is a full expression of this *mahanmana* is called *mahātmā*, *mahāpuruṣa*, etc. This *mahanmana* is a strange and amazing phenomenon. It is the desire of *mahanmana*, which decides the quality of *ākṛti* (shape), *prakṛti* (nature) and *ahaṁkṛti* (ego-consciousness). While the desire of the external *prajñāna mana* named *sarvendriya* is called *jīva*'s will, the desire of this internal mind called *mahanmana* is *Īśvara*'s will, which is very powerful. According to the principle, मम योनिर्म्महद्ब्रह्म तस्मिन् गर्भं दधाम्यहम् (*mama yonirmmahadbrahma tasmin garbhaṁ dadhāmyaham* – The total material substance (*prakṛti*) is the womb. I impregnate it with the individual souls, and thus all living beings are born – *Bhagavadgītā* XIV.3) – *avyayeśvara*, which is the image of *śvovasīyas mana*, is placed in this *mahān* called *sattva mana*.

By taking the help of this *mahad icchā* (*mahad* will), man can even change his shape and nature. *Ṛṣi*s were able to achieve the impossible through the medium of this *mahanmana*. That which is the lunar *prajñāna* mind called *sarvendriya* and that which is called the internal mind in the popular language is the sacred pure *pārameṣṭhya mahanmana* which is full of *soma*. It is well known that a work which is done by the outer mind is never successful, while the work done by the internal mind never fails. In the *Gītā*, two words have been used to express these two states – *unmanā* and *manmanā*. The word *unmanā* is used in our Rājasthānī dialect also (a slight change in pronunciation). Various acts of *unmanā* person end in vain. Even if they are completed, they become the cause of a person's downfall, because they create attachment. It has, therefore, been stated:

मन्मना भव मद्भक्तो मद्याजी मां नमस्कुरु।
मामेवैष्यसि युक्त्वैवमात्मानं मत्परायणः ॥ – *गीता* ९.३४

manmanā bhava madbhakto madhyājī māṁ namaskuru ।
māmevaiṣyasi yuktvaivamātmānaṁ matparāyanaḥ ॥ – *Gītā* IX.34

Always think of Me, be devoted to Me, worship Me and offer obeisance to Me. Having dedicated your mind and body to Me, you will certainly come to Me.

This earthly *bhāsvara soma, candrasoma, pārameṣṭhya mahatsoma* and the centrally situated *rasa* (with *bala* in its ambit) become the material component of the four physiological divisions of the mind called – *indriya-mana* (organ mind), *sarvendriya-mana, mahanmana* and *avyaya-mana*, which are respectively called *mana, prajñāna, sattva* and *ātmā*. Terms like *indriya* mind, outer mind, internal mind and *śvovasīyas* mind are also used for them. It need not be said that while modern physiology rests and culminates at the outer, earthly sensual mind, Indian physiology, on the other hand, analyses the three deeper and farther branches and culminates at the *ātma-mana* called *śvovasīyas*, which we have called the basic foundation of the science of creation.

We have to submit something more regarding *pārameṣṭhya mahanmana*, which is inseparable from the *avyaya-mana* because, according to the principle, भूतं-भविष्यत् प्रस्तौमि महद्ब्रह्मैकमक्षरं (*bhūtaṁ-bhaviṣyat prastaumi mahadbrhamaikamakṣaram*), this *pārameṣṭhya mahan* which is in the form of *mahanmana* is the integrated picture of "all", the *kṣara* facets of one *akṣara* and is the cause of the emergence of *aśvattha* tree. *Pārameṣṭhya mahan* becomes the foundation, the place from where the *kāmamaya avyaya mana* emerges. Common meaning of *mahān* is great or elder. Who is great? Answer should point out to *māyī avyayeśvara* in whose ambit *akṣara, kṣara,* etc. are confined. Then, why, instead of calling it *mahān*, that *parameṣṭhi*, which is younger than *svayambhū* of the *kṣara* universe, has been called *mahān*. Try to analyse these questions in your mind. Elucidating the form of *mahān*, Bhagavān has said:

मम योनिर्महद्ब्रह्म तस्मिन्गर्भं दधाम्यहम् ।
संभवः सर्वभूतानां ततो भवति भारत ॥

सर्वयोनिषु कौन्तेय मूर्तयः संभवन्ति याः ।
तासां ब्रह्म महद्योनिरहं बीजप्रदः पिता ॥ – *गीता* १४.३-४

mam yonirmahadbrahma tasmingarbhaṁ dadhāmyaham ।
saṁbhavaḥ sarvabhūtānāṁ tato bhavati bhārata ॥

sarvayoniṣu kaunteya mūrtayaḥ saṁbhavanti yāḥ ।
tāsāṁ brahma mahadyonirahaṁ bījapradaḥ pitā ॥ – *Gītā* XIV.3-4

The total material substance (*prakṛti*) is the womb. I impregnate it with the individual souls, and thus all living beings are born. Oh son of Kuntī! for all species of life that are produced, the material nature is the womb, and I am the seed-giving Father.

You may consider today's subject dry. Therefore, I shall not go into further details. The *avyaya-puruṣa* is conceived in this *mahān*. What does it mean? It means that the elliptical circle is formed by the entry of vital *agni* in the form of triple Vedas, which emerged from *svayambhū* into *pārameṣṭhya mahān*, which includes Bhṛgu and Aṅgirā. It is only then that the *aśvattha*, which is in the form of an elliptical-shaped universe, emerges. That is why the principle of ऋतमेव परमेष्ठि-ऋतं नात्येति किञ्चन-सर्वमापोमयं जगत् (*ṛtameva parameṣṭhi-ṛtaṁ nātyeti kiñcana-sarvamāpomayaṁ jagat*) has been established. That is why in all cultural rites of Indians, water becomes the first base of *saṅkalpa* (determined decision), a particular religious rite. *Prāṇa* says, "I am afraid of the ostensibility of nakedness". *Prāṇa* is asked, "What is the cover of your nakedness?". Answer comes forth "Water is my cover of nakedness". That is why in *yajña*, the act of accepting a *vrata apāṁpraṇayana* rite is performed. That is why in the *yajña* in which food is fuel and vital *agni* is fire, in the act of taking food, it is directed that in the beginning and in the end there should be triple *ācamana* (act of taking some water in a particular way). Vital-force can be held by water only. The whole earth becomes full of vitality and vigour by the touch of water. When it rains every leaf dances. It is due to these reasons that water continues to be the basic seed of creation. The basic seed is *kāmamaya avyaya mana*. But he is able to quicken the seed only by entering the womb of *mahān* (which is watery) through the medium of vital phenomenon of Veda. Thus the basic seed of this *manomaya kāma* is also dependent on the watery *mahān* seed and grows by water. According to the principle of Ambhovāda, in the natural process of creation *avyaya-mana* has to convert itself into the form of an *aśvattha* tree. It is obvious that to convert itself in the form of tree, it has to associate itself with essential water. This is the greatness of *pārameṣṭhya mahān*, which has included the *avyayeśvara*, which is the base of all and greatest song all, in its ambit (womb) and has converted it into the tree of the universe.

Rotation of Sun Around Parameṣṭhi

This *parameṣṭhi mahān* has been accepted as situated above the sun. Around it, the sun is rotating, keeping the earth and the moon in the sphere of envelope. What happens by these rotations? Hear the answer also श्रुतं हरति पापानि (*śrutaṁ harati pāpāni* – Hearing the narration of my glories will remove all diseases and infirmities – *Durgā Śaptasatī* 12.12). What more is possible only by listening to such lectures (except the disappearance of consequences of evil acts)? By the earthly ingredient, the characteristic of shape emerges in the *pārameṣṭhya mahān*, by the lunar ingredient the sense of "I", "ego", emerges. This sense of "I" has nothing to do with the popularly known characteristic of self-consciousness or egoism. As the earth has only inherited lustre, it has *tamo* traits (of the lowest type), moon has the traits of reflected lustre and therefore it has *rajo* traits (of the medium type) and the sun having all its self-lustre has *sattva* traits (of the highest type). Thus, due to these three – the earth, the moon and the sun, three characteristics also become integrated in the *pārameṣṭhya mahān* along with the three characteristics of shape, nature and "I". Therefore, by the rotation of the earth, the moon and the sun known as *darśapūrṇamāsa yajña*, the *pārameṣṭhya mahān* acquires six facets.

A few words to explain a relevant issue in this context. The five-divisional universe has also been accepted as six-divisional from the viewpoint of divisions based on *amṛta* and *mṛtyu* (immortality and mortality) due to this six-functional *mahān*. The aggregate of *svayambhū*, *parameṣṭhi* and the sun is the *amṛta* universe and the aggregate of the sun, the moon and the earth is the *martya* universe. Above the sun, the *amṛta rasa* essential predominates and below the sun, the *mṛtya-bala* essential predominates as is clear from the *śruti* – तद्यत् किञ्चार्वाचीनमादित्यात् सर्वं तन्मृत्युनाऽऽप्तम् (*tadyat kiñcārvācīnamādityāt sarvaṁ tanmṛtyunā 'ptam.*). The sun is situated in the centre of this *amṛta–mṛtya* universe. Therefore, according to निवेशयन्नमृतं मर्त्यञ्च (*niveśayannamṛtaṁ martyañca*), it has been described as possessing both characteristics (of *amṛta* and *mṛtyu*). The vital forces of *svayambhū* are *ṛṣi*s, the vital forces of *parameṣṭhi* are *pitṛ*s and the immortal, mortal solar vital forces are the *devatā*s. The three divisions of the mortal universe, the sun, the moon and the earth, are related to *ṛṣi-prāṇa*, *deva-prāṇa* and *pitṛ-prāṇa* respectively. Therefore, it can be stated that the sun bears the *ṛṣi-prāṇa* as is proved by तेऽङ्गिरसः सूनवः (*te'ṅgirasaḥ sūnavaḥ*). The moon is the initiator of *deva-prāṇa*, as is provided by चन्द्रमा वै देवानां वसु (*candramā vai devānāṁ vasu*). The earth holds within it the *pitṛ-prāṇa* as is clear from पृथिवी-गार्हपत्य-गृहाणां वै पितर ईशते (*pṛthivī-gārhapatya-gṛhāṇām vai pitar īśate*).

Thus, the three vital forces (*prāṇa*s) known as *ṛṣi*, *pitṛ* and *deva* are inspired in our mortal *trilokī* (aggregate of three worlds or three divisions of the universe) by the sun, the moon and the earth. These three vital forces become related to the three characteristics of shape, nature and "I am" (ego). The earthly shape is related to *pitṛ-prāṇa*, the lunar nature to *deva-prāṇa* and the solar ego to *ṛṣi-prāṇa*. At this stage, something else has also to be understood carefully.

Formation of Body, Mind and Intellect

By the characteristic of the shape of *pārameṣṭhya mahān*, which is integrated with the earthly *pitṛ-prāṇa* associated with *tamo-guṇa*, the body of the being is formed. By the "nature" characteristic of *mahān* integrated with *deva-prāṇa* associated with *rajo-guṇa*, the mind is formed. And by the "ego" of *mahān* integrated with *ṛṣi-prāṇa* associated with *sattva-guṇa* the intellect of man is made. Now remains the *cidātmā* named *avyayātmā*, conceived and concealed in the womb of *mahad*, which is beyond all traits and characteristics and *ṛṣi*, *pitṛ*, *deva prāṇa*, and thus beyond all. His form has found expression only in man, as has been explained in the third lecture. The body of man is earthly, is dominated by the *tamo* trait, is associated with the shape characteristic and here the *pitṛ-prāṇa* is well-placed and by it the *jāti* (race) of man has emerged which has body as its base. On this basis, the whole of mankind is one race. From the viewpoint of one human race, none is higher and none is lower. It is on this basis that the Vedic principle, *kṛṇavanto viśvamāryam* (कृण्वन्तो विश्वमार्यम्।) has been enunciated. As far as the body is concerned and the earthly acts of food, housing, etc. are concerned, all men have in this context equal rights. Due to nature? No, due to the body which has been clearly stated in the principle (सह नाववतु सह नौ भुनक्तु सह वीर्यं करवावहै – *saha nāvavatu saha nau bhunaktu saha vīryaṁ karvāvahai* (*Kaṭha Upaniṣad*, *Śāntipāṭha*) and समानेन वो हविषा जुहोमि – *samānena vo haviṣā juhomi* (*ṚV* X.191.3)).

May He protect us both together; may He nourish us both together;
May we work conjointly with great energy,
May our study be vigorous and effective;
May we not mutually dispute (or may we not hate any).
Auṁ! *Let there be peace in me!*

Emergence of Varṇa

Does the whole form of man end at this concept of "human race", based on body and related only to earthly "shape" characteristics? No, it can never be so. Until this stage only one manifest division of the universe, viz. earth, has been taken into account. Let us proceed further. The second division is that of the moon. The mind of man is lunar, it has predominantly *rajo-guṇa* traits and is related to subtle unmanifest characteristics of nature. Here, the lunar *deva-prāṇa* is well placed and from here the *varṇa* of man based on "nature" or mind emerges, which is different in each man. The *deva-prāṇa*s based on nature are different and due to this division of classes, men are placed in various categories and groups. The human *varṇa*, based on the nature of man, cannot be incorporated in the human race which is based on the body of man. Body can, to a slight extent, be accepted as based on "act" and thus the whole human race can be accepted as based on acts. But the *varṇa* related to mind and *deva-prāṇa* based on nature is entirely dependent on birth. While the whole human race is one from the point of view of the body; it is divided into eight. The *varṇa–avarṇa* categories are determined from the point of view of nature. On its basis, the conduct and characteristics of men belonging to various categories of *varṇa*s are determined. Does the definition of man's nature end at this system, which is the basis of *varṇa*?

Emergence of Gotra

After the moon comes the sector of the sun, from which the intellectual facet of man is formed, according to *dhiyo yonaḥ pracodayāt*. Intellect of man is solar, has the *sattva* characteristic in its original form and it is integrated with the subtle *ahaṁkṛti* (sense of "I") characteristic of *mahān*. Solar *ṛṣi-prāṇa*s are located here and from it the *gotra* of man emerges, which is based on intellect, and the "I" sense which is different in different family lines. After the sun, we have the division *avyayātmā*, concealed in the ambit of *mahān*, which in spite of being the initiator of *gotra*, *varṇa* and *jāti* is in its own form, completely beyond *agotra* and *varṇa* and is equal. The race, *varṇa* and *gotra* characteristics of man are based on shape, nature and sense of man, which are also continuously integrated with *ṛṣi*, *pitṛ* and *deva-prāṇa* by the obvious and ostensibly visible subtle mind and the most subtle intellect. *Varṇa* is superior to *jāti* and *gotra* is superior to *varṇa* and from all these three the "self" is superior, which is based on equality in seeing various beings. Forgetting this fact, man of today is committing the terrible blunder of making human race or mankind related to the concept of body only as the foundation of humanity and has turned away from the basic foundations – *varṇa* based on nature, *gotra* based on *ahaṁkṛti*, and equality of vision based on self.

Real Aim: Expansion of Gotra

What a terrible tragedy! Expansion of race, multiplying human race, has never been accepted as the desired object of man. Such expansion in the number of bodies has been desired as condemnable, because it is a useless expansion. Development of *varṇa* is also not its specific aim. "Expansion of *gotra*" is the main aim of the Indian intellect. Traditional ideal of this land is गोत्रं नोऽभिवर्द्धताम् (*gotraṁ no 'bhivarddhatām*) which is related to *ṛṣi-prāṇa*. *Ṛṣi-prāṇa* is the basic foundation of meditation of this land. Disappearance of this *prāṇa* has caused humanity to lose its core characteristics.

This is not an easy subject to grasp. We cannot understand the Vedaśāstra unless we can marshal all our senses. To partake the *amṛta*-like fruits of this wisdom, we need to work hard on ourselves. Like the tree *aśvattha* cannot grow and flourish on its own, we cannot understand the true meaning of Vedaśāstra without a determined pursuit of knowledge.

Ṣoḍaśī Prajāpati Conceived Creation

From this conception, five elements were brought about – these were *prāṇa, āpa, vāk, annāda* and *annam*. Since these were the materials from which the universe was created, they came to be known as *viśvasṛt*. These five elements then multiplied by five and in each of these additions, four were consumed, leaving only one. In the process, five elements remained which were called *pañcajana*. Once again, these five elements multiplied by five and from these emerged twenty-five *kalā*s in each. These came to be known as *purañjana*. From *pañcajana* named *prāṇa* came *veda-purañjana*, from *āpa* came *loka-purañjana*, from *vāk* came *deva-purañjana*, from *annāda-pāñcajana* came *bhūta-purañjana* and from *anna* came *paśu-purañjana*. These five *purañjana*s multiplied by five and these came to be known as *brahmapura*. A *pura* denotes an egg-shaped oval form. *Svayambhūpura* was created from *veda-purañjana*, *parameṣṭhipura* from *loka-purañjana*, *sūryapura* from *deva-purañjana*, *pṛthvīpura* from *bhūta-purañjana* and *candrapura* from *paśu-purañjana*. Please understand that these are different from the earth, the sun and the moon we know. Within these *pura*s reside five *mahābhūta*s – *ākāśa, vāyu, teja, jala* and *pṛthvī*. The earth we see is based on *pṛthvīpura*. In yājñic terms, the five *brahmapura*s are known as *paramākāśa, mahāsamudra, saṁvatsara, ānda* and *nakṣatra*. There are other nomenclatures for these elements.

Thus from Ṣoḍaśī Prajāpati, resembling *aśvattha* tree with several branches, emerged five elements, the five *mahābhūta*s which are the basis of creation. From a tiny seed, such a vast expanse of materials had converged and this is known as *brahmavistāra*. It is not possible for us to know the true workings of these processes. One can merely refer to it.

को अद्धा वेद क इह प्र वोचत्।
यो अस्याध्यक्षः परमे व्योमन्त्सोऽङ्ग वेद यदि वा न वेद॥

ko addhā veda ka iha pra vocat ।
yo asyādhyakṣaḥ parame vyomantso 'ṅga veda yadi vā na veda ॥

Who knows, who can tell how this creation came about? When did it begin and when will it end? Who knows when this creation became manifest?

It is said that *pārameṣṭhya mahān* is the birthplace of *avyayāśvattha*. *Pārameṣṭhya soma* named Brahamaṇaspati is the form of *mahān*. All herbs are *soma*-dominant, especially those grown in the north. It is this herb-infused *mahān* which makes the *aśvattha* seed into such a large tree. *Ṛṣis* have referred to this secret of *aśvattha-vidyā* thus:

अश्वत्थे वो निषदनं पर्णे वो वसतिष्कृता ।
गोभाज इत्किलासथ यत्सनवथ पूरुषम् ॥ – ऋ० १०.९७.५

aśvatthe vo niṣadanaṁ parṇe vo vasatiṣkṛtā ।
gobhāja itkilāsatha yatsanavatha pūruṣam ॥ – *ṚV* X.97.5

Your abode is in the *aśvattha*, your dwelling is established in the *palāśa*, you are assuredly the distributor of cattle, inasmuch as you bestow them on the physician.

The liquid-like *parameṣṭhi maṇḍala* in *akṣara-vidyā* is related to "Viṣṇu". Here resides the *soma*-infused *mahān*. It is the one which sets in motion *aśvattha-vistāra* (development of *aśvattha*). It is also therefore called *viṣṇu-vidyā*. That is the reason why in the Purāṇaśāstra, *aśvattha* tree (*pīpala*) is considered important in the Vedas. That is the reason for using the *aśvattha* tree as a symbol to explain the Vedaśāstra. Among the trees, *aśvattha* tree through touch, shade and worship makes us stronger and inspires us to achieve spiritual strength. We should thus offer our obeisance to the Viṣṇu-*pradhāna aśvattha* tree thus:

मूलतो ब्रह्मरूपाय मध्यतो विष्णुरूपिणे ।
अग्रतः शिवरूपाय अश्वत्थाय नमो नमः ॥ – पुराण

mūlato brahmarūpāya madhyato viṣṇurūpiṇe ।
agrataḥ śivarūpāya aśvatthāya namo namaḥ ॥ – *Purāṇa*

To you, the king of trees who takes on the form of Brahmā at the roots, Viṣṇu in the middle and Śiva at the extremes, our salutations.

Svayambhū is in Brahmā, *parameṣṭhi* in Viṣṇu and in the womb of ocean resides Sūryanārāyaṇa, the Sun Lord. This is the form of *ādhidaivika aśvattha*.

Vedaśāstra in Relation to Purāṇaśāstra through the Medium of Tattva-svarūpa of Rasa

It seems the discussion on *ātma-buddhi* has disappointed you and I seek your forgiveness. I do not want you to abandon this dry discussion on *tattva*. I am aware that often during such presentations, lighter moments are introduced to hold the attention of the audience. In our Bhāratīya (Indian) culture, even these moments have a special importance. Only the praise of *Bhagavān* brings joy to the heart of the listener. The intelligent remain true to the spiritual and physical aspects. Can there be night without the moon? Can a woman be complete without her love for her husband? A poet has expressed this in these words:

> या राका शशिशोभना, गतघना, सा यामिनी यामिनी।
> या सौन्दर्य्यगुणान्विता पतिरता, सा कामिनी कामिनी॥
>
> या गोविन्द-रस-प्रमोद-मधुरा, सा माधुरी माधुरी।
> या लोकद्वयसाधिनी तनुभृतां, सा चातुरी चातुरी॥ – *कविसूक्तिः*
>
> *yā rākā śaśiśobhanā, gataghanā, sā yāminī yāminī* ।
> *yā saundaryya-guṇānvitā patiratā, sā kāminī kāminī* ॥
>
> *yā govinda-rasa-pramoda-madhurā, sā mādhurī mādhurī* ।
> *yā lokadvayasādhinī tanubhṛtāṁ, sa cāturī cāturī* ॥ – *Kavisūktiḥ*
>
> That night when the moon is full and the full moon is cool, pure light shines brightly on a cloudless sky, that night is the real night. The one who weds in front of *agni* is *kāminī*, a woman who is desirable. The one who entices her husband with her physical and emotional charms is *kāminī*. The one who expresses deep devotion for Kṛṣṇa is *mādhurī*. The one who balances between the desires of the body and the yearning for other-worldly awareness is *cāturī*.

Today, someone had raised a question, what would be today's *kathā*? I said simply that we would talk about the *pīpala* tree. This reference to *kathā* reminded me of the fact that the only medium to disseminate knowledge of *tattva* was tales from the Purāṇas. Those who cannot take out time to reflect on *tattva*, there is no better way to keep their faith than *purāṇa-kathā*. The stories of Purāṇas are considered an eternal means of propagation. History is witness to the fact that Vedaśāstra had no following in public. It has remained solely with those *ācārya* (teachers) who studied it with great concentration and focus.

In *naimiṣāraṇya* (a forest), in front of 60,000 *maharṣis*, a dialogue took place between the disciple of *purāṇa-puruṣa* Bhagavān Vyāsa, expert in Purāṇaśāstra, Mahābhāga Sūta and the melodious teller of tales, Śaunaka. It was how the tradition of *purāṇa-kathās* began. It is the reason why Bhagavān Bādarāyaṇa (Vyāsa), who is considered the sole exponent of *bhāratīya saṁskṛti* since the Vedic ages, is known as the *purāṇa-puruṣa* and not *veda-puruṣa*.

With the loss of the fundamental meanings of Vedic terms, the Vedaśāstra has become *abhva* – ever-changing and mortal. Likewise, the disappearance of the Paurāṇic terminology and meanings have unfortunately left the Purāṇas at the risk of derision. Those gentlemen, full of themselves with Vedic knowledge, who are quick to dub the Purāṇas as "gossip", are not aware of the secrets contained in the Purāṇas which have direct references in the Vedas. Hence, condemning the Purāṇas is equal to humiliating the Vedas. But we need not pay much attention to these distortions in our pleasant talk today. I would rather inform the sensitive audience to the equal importance of the Vedas and Purāṇas.

Which of the Paurāṇic tales would suffice to explain *aśvattha-vidyā*? This is the question before us.

On the one hand is the need for pleasure, on the other hand, is the need to understand *aśvattha-vidyā*. And how can we not ignore the need for entertainment in today's meetings? Is there a tale in the Purāṇas which can satisfy all these three requirements?

The Purāṇaśāstra is as eternal and *sanātana* (unblemished) as the Vedaśāstra. As the Vedaśāstra has guided mankind towards the eternal truth, even the most perceptive of believers would not harbour any doubt, today or in the future, that Purāṇaśāstra too has an identical quality. These perceptive believers understood the meaning of the quotation, *saṁśayātmā vinaśyati* (doubt invites destruction).

Knowingly or unknowingly, despite enormous odds, the ancient *ṛṣi*s in this country, by toiling day and night, have kept alive their passion for Purāṇaśāstra. So, which is that Purāṇa-*kathā* which contains the essence of *avyaya-aśvattha* related to *soma*-infused *mahān* and is entertaining within our sense of decency and contains elements of song and dance? Such a tale is the *Śrīmad-Bhāgavata rasakrīḍā kathānaka* (tale of playful dance) whose *sūtradhāra* (lead narrator) is Bhagavān Kṛṣṇa, the complete incarnation of *saumya-avyaya-aśvattha*. Although this great tale's objective was to please the heart and therefore includes musical instruments like flute (*baṅsī*), in reality it calms carnal passion. So, let me introduce, with all humility and respect, an outline of the episode of this celestial playful dance.

Māṅgalika Saṁsmaraṇa

जन्माद्यस्य यतोऽन्वयादितरतश्चार्थेष्वभिज्ञः स्वराट्-
तेने ब्रह्म हृदा च आदिकवये मुह्यन्ति यत्सूरयः ।

तेजोवारिमृदां यथा विनिमयो यत्र त्रिसर्गोऽमृषा-
धाम्ना स्वेन सदा निरस्तकुहकं सत्यं परं धीमहि ॥

धर्म्मः प्रोज्झित-कैतवोऽत्र परमो निर्म्मत्सराणां सतां-
वेद्यं वास्तवमत्र वस्तु शिवदं तापत्रयोन्मूलनम् ।
श्रीमद्भागवते महामुनिकृते किं वा परैरीश्वरः-
सद्यो हृद्यवरुध्यतेऽत्र कृतिभिः शुश्रूषुभिस्तत्क्षणात् ॥

निगम-कल्पतरोर्गलितं फलंशुकमुखादमृतद्रवसंयुतम् ।
पिबत भागवतं रसमालयंमुहुरहो रसिका भुवि भावुकाः ॥ – *श्रीमद्भागवत* १.१.१-३

janmādyasya yato 'nvayāditaraścārtheṣvabhijñaḥ svarāṭ-
tene brahma hṛdā ca ādikavaye muhyanti yatsūrayaḥ ।
tejovārimṛdāṁ yathā vinimayo yatra trisargo 'mṛṣā-
dhāmnā svena sadā nirastakuhakaṁ satyam paraṁ dhīmahi ॥

dharmmaḥ projjhita-kaitavo 'tra paramo nirmmatsarāṇāṁ satāṁ-
vedyaṁ vāstavamatra vastu śivadaṁ tāpatrayonmūlanam ।
śrīmadbhāgavate mahāmunikṛte kiṁ vā parairīśvaraḥ-
sao hṛdyavarudhyate 'tra kṛtibhiḥ śuśrūṣubhistatkṣaṇāt ॥

nigama-kalpatarorgalitaṁ phalaṁsukamukhādamṛtadravasaṁyutam ।
pibata bhāgavataṁ rasamālayaṁmuhuraho rasikā bhuvi bhāvukā ॥
– *Śrīmad-Bhāgavata* 1.1.1-3

Oh my Lord! Śrī Kṛṣṇa, son of Vasudeva, Oh all-pervading Personality of Godhead! I offer my respectful obeisances unto You.

I meditate upon Lord Śrī Kṛṣṇa because He is the Absolute Truth and the primeval cause of all causes of the creation, sustenance and destruction of the manifested universes. He is directly and indirectly conscious of all manifestations, and He is independent because there is no other cause beyond Him.

It is He only who first imparted the Vedic knowledge unto the heart of Brahmājī, the original living being. By Him even the great sages and demi-gods are placed into illusion, as one is bewildered by the illusory representations of water seen in fire, or land seen on water.

Only because of Him do the material universes, temporarily manifested by the reactions of the three modes of nature, appear factual, although they are unreal.

I therefore meditate upon Him, Lord Śrī Kṛṣṇa, who is eternally existent in the transcendental abode, which is forever free from the illusory representations of the material world. I meditate upon Him, for He is the Absolute Truth.

Completely rejecting all religious activities which are materially motivated, this *Bhāgavata Purāṇa* propounds the highest truth, which is understandable by those devotees who are fully pure in heart.

The highest truth is reality distinguished from illusion for the welfare of all.

Such truth uproots the threefold miseries.

This beautiful *Bhāgavatam*, compiled by the great sage Vyāsadeva (in his maturity), is sufficient in itself for God realization.

What is the need of any other scripture?

As soon as one attentively and submissively hears the message of *Bhāgavatam*, by this culture of knowledge the Supreme Lord is established within his heart.

Oh expert and thoughtful men! relish *Śrīmad-Bhāgavatam*, the mature fruit of the desire tree of Vedic literatures. It emanated from the lips of Śrī Śukadeva Gosvāmī.

Therefore this fruit has become even more tasteful, although its nectarean juice was already relishable for all, including liberated souls.

यं प्रव्रजन्तमनुपेतमपेतकृत्यं द्वैपायनो विरहकातर आजुहाव।
पुत्रेति तन्मयतया तरवोऽभिनेदुस्तं सर्वभूतहृदयं मुनिमानतोऽस्मि॥

यः स्वानुभावमखिलश्रुतिसारमेकमध्यात्मदीपमतितितीर्षतां तमोऽन्धम्।
संसारिणां करुणयाऽह पुराणगुह्यंतं व्याससूनुमुपयामि गुरुं मुनीनाम्॥
– *श्रीमद्भागवत* १.२.२-३

yaṁ pravrajantamanupetamapetakṛtyaṁ
dvaipāyano virahakātara ājuhāva ।
putreti tanmayatayā tarvo 'bhinedustaṁ
sarvabhūtahṛdayaṁ munimānato 'smi ॥

yaḥ svānubhāvamakhilaśrutisārameka-
madhyātmadīpamatititīrṣatāṁ tamo 'ndham ।
saṁsāriṇāṁ karuṇayā 'ha purāṇaguhyaṁtaṁ
vyāsasūnumupayāmi guruṁ munīnāma ॥
– *Śrīmad-Bhāgavata* 1.2.2-3

Let me offer my respectful obeisances unto that great sage (Śukadeva Gosvāmī) who can enter the hearts of all. When he went away to take up the renounced order of life (*saṁnyāsa*), leaving home without undergoing reformation by the sacred thread or the ceremonies observed by the higher castes, his father, Vyāsadeva, fearing separation from him, cried out, "Oh my son!" Indeed, only the trees, which were absorbed in the same feelings of separation, echoed in response to the bereaved father.

Let me offer my respectful obeisances unto him (Śuka) the spiritual master of all sages, the son of Vyāsadeva, who, out of his great compassion for those gross materialists who struggle to cross over the darkest regions of material existence, spoke this most confidential supplement to the cream of Vedic knowledge, after having personally assimilated it by experience.

यां यां शक्तिमुपाश्रित्य पुरुशक्तिः परः पुमान्।
आत्मानं क्रीडयन् क्रीडन् करोति विकरोति च॥

नूनं भगवतो ब्रह्मन् हरेरद्भुतकर्म्मणः।
दुर्विभाव्यमिवाभाति कविभिश्चापि चेष्टितम्॥

यथा गुणांस्तु प्रकृतेर्युगपत् क्रमशोऽपि वा ।
बिभर्ति भूरिशस्त्वेकः कुर्वन् कर्म्माणि जन्मभिः॥

विचिकित्सितमेतन्मे ब्रवीतु भगवान् यथा।
शाब्दे ब्रह्मणि निष्णातः परस्मिंश्च भवान् खलु॥

सूत उवाच
इत्युपामन्त्रितो राज्ञा गुणानुकथने हरेः।
हृषीकेशमनुस्मृत्य प्रतिवक्तुं प्रचक्रमे॥

श्रीशुक उवाच
नमः परस्मै पुरुषाय भूयसे सदुद्भवस्थाननिरोधलीलया।
गृहीतशक्तित्रितयाय देहिनामन्तर्भवायानुपलक्ष्यवर्त्मने॥

भूयो नमः सद्वृजिनच्छिदेऽसतामसंभवायाखिलसत्त्वमूर्तये।
पुंसां पुनः पारमहंस्य आश्रमेव्यवस्थितानामनुमृग्यदाशुषे॥

नमो नमस्तेऽस्त्वृषभाय सात्वतांविदूरकाष्ठाय मुहुः कुयोगिनाम्।
निरस्तसाम्यातिशयेन राधसास्वधामनि ब्रह्मणि रंस्यते नमः॥

यत्कीर्तनं-यत्स्मरणं-यदीक्षणं-यद्वन्दनं यच्छ्रवणं यदर्हणम्।
लोकस्य सद्यो विधुनोति कल्मषंतस्मै सुभद्रश्रवसे नमो नमः॥

विचक्षणा यच्चरणोपसादनात्सङ्गं व्युदस्योभयतोऽन्तरात्मनः।
विन्दन्ति हि ब्रह्मगतिं गतक्लमास्तस्मै सुभद्रश्रवसे नमो नमः॥

तपस्विनो दानपरा यशस्विनो-मनस्विनो मन्त्रविदः सुमङ्गलाः।
क्षेमं न विन्दन्ति विना यदर्पणंतस्मै सुभद्रश्रवसे नमो नमः॥

किरात-हूणान्ध्र-पुलिन्द-पुल्कसा-आभीरकङ्का यवनाः खसादयः।
येऽन्ये च पापा यदपाश्रयाश्रयाःशुध्यन्ति तस्मै प्रभविष्णवे नमः॥

स एष आत्माऽऽत्मवतामधीश्वरस्त्रयीमयो धर्म्ममयस्तपोमयः।
गतव्यलीकैरजशङ्करादिभिर्वितर्क्यलिङ्गो भगवान् प्रसीदताम्॥

श्रियःपतिर्यज्ञपतिः प्रजापतिर्धियांपतिर्लोकपतिर्धरापतिः ।
पतिर्गतिश्चान्धकवृष्णिसात्वतांप्रसीदतां मे भगवान् सतां पतिः ॥

यदङ्घ्र्यनुध्यानसमाधिधौतयाधियाऽनुपश्यन्ति हि तत्त्वमात्मनः ।
वदन्ति चैतत् कवयो यथारुचं स मे मुकुन्दो भगवान् प्रसीदताम् ॥

प्रचोदिता येन पुरा सरस्वती वितन्वताऽजस्य सतीं स्मृतिं हृदि ।
स्वलक्षणा प्रादुरभूत्-किलास्यतः स मे ऋषीणामृषभः प्रसीदताम् ॥

भूतैर्महद्भिर्य इमाः पुरो विभुर्निर्माय शेते यदमूषु पूरुषः ।
भुङ्क्ते गुणान् षोडश षोडशात्मकः-सोऽलङ्कृषीष्ट भगवान् वचांसि मे ॥

नमस्तस्मै भगवते व्यासायामिततेजसे ।
पशुर्ज्ञानमयं सौम्या यन्मुखाम्बुरुहासवम् ॥

एतदेवात्मभू राजन्! नारदाय विपृच्छते ।
वेदगर्भोऽभ्यधात् साक्षात् यदाह हरिरात्मनः ॥ – *श्रीमद्भागवत* २.४.७-२५

yāṁ yāṁ śaktimupāśritya puruśaktiḥ paraḥ pumān ।
ātmānaṁ krīḍayan krīḍan karoti vikaroti ca ॥

nūnaṁ bhagavato brahman hareradbhutakarmmaṇaḥ ।
durvibhāvyamivābhāti kavibhiścāpi ceṣṭitam ॥

yathā guṇāṁstu prakṛteryugpat kramaśo 'pi vā ।
bibharti bhūriśastvekaḥ kurvan karmāṇi janmabhiḥ ॥

vicikitsitametanme bravītu bhagavān yathā ।
śābde brahmaṇi niṣṇātaḥ parasmiṁśca bhavān khalu ॥

sūta uvāca
ityupāmantrito rājñyā guṇānukathane hareḥ ।
hṛṣikeśamanusmṛtya prativaktuṁ pracakrame ॥

śrīśuka uvāca
namaḥ parasmai puruṣāya bhūyase
sadudbhavasthānanirodhalīlayā ।
gṛhīta-śākti-tritayāya dehināmantar-
bhavāyānupalakṣyavartmane ॥

bhūyo namaḥ sadvṛjinacchide 'satāma-
saṁbhavāyākhilasattvamūrtaye ।
puṁsāṁ punaḥ pāramahaṁsya āśrame-
vyavasthitānāmanumṛgyadāśuṣe ॥

namo namaste 'stvṛṣabhāya sātvatāṁ-
vidūra-kāṣṭhāya muhuḥ kuyogināṁ ।
nirasta-sāmyātiśayena rādhasāsvadhāmani
brahmaṇi raṁsyate namaḥ ॥

yatkīrtanaṁ-yatsmaraṇaṁ-yadīkṣaṇaṁ-
yadvandanaṁ yacchravaṇaṁ yadarhaṇam ।
lokasya sadyo vidhunoti kalmaṣaṁ-
tasmai subhadraśravase namo namaḥ ॥

vicakṣaṇā yaccaraṇopasādanāt-
saṅgaṁ vyudasyobhayato 'ntarātmanaḥ ।
vindanti hi brahmagatiṁ gataklamās-
tasmai subhadraśravase namo namaḥ ॥

tapasvino dānaparā yaśasvino-
manasvino mantravidaḥ sumaṅgalāḥ ।
kṣemaṁ na vindanti vinā yadarpaṇaṁ-
tasmai subhadraśravaso namo namaḥ ॥

kirāta-hūṇāndhra-pulinda-pulkasā-
ābhīrakaṅkā yavanāḥ khasādayaḥ ।
ye 'nye ca pāpā yadapāśrayāśrayāḥ-
śudhyanti tasmai prabhaviṣṇave namaḥ ॥

sa eṣa ātmā 'tmavatāmadhīśvaras-
trayīmayo dharmmamayastapomayaḥ ।
gatavyalīkairajaśaṅkarādibhir-
vitarkyaliṅgo bhagavān prasīdatām ॥

śriyaḥpatiryagjñapatiḥ prajāpatir-
dhiyāṁpatirlokapatirdharāpatiḥ ।
patirgatiścāndhaka-vr̥ṣni-sātvatāṁ-
prasīdatāṁ me bhagavān satāṁ patiḥ ॥

yadaṅghryanudhyānasamādhidhautayā-
dhiyā 'nupaśyanti hi tattvamātmanaḥ ।
vadanti caitat kavayo yathārucaṁ sa
me mukundo bhagavān prasīdatām ॥

pracoditā yena purā sarasvatī
vitanvatā 'jasya satīṁ smr̥tiṁ hr̥di ।
svalakṣaṇā prādurabhūta-kilāsyataḥ
sa me r̥ṣīṇamr̥ṣabhaḥ prasīdatām ॥

bhūtairmahadbhirya imāḥ puro vibhur-
nirmāya śete yadamūṣu pūruṣaḥ ।
bhuṅkte guṇān ṣoḍaśa ṣoḍaśātmakaḥ-
so 'laṅkr̥ṣīṣṭa bhagavān vacāṁsi me ॥

namastasmai bhagavate vyāsāyāmitatejase ।
paśurjñānamayaṁ saumyā yanmukhāmburuhāsavam ॥

etadevātmabhū rājan! nāradāya vipṛcchate ।
vedagarbho 'bhyadhāt sākṣāt yadāha harirātmanaḥ ॥
– *Śrīmad-Bhāgavata* 2.4.7-25

His different energies and different expansions in maintaining and again winding up the phenomenal world in the sporting spirit of a player. Oh learned brāhmaṇa! the transcendental activities of the Lord are all wonderful, and they appear inconceivable because even great endeavours by many learned scholars have still proved insufficient for understanding them. The Supreme Personality of godhead is one, whether He alone acts with the modes of material nature, or simultaneously expands in many forms, or expands consecutively to direct the modes of nature.Kindly clear up all these doubtful inquiries, because you are not only vastly learned in the Vedic literatures and self-realized in transcendence, but are also a great devotee of the Lord and are therefore as good as the Personality of godhead.

Sūta Gosvāmī said: When Śukadeva Gosvāmī was thus requested by the king to describe the creative energy of the Personality of godhead, he then systematically remembered the master of the senses (Śrī Kṛṣṇa), and to reply properly he spoke thus.

Śukadeva Gosvāmī said: Let me offer my respectful obeisances unto the Supreme Personality of Godhead, who, for the creation of the material world, accepts the three modes of nature. He is the complete whole residing within the body of everyone, and His ways are inconceivable.

I again offer my respectful obeisances unto the form of complete existence and transcendence, who is the liberator of the pious devotees from all distresses and the destroyer of the further advances in atheistic temperament of the non-devotee (demons). For the transcendentalists who are situated in the topmost spiritual perfection, He grants their specific destinations.

Let me offer my respectful obeisances unto Him who is the associate of the members of the Yadu dynasty and who is always a problem for the non-devotees. He is the supreme enjoyer of both the material and spiritual worlds, yet He enjoys His own abode in the spiritual sky. There is no one equal to Him because His transcendental opulence is immeasurable.

Let me offer my respectful obeisances unto the all-auspicious Lord Śrī Kṛṣṇa, about whom glorification, remembrances, audience, prayers, hearing and worship can at once cleanse the effects of all sins of the performer.

Let me offer my respectful obeisances again and again unto the all-auspicious Lord Śrī Kṛṣṇa. The highly intellectual, simply by surrendering unto His lotus feet, are relieved of all attachments to present and future existences and without difficulty progress toward spiritual existence.

Let me offer my respectful obeisances unto the all-auspicious Lord Śrī Kṛṣṇa again and again because the great learned sages, the great performers of charity, the great workers of distinction, the great philosophers and mystics, the great chanters of the Vedic hymns and the great followers of Vedic principles cannot achieve any fruitful result without dedication of such great qualities to the service of the Lord.

Kirāta, Hūṇa, Āndhra, Pulinda, Pulkaśa, Ābhīra, Śumbha, Yavana, members of the Khasa races and even others addicted to sinful acts can be purified by taking shelter as the devotees of the Lord, due to His being the supreme power. I beg to offer my respectful obeisances unto Him.

He is the Supersoul and the Supreme Lord of all self-realized souls. He is the personification of the Vedas, religious scriptures and austerities. He is worshiped by Lord Brahmā and Śiva and all those who are transcendental to all pretensions. Being so revered with awe and veneration, may that Supreme Absolute be pleased with me.

May Lord Śrī Kṛṣṇa, who is the worshippable Lord of all devotees, the protector and glory of all the kings like Andhaka and Vṛṣṇi of the Yadu dynasty, the husband of all goddesses of fortune, the leader of all sacrifices and therefore the leader of all living entities, the controller of all intelligence, the proprietor of all planets, spiritual and material, and the supreme incarnation on the earth (the supreme all in all), be merciful upon me.

It is the Personality of godhead Śrī Kṛṣṇa who gives liberation. By thinking of His lotus feet at every second, following in the footsteps of authorities, the devotee in trance can see the Absolute Truth. The learned mental speculators, however, think of Him according to their whims. May the Lord be pleased with me.

May the Lord, who in the beginning of the creation amplified the potent knowledge of Brahmā from within his heart and inspired him with full knowledge of creation and of His own Self, and who appeared to be generated from the mouth of Brahmā, be pleased with me.

May the Supreme Personality of godhead, who enlivens the materially created bodies of the elements by lying down within the universe, and who in His *Puruṣa* incarnation causes the living being to be subjected to the sixteen divisions of material modes which are his generator, be pleased to decorate my statements.

I offer my respectful obeisances unto Śrīla Vyāsadeva, the incarnation of Vāsudeva who compiled the Vedic scriptures. The pure devotees drink up the nectarean transcendental knowledge dropping from the lotus-like mouth of the Lord.

My dear king, Brahmā, the firstborn, on being questioned by Nārada, exactly apprised him on this subject as it had been directly spoken by the Lord to His own son, who was impregnated with Vedic knowledge from his very birth.

नौमीड्य तेऽभ्रवपुषे तडिदम्बराय-गुञ्जावतंस-परिपिच्छ-लसन्मुखाय।
वन्यस्रजे कवल-वेत्रविषाण-वेणु-लक्ष्मश्रिये मृदुपदे पशु-पाङ्गजाय॥

अस्यापि देव वपुषो मदनुग्रहस्य-स्वेच्छामयस्य न तु भूतमयस्य कोऽपि।
नेशे महित्ववसितुं मनसाऽऽन्तरेण-साक्षात्तवैव किमुतात्मसुखानुभूतेः॥

ज्ञाने प्रयासमुदपास्य नमन्त एवजीवन्ति सन्मुखरितां भवदीयवार्ताम्।
स्थाने स्थिताः श्रुतिगतां तनुवाङ्मनोभिर्ये प्रायशोऽजित जितोऽप्यसि तैस्त्रिलोक्याम्॥
– *श्रीमद्भागवत* १०.१४.१-३

naumīḍya te 'bhravapuṣe taḍidambarāya-
guñjāvataṁsa-paripiccha-lasanmukhāya ।
vanyasraje kavala-vetraviṣāṇa-veṇu-
lakṣmaśriye mṛdupade paśu-pāṅgajāya ॥

asyāpi deva vapuṣo madanugrahasya-
svecchāmayasya na tu bhūtamayasya ko 'pi ।
neśe mahitvavasituṁ manasā 'ntareṇa-
sākṣāttavaiva kimutātmasukhānubhūteḥ ॥

jñāne prayāsamudapāsya namanta eva-
jīvanti sanmukharitāṁ bhavadīyavārtām ।
sthāne sthitāḥ śrutigatāṁ tanuvāṅgamanobhirye
prāyaśo 'jita jito 'pyasi taistrilokyām ॥ – *Śrīmad-Bhāgavata* 10.14.1-3

My dear Lord, You are the only worshippable Lord, the Supreme Personality of godhead, and therefore I offer my humble obeisances and prayers just to please You. Oh son of the king of the cowherds! Your transcendental body is dark blue like a new cloud, Your garment is brilliant like lightning, and the beauty of Your face is enhanced by

Your *guñjā* earrings and the peacock feather on Your head. Wearing garlands of various forest flowers and leaves, and equipped with a herding stick, a buffalo horn and a flute, You stand beautifully with a morsel of food in Your hand.

My dear Lord, neither I nor anyone else can estimate the potency of this transcendental body of Yours, which has shown such mercy to me and which appears just to fulfil the desires of Your pure devotees. Although my mind is completely withdrawn from material affairs, I cannot understand Your personal form. How, then, could I possibly understand the happiness You experience within Yourself?

Those who, even while remaining situated in their established social positions, throw away the process of speculative knowledge and with their body, words and mind offer all respects to descriptions of Your personality and activities, dedicating their lives to these narrations, which are vibrated by You personally and by Your pure devotees, certainly conquer Your Lordship, although You are otherwise unconquerable by anyone within the three worlds.

क्वाहं तमोमहमदं खचराग्निवार्भूसंवेष्टिताण्ड-घट-सप्त-वितस्तिकायः ।
क्वेदृग्विधा-विगणिता-ताण्ड-पराणुचर्य्या-वाताध्वरोमविवरस्य च ते महित्वम् ॥
– *श्रीमद्भागवत* १०.१४.११

kvāhaṁ tamomahamadaṁ khacarāgnivārbhū-
saṁveṣṭitāṇḍa-ghaṭa-sapta-vitastikāyaḥ ।
kvedṛgvidhā-vigaṇitā-tāṇḍa-parāṇucaryyā-
vātādhvaromavivarasya ca te mahitvam ॥ – *Śrīmad-Bhāgavata* 10.14.11

अहोऽतिधन्या व्रजगोरमण्यःस्तन्यामृतं पीतमतीव ते मुदा ।
यासां विभो वत्सतरात्मजात्मना यत्तृप्तयेऽद्यापि न चालमध्वराः ॥
– *श्रीमद्भागवत* १०.१४.३१

aho 'tidhanyā vrajagoramaṇyaḥstanyāmṛtaṁ pītamatīva te mudā ।
yāsāṁ vibho vatsatarātmajātmanā yattṛptye 'dyāpi na cālamadhvarāḥ ॥
– *Śrīmad-Bhāgavata* 10.14.31

Oh almighty Lord! how greatly fortunate are the cows and ladies of Vṛndāvana, the nectar of whose breast milk You have happily drunk to Your full satisfaction, taking the form of their calves and children! All the Vedic sacrifices performed from time immemorial up to the present day have not given You as much satisfaction.

श्यामं हिरण्यपरिधिं वनमाल्यबर्हधातु-प्रवाल-नट-वेषमनुव्रतांसे ।
विन्यस्तहस्तमितरेण धुनानमब्जं कर्णोत्पलालककपोल-मुखाब्जहासम् ॥

प्रायः श्रुतप्रियतमोदयकर्णपूरैर्यस्मिन् निमग्न-मनसस्तमथाक्षिरन्ध्रैः ।
अन्तः प्रवेश्य सुचिरं परिरभ्य तापं-प्राज्ञं यथाभिमतयो विजहुर्नरेन्द्र! ॥
– *श्रीमद्भागवत* १०.२३.२२-२३

śyāmaṁ hiraṇyaparidhiṁ vanamālyabarha-
dhātu-pravāla-naṭa-veṣamanuvratāṁse ।
vinyastahastamitareṇa dhunānamabjaṁ
karṇotpalālakakapola-mukhābjahāsam ॥

prāyaḥ śrutapriyatamodayakarṇapūrair-
yasmin nimagna-manasastamathākṣirandhraiḥ ।
antaḥ praveśya suciraṁ parirabhya tāpaṁ-
prājñaṁ yathābhimatayo vijahurnarendra! ॥
– *Śrīmad-Bhāgavata* 10.23.22-23

His complexion was dark blue and His garment golden. Wearing a peacock feather, coloured minerals, springs of flower buds, and a garland of forest flowers and leaves, He was dressed just like a dramatic dancer. He rested one hand upon the shoulder of a friend and with the other twirled a lotus. Lilies graced His ears, His hair hung down over His cheeks, and His lotus-like face was smiling.

Oh ruler of men! for a long time those brāhmaṇa ladies had heard about Kṛṣṇa, their beloved, and His glories had become the constant ornaments of their ears. Indeed, their minds were always absorbed in Him. Through the apertures of their eyes they now forced Him to enter within their hearts, and then they embraced Him within for a long time. In this way they finally gave up the pain of separation from Him, just as sages give up the anxiety of false ego by embracing their innermost consciousness.

आसामहो चरण-रेणु-जुषामहं स्यां-वृन्दावने किमपि गुल्म-लतौषधीनाम् ।
या दुस्त्यजं स्वजनमार्य्यपथं च हित्वा-भेजेर्मुकुन्दपदवीं श्रुतिभिर्विमृग्याम् ॥
– *श्रीमद्भागवत* १०.४७.६१

āsāmaho caraṇa-reṇu-juṣāmahaṁ syāṁ-
vṛndāvane kimapi gulma-latauṣadhīnām ।
yā dustyajaṁ svajanamāryyapathaṁ ca hitvā-
bhejermukundapadavīṁ śrutibhirvimṛgyām ॥
– *Śrīmad-Bhāgavata* 10.47.61

The *gopīs* of Vṛndāvana have given up the association of their husbands, sons and other family members, who are very difficult to give up, and they have forsaken the path of chastity to take shelter of the lotus feet of Mukunda, Kṛṣṇa, which one should search for by Vedic knowledge.

Oh! let me be fortunate enough to be one of the bushes, creepers or herbs in Vṛndāvana, because the *gopīs* trample them and bless them with the dust of their lotus feet.

यो यज्ञो दिवि परमेष्ठि-गोसवात्मा-विज्ञानं समुपदिदेश गीतया यः।
आनन्द जनयतु विश्वतो ममायं-गोविन्दः स हि मयि सन्निधानमेतु॥

अहो बकीयं स्तन-कालकूटं-जिघांसयाऽपाययदप्यसाध्वी।
लेभे गतिं धात्र्युचितां ततोऽन्यं कं वा दयालुं शरणं व्रजेम॥
– *श्रीमद्भागवत* ३.२.२३-२४

yo yajño divi parameṣṭhi-gosavātmā-
vijñānaṁ samupadideśa gītayā yaḥ ।
ānanda janayatu viśvato mamāyaṁ-
govindaḥ sa hi mayi sannidhānametu ॥

aho bakīyaṁ stana-kālakūtaṁ-
jighāṁsayā 'pāyayadapyasādhvī ।
lebhe gatiṁ dhātryucitāṁ tato 'nyaṁ
kaṁ vā dayāluṁ śaraṇaṁ vrajema ॥
– *Śrīmad-Bhāgavata* 3.2.23-24

Alas! how shall I take shelter of one more merciful than He who granted the position of mother to a she-demon (Pūtanā) although she was unfaithful and she prepared deadly poison to be sucked from her breast?

ब्रह्मादि-जय-संरूढ-दर्प-कन्दर्प-दर्पहा।
जयति श्रीपतिर्गोपीरासमण्डल-मण्डनः॥

को वेत्ति भूमन् भगवन् परात्मन् योगेश्वरोऽन्तर्भवतस्त्रिलोक्याम्।
क्व वा, कथं वा, कति वा, कदेति-विस्तारयन् क्रीडसि योगमायाम्॥
– *श्रीमद्भागवत* १०.१४.२१

प्रह्लाद-नारद-पराशर-पुण्डरीक-व्यासा-ऽम्बरीष-शुक-शौनक-भीष्म-दाल्भ्यान्।
रुक्माऽङ्गदाऽर्जुन-वसिष्ठ-विभीषणादीन् पुण्यानिमान् परम-भागवतान्नतोऽस्मि॥

brahmādi-jaya-saṁrūḍha-darpa-kandarpa-darpahā ।
jayati śrīpatirgopīrāsamaṇḍala-maṇḍanaḥ ॥

ko vetti bhūman bhagavan parātman
yogeśvaro 'ntarbhavatastrilokyām ।
kva vā, kathaṁ vā, kati vā, kadeti-
vistārayan krīḍasi yogamāyām ॥
– *Śrīmad-Bhāgavata* 10.14.21

Oh supreme great one! Oh Supreme Personality of godhead! Oh Supersoul, master of all mystic power! Your pastimes are taking place continuously in these three worlds, but who can estimate where, how and when You are employing Your spiritual energy and performing these innumerable pastimes? No one can understand the mystery of how Your spiritual energy acts.

prahlāda-nārada-parāśara-puṇḍarīka-vyāsā-
'mbarīṣa-śuka-śaunaka-bhīṣma-dālbhyān ।
rukmā 'ṅgadā 'rjuna-vasiṣṭha-vibhīṣaṇādīn
puṇyānimān paramabhāgvatānnato 'smi ॥

I meditate upon the Bhāgavatas, Nārada, Prahlāda, Parāśara, Puṇḍarīka, Vyāsa, Ambarīṣa, Śuka, Śaunaka, Dhīṣma, Rukma, Aṅgada, Arjuna, Vasiṣṭha, Vibhīṣaṇa – all the virtuous souls.

We are going to talk about the *sat-cit-ānanda-ghana-parabrahma satya* which is omnipresent and infinite and is the core of all materials and the very existence itself. We find a clear description of *avyaya* in the form of Vasudeva Kṛṣṇa, in the *Śrīmad Bhagavadgītā*, which is part of the fifth *saṁhitā*, the *Purāṇa-saṁhitā*, authored by Bhagavān Vyāsadeva who is known as the *purāṇa-puruṣa*. Those who spend time immersed in the *Bhagavadgītā* become closer to Kṛṣṇa and are extraordinarily blessed. Such blessed souls need nothing else to fulfil their lives in this world and the world beyond.

Oh superior beings! immersed in the joys of worship, enjoy forever the *Bhāgavata* which is the sweet fruit filled with *amṛta* from the *kalpavṛkṣa*-like Vedaśāstra. The *Bhāgavata*, the summary of Vedaśāstra offered by Muni Śukra, is like the sweetest fruit pecked by a parrot which falls to the ground. Having been touched by the lips of Śukra Muni, the Bhāgavata-Kathā becomes sweet and gratifying. This is what is being served today.

Let us begin by respectfully bowing before the seer who has, with extraordinary dedication and sacrifice, presented the essence of the *Śrīmad Bhagavadgītā*.

King Parīkṣit is seeking an answer from Śukradeva, Oh! great sage! please tell us the secret of the genesis of the universe which came into existence with the power of *parā* (*akṣara*) and *aparā* (*kṣara*). Hey! *Brahman*, you have been able to understand the secrets of creation which even men of great intellect could not fathom.

Oh Bhagavān! please satisfy our curiosity about the universe, because you alone have the power to know what is visible and what is not, and you alone have the words to explain the mysteries of *brahma-tattva*.

Responding to the entreaties of King Parīkṣit, Sage Śukra, reminiscing Kṛṣṇa, said:

> We bow before that supreme *Puruṣa* who created the universe with *akṣara*, infused it with three natural principles of *sat*, *raja* and *tama* and became *antarayāmī* (inner witness) through the medium of three *devatā*s – Viṣṇu, Indra and Yama.

We once again pay obeisance to the supreme being Kṛṣṇa who can see through noble deeds in a moment, stop ignoble deeds forever and offer the light of *brahma-jñāna* to the devoted seeker of truth.

To the supreme being who always protects the humble devotees, the one who remains hidden from the eyes of the non-believers, the one whose glory is unmatched, we offer our veneration.

Adoring devotees believe that Bhagavān Kṛṣṇa liked Vrajadhāma more than any other place in the universe. So let us proceed towards this place where Kṛṣṇa is playing his flute, with a herd of cows wandering about.

> व्रज तज या संसार में प्रिय न दूसरो ठाम।
> पात पात में रम रहा राधा राधा नाम॥
>
> *vraja taja yā saṁsāra meṅ priya na dūsaro ṭhāma* ।
> *pāta pāta meṅ rama rahā rādhā rādhā nāma* ॥

According to *aśvattha-vidyā*, the place where the sun is established in the great ocean is known as *parameṣṭhi* which is related to *viṣṇu-akṣara*. Similar to the three elements born out of mind in *parameṣṭhi*, *bhṛgu-aṅgirā-atri*, there are three other elements born out of mind – हट्-ऊर्क-भोगाः (*haṭ-ūrk-bhogāḥ*). The sun with a thousand rays was born from the *saumya-prāṇa* which is *gau-tattva* infused with *viṣṇu-akṣara* in *parameṣṭhi*. Hence, the sun is also known as *gau* and *gopatha* as narrated in the following *mantras* – आयं गौः पृश्निरक्रमीत् (*āyaṁ gauḥ pṛśnirakramīt*) and अयं वै गोपाः (*ayaṁ vai gopāḥ*).

Subsequently, it was *pārameṣṭhya gau-tattva*, in the form of *ṛtu*, born from *āṅgirasa* and *bhārgava*, which came to be called गच्छतीति गौः (*gacchatīti gauḥ*). What speed (*gati*)? That which is beyond measure and whose expanse cannot be explained. Speed gets limited in solid mass but when it is freed from mass, it becomes limitless and such is the speed of *gau-prāṇa*, in the form of *aṅgirā* and *bhṛgu* waves in the limitless *pārameṣṭhya* ocean. In popular language, it means before the solar system was born, there was a *pārameṣṭhya* ocean in which countless, hot and glowing orbs rotated with great speed. These vaporous, rare, watery comets marked by signs of smoke became well known as *dhūmaketu*. These celestial elements embellished the watery *pārameṣṭhya* ocean. This *pārameṣṭhya* ocean has not changed, it still remains as it is, as the *śruti* explains:

आपो भृग्वङ्गिरोरूपमापो भृग्वङ्गिरोमयम् ।
अन्तरैते त्रयो वेदा भृगूनङ्गिरसोऽनुगाः ॥ – *गो०ब्रा०*, पूर्वभाग १.३९

āpo bhṛgvaṅgirorūpamāpo bhṛgvaṅgiromayam ।
antaraite trayo vedā bhṛgūnaṅgiraso 'nugā ॥ – *GoBrā* 1.39

This *dhūmaketu* in time transformed into *hiraṇyagarbha-sūrya*.

This is the history of the birth of *sūrya* in Hiraṇyagarbha Prajāpati. The reference to these events is made here to draw your attention to *pārameṣṭhya gau-tattva* and the long waves on which it floats in the celestial ocean:

या ते धामान्युश्मसि गमध्यै यत्र गावो भूरिशृङ्गा अयासः ।
अत्राह तदुरुगायस्व विष्णोः परमं पदमवभारि भूरि ॥ – *यजुःसंहिता* ६.३

yā te dhāmānyuśmasi gamadhyai yatra gāvo bhūriśṛṅgā ayāsaḥ ।
atrāha tadurugāyasva viṣṇoḥ paramaṁ padamavabhāri bhūri ॥
– *Yajuḥsaṁhitā* 6.3

As the earthly acrid water is called *māra*, *saumya* infused liquid element is called *śraddhā*, liquid element in *pārameṣṭhya* is called *ambha*, liquid element with characteristics of fire born out of the clash of sun's rays is called *marīci* – Bhagavān Aitareya showed us all these four waters. The water from a tap, a stream and a river is *māra*, the liquid element in medicinal herbs is *śraddhā*, water from the Gaṅgā is *ambha* and the Yamunā represents *marīci*.

The *āpa-tattva* from *parameṣṭhi*, the integral part of the sphere of sun's rays, is called *vena* and this *vena* in the form of *marīci* is the elemental form of Yamunā. *Marīci* is the *āpa-tattva* with the characteristics of *agni*, created from the meeting of sun's rays. Therefore, Vrajabhūmi is the place where cows from *parameṣṭhi-loka* amble about on the banks of Yamunā. What kind of *parameṣṭhi-loka* is this? This is the place where Viṣṇu is established and is present in the form of *akṣara*.

This is the Vrajadhāma. Is this definition a mere creation of our imagination? Every word here reveals the fundamental truth of creation. What is defined as *gau-loka* in the Purāṇas is mentioned in the Vedas as Vraja. Is this nomenclature our imagination? Never! Never! Here every word holds the secret and mystery of creation.

What is in the Purāṇas mentioned as *gau-loka*, *gauṣṭa* is what is referred to in the Vedas as Vraja. Here are *mantras* which will make it clear that Vraja is synonymous with *parameṣṭhi-loka*.

अपाररु पृथिव्यै देवयजनाद्वध्यासं व्रजं गच्छ गोष्ठानम् ।
वर्षतु ते द्यौर्वधान देव सवितः परमस्यां पृथिव्याम् ॥

अररो! दिवं मा पप्तः, द्रप्सस्ते द्यां मा स्कन् ।
व्रजं गच्छ गोष्ठानं वर्षतु ते द्यौर्वधान देव सवितः ॥ – *यजुःसंहिता* १.२६

apāraru pṛthivyai deva-yajanādvadhyāsaṁ vrajaṁ gaccha goṣṭhānam ।
varṣatu te dyorvadhāna deva savitaḥ paramasyāṁ pṛthivyām ॥

araro! divaṁ mā paptaḥ, drapsaste dyāṁ mā skan ।
vrajaṁ gaccha goṣṭhānaṁ varṣatu te dyaurvadhāna deva savitaḥ ॥
– *Yajuḥsaṁhitā* 1.26

May I drive away the devilish enemy from this earth, the place of divine worship. Go to the pen, cowshed. May heaven send rain for you. Oh Creator! God! Here on this earth, bind with 100 letters, the enemy who is hostile to us, do not release him. Oh enemy! may your progeny be also deprived of light.

पृथिवी देव-यजन्योषध्यास्ते मूलं मा हिंसिषम् ।
व्रजं गच्छ गोष्ठानं वर्षतु ते द्यौः ॥ – *यजुःसंहिता* १.२५

pṛthivī deva-yajanyoṣadhyāste mūlaṁ mā hiṁsiṣam ।
vrajaṁ gaccha goṣṭhānaṁ varṣatu te dauḥ ॥ – *Yajuḥsaṁhitā* 1.25

Learned men should ensure that *yajña* and herbs are not destroyed on the earth. The *yajña* in which offerings are made which purifies the air should never be abandoned. All men should give up jealousy and bitterness and live in harmony.

त्वामग्ने ! यजमाना अनु द्यून् विश्वा वसु दधिरे वार्याणि ।
त्वया सह द्रविणमिच्छमाना व्रजं गोमन्तमुशिजो विवव्रुः ॥ – *यजुःसंहिता* १२.२८

tvāmagne! yajamānā anu dyūn viśvā vasu dadhire vāryāṇi ।
tvayā saha draviṇamicchamānā vrajaṁ gomantamuśijo vivavruḥ ॥
– *Yajuḥsaṁhitā* 12.28

The wise sage, by worshipping you day and night and making all sacrifices, in your presence, has discovered the path of enlightenment.

अति विश्वाः परिष्ठाः स्तेन इव व्रजमक्रमुः ।
ओषधीः प्राचुच्यवुर्यत्किंच तन्वोरपः ॥ – *यजुःसंहिता* १२.८४

ati viśvāḥ pariṣṭhāḥ stena iva vrajamakramuḥ ।
oṣadhīḥ prācucyavuryatkiñca tanvorapaḥ ॥ – *Yajuḥsaṁhitā* 12.84

As soon as I take up these herbs in my hand to restore the strength of the patient, the soul of the wasting disease is destroyed, just as a condemned creature dies before its time.

Two streams of conception emanate from this *parameṣṭhi-loka* known as Vraja – *aṅgirā* and *bhṛgu*. Vāk (word) is born from *aṅgirā* and from *bhṛgu* comes wealth. Both are known as Sarasvatī and Āmbhraṇī. Āmbhraṇī is Lakṣmī who is described as Rādhā in the Purāṇas. Sarasvatī is the creator of speech and is known as Śrī. Sarasvatī in the form of Śrī gave birth to *nāda-dhvani* (sound which gives life to the word). This element has a deep relationship with the master of *gau-loka*, Govinda Kṛṣṇa (Viṣṇu). Is it therefore surprising to witness the divine play of Bhagavān Kṛṣṇa in Vrajadhāma? These divine actions are the characteristics of a divine being. Not everyone can understand the secrets of these divine mysteries. Bhāratavarṣa has been blessed by these divine actions of Kṛṣṇa. Vrajadhāma has therefore become a sacred place of worship. Can anyone extol the majesty of the true *Saguṇa-Brahman*? We can only reflect on the flute playing, eager custodian of cows, Kṛṣṇa's *pārameṣṭhya līlā*. Sage Śukra says:

तत्रोद्वहत्पशुपवंश-शिशुत्व-नाट्यं-
ब्रह्माद्वयं परमनन्तमगाधबोधम्।
वत्सान् सखीनिव पुरा परितो विचिन्व-
देक सपाणिकवलं परमेष्ठ्यचष्ट ॥ – *श्रीमद्भागवत्* १०.१३.६१

tatrodvahatpaśupavaṁśa-śiśutva-nāṭyaṁ-
brahmādvayaṁ paramanantamagādhabodham ।
vatsān sakhīniva purā parito vichinva-
deka sapāṇikavalaṁ parameṣṭyacaṣṭa ॥ – *Śrīmad-Bhāgavata* 10.13.61

Then Lord Brahmā saw the Absolute Truth – who is one without a second, who possesses full knowledge and who is unlimited – assuming the role of a child in a family of cowherd men and standing all alone, just as before, with a morsel of food in His hand, searching everywhere for the calves and His cowherd friends.

Bhagavān Brahma with his insight saw-experienced that Avyaya-Brahma in a different form was searching for his cowherd friends and calves. He is the physical incarnation of Parameṣṭhi Viṣṇu. Brahmā eulogizes *Bhagavān* in these words:

नौमीड्य तेऽभ्रवपुषे तडिदम्बराय-
गुञ्जावतंस-परिपिच्छ-लसन्मुखाय।

वन्यस्रजे कवल-वेत्र-विषाण-वेणु-
लक्ष्मश्रिये मृदुपदे पशुपाङ्गजाय ॥ – *श्रीमद्भागवत* १०.१४.१

naumīḍya te 'bhravapuṣe taḍidambarāya-
guñjāvataṁsa-paripiccha-lasanmukhāya ।
vanyasraje kavala-vetra-viṣāṇa-veṇu-
lakṣmaśriye mṛdupade paśupāṅgajāya ॥ – *Śrīmad-Bhāgavata* 10.14.1

My dear Lord, You are the only worshippable Lord, the Supreme Personality of godhead, and therefore I offer my humble obeisances and prayers just to please You. Oh son of the king of the cowherds! Your transcendental body is dark blue like a new cloud, Your garment is brilliant like lightning, and the beauty of Your face is enhanced by Your *guñjā* earrings and the peacock feather on Your head. Wearing garlands of various forest flowers and leaves, and equipped with a herding stick, a buffalo horn and a flute, You stand beautifully with a morsel of food in Your hand.

Today's subject is the relationship between Vedaśāstra and Purāṇaśāstra. Hence, it has become necessary to show relevant glimpses of Vedic *tattva* in between narrating stories from the Purāṇas.

So where does Kṛṣṇa's Bhārata come in this nation of fire, Bhāratavarṣa? Wait! How has the word "Kṛṣṇa" come about with "Bhārata-agni"? In fact, the *pārameṣṭhya-angirasa agni* mentioned earlier is nothing but the inexplicable *kṛṣṇabhāvāpanna* (spirit of Kṛṣṇa). The heat produced by the sun is known as Kṛṣṇa. Because of the spirit of Kṛṣṇa embedded in *agni* that it became *kṛṣṇamṛga* (black antelope). The Vedas prove this in मृगो न भीमः कुचरो गरिष्ठाः (*mṛgo na bhīmaḥ kucaro gariṣṭhāḥ* – You, Indra, who live in the mountains like the lion and destroy the enemy from all sides with great speed – *ṚV* 10.150.2) and अग्निर्वै कृष्णो भूत्वा चचार (*agnirvai kṛṣṇo bhūtvā cachāra*), etc.

The animal which exhibits Kṛṣṇa-*tattva* too has become sacred. Without the use of its black skin, sacrificial rites like *havi-peṣaṇa* cannot be performed. Nor can anyone study the Vedas without its use. How lucky is Bhāratavarṣa where such animals roam around freely. It used to be. It is possible that with the blessing of Sanskrit lover President, we would see a return to such glorious days as Rājarṣi Manu had said:

कृष्णसारस्तु चरति मृगो यत्र स्वभावतः ।
स ज्ञेयो यज्ञियो देशः म्लेच्छेदेशस्त्वतः परः ॥ – *मनु*० २.२३

kṛṣṇasārastu carati mṛgo yatra svabhāvataḥ ।
sa jñeyo yajñiyo deśaḥ mlecchedeśastvataḥ paraḥ ॥ – *Manu* 2.23

> But the region where the spotted deer roams by nature is to be known as the "land fit for sacrificial acts"; beyond that is the "land of the *mlecchas*".

About 5,000 years ago, when Tattvavāda gave way to *adharma*, two opinions emerged. One said only *dharma* was supreme while the other held that *karma* (action) superceded everything. To illustrate from the *Mahābhārata*, Duryodhana stood for the second while Yudhiṣṭhira represented the first view. We all know what grave consequences resulted in the clash between these two ideologies. We are yet to recover from the consequences of that epic battle. If a nation's honour and destiny could be destroyed by the battle between two sections, what would become if all sections of a society or a nation were at conflict with each other. It is terrifying even to imagine such a situation. Such a situation of great disquiet had happened some 5,000 years ago. We were saved by Bhagavān Kr̥ṣṇa alone when he took the form of a human. We, therefore, remember *pūrṇeśvara bhagavān* (complete God) through his *rāsa-krīḍā* for which he has been known since.

Bhagavān Kr̥ṣṇa took the form of a human being to save the world from *adharma* and to re-establish the role of *dharma*. *Bhagavān* needs no assertion of his divinity. We, humans, however need such validations to steer clear of *adharma*. *Bhagavān* assumes an *avatāra* (form of human) whenever *dharma* is under threat. *Bhagavān* is not proving his divinity by taking the form of a human; his objective is to keep the humans on the path of *dharma*.

The human form, adopted by *Bhagavān*, has four elements – *ātmā*, *buddhi*, *mana* and *śarīra* (body). As explained in the third discourse, these four elements create two sides of a human – *antarniṣṭha* (introspective) and *bahirbhāvuka-rūpa* (external emotional side). *Ātmā* and intellect enable a man to introspect and the combination of *mana* and *śarīra* makes him emotional. Both these characteristics are not fully developed in all humans. Many remain in the first category while others know only the second side throughout their lives. The thinking, contemplative individuals relying on *ātmā* and *buddhi* remain *antarniṣṭha* and those who rely on mind and body are known as *bahirniṣṭha*.

Siṇce *Bhagavān* has taken the human form to help all humans, he must address both types of humans. Among all the incarnations of *Bhagavān* who has blessed the earth of Bhārata, Kr̥ṣṇa's human *avatāra* alone has addressed these differences. Only Kr̥ṣṇa divided his human self into two – Yogeśvara and Bhogeśvara – to appease the two different types of humans. Hence, he is known as *pūrṇa-avatāra* (complete incarnation).

This can be explained in simpler terms. In the Purāṇas, Kṛṣṇa has been depicted in two forms, Nandanandana and Vasudevanandana. The one who follows his mind and body is Nandanandana, who is worshipped by devotees, women and others who are simple-minded. Kṛṣṇa's *bāla-līlā*s (playful actions of childhood) are nothing but an expression of his self as Nandanandana. Vasudevanandana is the other-wordly, non-human form of Kṛṣṇa which only *ātmā* and intellect can understand. He is known to *yogī*s as Vasudeva. He is the custodian of *bhaga-vidyā* – *ārṣa-vidyā*, *siddha-vidyā*, *rājarṣi-vidyā* and *rāja-vidyā* – which is animated by four famous *bhaga* qualities – *dharma*, *jñāna*, *vairāgya* (renunciation) and *aiśvarya* (prosperity). He became well-known as Yogeśvara as mentioned in this *sūkti*: यत्र योगेश्वरः कृष्णो यत्र पार्थो धनुर्धरः (*yatra yogeśvaraḥ kṛṣṇo yatra pārtho dhanurdharaḥ*). Kṛṣṇa's physical acts made him famous as Bhogeśvara in the *Bhāgavata* stories. Poet Jaideva, an emotional person, depicted and praised Kṛṣṇa in the Bhogeśvara form. His epic poem, *Gīta Govinda*, exudes great influence on tender-hearted devotees of Kṛṣṇa as is clear from the book's first verse itself:

> मेघैर्मेदुरमम्बरं वनभुवः श्यामास्तमालद्रुमै-
> नर्क्तं भीरुरयं त्वमेव तदिमं राधे! गृहं प्रापय।
> इत्थं नन्द-निदेशतश्चलितयोः प्रत्यध्व-कुञ्ज-द्रुमं
> राधामाधवयोर्जयन्ति यमुनाकूले रहः केलयः ॥ – १.१
>
> *meghairmeduramambaraṁ vanabuvaḥ śyāmāstamāladrumair-*
> *naktaṁ bhīrurayaṁ tvameva tadimaṁ rādhe! gṛhaṁ prāpaya* ।
> *itthaṁ nanda-nideśataścalitayoḥ pratyadhva-kuñja-drumaṁ*
> *rādhāmādhavayorjayanti yamunākūle rahaḥ kelayaḥ* ॥ – 1.1
>
> यदि हरिस्मरणे सरसं मनो यदि विलासकलासु कुतूहलम्।
> मधुर-कोमल-कान्त-पदावलीं शृणु तदा जयदेव-सरस्वतीम् ॥ – १.३
>
> *yadi harismaraṇe sarasaṁ mano yadi vilāsakalāsu kutūhalam* ।
> *madhura-komala-kānta-padāvalīṁ śṛṇu tadā jayadeva-sarasvatīm* ॥
> – 1.3

The playful Nandanandakumāra, with his inseparable companion, Śrī Rādhe, has taken permission from his father, Bābā Nanda, to play in the gardens on the banks of Yamunā. Kṛṣṇa is young (10-11 years of age). Śrī Rādhe is older to Kṛṣṇa. Bābā Nanda said to Rādhā:

Oh Rādhā! you are going to the garden. But do not forget my

> request to take care of my innocent Kr̥ṣṇa. The night is getting darker and dark clouds are crowding in the skies. Big trees make the garden forbidding. Young Kr̥ṣṇa gets easily frightened. So take care of him and you have to escort him back to home with great care.

Learned men have explained how the worldly form of Kr̥ṣṇa is in itself other-worldly also.

> किं कस्मै कथनीयं, कस्य मनः प्रत्ययो भवतु ।
> गो-धूलि-धूसराङ्गो नृत्यति वेदान्त-सिद्धान्तः ॥
>
> *kiṁ kasmai kathanīyaṁ, kasya manaḥ pratyayo bhavatu* ।
> *go-dhūli-dhūsarāṅgo nr̥tyati vedānta-siddhāntaḥ* ॥

It is said that once a learned *saṁnyāsī* came to the doorstep of Kr̥ṣṇa's residence. In the dusty courtyard, he saw the young Kr̥ṣṇa playing and realised that the young boy was no one else but the very God he was meditating on. He exclaimed suddenly, "Whom do I tell? Who will believe me? I found the 'Vedānta Puruṣa' in human form dancing in a dusty courtyard!"

In the *Bhagavadgītā*, there is a vivid description of both the characteristics of Kr̥ṣṇa's human form. Ordinary people are quite content with listening to the glory of *Bhagavān*. The *yogī*s, on the other hand, contemplate on the Yogeśvara aspect of Kr̥ṣṇa. Bhagavān himself has revealed in *Bhagavadgītā* VII.19 his form as Vāsudeva and several of its incarnations:

> बहूनां जन्मनामन्ते ज्ञानवान्मां प्रपद्यते ।
> वासुदेवः सर्वमिति स महात्मा सुदुर्लभः ॥
>
> *bahūnāṁ janmanāmante jñānavānmāṁ prapadyate* ।
> *vāsudevaḥ sarvamiti sa mahātmā sudurlabhaḥ* ॥
>
> After many births of spiritual practice, one who is endowed with knowledge surrenders unto Me, knowing Me to be all that is. Such a great soul is indeed very rare.

In the *Bhagavadgītā*'s tenth chapter, there are descriptions of Bhagavān Kr̥ṣṇa's playfulness in younger days which seems to represent Bhagavān's Bhogeśvara form but in essence, if viewed minutely, the same episodes draw our attention to his Yogeśvara form. As it is evident in the following verses: आत्मन्यवरुद्धसौरतः (*ātmanyavaruddhasaurataḥ*), आत्मारामोऽप्यरीरमत् (*ātmārāmo 'pyarīramat*), यथार्मकः स्वप्रतिबिम्बविभ्रमः (*yathārmakaḥ svapratibimbavibhramaḥ*). In the entire *Bhāgavata*, the chapter on "Rāsapañcādhyāyī" is the only amazing part in which Bhagavan's both forms have been depicted as one. So, let us now listen and introspect on some of the key elements of this section on *rasa*.

It is said that when Kṛṣṇa took the form of a human to save humanity from *adharma*, Brahmā, Indra and other *devatā*s decided to put this *pūrṇāvatāratva* to test. The *devatā*s were soon satisfied with the result of their test and found themselves blessed. Such a thing had never happened in the world – even the master of the triadic world, Viṣṇu and the great Śiva had failed to measure up to the expectations of the *devatā*s. As a poet imagined:

क्रोधं प्रभो! संहर संहरेतियावद्गिरः खे मरुतां चरन्ति ।
तावत्स वह्निर्भवनेत्रजन्माभस्मावशेषं मदनं चकार ॥ – *कुमारसम्भव* ३.७२

krodhaṁ prabho! saṁhara saṁharetiyāvadgiraḥ khe marutāṁ caranti ।
tāvatsa vahnirbhavanetrajanmā-bhasmāvaśeṣaṁ madanaṁ cakāra ॥
– *Kumārasambhava* 3.72

Even the epitome of righteousness, Bhagavān Rāma could not escape the wiles of Kāmadeva and was forced to cry out:

रे वृक्षाः पर्वतस्था गिरि-गहन-लता वायुना वीज्यमानाः
रामोऽहं व्याकुलात्मा दशरथतनयः शोकशुक्रेण दग्धः ।
बिम्बोष्ठी चारुनेत्री सुविपुलजघना बद्धनागेन्द्रकाञ्ची-
हा! सीता केन नीता मम हृदयगता को भवान् केन दृष्टा ॥

re vṛkṣāḥ parvatasthā giri-gahana-latā vāyunā vījyamānāḥ
rāmo 'haṁ vyākulātmā daśarathatanayaḥ śokaśukreṇa dagdaḥ ।
bimboṣṭhī cārunetrī suvipulajaghanā baddhanāgendrakāñcī-
hā! sītā kena nītā mama hṛdayagatā ko bhavān kena dṛṣṭā ॥

When Kāmadeva, full of his victories across the world, heard the appearance of a person in Vraja who had bested even *devatā*s like Brahmā and Indra, he became upset and angry. Not able to restrain showing his power, Kāmadeva made the blunder of appearing before Bhagavān Kṛṣṇa. *Bhagavān* very cordially, with a smile on his face, welcomed Kāmadeva. Abandoning all manners and courtesy, Kāmadeva blurted out:

> I have heard that you are a *pūrṇāvatāra*. It is said that you have saved the people of Vraja by lifting the Govardhana mountain and rescued Brahmā's lost cows. By performing these petty acts, you claim to outwit the *devatā*s. But all those acts are worthless unless you do not face the power of Kāmadeva. You must

remember that no one has been able to defeat Kāmadeva in all the three worlds. It is clear that till you defeat me, you cannot be called a *pūrṇāvatāra*. Answer me, answer me now. Do you accept my challenge?

Bhagavān heard him with little interest but silently accepted his challenge. Kāmadeva set the rules of the duel:

1. The duel will be held in early autumn, a season in which Kāmadeva has maximum power of influence.
2. The duel will take place in the open; there will be no fort or any other shelter.
3. I will be armed but not you.
4. I can also summon armed soldiers in case I feel so but not you.

Such a one-sided set of conditions was accepted and agreed upon. Both the individuals returned to their respective places. So what happened when the appropriate time came about? Hear what *Bhagavān* has to say in the voice of Śukra Muni:

भगवानपि ताः रात्रीः शरदोत्फुल्ल-मल्लिकाः ।
वीक्ष्य रन्तुं मनश्चक्रे योगमायामुपाश्रिताः ॥ – *श्रीमद्भागवत* १०.२९.१

bhagavānapi tāḥ rātrīḥ śaradotphulla-mallikāḥ ।
vīkṣya rantuṁ manaścakre yogamāyāmupāśritāḥ ॥
– *Śrīmad-Bhāgavata* 10.29.1

Oh Parīkṣit! Those nights in which *mallikā* flowers bloom, those nights which are aglow with autumn light, *Bhagavān* decided to take a stroll.

Kāmadeva had by then forgotten the time he himself had set for the duel. How can Yogeśvara Bhagavān forget his promise? Pay attention to this *tā rātri* (those nights)! Which nights? Those nights which *Bhagavān* and Kāmadeva had agreed upon. Every word, every sentence is loaded with mystery here. You need close study of Vedaśāstra and Purāṇaśāstra. It is not possible to understand these mysteries with simple stories. Take, for example, the word *mallikā*. The flower is commonly known as *belā* or *mogarā*. In Sanskrit, it is called *mallikā*. There is a whole section devoted to this flower in Purāṇaśāstra. It is written there that when Kāmadeva was making attempts to target Bhagavān Śaṅkara, he almost got burnt by the third eye of Śiva. Kāmadeva's weapon caught fire first and broke up into five trees. The upper part of the weapon adorned with *cidruma-maṇi* turned into *mallikā*.

> ऊर्ध्वं मुष्ट्या अधः कट्या स्थानं विद्रुमभूषितम् ।
> तस्माद्बहुपुटा मल्ली सञ्जाता विविधा मुने! ॥
>
> *ūrdhvaṁ muṣṭyā adhaḥ kaṭyā sthānaṁ vidrumabhūṣitam* ।
> *tasmādbahupuṭā mallī sañjātā vividhā mune!* ॥

Hence, Indian poets have depicted *mallikā* as the flower of Kāmadeva.

> मल्लिका-मुकुले चण्डि ! भाति गुञ्जन् मधुव्रतः ।
> प्रयाणे पञ्चबाणस्य शङ्खमापूरयन्निव ॥ – *काव्यादर्श*
>
> *mallikā-mukule caṇḍi! bhāti guñjan madhuvrataḥ* ।
> *prayāṇe pañcabāṇasya śaṅkhamāpūrayanniva* ॥ – *Kāvyādarśa*

The meaning of this verse is this:

> When Kāmadeva starts on his travels to entrap someone, his associates announce his arrival by blowing the conch.

The reference in the *Bhāgavata* about *śaradotphulla-mallikā* is to indicate the movement of desire. Now an important question needs to be addressed – of all the six seasons, poets have indicated the monsoon as the season of Kāmadeva or desire. Hence, this season is known as *ṛturāja* (king of seasons).

> द्रुमाः सपुष्पाः सलिलं सपद्मं स्त्रियः सकामाः पवनः सुगन्धिः ।
> सुखाः प्रदोषा दिवसाश्च रम्याः सर्व्वं प्रिये! चारुतरं वसन्ते ॥ – ऋतुसंहार
>
> *drumāḥ sapuṣpāḥ salilaṁ sapadmaṁ*
> *striyaḥ sakāmāḥ pavanaḥ saugandiḥ* ।
> *sukhāḥ pradoṣā divasāśca ramyāḥ*
> *sarvvaṁ priye! cārutaraṁ vasante* ॥ – *Ṛtusaṁhāra*

If the monsoon season is Kāmadeva's season, then why does the *Bhāgavata* mention autumn? The answer to this question can be found in the most subtle of Tattvavāda (discourse on reality). It is related to *vaidika* astronomy which is beyond the scope of the present discourse. We should be content with this simple fact that Bhagavān Kṛṣṇa was a *pūrṇāvatāra*. It means all the incarnations in the world are embodied in one *avatāra puruṣa*. The foundational element of Svayambhū Prajāpati is located in Govardhana. So is a part of *parameṣṭhi*. The *Bhāgavata* is famous throughout the world as *pārameṣṭhya-sārasvat-kalpa*.

Flute playing is representative of this *pārameṣṭhya dharma* which is related to *parameṣṭhi-sarasvatī-vāk*. *Hiraṇyamūrti sūrya* is also part of *sarvātmana* (supreme spirit) which is manifested materially as *pītāmbara* and in *prāṇa*-infused form as the essence of *Bhagavadgītā*. Animated by the sun's sphere, the *Kenopaniṣad*'s Haimavatī Umā is known as Śrīśrīpītāmbarā Bhagavatī in the Āgamaśāstra. *Cāndra-dharma* is reflected in the supreme spirit and so are *svayambhū, parameṣṭhi, sūrya, bhūpiṇḍa* and *candra* which are reflected in *Bhagavān*'s *pūrṇāvatāra*. These elements are related to Bhagavān's *rāsa-krīḍā* and therefore I am presenting a few words on this mystery.

ब्रह्मा कृष्णश्च नोऽवतु (*brahmā kṛṣṇaśca no 'vatu*) – according to this *Yajurveda mantra*, *candramā* is considered as the Brahmā of daily rituals of nature and its material form is Kṛṣṇa. The moonlight is nothing but the reflection of the sun's light – it is clear from this *śruti* in *Ṛgveda* I.84.15:

अत्राह गोरमन्वत नाम त्वष्टुरपीच्यम्।
इत्था चन्द्रमसो गृहे॥

atrāha goramanvata nāma tvaṣṭurapīcyam ।
itthā candramaso gṛhe ॥

तरणि-किरणसङ्गादेष-पानीयपिण्डो-दिनकरिदिशि चच्चच्चन्द्रिकाभिश्चकास्ते (*taraṇi-kiraṇasaṅgādeṣa-pānīyapiṇḍo-dinakaridiśi caccaccandrikābhiścakāste*) is well known. Candramā is Kṛṣṇa and this is the Rāsabihārī Kṛṣṇacandra of *adhidaivata maṇḍala*. What *rāsa* can happen without Rādhā? Rādhā is the daughter of Vṛṣabhānu. Who is she? Where does she belong in this *ādhidaivika rāsa*? Investigate through astronomy. Beginning from Aśvinī (star) to Revatī in the vast skies, there are twenty-seven stars. These stars are divided into 9-9-9 in three divisions. Of these, one star is known as Viśākhā. It is also known as Rādhā as is clear from राधा-विशाखा-पुण्ये तु (*rādhā-viśākhā-puṇye tu*). Why was it called Rādhā? Rādhā means the material wealth of the universe, in other words the earth, the round orb and the sun, the celestial orb. The earth's source of life is *agni* (fire) and the sun's life force is Indra as is said, यथाग्निगर्भा पृथिवी तया द्यौरिन्द्रेण गर्भिणी (*yathāgnigarbhā pṛthivī tayā dyaurindreṇa garbhiṇī*). The life-force of the earth and its sphere is Indrāgni which is established in the star, Viśākhā. The Jyotiṣa-śāstra has accepted Indrāgni as the deity of Viśākhā as it is clear from the following:

नासत्यान्तक-वह्नि-धातृ-शशभृद्-रुद्रादितिज्योरगा-
ऋक्षेशाः पितरोऽर्य्यमा भगरवी त्वष्टा समीरः क्रमात्।
शक्राग्नी त्वथ इन्द्रमित्र-निर्ऋति-क्षीराणि विश्वेविधि-
र्गोविन्दो वसुतोयपाजचरणाहिर्बुध्न्यपूषाभिधाः॥

nāsatyāntaka-vahni-dhātṛ-śaśabhṛd-rudrāditijyoragā-
ṛkṣeśāḥ pitro 'ryyamā bhagaravi tvaṣṭā samīraḥ kramāt ।

śakrāgnī tvatha indramitra-nirṛti-kṣīrāṇi viśvevidhir-
govindo vasutoyapājacaraṇāhirbudhnyapūṣābhidhāḥ ॥

Viśākhā is therefore the centre of great resources and is certainly the star Rādhā. That is why the next star in line is called Anurādhā. In the centre is the star Rādhā, on its eastern side are four sub-stars – Uttarāphālgunī, Hastā, Citrā, Svāti; on its north are Anurādhā, Jyeṣṭhā, Mūlā, Pūrvāṣāḍhā. All these stars are part of a constellation with star Rādhā in the centre. The constellation faces Kṛṣṇacandra of autumn and the same season's *sūrya* of Vṛṣa *rāśi*. The star Viśākhā is right in front of this formation. पश्यन्ति सप्तमं सर्वे शनिजीवकुजाः पुनः (*paśyanti saptamaṁ sarve śanijīvakujāḥ punaḥ*). The relationship between Viśākhā and the sun is clear and thus Rādhā has become Vṛṣabhānusutā[1] and with whom the autumnal Kṛṣṇacandra is dancing. Kṛṣṇa has eight friends, so does Rādhā.

With these "friends" (stars) in the heavens, Kṛṣṇacandra is leading the *rāsa-maṇḍala*, the circular space in which Kṛṣṇa is engaged in *rāsa-līlā* with the *gopīs*. This cosmic dance induces a continuous rain of seven *rāsas* like *dadhi* (curd), *ghṛta* (*ghee* or clarified butter), *madhu* (honey) and *ikṣu* (nectar of sugar cane).

In the Purāṇas, seven oceans are mentioned. Are they imaginary? No. So where are these oceans of *ghee*, *dūdha*, *madhu* on this earth? Modern geologists have not been able to find these oceans despite advances in technology. Although scientists know about the earth, they are still in the dark about the vast earthly sphere which begins from the core of the earth and spreads beyond the sun. According to Indian scientists, the shape of the earth resembles two halves of an egg (*aṇḍa kaṭāha*). From the perspective of the lower half, the Purāṇas say the earth looks flat. The Purāṇas mention seven islands and their vast expanse which modern science believes to be imaginary. But these geographical features do exist in the *pṛthvī maṇḍala* which envelopes even the sun. This sphere constantly witnesses showers of *rasa*. One such *rasa* is *cāndrarasa* which creates Śarada *ṛtu* (winter season). Bhagavān Kṛṣṇa symbolizes this *candra-tattva*. As Bhagavān Kṛṣṇa took a human form to engage in *rāsa-krīḍā* on this earth, the moon and the heavens are his

---

[1] *kenacitkaraṇenaiva rādhāvṛndāvane vane* ।
vṛṣabhānusutā jātā golokasthāyinī sadā ॥ – *Devī Bhāgavata Purāṇa* 9.50.43

kārttikyāṁ pūrṇimāyāṁ tu rādhā-rāsa-mahotsavaḥ ।
kṛṣṇa sampūjyatāṁ rādhāmuvāsa rāsamaṇḍale ॥ – Ibid. 9.12.47-48

constant companions. This mystery of this balance between *ādhidaivika* and *ādhibhautika* form of Bhagavān has been indicated by Mahāmuni Śukadeva in these words:

> तदोडुराजः ककुभः करैर्मुखंप्राच्या विलिम्पन्नरुणेन शन्तमैः ।
> स चर्षणीनामुदगाच्छुचो मृजन्प्रियः प्रियाया इव दीर्घदर्शनः ॥ – *श्रीमद्भागवत* १०.१९.२
>
> *tadoḍurājaḥ kakubhaḥ karairmukhaṁ-*
> *prācyā vilimpannaruṇena śantamaiḥ* ।
> *sa carṣaṇīnāmudagācchuco mṛjan-*
> *priyaḥ priyāyā iva dhīrghadarśanaḥ* ॥ – *Śrīmad-Bhāgavata* 10.19.2
>
> The moon then rose, anointing the face of the eastern horizon with the reddish hue of his comforting rays, and thus dispelling the pain of all who watched him rise. The moon was like a beloved husband who returns after a long absence and adorns the face of his beloved wife with red *kumkum*.

Hear, what happened next:

> दृष्ट्वा कुमुद्वन्तमखण्ड मण्डलं-रमाननाभं नवकुङ्कुमारुणम् ।
> वनं च तत्कोमल-गोभिरञ्जितं-जगौ कलं वामदृशां मनोहरम् ॥ – *श्रीमद्भागवत* १०.२९.३
>
> *draṣṭvā kumudvantamakhaṇḍa maṇḍalaṁ-*
> *ramānanābhaṁ navakuṅkumāruṇam* ।
> *vanaṁ ca tatkomala-gobhirañjitaṁ-*
> *jagau kalaṁ vāmadṛśāṁ manoharam* ॥ – *Śrīmad-Bhāgavata* 10.29.3
>
> Lord Kṛṣṇa saw the unbroken disk of the full moon glowing with the red effulgence of newly applied vermilion, as if it were the face of the Goddess of fortune. He also saw the *kumuda* lotuses opening in response to the moon's presence and the forest gently illumined by its rays. Thus the Lord began to play sweetly on His flute, attracting the minds of the beautiful-eyed *gopī*s.

In the moonlit night on the banks of Yamunā, Bhagavān Kṛṣṇa is playing his flute. By playing the flute, *Bhagavān* was calling Kāmadeva and challenging him. At once Kāmadeva appeared and said:

> Why have you gone on the offensive? We had promised not to use any weapon in our battle. And nor will there be any troops. Then why are you using your flute as the weapon and silent admirers of your music as soldiers?

Truly, Kāmadeva is not only formless (*anaṅga*) but is also blind. He is oblivious to reality. Is flute a weapon? Are the fair-eyed *gopī*s *Bhagavān*'s soldiers? No, certainly not. This music, these fair-eyed music lovers are in fact allied with Kāmadeva. *Bhagavān*, by playing his flute, was in fact supporting Kāmadeva. Śukra Muni explains this in a verse:

निशम्य गीतं तदनङ्गवर्धनं व्रजस्त्रियः कृष्ण-गृहीत-मानसाः ।
आजग्मुरन्योऽन्यमलक्षितोद्यमाः स यत्र कान्तो जवलोल-कुण्डलाः ॥
– *श्रीमद्भागवत* १०.२९.४

niśamya gītaṁ tadanaṅga-vardhanaṁ
vrajastriyaḥ kṛṣṇa-grahīta-mānasāḥ ।
ājagmuranyo 'nyamalakṣitodyamāḥ
sa yatra kānto javalola-kuṇḍalāḥ ॥ – *Śrīmad-Bhāgavata* 10.29.4

When the young women of Vṛndāvana heard Kṛṣṇa's flute-song, which arouses romantic feelings, their minds were captivated by the Lord. They went to where their lover waited, each unknown to the others, moving so quickly that their earrings swung back and forth.

What kind of music was it that drew the *gopī*s to Kṛṣṇa? तदनङ्गवर्धनम् (*tadanaṅgavardhanam*) – the one which gave strength to Anaṅga or Kāmadeva. The *gopī*s were attracted to such music and it was as if they had revolted against their commander. Bhagavān Kṛṣṇa is God, is *ātmā* and being attracted to Him is in itself Kāmadeva's failure. Desires take man and woman away from the reality of life. When our lives are blessed with *Bhagavān*, we are drawn towards Him. Śukra Muni says:

दुहन्त्योऽभिययुः काश्चिद्दोहं हित्वा समुत्सुकाः ।
पयोऽधिश्रित्य संयावमनुद्वास्यापरा ययुः ॥

परिवेषयन्त्यस्तद्धित्वा पाययन्त्यः शिशून्पयः ।
शूश्रूषन्त्यः पतीन्काश्चिदश्नन्त्योऽपास्य भोजनम् ॥

लिम्पन्त्यः प्रमृजन्त्योऽन्या अञ्जन्त्यः काश्च लोचने ।
व्यत्यस्त-वस्त्राभरणाः काश्चित्कृष्णान्तिकं ययुः ॥

ता वार्य्यमाणाः पतिभिः पितृभिर्भ्रातृ-बन्धुभिः ।
गोविन्दापहृतात्मानो न न्यवर्तन्त मोहिताः ॥

अन्तर्गृहगताः काश्चिद्गोप्योऽलब्ध-विनिर्गमाः ।
कृष्णं तद्भावना-युक्ता दध्युर्मीलित-लोचनाः ॥

दुःसहप्रेष्ठ-विरह-तीव्र-तापधुता-शुभाः ।
ध्यानप्राप्ताच्युताश्लेष-निर्वृत्या क्षीण-मङ्गलाः ॥

तमेव परमात्मानं जरा (लोक) बुद्ध्यापि सङ्गताः
जहुर्गुणमयं देहं सद्यः प्रक्षीण-बन्धनाः ॥ – *श्रीमद्भागवत* १०.२९.५-११

duhantyo 'bhiyayuḥ kaśiciddohaṁ hitvā samutsukāḥ ।
payo 'dhiśritya saṁyāvamanudvāsyāparā yayuḥ ॥

pariveṣayantyastaddhitvā pāyayantyaḥ śiśūnpayaḥ ।
śūśruṣantyaḥ patīnkāścidaśnantyo 'pāsya bhojanam ॥

limpantyaḥ pramṛjantyo 'nyā ajñjantyaḥ kāśca locane ।
vyatyasta-vastrābharaṇāḥ kāścitkṛṣṇāntikaṁ yayuḥ ॥

ta vāryyamāṇāḥ patibhiḥ pitṛbhirbhrātṛ-bandhubhi ।
govindāpahṛtātmāno na nyavartanta mohitāḥ ॥

antargrahagatāḥ kāścidgopyo 'labdha-vinirgamāḥ ।
kṛṣṇaṁ tadbhāvanā-yuktā dadhyurmīlita-locanāḥ ॥

duḥ-sahapreṣṭha-viraha-tīvra-tāpadhutā-śubhāḥ ।
dhyānaprāptācyutāśleṣa-nirvṛtyā kṣīṇamaṅgalāḥ ॥

tameva paramātmānaṁ jarā (loka) buddhyāpi saṅgatāḥ ।
jahurguṇamayaṁ dehaṁ sadyaḥ prakṣīṇa-bandhanāḥ ॥
– *Śrīmad-Bhāgavata* 10.29.5-11

The meaning of these verses is clear:

> She left whatever domestic work she was doing – milking cow, boiling milk, food being cooked in a pot, feeding milk to a baby – to see Kṛṣṇa. Those who were stopped, their sins turned into ashes with the fierce heat of *agni* and they became one with *Bhagavān*.

Ignorant of this *ādhyātmika* (spiritual) truth, King Parīkṣit had the temerity to pose such a question to Śukra Muni.

कृष्णं विदुः परं कान्तं न तु ब्रह्मतया मुने! ।
गुण-प्रवाहोपरमस्तासां गुणधियां कथम्? ॥ – *श्रीमद्भागवत* १०.२९.१२

kṛṣṇaṁ viduḥ paraṁ kāntaṁ na tu brahmatayā mune! ।
guṇa-pravāhoparamastāsāṁ guṇadiyāṁ katham? ॥
– *Śrīmad-Bhāgavata* 10.29.12

> Oh sage, the *gopī*s knew Kṛṣṇa only as their lover, not as the Supreme Absolute Truth. So how could these girls, their minds caught up in the waves of the modes of nature, free themselves from material attachment?

Parīkṣit made the common mistake of believing that *gopī*s' attraction towards Kṛṣṇa was romantic. With his erroneous notion, he asks the *muni*, oh *muni*! the *gopī*s did not see Kṛṣṇa as Brahmā. They saw Kṛṣṇa as a lover. So how did they, nursing such feelings, could attain the state of Brahmā? Śukra Muni got upset with his questions and said in a tone of admonition:

उक्तं पुरस्तादेतत्ते चैद्यः सिद्धिं यथा गतः।
द्विषन्नपि हृषीकेशं किमुताधोक्षजप्रियाः॥

नृणां निःश्रेयसार्थाय व्यक्तिर्भगवतो नृप।
अव्ययस्याप्रमेयस्य निर्गुणस्य गुणात्मनः॥

कामं क्रोधं भयं स्नेहमैक्यं सौहृदमेव च।
नित्यं हरौ विदधतो यान्ति तन्मयतां हि ते॥

न चैवं विस्मयः कार्यो भवता भगवत्यजे।
योगेश्वरेश्वरे कृष्णे यत एतद्विमुच्यते॥ – *श्रीमद्भागवत* १०.२९.१३-१६

uktaṁ purastādetatte caidyaḥ siddhiṁ yathā gataḥ ।
dviṣannapi hṛṣikeśaṁ kimutādhokṣajapriyāḥ ॥

nṛṇāṁ niḥśreyasārthāya vyaktirbhagavato nṛpa ।
avyayasyāprameyasya nirguṇasya guṇātmanaḥ ॥

kāmaṁ krodhaṁ bhayaṁ snehamaikyaṁ sauhṛdameva ca ।
nityaṁ harau vidadhato yānti tanmayatāṁ hi te ॥

na caivaṁ vismayaḥ kāryo bhavatā bhagavatyaje ।
yogeśvareśvare kṛṣṇe yata etadvimucyate ॥
– *Śrīmad-Bhāgavata* 10.29.13-16

Oh king! beware, you are again going astray. It has already been explained that Kṛṣṇa was not a human being. He is Yogeśvara Brahma. It is therefore a fundamental mistake to assume that *gopī*s were attracted to Kṛṣṇa because of his masculinity. Even if one were to assume, for a moment, that you are not wrong, your questions would still be fallacious because when Śiśupāla took up cudgels against *Bhagavān*, he became free of the cycle of life and death, so did Pūtanā when she fed *Bhagavān* poison, so why cannot the *gopī*s attain *mukti*, by loving Kṛṣṇa? Do not forget that Kṛṣṇa took the form of human to free humanity from bondage.

Those, who become connected to *Bhagavān* through anger, longing, desire, fear and friendship, would achieve freedom. So, abandon your question and listen to what happened next?

ता दृष्ट्वान्तिकमायाता भगवान् व्रजयोषितः।
अवदत्-वदतां श्रेष्ठो वाचः पेशैर्विमोहयन्॥ – *श्रीमद्भागवत* १०.२९.१७

tā draṣṭvāntikamāyātā bhagavān vrajayoṣitaḥ ।
avadat-vadatāṁ śreṣṭho vācaḥ peśairvimohayan ॥
– *Śrīmad-Bhāgavata* 10.29.17

Seeing that the girls of Vraja had arrived, Lord Kṛṣṇa, the best of speakers, greeted them with charming words that bewildered their minds.

Drawn by the melody of Kṛṣṇa's flute, *gopī*s reached the banks of Yamunā. Among the *gopī*s stood Kṛṣṇa. Kāmadeva could not resist mulling:

> Now you know the power of Kāmadeva. Who will deny that Kṛṣṇa standing amongst fair-eyed *gopī*s longingly looking at him on the moonlight banks of Yamunā is not Kāmadeva's victory?

Sensing the thought of Kāmadeva, *Bhagavān* said:

> स्वागतं वो महाभागाः! प्रियं किं करवाणि वः? ।
> व्रजस्यानामयं कच्चित्! ब्रूतागमनकारणम् ॥ – *श्रीमद्भागवत* १०.२९.१८
>
> *svāgataṁ vo mahābhāgāḥ! priyaṁ kiṁ karavāṇi vaḥ* ।
> *vrajasyānāmayaṁ kaccit! brūtāgamanakāraṇam* ॥
> – *Śrīmad-Bhāgavata* 10.29.18
>
> Come, come *gopī*s, I welcome you all with respect. Tell me, what can I do for you? Is there a new calamity on Vraja? Tell me, tell me, why have you all come so suddenly?

Pay attention to *svāgataṁ vo mahāghāgāḥ* and *priyaṁ kiṁ karavāṇi vaḥ* ... how noble are these thoughts. There is not an iota of romance in these words, nor any desire. When we meet whom we love, we are inclined to rush towards them in anticipation. Here there are no such sentiments. The *gopī*s have not come to Kṛṣṇa for the first time. Whenever people of Vraja experienced trouble, they sought help from Kṛṣṇa. In such a relationship, even an inkling of desire is forbidden. This is clarified here:

> रजन्येषा घोररूपा घोरसत्त्व-निषेविता ।
> प्रतियात व्रजं नेह स्थेयं स्त्रीभिः सुमध्यमाः ॥
>
> मातरः पितरः पुत्रा भ्रातरः पतयश्च वः ।
> विचिन्वन्ति ह्यपश्यन्तो मा कृध्वं बन्धुसाध्वसम् ॥ – *श्रीमद्भागवत* १०.२९.१९
>
> *rajanyeṣā ghorarūpā ghorasattva-niṣevitā* ।
> *pratiyāta vrajaṁ neha stheyaṁ strībhiḥ sumadhymāḥ* ॥
>
> *mātaraḥ pitaraḥ putrā bhrātaraḥ patayaśca vaḥ* ।
> *vicinvanti hyapaśyanto mā kṛdhvaṁ bandhusādhvasam* ॥
> – *Śrīmad-Bhāgavata* 10.29.19
>
> Look around you, there are no humans on this deserted stretch of the riverbank. The night is dark and deep and wild animals

are roaming around freely. Return without a moment's delay. This is not a place for young women to be.

दृष्टं वनं कुसुमितं राकेश-कर-रञ्जितम् ।
यमुना-निल-लीलैजत्तरुपल्लव-शोभितम् ॥ – *श्रीमद्भागवत* १०.२९.२०

dṛṣṭaṁ vanaṁ kusumitaṁ rākeśa-kara-rañjitam ।
yamunā-nila-līlaijattarupallava-śobhitam ॥
– *Śrīmad-Bhāgavata* 10.29.20

Oh, I see! you have come to enjoy the moonlight banks of River Yamunā. Now that you have seen it. You have seen the *mallikā* flowers shining in the moonlight and enjoyed the cool and scented breeze from the forest.

Look at the manner in which Kāmadeva is led to his defeat by a playful Kṛṣṇa.

तद्यात! मा चिरं गोष्ठं-शुश्रूषध्वं पतीन्सतीः ।
क्रन्दन्ति वत्सा, बालाश्च-तान्पाययत दुह्यत ॥ – *श्रीमद्भागवत* १०.२९.२२

tadyāta! mā ciraṁ goṣṭhaṁ-śuśrūṣadhvaṁ patīnsatīḥ ।
krandanti vatsā, bālāśca-tānpāyayata duhyat ॥
– *Śrīmad-Bhāgavata* 10.29.22

Go back from here. Return home immediately. *Gopī*s, you have seen the majesty of the forest. Now go back, now. How can you forget your calves and your babies? Go back. Without milk, calves would be moaning. Children would be crying. Milk the cows. Feed your babies.

A woman's life has many aspects. She has the right to enjoy the vistas of forests and natural surroundings. She is also a mother, her responsibility towards her children is supreme. *Gopī*s are mothers, not women alone. Can Kāmadeva understand this? Women have many characteristics and each is unique. They can be women, mothers and yet retain the right to enjoy the pleasures of nature. Says *Bhagavān*:

अथवा मदभिस्नेहाद् भवत्यो यन्त्रिताशयाः ।
आगताः ह्युपपन्नं वः प्रीयन्ते मयि जन्तवः ॥

भर्तुः शुश्रूषणं स्त्रीणां परो धर्मो ह्यमायया ।
तद्बन्धूनां च कल्याण्यः प्रजानां चानुपोषणम् ॥

दुःशीलो दुर्भगो वृद्धो जडो रोग्यधनोऽपि वा ।
पतिः स्त्रीभिर्न हातव्यो लोकेप्सुभिरपातकी ॥ – *श्रीमद्भागवत* १०.२९.२३-२५

athavā madabhisnehād bhavatyo yantritāśayāḥ ।
āgatāḥ hyupapannaṁ vaḥ prīyante mayi jantavaḥ ॥

bhartuḥ śuśrūṣaṇaṁ strīṇāṁ paro dharmo hyamāyayā ।
tadbandhūnāṁ ca kalyāṇyaḥ prajānāṁ cānupoṣaṇam ॥

duḥśīlo durbhago vṛddho jaḍo rogyadhano 'pi vā ।
patiḥ strībhirna hātavyo lokepsubhirapātakī ॥
– *Śrīmad-Bhāgavata* 10.29.23-25

I am aware of your fondness for me. I also know that you have come to meet me drawn by that love. You have not come with any desire. You have come as a mother, as a devotee.

Do you know why *Bhagavān* is loved? If not, then let me tell you what Śāstras have said about the role of women.

According to the Śāstras, a woman in her marital life should love her husband and observe religious traditions. Being with her husband is her true devotion. She has no independent role as per the Śāstras. So "return home, immediately". You have one question left to be answered. So listen:

श्रवणाद्दर्शनाद्ध्यानान्मयि भावोऽनुकीर्तनात् ।
न तथा सन्निकर्षेण, प्रतियात ततो गृहान् ॥ – *श्रीमद्भागवत* १०.२९.२७

śravaṇāddarśanāddhyānānmayi bhāvo 'nukīrtanāt ।
na tathā sannikarṣeṇa, pratiyāta tato gṛhān ॥
– *Śrīmad-Bhāgavata* 10.29.27

You can say that as long as *Bhagavān*'s physical form is not visible, a woman should follow the path of worship (*bhakti*) along with her husband. But when *Bhagavān* appears in physical form, then these rules become irrelevant. Here I must clarify the true meaning of *bhakti*. Praying, contemplating and listening to praises of *Bhagavān* are true forms of *bhakti* and not meeting *Bhagavān* in flesh. I tell you therefore to return to your homes at once. To know the answers to mysterious questions, meditate with faith and respect on the chapter on *rāsa*. Since time is short, I will conclude today's discourse with a few auspicious recollections.

इति विप्रियमाकर्ण्य गोप्यो गोविन्दभाषितम् ।
विषण्णा भग्न-संकल्पाश्चिन्तामापुर्दुरत्ययाम् ॥ – *श्रीमद्भागवत* १०.२९.२८

iti vipriyamākarṇya gopyo govindabhāṣitam ।
viṣaṇṇā bhagna-saṅkalpāścintāmāpurduratyayām ॥
– *Śrīmad-Bhāgavata* 10.29.28

> Hearing these unpleasant words spoken by Govinda, the *gopī*s became morose. Their great hopes were frustrated and they felt insurmountable anxiety.

The *gopī*s were heartbroken by *Bhagavān*'s exhortations. They did not expect to be scolded and asked to return home. They did not realise that Kṛṣṇa was determined to break Kāmadeva's arrogance.

> कृत्वा मुखान्यव शुचः श्वसनेन शुष्यद्-
> बिम्बाधराणि चरणेन भुवं लिखन्त्यः ।
> अस्रैरुपात्तमदिभिः कुच-कुङ्कुमानि
> तस्थुर्मृजस्य उरुदुःखभरा स्म तूष्णीम् ॥ – *श्रीमद्भागवत* १०.२९.२९
>
> *kṛtvā mukhānyava śucaḥ śvasanena śuṣyad-*
> *bimbādharāṇi caraṇena bhuvaṁ likhantyaḥ* ।
> *asrairupāttamadibhiḥ kuca-kuṁkumāni*
> *tasthurmṛjasya uruduḥkhabharā sma tūṣṇīm* ॥
> – *Śrīmad-Bhāgavata* 10.29.29

The *gopī*s became sad at this unbearable, painful rejection. Tears began to flow. Silently they all stood, drawing listlessly on the sand with their toes.

The reality is this – Kṛṣṇa-*tattva* or the essence of Bhagavān Kṛṣṇa could not be understood by feeling amorous towards the human form of Kṛṣṇa. The *gopī*s have only seen Kṛṣṇa's human form, the Nandanandana form and hence they could never see the divine side of *Bhagavān*. When the *gopī*s saw this divine view of *Bhagavān*, they cried out:

> प्रेष्ठं प्रियेतरमिव प्रतिभाषमाणं
> कृष्णं तदर्थ-विनिवर्तित-सर्वकामाः ।
> नेत्रे विमृज्य रुदितोपहते स्म किञ्चित्
> संरम्भ-गद्गद्गिरोऽब्रुवतानुरक्ताः ॥ – *श्रीमद्भागवत* १०.२९.३०
>
> *preṣṭham priyetaramiva pratibhāṣamāṇaṁ*
> *kṛṣṇaṁ tadartha-vinivartita-sarvakāmāḥ* ।
> *netre vimṛjya ruditopahate sma kiñcit*
> *saṁrambha-gadgadgiro 'bruvatānuraktāḥ* ॥
> – *Śrīmad-Bhāgavata* 10.29.30

> Although Kṛṣṇa was their beloved, and although they had abandoned all other objects of desire for His sake, He had been speaking to them unfavourably. Nonetheless, they remained unflinching in their attachment to Him. Stopping their crying, they wiped their eyes and began to speak, their voices stammering with agitation.

The *gopī*s were stunned at the dramatic change in Kṛṣṇa, who had been so kind and generous towards them. They had never seen such a cruel, heartless side of Kṛṣṇa. They were shell shocked. (How would the *gopī*s know that Bhagavān Kṛṣṇa was about to establish how humans can pursue marital duties even after suppressing desires?) If the *gopī*s had come to meet Kṛṣṇa with desire in their mind, then it would have been a different matter. Do you know what brought the *gopī*s to Kṛṣṇa? Would you, today's modern, educated Indian, like to know why? Then they should at least try to know the literal meaning of कृष्णं तदर्थविनिवर्त्तितसर्वकामाः (*kṛṣṇaṁ tadarthavinivarttitasarvakāmāḥ*).

As the *gopī*s began to realize the true nature of Kṛṣṇa, their shock and sadness began to dissipate. Kṛṣṇa came into their hearts where Kāmadeva was to be as if the enemy was defeated in his own home. The *gopī*s, wiping their tears, in voice broken by sobs, exclaimed:

भैवं विभोऽर्हति भवान् गदितुं नृशंसं!
सन्त्यज्य सर्वविषयांस्तव पादमूलम्।
भक्ता, भजस्व! दुरवग्रह मा त्यजास्मान्!
देवो यथादिपुरुषो भजते मुमुक्षून्॥ – *श्रीमद्भागवत* १०.२९.३१

bhaivaṁ vibho 'rhati bhavān gadituṁ nṛśaṁsaṁ!
santyajya sarvaviṣayāṁstava pādamūlam ।
bhaktā, bhajasva! duravagraha mā tyajāsmān!
devo yathādipuruṣo bhajate mumukṣūn ॥
– *Śrīmad-Bhāgavata* 10.29.31

Oh all-powerful one! You should not speak in this cruel way. Do not reject us, who have renounced all material enjoyment to render devotional service at Your lotus feet. Reciprocate with us, Oh stubborn one! just as the primaeval Lord, Śrī Nārāyaṇa, reciprocates with His devotees in their endeavours for liberation.

Oh! the intelligent people who laugh at the Bhāgavata Rāsalīlā! Pay attention to this soulful cry of the *gopī*s. Oh masters of debate! learn something from this address. At least try to give up your stubbornness which has taken man away from a life of *jñāna-vijñāna*.

What are the *gopī*s saying? Listen to their words carefully. Oh the one who is all-pervasive, Sarveśvarapūrṇa Brahma! Have you thought that we see you only as a lover and we have come to meet you, abandoning our honour and domestic duties? Remove this wishful thinking. If you have scolded us keeping this in mind, then remember, we have come to worship you after renouncing worldly desires. We are not your lovers, we are your *bhakta*s (devotees) – *bhaktāḥ bhajasva duravagraha mā tyajāsmān*.

Do not forsake us. Do not ignore us. (You cannot leave us in the lurch.) Do you want any more clarifications from us? Then *devo yathādipuruṣo bhajate mumukṣūn* is enough. As you bless those who seek *mokṣa*, you should treat us with the same respect. We too have come to you for *mukti*. The *gopī*s then said:

प्रेष्ठो भवांस्तनुभृतां किल बन्धुरात्मा
तन्नः प्रसीद परमेश्वर! मा स्म छिन्द्या
ध्यानेन याम पदयोः पदवीं सखे ते
तद्वद्वयं च तव पादरजः प्रपन्नाः
प्राप्ता विसृज्य वसतीस्त्वदुपासनाशाः
तप्तात्मनां पुरुषभूषण! देहि दास्यम्
– *श्रीमद्भागवत* १०.२९.३२-३३, ३५, ३७-३८

preṣṭho bhavāṁstanubhr̥tāṁ kila bandhurātmā
tannaḥ prasīda parameśvara! mā sma chindyā
dhyānena yāma padayoḥ padavīṁ sakhe te
tadvadvayaṁ ca tava pādarajaḥ prapannāḥ
prāptā visr̥jya vasatīstvdupāsanāśāḥ
taptātmanāṁ puruṣabhuṣaṇa! dehi dāsyam!
– *Śrīmad-Bhāgavata* 10.29.32-33, 35, 37-38

You are the dearmost friend of all embodied souls. You are their most intimate relative and indeed their very Self.

Oh supreme controller! grant us Your mercy. Oh lotus-eyed one! please do not cut down our long-cherished hope to have Your association.

And thus like *yogī*s attain to the abode of Your lotus feet by meditation.

We have approached the dust of Your lotus feet for shelter.

Our hearts are burning with intense desires generated by Your beautiful smiling glances.

O jewel among men, please make us Your maidservants.

Thus Bhagavān Kr̥ṣṇa presented his pure *ādhyātmika* form, initiating *mahārāsa* which had the power to remove every human ill. Remember that this Rāsalīlā is the physical manifestation of *ādhidaivika* Kr̥ṣṇacandra as has been explained in the Vedic astrology. Śukra Muni has clarified further:

ताभिः समेताभिरुदारचेष्टितः प्रियेक्षणोत्फुल्लमुखीभिरच्युतः ।
उदारहासद्विजकुन्द-दीधितिर्व्यरोचतैणाङ्क इवोडुभिर्वृतः ॥ – *श्रीमद्भागवत* १०.२९.४३

tābhiḥ sametābhirudāraceṣṭitaḥ
priyekṣaṇotphullamukhībhiracyutaḥ ।

udārahāsadvijakunda-dīdhitir-
vyarocataiṇāṅka evoḍubhirvṛtaḥ ॥ – *Śrīmad-Bhāgavata* 10.29.43

Among the assembled *gopīs*, the infallible Lord Kṛṣṇa appeared just like the moon surrounded by stars. He whose activities are so magnanimous made their faces blossom with His affectionate glances, and His broad smiles revealed the effulgence of His jasmine-bud-like teeth.

As *rāsa* began, Kāmadeva's strength started waning, as if Kṛṣṇa was determined to defeat Kāmadeva. How?

बाहु-प्रसार-परिरम्भ-कराल-कोरु-नीवीस्तनालभन-नर्म-नखाग्रपातैः ।
क्ष्वेल्याऽवलोक-हसितैर्व्रजसुन्दरीणां उत्तम्भयन् रतिपतिं रमयाञ्चकार ॥
– *श्रीमद्भागवत* १०.२९.४६

bāhu-prasāra-parirambha-karāla-koru-
nīvīstanālabhana-narma-nakhāgrapātaiḥ ।
kṣvelyā 'valoka-hasitairvrajasundarīṇāṁ
uttambhayan ratipatiṁ ramayāñcakāra ॥
– *Śrīmad-Bhāgavata* 10.29.46

There Kṛṣṇa threw His arms around the *gopīs* and embraced them. He aroused Cupid in the beautiful young ladies of Vraja by touching their hands, hair, thighs, belts and breasts, by playfully scratching them with His fingernails, and also by joking with them, glancing at them and laughing with them. In this way the Lord enjoyed His pastimes.

Can there be a more glorious example of victory in this world? Impossible. Aśīti could declare himself to be free of *kāma* only when he turned 80. It is no great feat to defeat desire by drinking *kelpātra*. But to live with all the sensual feelings and to carry out marital duties amidst beautiful natural surroundings and not to be swayed by desire is the true victory over senses. To tame sensual senses is true victory over desire and not giving up desires. काम्यानां कर्म्मणां-न्यासं संन्यासं कवयो विदुः (*kāmyānāṁ karmmaṇāṁ-nyāsaṁ saṁnyāsaṁ kavayo viduḥ*) is the real definition of *saṁnyāsa* as established by *Bhagavān*'s Rāsalīlā. To live without desire in the world of beauty and desire is the true definition of *tyāga* (renunciation) which, unfortunately, has been lost in today's world. Now it is either forced elimination of desire or living a rule-bound marital life which are boastfully claimed as achievements. The true characteristic of *tyāga* is to amass but not to get swayed by greed. While keeping desires under check, to work selflessly for the welfare of the nation has been the age-old tradition in this nation. Declaring oneself as *tyāgī* or *tapasvī*, without having experienced worldly as well as spiritual sides of life, has no meaning. Such people are not worthy of even speaking the word *tyāga*.

This is what happened to our great, spiritually endowed Bhārata over the last 3,000 years. Such fraudulent *tapa*, *tapasyā*, brought only ignominy to our great nation, deprived us of the wisdom of *jñāna* and *vijñāna* and left us nowhere. It is our fortune that we have retrieved our lost glory once again and with the blessings of our Vedic wisdom and tradition, a greater future for our nation is in the making. We must be cautious and not let complacency and ignorance drag us back to slavery and rejection. This is what today's discourse on *rāsa* reminds us of. *Bhagavān*, with his vanquishing *rāsa-krīḍā* (celestial dance), cautions the *gopī*s of becoming arrogant and insolent.

तासां तत्सौभगमदं वीक्ष्य मानं च केशवः ।
प्रशमाय प्रसादाय तत्रैवान्तरधीयत ॥ – *श्रीमद्भागवत* १०.२९.४८

tāsāṁ tatsaubhagamadaṁ vīkṣya mānaṁ ca keśavaḥ ।
praśamāya prasādāya tatraivāntaradhīyata ॥
– *Śrīmad-Bhāgavata* 10.29.48

Lord Keśava, seeing the *gopī*s too proud of their good fortune, wanted to relieve them of this pride and show them further mercy. Thus He immediately disappeared.

If man becomes arrogant because of the wealth and prestige he got with the blessings of *Īśvara*, such wealth and honour would not last long. This is the moral lesson that can be drawn from the above verse. *Bhagavān* meets the *gopī*s again, but with great restraint. Greed, arrogance, jealousy and deception makes a man weep for the loss of wealth and honour. Like the *gopī*s did when they could not find *Bhagavān*. It was only when the *gopī*s gave up their arrogance, did *Bhagavān* appear before them. How did they manage to keep *Bhagavān* with them, hear from Śukra Muni:

इति गोप्यः प्रगायन्त्यः प्रलपन्त्यश्च चित्रधा ।
रुरुदुः सुस्वरं राजन्! कृष्ण-दर्शन-लालसाः ॥

तासामाविरभूच्छौरिः स्मयमानमुखाम्बुजः ।
पीताम्बरधरः स्रग्वी साक्षान्मन्मथमन्मथः ॥ – *श्रीमद्भागवत* १०.३२.१-२

iti gopyaḥ pragāyantyaḥ pralapantyaśca citradhā ।
ruruduḥ susvaraṁ rājan! kṛṣṇa-darśana-lālasāḥ ॥

tāsāmāvirabhūcchauriḥ smayamānamukhāmbujaḥ ।
pītāmbaradharaḥ sragvī sākṣānmanmathamanmathaḥ ॥
– *Śrīmad-Bhāgavata* 10.32.1-2

> Oh king! having thus sung and spoken their hearts out in various charming ways, the *gopīs* began to weep loudly. They were very eager to see Lord Kr̥ṣṇa.

Here, Kāmadeva was completely vanquished. He accepted defeat and became part of *Bhagavān*'s *ātmasīmā* (boundaries of self). In this new form, *Bhagavān* is neither Nandanandana nor Vasudevanandana. He is in fact Śauri Bhagavān. In India's ancient traditions, a brave victor is known not by his father's name but by the honour of his forefathers. Bhagavān Rāma is thus known as Raghuvaṁśī. The great soldier, Mahārāṇā Pratāp, is known by his lineage to Bappāravāla. *Bhagavān*'s act of quelling *kāma* (desire) has been a landmark in human history. Kāmadeva had to concede that Kr̥ṣṇa was truly Śauri.[2] Kr̥ṣṇa was an illustrious descendant of the great warrior king, Śūrasena, and hence his name, "Śauri". By crushing the arrogance (*mada*) of Kāmadeva, Kr̥ṣṇa came to be known as "Manmathamanmatha". Oh, *Bhagavān*! the same Kāmadeva who has tempted everyone was himself enticed by you and hence you became famous as "Madanamohana". Even Śiva failed to reject desire completely but you have proved to be different; you are truly Pārameṣṭhya Pītāmbara, you are Pūrṇeśvara (complete God) symbolized as the *aśvattha* tree.

Do you still harbour any doubts? If so, then pay attention to the following:

> न खलु गोपिकानन्दनो भवान् अखिलदेह्निामन्तरात्मदृक् ।
> विखनसाऽर्थितो विश्वगुप्तयेसख उदेयिवान्सात्वतां कुले ॥ – *श्रीमद्भागवत* १०.३१.४
>
> *na khalu gopikānandano bhavān akhiladehināmantarātmadr̥k* ।
> *vikhanasā 'rthito viśvaguptayesakha udeyivānsātvatāṁ kule* ॥
> – *Śrīmad-Bhāgavata* 10.31.4
>
> You are not actually the son of the *gopī* Yaśodā, Oh friend! but rather the indwelling witness in the hearts of all embodied souls. Because Lord Brahmā prayed for You to come and protect the universe, You have now appeared in the Sātvata dynasty.
>
> तत्रोपविष्टो भगवान् स ईश्वरोयोगेश्वरान्तर्हृदि कल्पितासनः ।
> चकास गोपीपरिषद्गतोऽर्चितस्त्रैलोक्यलक्ष्म्येकपदं वपुर्दधत् ॥
> – *श्रीमद्भागवत* १०.३२.१४

---

[2] Kr̥ṣṇa is known as Vāsudeva, Govinda and Kr̥ṣṇa Śauri of the Vr̥ṣṇis. The Vr̥ṣṇis were the rulers of Dvārakā, a submerged island-state off-coast, modern Gujarat, India.

> Lord Kṛṣṇa, the Supreme Personality of godhead, for whom the great masters of mystic meditation arrange a seat within their hearts, took His seat in the assembly of *gopīs*. His transcendental body, the exclusive abode of beauty and opulence within the three worlds, shone brilliantly as the *gopīs* worshipped Him.
>
> *tatropaviṣṭo bhagavān sa īśvaroyogeśvarāntarhṛdi kalpitāsanaḥ* ।
> *cakāsa gopīpariṣadgato 'rcitastrailokyalakṣmyekapadaṁ vapurdadhat* ॥
> – *Śrīmad-Bhāgavata* 10.32.14
>
> एवं परिष्वङ्गकराभिमर्शस्निग्धेक्षणोद्दामविलासहासैः ।
> रेमे रमेशो व्रजसुन्दरीभिर्यथार्भकः स्वप्रतिबिम्बविभ्रमः ॥ – *श्रीमद्भागवत* १०.३३.१७
>
> *evaṁ pariṣvaṅgakarābhimarśasnigdhekṣaṇoddāmavilāsahāsaiḥ* ।
> *reme rameśo vrajasundarībhiryathārbhakaḥ svapratibimbavibhramaḥ* ॥
> – *Śrīmad-Bhāgavata* 10.33.17
>
> Although the *gopīs* were firmly attached to Lord Kṛṣṇa, whose desires are always fulfilled, the Lord was not internally affected by any mundane sex desire. Still, to perform His pastimes the Lord took advantage of all those moonlit autumn nights, which inspire poetic descriptions of transcendental affairs.
>
> एवं शशाङ्कांशुविराजिता निशाः स सत्यकामोऽनुरताबलागणः ।
> सिषेव आत्मन्यवरुद्धसौरतः सर्वाः शरत्काव्यकथारसाश्रयाः ॥ – *श्रीमद्भागवत* १०.३३.२५
>
> *evaṁ śaśāṅkāṁśuvirājitā niśāḥ sa satyakāmo 'nuratābalāgaṇaḥ* ।
> *siṣeva ātmanyavaruddha-sauratạḥ sarvāḥ śaratkāvyakathārasāśrayāḥ* ॥
> – *Śrīmad-Bhāgavata* 10.33.25

Realizing the *brahmasvarūpa* of Kṛṣṇa, the *gopīs* pleaded with him thus:

> Oh *Bhagavān*! we realise you are not only Gopikānandana, or Yaśodānandana but you are the soul of every being. You are truly a *sakhā* (friend), who has taken the form of human on the prayers of Brahmā.

The same *Bhagavān*, who lives in the heart of the *gopīs*, is today resplendent in his divine form.

At different places, cups filled with water and mirrors are kept. A playful child reaches there and goes to each of the cups. He sees his reflection in them. He displays his happiness by clapping and laughing out loud. This is what is happening in today's Rāsalīlā. Young Kṛṣṇa, nine to ten years old, is *Saguṇa-Brahman* himself and the cups filled with water around him are *mahadbrahma prakṛti gopīs*. The conscious part of their living being is a reflection of *Saguṇa-Brahman* and Kṛṣṇa is thus playing with his own reflection. Verses like एवं परिष्वङ्गकराभिमर्शस्निग्धेक्षणोद्दामविलासहासैः

(*evaṁ pariṣvaṅgakarābhimarśasnigdhekṣaṇoddāmavilāsahāsaiḥ*) clearly indicate the communion between *cidātmā* (supreme being) and *cidābhāsa* (reflection of Brahmā).

The Vedas can only be learned through self-study. *Kathā* is drawn from the Purāṇas. I believe this vivid description of *Bhagavān*'s Rāsalīla has been understood by you all. There would be doubts. Doubts are a part of the human mind. That was the reason why Parīkṣit, blinded by the curse of a brāhmaṇa, nursed doubts and was compelled to ask:

संस्थापनाय धर्म्मस्य प्रशमायेतरस्य च।
अवतीर्णो हि भगवान्-अंशेन जगदीश्वरः॥

स कथं धर्म्मसेतूनां वक्ता कर्त्ताभिरक्षिता।
प्रतीपमाचरद् ब्रह्मन्! परदाराभिमर्शनम्॥

आप्तकामो यदुपतिः कृतवान्वै जुगुप्सितम्।
किमभिप्राय एतं नः संशयं छिन्धि सुव्रत॥ – *श्रीमद्भागवत* १०.३३.२७-२९

saṁsthāpanāya dharmmasya praśamāyetarasya ca ।
avatīrṇo hi bhagavān-aṁśena jagadīśvaraḥ ॥

sa kathaṁ dharmmasetūnāṁ vaktā karttābhirakṣitā ।
pratīpamācarad brahman! paradārābhimarśanam ॥

āptakāmo yadupatiḥ kṛtavānvai jugupistam ।
kimabhiprāya etaṁ naḥ saṁśayaṁ chindhi suvrata ॥
– *Śrīmad-Bhāgavata* 10.33.27-29

Parīkṣit raises his doubts with Śukra Muni thus:

> Oh *muni*! Bhagavān Kṛṣṇa assumed the human form to free the world of *adharma*. So why did he cohabit with other women? It was against *dharma* which he himself had established. Why did he indulge in this sinful act? Please enlighten me.

Śukra Muni clarified his doubts but we do not have time to go into it in detail. We will confine ourselves to the following:

यत् पाद-पङ्कज-पराग-निषेवतृप्ता-योग-प्रभाव-विधुताखिल-कर्म्मबन्धाः।
स्वैरं चरन्ति मुनयोऽपि न नह्यमानास्तस्येच्छयात्तवपुषः कुत एव बन्धः॥
– *श्रीमद्भागवत* १०.३३.३५

yat pāda-paṅkaja-parāga-niṣevatṛptā-
yoga-prabhāva-vidhutākhila-karmmabandhāḥ ।
svairaṁ caranti munayo 'pi na nahyamānās-
tasyecchayāttavapuṣaḥ kuta eva bandhaḥ ॥
– *Śrīmad-Bhāgavata* 10.33.35

Oh King! Beware! You are again making a mistake. How can the one whose mere touch releases *yogīs* from *karmabandha* (bonds of action) and whose blessing enables *munis* to roam around freely in the world and not be bound by the physical body which *Bhagavān* himself has adopted? Even such a thought is *mahāpāpa* (great sin). Listen, listen carefully and you will be free of your curse!

गोपीनां तत्पतीनाञ्च सर्वेषामेव देहिनाम्।
योऽन्तश्चरति सोऽध्यक्षः क्रीडनेनेह देहभाक्॥ – *श्रीमद्भागवत* १०.३३.३६

gopīnāṁ tatpatīnāñca sarveṣāmeva dehinām ।
yo 'ntaścarati so 'dhyakṣaḥ krīḍaneneha dehabhāk ॥
– *Śrīmad-Bhāgavata* 10.33.36

That *kṛṣṇavyaya-tattva* which is in every *gopī*, their husbands and in fact in every human being as *cidābhāsa*, the same *avyayeśvara* has taken human form to establish *dharma* on this earth.

अनुग्रहाय भूतानां मानुषं देहमास्थितः।
भजते तादृशी क्रीडा याः श्रुत्वा तत्परो भवेत्॥

नासूयन् खलु कृष्णाय मोहितास्तस्य मायया।
मन्यमाना स्वपार्श्वस्थान् स्वान् स्वान् दारान् व्रजौकसः॥

ब्रह्मरात्र उपावृत्ते वासुदेवानुमोदिताः।
अनिच्छन्त्यो ययुर्गोप्यः स्वगृहान् भगवत्प्रियाः॥ – *श्रीमद्भागवत* १०.३३.३७-३९

anugrahāya bhūtānāṁ mānuṣaṁ dehamāsthitaḥ ।
bhajate tādṛśī krīḍā yāḥ śrutvā tatparo bhavet ॥

nāsūyan khalu kṛṣṇāya mohitāstasya māyayā ।
manyamānā svapārśvasthān svān svān dārān vrajaukasaḥ ॥

brahmarātra upāvṛtte vāsudevānumoditāḥ ।
anicchantyo yayurgopyaḥ svagṛhān bhagavatpriyāḥ ॥
– *Śrīmad-Bhāgavata*. 10.33.37-39

Oh Avyayeśvara Bhagavān! you carry out human acts in your human form for the benefit of living beings and by worshipping you we can become part of your *līlā*.

Do you think the husbands, sons and relatives of *gopīs* were worried about their absence? Ignorant are you. It seems you have not become free of the curse. Then hear! The *gopīs* and their families were together before the Yogamāyī Bhagavān. (So your question has no relevance.) After the *līlā*, the *gopīs* returned home as *Bhagavān* had asked them to.

नाकारणं हि शास्त्रेऽस्ति धर्म्मः सूक्ष्मोऽपि जाजले?।
कारणाद्धर्म्ममन्विच्छन् स लोकानाप्नुते शुभान्॥ – *वाल्मीकिरामायण*

nākāraṇaṁ hi śāstre 'sti dharmmaḥ sūkṣmo 'pi jājale? ।
kāraṇāddharmmamanvicchan sa lokānāpnute śubhān ॥
– *Vālmīki Rāmāyaṇa*

Oh Jājale! Even the most miniscule part of *dharma* is not without a reason. Only by knowing this mystery can you sense the reality of life.

The question now is what is the use of these stories from the Purāṇas and discussions on the Veda and Purāṇas in today's materialistic world? The question is serious, timely and debatable. There are several answers to this question, of which only one would be presented before you. Today, those who are engaged in nation building, have to work very hard. According to medical science, excessive labour causes pressure on the heart and leads to heart diseases. A weak heart is the cause of an unstable mind. Weakness of mind is the real cause of heart trouble, according to Vedic *vijñāna*. The *rāsa-krīḍā* establishes a direct link to Kṛṣṇacandra:

चन्द्रमा मनसो जातः मनश्चन्द्रेण लीयते हृत्पृष्ठं यदजिरं जविष्ठं तन्मे मनः शिवसंकल्पमस्तु ।

candramā manaso jātaḥ manaścandreṇa līyate hṛtpratiṣṭhaṁ yadajiraṁ javiṣṭhaṁ tanme manaḥ śivasaṅkalpamastu ।

These Vedic principles tell us that *candra-tattva* (essence of moon) is beneficial to our heart and mind. We have also heard from "historians" that material pleasure also strengthens the heart. This could be the reason why our nation hosts many events of entertainment. Perhaps one is mistaken. But I have a firm belief that the heart and mind can only be strengthened by *candra-tattva*. It is not an imaginary tale. Remember the mystery in Śukra Muni's advice:

विक्रीड़ितं व्रजवधूभिरिदं च विष्णोः श्रद्धान्वितोऽनुशृणुयादथ वर्णयेद्यः ।
भक्तिं परां भगवति प्रतिलभ्य कामं हृद्रोग माश्वपहिनोत्यचिरेण धीरः ॥
– *श्रीमद्भागवत* १०.३३.४०

vikrīḍitaṁ vrajavadhūbhiridaṁ ca viṣṇoḥ
śraddhānvito 'nuśṛṇuyādatha varṇayedyaḥ ।
bhaktiṁ parāṁ bhagavati pratilabhya kāmaṁ
hṛdroga māśvapahinotyacireṇa dhīraḥ ॥
– *Śrīmad-Bhāgavata* 10.33.40

"Those who listen to this *śarat kāvya kathā* with great attention are capable of saving themselves from heart trouble." This is an example of the Vedaśāstra's relationship with Purāṇaśāstra. But there are people who have made their life's mission to be doubtful of everything. Is there a response in the Vedaśāstra for such people? The Vedaśāstra would be amiss if it failed to respond to such sceptics.

इत्येवं श्रुति-नीति-संप्लव-जलैर्भूयोभिराक्षालिते
येषां नास्पदमादधासि हृदये ते शैलसाराशयाः ।
किन्तु प्रस्तुत-विप्रतीप-विधयोऽप्युच्चैर्भवच्चिन्तकाः
काले कारुणिक! त्वयैव कृपया ते भावनीया नराः ॥ – *न्यायकुसुमाञ्जलिः* ५.१८

ityevaṁ śruti-nīti-saṁplava-jalairbhūyobhirākṣālite
yeṣāṁ nāspadamādadhāsi hṛdaye te śailasārāśayāḥ ।
kintu prastuta-vipratīpa-vidhayo 'pyuccairbhavaccintakāḥ
kāle kāruṇika! tvayaiva kṛpayā te bhāvanīyā narāḥ ॥
– *Nyāyakusumāñjali* 5.18

Udayanācārya,[3] addressing *Īśvara*, said, *Bhagavān*, we have tried to convince atheists and sceptics through various reasonings about your existence. Is their heart made of stone? No. Is their heart then made of dust? Or even a minute part of dust? Can our Veda–Purāṇa *jñāna* not irrigate these hearts? Can we not rescue them? We cannot let it be. You are the master of the universe, *Bhagavān*. You can say that they do not recognize you. Please forgive me, *Bhagavān*, if I were to argue that even they have accepted your existence in a way. In fact, I would even go to the extent of saying that they believe in you more than the believers. What proof? *Bhagavān*, your timelessness is the proof. Every time these sceptics shout that they do not believe in *Īśvara*, they are reinforcing your existence. Like Rāvaṇa, Śiśupāla and others who took cudgels against you but were blessed by merely taking your name, please bless these sceptics too. As for me:

अस्माकं तु निसर्ग-सुन्दर! चिराच्चेतो निमग्नं त्वयी-
त्यद्धाऽऽनन्दनिधे! तथापि तरलं नाद्यापि सन्तृप्यते ।
तन्नाथ! त्वरितं विधेहि करुणां येन त्वदेकाग्रतां
याते चेतसि नाप्नुयाम शतशो याम्याः पुनर्यातनाः ॥ – *न्यायकुसुमाञ्जलिः* ५.१९

asmākaṁ tu nisarga-sundara! cirācceto nimagnaṁ tvayī-
tyaddhā 'nandanidhe! tathāpi taralaṁ nādyāpi santṛpyate ।
tannātha! tvaritaṁ vidhehi karuṇāṁ yena tvadekāgratāṁ
yāte cetasi nāpnuyāma śataśo yāmyāḥ punaryātanāḥ ॥
– *Nyāyakusumāñjali* 5.19

---

[3] Udayanācārya was a well-known logician who lived near Darbhanga in today's Bihar in the tenth century. He tried to find a common thread between the two major schools of logic that were the sources of the Navya-Nyāya (New Nyāya) school of "right" reasoning, *Nyāyakusumāñjali* was authored by him where he presented reasonings for the existence of God.

Oh lord, we are immersed in your blessed being. But we are unable to become one with you. Please help us in achieving our goal and save us from the pain of death.

Respectable President,

I am failing in words to express my gratitude to you for hosting this five-day discourse on Veda–Purāṇa on the inspiration of Dr Vasudevasharan Agrawal in this august Rashtrapati Bhawan, a great symbol of our sovereignty.

This great library of *jñāna* and *vijñāna* of Indian culture is free of any sectarian or communal bias. In the last 2,000 to 3,000 years, we have managed to forget this fountainhead of wisdom through meaningless debates. It would be befitting if with your blessing and guidance, these timeless texts could be translated into all languages and promoted at the earliest. This proclamation of Bhagavān Manu should reverberate in all corners of the world.

एतद्देश-प्रसूतस्य सकाशादग्रजन्मनः ।
स्वं स्वं चरित्रं शिक्षेरन् पृथिव्यां सर्वमानवाः ॥ – *मनु०* २.२०

etaddeśa-prasūtasya sakāśādagrajanmanaḥ ।
svaṁ svaṁ caritraṁ śikṣeran pṛthivyāṁ sarvamānavāḥ ॥ – *Manu* 2.20

All men on the earth may learn their respective duties from the brāhmaṇa born in these countries.

It is with great pleasure that I present these verses in gratitude to you for holding the discourse.

इति दुरितविरामः कीर्तिकान्ताभिरामः
सुसुजन-हृदयरामः कोऽप्यभूत् यः स रामः ।
प्रकृतमनुसरामः पापपाशं तरामः
सुकृतभुवि चरामस्तस्य नाम स्मरामः ॥

iti duritavirāmaḥ kīrtikāntābhirāmaḥ
susujana-hṛdayarāmaḥ ko 'pyabhūt yaḥ sa rāmaḥ ।
prakṛtamanusarāmaḥ pāpapāśaṁ tarāmaḥ
sukṛtabhuvi carāmastasya nāma smarāmaḥ ॥

सर्वे भवन्तु सुखिनः सर्वे सन्तु निरामयाः ।
सर्वे भद्राणि पश्यन्तु मा कश्चिद् दुःखभाग्भवेत् ॥

sarve bhavantu sukhinaḥ sarve santu nirāmayāḥ ।
sarve bhadrāṇi paśyantu mā kaścid duḥkhabhāgbhavet ॥

दातारो नोऽभिवर्द्धन्ताम्!
वेदाः सन्ततिरेव च!
बहु देयं च नोऽस्तु!
अतिथींश्च लभेमहि!
श्रद्धा च मा नो व्यगमत्!
याचितारश्च नः सन्तु!
मा च याचिष्म कञ्चन!

dātāro no 'bhivarddhantām!
vedāḥ santatireva ca!
bahu deyaṁ ca no 'stu!
atithīṁśca labhemahi!
śraddhā ca mā no vyagamat!
yācitāraśca naḥ santu!
mā ca yaciṣma kañcana!

Let there be more generous people in our country,
Let more students of Vedaśāstra grow in our country,
Let there be more contribution to our national treasury,
Let us welcome respectable guests,
Let faith remain secure in our national consciousness,
Let others seek our aid, and
Let us not seek any help from anyone.

Thus concludes the fifth discourse.

APPENDIX

List of References Quoted from Vedic Text

अ

अग्निमीले पुरोहितं होतारं रत्नधातवम्। – *ऋक्संहिता* १.१.१ (मू॰ग्र॰ पृ॰ १६)

अग्नि-वायु-रविभ्यस्तु त्रयं ब्रह्म सनातनम्।
दुदोह यज्ञसिद्ध्यर्थं ऋग्-यजुः-सामलक्षणम्॥ – *मनु॰* १.२३ (मू॰ग्र॰ पृ॰ १२)

अग्निर्जागार तमृचः कामयन्ते अग्निर्जागार तमु सामानि यन्ति।
अग्निर्जागार तमयं सोम आह तवाहमस्मि सख्ये न्योकाः॥ – *ऋक्संहिता* ५.८५.१५ (मू॰ग्र॰ पृ॰ ४०, ६४)

अग्निं तं मन्ये यो वसुरस्तं यं यन्ति धेनवः।
अस्तमर्वन्तं आशवोऽस्तं नित्याशो वाजिन इषं स्तोतृभ्य आभर॥ – *वही* ५.६.१ (मू॰ग्र॰ पृ॰ १७)

अचिकित्वाञ्चिकितुषश्चिदत्र कवीन् पृच्छामि विद्मने न विद्वान्।
वि यस्तम्भ षडिमा रजस्यजस्य रूपे किमपि स्विदेकम्॥ – *वही* १.१६४.६ (मू॰ग्र॰ पृ॰ ५५)

अचिन्त्याः खलु ये भावा न तांस्तर्केण योजयेत्।
प्रकृतिभ्यः परं यच्च तदचिन्त्यस्य लक्षणम्॥ – *महाभारत* ६.६.११ (मू॰ग्र॰ पृ॰ १४)

अतद्व्यावृत्या यं चकितमभिधत्ते श्रुतिरपि। – *महिम्नस्तोत्र* २, (मू॰ग्र॰ पृ॰ १४४)

अति विश्वाः परिष्ठाः स्तेन इव व्रजमक्रमुः।
ओषधीः प्राचुच्यवुर्यत्किंच तन्वोरपः॥ – *यजुःसंहिता* १२.८४ (मू॰ग्र॰ पृ॰ १६९)

अतीन्द्रियानसंवेद्यान्पश्यन्त्यार्षेण चक्षुषा।
ये भावान्वचनं तेषां नानुमानेन बाधते॥ – *वाक्यपदीय* १३८ (मू॰ग्र॰ पृ॰ १४)

अत्राह गोरमन्वत नाम त्वष्टुरपीच्यम्।
इत्था चन्द्रमसो गृहे॥ – *ऋक्संहिता* १.८४.१५ (मू॰ग्र॰ पृ॰ १७७)

अथ तत ऊर्ध्वं उदेत्य-नैवोदेता नास्तमेता। एकल एव मध्ये स्थाता। – *छा॰उप॰* ३.११.१ (मू॰ग्र॰ पृ॰ ५१)

अथवा मदस्नेहाद् भवत्यो यन्त्रिताशयाः।
आगताः ह्युपपन्नं वः प्रीयन्ते मयि जन्तवः॥ – *श्रीमद्भागवत* १०.२९.२३ (मू॰ग्र॰ पृ॰ १८५)

अनाभ्यासेन वेदानां, आचारस्य च वर्जनात्।
आलस्यादन्नदोषाच्च मृत्युर्विप्राञ्चिघांसति॥ – *मनु॰* ५.४ (मू॰ग्र॰ पृ॰ ६२)

अन्तःसंज्ञा भवन्त्येते सुखदुःखसमन्विताः। – *वही* १.४९ (मू॰ग्र॰ पृ॰ २३)

अनुग्रहाय भूतानां मानुषं देहमास्थितः।
भजते तादृशीः क्रीडा याः श्रुत्वा तत्परो भवेत् ॥ – *श्रीमद्भागवत* १०.३३.३७ (मू.ग्र. पृ. १९३)

अन्तरं मृत्योरमृतं मृत्यावमृत आहितः। – *शत.ब्राह्मण* १०.५.२.४ (मू.ग्र. पृ. १३१)

अन्तर्गृहगताः काश्चिद्गोप्योऽलब्ध-विनिर्गमाः।
कृष्णं तद्भावना-युक्ता दध्युर्मीलित-लोचनाः ॥ – *श्रीमद्भागवत* १०.२९.९ (मू.ग्र. पृ. १८१)

अन्तश्चरति रोचनास्य प्राणदपानती। व्यख्यन्महिषो दिवम् ॥ – *ऋक्संहिता* १०.१८९.२ (मू.ग्र. पृ. ५)

अनेजदेकं मनसो जवीयो नैनद्देवा अप्नुवन् पूर्वमर्षत्।
तद्धावतोऽन्यानत्येति तिष्ठत्तस्मिन्नपो मातरिश्वा दधाति ॥ – *ईश.उप.* ४ (मू.ग्र. पृ. ५३, ११४)

अपां संघातो, विलयनं च तेजः संयोगात्। – वैशेषिकसूत्र ५.२.८ (मू.ग्र. पृ. ९)

अपाररुं पृथिव्यै देव-यजनाद्वध्यासं व्रजं गच्छ गोष्ठानम्।
वर्षतु ते द्यौर्बधान देव सवितः परमस्यां पृथिव्याम् ॥
अररो ! दिवं मा पप्तः, द्रप्सस्ते द्यां मा स्कन्।
व्रजं गच्छ गोष्ठानं वर्षतु ते द्यौर्बधान देव सवितः ॥ – *यजुःसंहिता* १.२६ (मू.ग्र. पृ. १६९)

अयमग्निर्वैश्वानरः – योऽयमन्तः पुरुषे (शरीरे प्रतिष्ठितः)। येनेदमन्नं पच्यते, यदिदमद्यते। तस्यैष घोषो भवति, यमेतत्कर्णावपिधाय। शृणोति। स यदा उत्क्रमिष्यन् भवति – नैतं घोषं शृणोति।
– *शत.ब्राह्मण* १४.८.१०.१ (मू.ग्र. पृ. १९)

अयं वाव यजुः – योऽयं पवते, एष हि यन्नेवेदं सर्वं जनयति, एतं यन्तमिदमनु प्रजायते, तस्माद्वायुरेव यजुः, अयमेवाकाशो जूः, यदिदमन्तरिक्षम्, एतं ह्याकाशमनु जवते, तदेतत्यजुर्वायुश्चान्तरिक्षञ्च, यच्च जूश्च, तस्माद्यजुः, तदेतत् ऋक्सामयोः प्रतिष्ठितम्, ऋक्सामे वहतः। – *वही* १०.३.५.१-२ (मू.ग्र. पृ. १६)

अर्वाग्बिलश्चमस ऊर्ध्वबुध्नस्तस्मिन् यशो निहितं विश्वरूपम्।
तस्यासत ऋषयः सप्त तीरे वागष्टमी ब्रह्मणा संविदाना ॥ – *वही* १४.५.२.५ (मू.ग्र. पृ. २८)

अविद्यामन्तरे वर्तमानाः स्वयं धीराः पण्डितं मन्यमानाः।
दन्द्रम्यमाणा परियन्ति मूढा अन्धेनैव नीयमाना यथान्धा ॥ – *मुण्ड.उप.* १.२.८ (मू.ग्र. पृ. १०२)

अव्यक्तनिधनान्येव तत्र का परिदेवना ॥ – *गीता* २.२८ (मू.ग्र. पृ. १२५)

अव्यक्ताद्व्यक्तयः सर्वाः प्रभवन्त्यहरागमे।
रात्र्यागमे प्रलीयन्ते तत्रैवाव्यक्तसंज्ञके ॥ – *वही* ८.१८ (मू.ग्र. पृ. १२५)

अव्यक्ता हि गतिर्दुःखं देहवद्भिरवाप्यते। – *वही* १२.५ (मू.ग्र. पृ. २२४)

अश्वत्थे वो निषदनं पर्णे वो वसतिष्कृता।
गोभाज इत् किलासथ यत्सनवथ पूरुषम् ॥ – *ऋक्संहिता* १०.९७.५ (मू.ग्र. पृ. १५६)

असतोऽधि मनोऽसृज्यत। मनः प्रजापतिमसृजत। प्रजापतिः प्रजा असृजत तद्वा इदं मनस्येव परमं प्रतिष्ठितम्। यदिदं किञ्च। तदेतत्-श्वोवस्यसं नाम ब्रह्म। – *तै.ब्राह्मण* २.२.९.१० (मू.ग्र. पृ. १४८)

असद्वा इदमग्र आसीत्। तदाहुः – किं तदसदासीदिति? ऋषयो वाव तदग्रेऽसदासीत्। के ते ऋषयः? प्राणा वा ऋषयः। ते यत् पुरा-अस्मात्-इदमिच्छन्तः श्रमेण तपसा-अरिषन्-तस्मात्-ऋषयः।

– *शत.ब्रा.* ६.१.१.१ (मू.ग्र. पृ. २७)

असन्नेव स भवन्ति असद् ब्रह्मेति वेद चेत्।
अस्ति ब्रह्मेति चेद्वेद सन्तमेनं ततो विदुः॥ – *तै.उप.* २.६.१ (मू.ग्र. पृ. १०५)

अस्यापि देव वपुषो मदनुग्रहस्य
स्वेच्छामयस्य न तु भूतमयस्य कोऽपि।
नेशे महित्ववसितुं मनसाऽऽन्तरेण-
साक्षात्तवैव किमुतात्म-सुखानुभूतेः॥ – *श्रीमद्भागवत* १०.१४.२, (मू.ग्र. पृ. १६३)

अस्माकं तु निसर्ग-सुन्दर! चिराच्चेतो निमग्नं त्वयी-
त्यद्धाऽऽनन्दनिधे! तथापि तरलं नाद्यापि सन्तृप्यते।
तन्नाथ! त्वरितं विधेहि करुणां येन त्वदेकाग्रता
याते चेतसि नाप्नुयाम शतशो याम्याः पुनर्यातनाः॥ – *न्यायकुसुमाञ्जलिः* ५.१९ (मू.ग्र. पृ. १९६)

अहमस्मि प्रथमजा ऋतास्य पूर्वं देवेभ्योऽमृतस्य नाम।
यो मा ददाति स इ देव मा वाः अहमन्नमन्नमदन्तमद्मि॥ – *तै.उप.* ३.१०.६ (मू.ग्र. पृ. ३५)

अहोऽतिधन्या व्रजगोरमण्यःस्तन्यामृतं पीतमतीव ते मुदा।
यासां विभो वत्सतरात्मजात्मनायत्तृप्तयेऽद्यापि न चालमध्वराः॥ – *श्रीमद्भागवत* १०.१४.३१, (मू.ग्र. पृ. १६४)

अहो बकीयं स्तन-कालकूटं जिघांसयाऽपाययदप्यसाध्वी।
लेभे गतिं धात्र्युचितां ततोऽन्यं कं वा दयालुं शरणं व्रजेम॥ – *वही* ३.२.२३, (मू.ग्र. पृ. १६५)

आ

आ कृष्णेन रजसा वर्तमानो निवेशयन्नमृतं मर्त्यञ्च।
हिरण्येन सविता रथेनादेवो याति भुवनानि पश्यन्॥ – *यजुःसंहिता* ३३.४३ (मू.ग्र. पृ. ५०)

आख्यानैश्चाप्युपाख्यानैर्गाथाभिः कल्पशुद्धिभिः॥
पुराणसंहिताञ्चक्रे भगवान् बादरायणः॥ – *वि.पु.* ३.६.१५ (मू.ग्र. पृ. ४२)

आत्मैव देवताः सर्वाः सर्वमात्मन्यवस्थितम्।
आत्मा हि जनयत्येषां कर्मयोगं शरीरिणाम्॥ – *मनु.* १२.११९ (मू.ग्र. पृ. ७७)

आनन्दमित्युपास्व। – *तै.उप.* १.६ (मू.ग्र. पृ. १२६)

आनन्दाद्ध्येव खल्विमानिभूतानि जायन्ते।
आनन्देन जातानि जीवन्ति।
आनन्दं प्रयन्त्यभिसंविशन्ति॥ – *वही* ३.६ (मू.ग्र. पृ. १२६)

आप्तकामो यदुपतिः कृतवान्वै जुगुप्सितम्।
किमभिप्राय एतं नः संशय छिन्धि सुव्रत॥ – *श्रीमद्भागवत* १०.३३.२७-२९ (मू.ग्र. पृ. १९४)

आ ब्रह्मन् ब्राह्मणो ब्रह्मवर्चसी जायताम्!
आ राष्ट्रे राजन्यः शूर इषव्योऽतिव्याधी महारथो जायताम्!
दोग्ध्री धेनुः, वोढानड्वान्, आशुः सप्तिः!
पुरन्धिर्योषा! जिष्णू रथेष्ठा!
सभेयो युवास्य यजमानस्य वीरो जायताम्!
निकामे निकामे नः पर्जन्यो वर्षतु!
फलवत्यो न ओषधयः पच्यन्ताम्!
योगक्षेमो नः कल्पताम्! – *यजुःसंहिता* (मू॰ग्र॰ पृ॰ ९९)

आयङ्गौः पृश्निरक्रमीदसदन् मातरम्पुरः।
पितरञ्च प्रयन्त्स्वः॥ – *ऋग्वेद* १०.१८९.१ (मू॰ग्र॰ पृ॰ ४)

आविर्भूतप्रकाशानां अनुपप्लुतचेतसाम्।
अतीतानागतज्ञानं प्रत्यक्षान्न विशिष्यते ॥ – *वाक्यपदीय* १.३७ (मू॰ग्र॰ पृ॰ १४)

आसामहो चरण-रेणु-जुषामहं स्यां-
वृन्दावने किमपि गुल्म-लतौषधीनाम्।
या दुस्त्यजं स्वजनमार्यपथं च हित्वा-
भेजेर्मुकुन्दपदवीं श्रुतिभिर्विमृग्याम्॥ – *श्रीमद्भागवत* १०.४७.६१ (मू॰ग्र॰ पृ॰ १६५)

इ

इति दुरितविरामः कीर्तिकान्ताभिरामः
सुसुजन-हृदयरामः कोऽप्यभूत् यः स रामः।
प्रकृतमनुसरामः पापपाशं तरामः
सुकृतभुवि चरामस्तस्य नाम स्मरामः॥ – क्षेमेन्द्र, *रामायणमञ्जरी*, उत्तरकाण्ड, १२६३ (मू॰ग्र॰ पृ॰ १९७)

इति गोप्यः प्रगायन्त्यः प्रलपन्त्यश्च चित्रधा।
रुरुदुः सुस्वरं राजन्! कृष्ण-दर्शन-लालसाः ॥ – *श्रीमद्भागवत* १०.३१.१ (मू॰ग्र॰ पृ॰ १९०)

इति विप्रियमाकर्ण्य गोप्यो गोविन्दभाषितम्।
विषण्णा भग्न-संकल्पाश्चिन्तामापुर्दुरत्ययाम् ॥ – *वही* १०.२९.२८ (मू॰ग्र॰ पृ॰ २२९)

इत्युपामन्त्रितो राज्ञा गुणानुकथने हरेः।
हृषीकेशमनुस्मृत्य प्रतिवक्तुं प्रचक्रमे ॥ – *वही* २.४.११ (मू॰ग्र॰ पृ॰ १६०)

इत्येवं श्रुति-नीति-संप्लव-जलैर्भूयोभिराक्षालिते
येषां नास्पदमादधासि हृदये ते शैलसाराशयाः।
किन्तु प्रस्तुत-विप्रतीप-विधयोऽप्युच्चैर्भवच्चिन्तकाः
काले कारुणिक! त्वयैव कृपया ते भावनीया नराः॥ – *न्यायकुसुमाञ्जलिः* ५.१८ (मू॰ग्र॰ पृ॰ १९५)

इन्द्रियेभ्यो परा ह्यर्थाः, अर्थेभ्यश्च परं मनः।
मनस्तु परा बुद्धिः बुद्धेरात्मा महान् परः॥ – *कठ॰उप॰* १.३.१०, (मू॰ग्र॰ पृ॰ ५९)

इन्द्रो-धाता-भगः-पूषा-मित्रोऽथ-वरुणोऽर्यमा।
अंशुर्विवस्वान्-त्वष्टा च, सविता-विष्णुरेव॥ – *ब्रह्माण्ड पु*., पूर्वभाग, २४.३३-३४ (मू.ग्र. पृ. १२)

इयं विसृष्टिर्यत आबभूव यदि वा दवे, यदि वा न।
योऽस्याध्यक्षः परमे व्योमन्त्सो अङ्ग वेद यदि वा न वेद॥ – *ऋक्संहिता* १०.१२९.७ (मू.ग्र. पृ. १६१)

इह चेदवेदीदथ सत्यमस्ति न चेदवेदीन्महती विनष्टिः।
भूतेषु भूतेषु विचित्य धीराः प्रेत्यास्माल्लोकादमृता भवन्ति ॥ – *केन.उप*. २.२.५ (मू.ग्र. पृ. १०३)

उ

उक्तं पुरस्तादेतत्ते चैद्यः सिद्धिं यथा गतः।
द्विषन्नपि हृषीकेशं किमुताधोक्षजप्रियाः॥ – *श्रीमद्भागवत* १०.२९.१३ (मू.ग्र. पृ. १८२)

उत्तमः पुरुषस्त्वन्यः परमात्मेत्युदाहृतः।
यो लोकत्रयमाविश्य बिभर्त्यव्यय ईश्वरः॥ – *गीता* १५.१७ (मू.ग्र. पृ. १३९)

उपद्रष्टानुमन्ता च भर्ता भोक्ता महेश्वरः।
परमात्मेति चाप्युक्तो देहेऽस्मिन् पुरुषः परः॥ – *वही* ९.२२ (मू.ग्र. पृ. १४८)

उभा जिग्यथुर्नपराजयेथे, न पराजिग्ये कतरश्चः नैनोः।
इन्द्रश्च विष्णो यदपस्पृधेथां त्रेधा सहस्रं वि तदैरयेथाम् ॥ – *ऋक्संहिता* ६.६९.८ (मू.ग्र. पृ. १०९)

उपायाः शिक्षमाणानां बालानामुपलालनाः।
असत्ये वर्तमनि स्थित्वा ततः सत्यं समीहते॥ – *वाक्यपदीय* २.२३८ (मू.ग्र. पृ. ७)

ऊ

ऊर्ध्वमूलमधःशाखमश्वत्थं प्राहुरव्ययम्।
छन्दांसि यस्य पर्णानि यस्तं वेद, स वेदवित्॥ – *गीता* १५.१ (मू.ग्र. पृ. १४१)

ऊर्ध्वमूलोऽवाक्शाख एषोऽश्वत्थः सनातनः।
तदेव शुक्रं तद्ब्रह्म-तदेवामृतमुच्यते।
तस्मिँल्लोकाः श्रिताः सर्वे, तदु नात्येति कश्चन।
एतद्वै तत्। – *कठ.उप*. २.३.१ (मू.ग्र. पृ. १४१)

ऊर्ध्वं प्राणमुन्नयति अपानं प्रत्यगस्यति।
मध्ये वामनमासीनं सर्वे देवा उपासते। – *वही* २.२.३ (मू.ग्र. पृ. ४)

ऊर्ध्वं मुष्ट्या अधः कट्या(कोट्योः) स्थानं विद्रुमभूषितम्।
तस्माद्बहुपुटा मल्ली सञ्जाता विविधा मुने!॥ – *वामन पु*. ६.१०२ (मू.ग्र. पृ. १७६)

ऋ

ऋग्भ्यो जातां सर्वशो मूर्तिमाहुःसर्वा गतिर्याजुषीं हैव शश्वत्।
सर्वं तेजः सामरूप्यं ह शश्वत्सर्वं हेदं ब्रह्मणा हैव सृष्टम्॥ – *तै. ब्राह्मण* ३.१२.९.१ (मू.ग्र. पृ. ८)

ऋतमेव परमेष्ठी ऋतं नात्येति किञ्चन। – *वही* १.५.५.१ (मू॰ग्र॰ पृ॰ १५१)

ऋतं च सत्यं चाभीद्धात्तपसोऽध्यजायत।
ततो रात्र्यजायत ततः समुद्रो अर्णवः॥ – *ऋक्संहिता* १०.१९१.१ (मू॰ग्र॰ पृ॰ ३९)

ए

एतदेवात्मभू राजन्! नारदाय विपृच्छते।
वेदगर्भोऽभ्यधात् साक्षात् यदाह हरिरात्मनः॥ – *श्रीमद्भागवत* २.४.२५ (मू॰ग्र॰ पृ॰ १६१)

एतद्देश-प्रसूतस्य सकाशादग्रजन्मनः।
स्वं स्वं चरित्रं शिक्षेरन् पृथिव्यां सर्वमानवाः॥ – *मनु॰* २.२० (मू॰ग्र॰ पृ॰ ३०, १९७)

एतमेके वदन्त्यग्निं मनुमन्ये प्रजापतिम्।
इन्द्रमेके, परे प्राणमपरे ब्रह्म शाश्वतम्॥ – *वही* १२.१२३ (मू॰ग्र॰ पृ॰ ७७)

एवं परिष्वङ्गकराभिमर्शस्निग्धेक्षणोद्दामविलासहासैः।
रेमे रमेशो व्रजसुन्दरीभिर्यथार्भकः स्वप्रतिबिम्ब-विभ्रमः॥ – *श्रीमद्भागवत* १०.३३.१७ (मू॰ग्र॰ पृ॰ १९१)

एवं शशाङ्कांशुविराजिता निशाः स सत्यकामोऽनुरताबलागणः।
सिषेव आत्मन्यवरुद्ध-सौरतः सर्वाः शरत्काव्यकथारसाश्रयाः॥ – *वही* १०.३३.२६ (मू॰ग्र॰ पृ॰ १९१)

एष सर्वाणि भूतानि पञ्चभिर्व्याप्य तिष्ठति।
जन्म-वृद्धि-क्षयैर्नित्यं संसारयति चक्रवत्॥ – *मनु॰* १२.१२४ (मू॰ग्र॰ पृ॰ ७७)

एषा ब्राह्मी स्थितिः पार्थ! नैनं प्राप्य विमुह्यति। – *गीता* २.७२ (मू॰ग्र॰ पृ॰ १३१)

एहि! इमं विद्धि! अयं वै सर्वविद्या। तस्मै हैतमग्निं सावित्रमुवाच। एषा उ वा त्रयी विद्या। तं विदित्वा (भरद्वाजः) अमृतो भूत्वा स्वर्गं लोमियाय आदित्यस्य सायुज्यम्। – *तै॰ ब्राह्मण* ३.१०.११.४-५ (मू॰ग्र॰ पृ॰ ३९)

औ

औत्पत्तिकस्तु शब्दस्यार्थेन सम्बन्धस्तस्य ज्ञानमुपदेशोऽव्यतिरेकश्चार्थेऽनुपलब्धे तत्प्रमाणं बादरायणस्य-अनपेक्षत्वात्। – *पूर्वमीमांसासूत्र* १.१.५ (मू॰ग्र॰ पृ॰ १४)

क

काकैर्निष्कुषितं श्वभिः कवलितं गोमायुभिर्लिण्ठितं
  स्रोतोभिश्चलितं तटाम्बुलुबितं वीचीभिरान्दोलितम्।
दिव्यस्त्री-करचारुचामरमरुत्संवीज्यमानः कदा
  द्रक्ष्येऽहं परमेश्वरि त्रिपथगे भागीरथी स्वं वपुः॥ – *गङ्गाष्टकम्* ४ (मू॰ग्र॰ पृ॰ ६८)

कामस्तदग्रे समवर्तताधि मनसो रेतः प्रथमं यदासीत्।
सतो बन्धुमसति निरविन्दन् हृदि प्रतीष्या कवयो मनीषा॥ – *ऋक्संहिता* १०.१२९.४ (मू॰ग्र॰ पृ॰ १३५)

कामं क्रोधं भयं स्नेहमैक्यं सौहृदमेव च।
नित्यं हरौ विदधतो यान्ति तन्मयतां हि ते॥ – *श्रीमद्भागवत* १०.२९.१५ (मू॰ग्र॰ पृ॰ १८२)

काम्यानां कर्मणां न्यासं संन्यासं कवयो विदुः। – *गीता* १८.२ (मू.ग्र. पृ. १८९)

किरात-हूणान्ध्र-पुलिन्द-पुल्कसा-आभीरकङ्का यवनाः खसादयः।
येऽन्ये च पापा यदपाश्रयाश्रयाःशुध्यन्ति तस्मै प्रभविष्णवे नमः ॥ – *श्रीमद्भागवत* २.४.१८ (मू.ग्र. पृ. १६१)

कृष्णं विदुः परं कान्तं न तु ब्रह्मतया मुने !।
गुण-प्रवाहोपरमस्तासां गुणधियां कथम् ॥ – *वही* १०.२९.१२ (मू.ग्र. पृ. १८२)

कृत्वा मुखान्यव शुचः श्वसनेन शुष्यद्बिम्बाधराणि चरणेन भुवं लिखन्त्यः।
अस्रैरुपात्तमषिभिः कुच-कुङ्कुमानि तस्थुर्मृजस्य उरुदुःखभरा स्म तूष्णीम् ॥ – *वही* १०.२९.२९ (मू.ग्र. पृ. १८६)

किंस्विद्वनं क उ स वृक्ष आस यतो द्यावापृथिवी निष्टतक्षुः।
मनीषिणो मनसा पृच्छतेदु तत् यदध्यतिष्ठद्भुवनानि धारयन् ॥ – *ऋक्संहिता* १०.८१.४ (मू.ग्र. पृ. १४४)

को अद्धा वेद क इह प्र वोचत्।
यो अस्याध्यक्षः परमे व्योमन्त्सोऽङ्ग वेद यदि वा न वेद ॥ – *वही* १०.१२९.६-७ (मू.ग्र. पृ. १५६)

को अद्धा वेद, क इह प्रवोचत्कुत आजाता कुत इयं विसृष्टिः।
अर्वाग्देवा विसर्जनेअस्यनाथा को वेद यत आबभूव ॥ – *वही* १०.१२९.६ (मू.ग्र. पृ. १४६)

को वेत्ति भूमन् भगवन् परात्मन् योगेश्वरोऽन्तर्भवतस्त्रिलोक्याम्।
क्व वा, कथं वा, कति वा, कदेतिविस्तारयन् क्रीडसि योगमायाम् ॥ – *श्रीमद्भागवत* १०.१४.२१ (मू.ग्र. पृ. १८४)

क्रोधं प्रभो! संहर संहरेति-यावद्गिरः खे मरुतां चरन्ति।
तावत्स वह्निर्भवनेत्रजन्मा भस्मावशेषं मदनं चकार ॥ – *कुमारसम्भव* ३.७२ (मू.ग्र. पृ. १७४)

कृष्णसारस्तु चरति मृगो यत्र स्वभावतः।
स ज्ञेयो यज्ञियो देशः म्लेच्छ-देशस्त्वतः परः ॥ – *मनु*. २.२३ (मू.ग्र. पृ. १७१)

किंस्विदासीदधिष्ठानमारम्भणं कतमत्स्वित् कथासीत्।
यतो भूमि जनयन् विश्वकर्मा विद्यामौर्णोन् महिना विश्वचक्षाः ॥ – *ऋक्संहिता* १०.१८.१४ (मू.ग्र. पृ. १४५)

क्वाहं तमो महदहंखचराग्निवार्भू-संवेष्टिताण्ड-घट-सप्त-वितस्ति-कायः।
क्वेदृग्विधा-विगणिताण्ड-पराणुचर्यावाताध्वरोमविवरस्य च ते महित्त्वम् ॥
– *श्रीमद्भागवत* १०.१४.११ (मू.ग्र. पृ. ५६, १६४)

किं तत्सहस्रमिति? – इमे लोकाः, इमे वेदाः, अथो वागितिब्रूयात् (ब्राह्मण)
– *ऐत*. *ब्राह्मण* ६.१४ (मू.ग्र. पृ. ११०)

ग

गतिर्भर्ता-प्रभुः साक्षी-निवासः शरणं सुहृत्।
प्रभवः प्रलयः स्थानं निधानं बीजमव्ययम् ॥ – *गीता* ९.१८ (मू.ग्र. पृ. १४७)

गोत्रं नोऽभिवर्द्धन्ताम्। – *अग्नि*. *पु*. ११७.२५ (मू.ग्र. पृ. १५५)

गोपीनां तत्पतीनाञ्च सर्वेषामेव देहिनाम्।
योऽन्तश्चरति सोऽध्यक्षः क्रीडनेनेह देहभाक् ॥ – *श्रीमद्भागवत* १०.३३.३६ (मू॰ग्र॰ पृ॰ १९३)

च

चन्द्रमा मनसो जातः। – *ऋग्वेद* १०.९०.१३-६१, १९५ (मू॰ग्र॰ पृ॰ ६१, १९५)

ज

जन्माद्यस्य यतोऽन्वयादितरतश्चार्थेष्वभिज्ञः स्वराट्-
तेने ब्रह्म हृदा य आदिकवये मुह्यन्ति यत्सूरयः।
तेजोवारिमृदां यथा विनिमयो यत्र त्रिसर्गोऽमृषा-
धाम्ना स्वेन सदा निरस्तकुहकं सत्यं परं धीमहि ॥ – *श्रीमद्भागवत* १.१.१ (मू॰ग्र॰ पृ॰ १५९)

ज्ञाने प्रयासमुदपास्य नमन्त एव
जीवन्ति सन्मुखरितां भवदीयवार्ताम्।
स्थाने स्थिताः श्रुतिगतां तनुवाङ्मनोभि-
र्ये प्रायशोऽजित जितोऽप्यसि तैस्त्रिलोक्याम्॥ – *वही* १०.१४.३ (मू॰ग्र॰ पृ॰ १६४)

ज्ञानं तेऽहं सविज्ञानमिदं वक्ष्याम्यशेषतः।
यज्ज्ञात्वा नेह भूयोऽन्यज् ज्ञातव्यमवशिष्यते॥ – *गीता* ७.२ (मू॰ग्र॰ पृ॰ १२४)

त

तत्र-अपरा-ऋग्वेदो यजुर्वेदः सामवेदोऽथर्ववेदः, शिक्शाकल्पो-व्याकरणं-निरुक्त-छन्दो ज्यौतिषमिति। अथ परा-यया तदक्षरमधिगम्यते। – *मुण्ड॰ उप॰* १.१.५ (मू॰ग्र॰ पृ॰ १२४)

तत्रोद्वहत्पशुपवंश-शिशित्व-नाट्यं ब्रह्माद्वयं परमनन्तमगाधबोधम्।
वत्सान् सखीनिव पुरा परितो विचिन्वदेक सपाणिकवलं परमेष्ठ्यचष्ट ॥
– *श्रीमद्भागवत्* १०.१३.६१ (मू॰ग्र॰ पृ॰ १९७)

तत्रोपविष्टो भगवान् स ईश्वरो योगेश्वरान्तर्हृदि कल्पितासनः।
चकास गोपीपरिषद्गतोऽर्चितस्त्रैलोक्यलक्ष्म्येकपदं वपुर्दधत्॥ – *वही* १०.३२.१४ (मू॰ग्र॰ पृ॰ १९१)

तदेजति, तन्नेजति, तद्दूरे तद्वन्तिके।
तदन्तरस्य सर्वस्य, तदु सर्वस्य बाह्यतः॥ – *ईश॰उप॰* ५ (मू॰ग्र॰ पृ॰ ५९, १४४)

तदेतत् त्रयं सदेकमयमात्मा। आत्मा उ एकः सन्नेतत् त्रयम्। तदमृतं सत्येन छन्नम्। प्राणो वा अमृतम्। नामरूपे सत्यम्। ताभ्यामयं प्राणश्छन्नः। – *बृ॰उप॰* ३.६.३ (मू॰ग्र॰ पृ॰ ४७)

तदोडुराजः ककुभः करैर्मुखं प्राच्या विलम्पन्नरुणेन शन्तमैः।
स चर्षणीनामुदगाच्छुचो मृजन्प्रियः प्रियाया इव दीर्घदर्शनः ॥ – *श्रीमद्भागवत* १०.२९.२ (मू॰ग्र॰ पृ॰ १७९)

तद्द्वयं च तव पादरजः प्रपन्नाः। – *वही* १०.२९.३७ (मू॰ग्र॰ पृ॰ १८८)

तद्यत् किञ्चार्वाचीनमादित्यात् सर्वं तन्मृत्युनाऽऽप्तम्। – *शत॰ ब्राह्मण* १०.५.१.५ (मू॰ग्र॰ पृ॰ १५३)

तद्यात ! मा चिरं गोष्ठं-शुश्रूषध्वं पतीन्सतीः।
क्रन्दन्ति वत्सा, बालाश्च तान्पाययत दुह्यत ॥ – *श्रीमद्भागवत* १०.२९.२२ (मू.ग्र. पृ. १८४)

तन्नः प्रसीद परमेश्वर ! मा स्म छिन्द्या। – *वही* १०.२९.३३ (मू.ग्र. पृ. १८८)

तपस्विनो दानपरा यशस्विनो मनस्विनो मन्त्रविदः सुमङ्गलाः।
क्षेमं न विन्दन्ति विना यदर्पणं तस्मै सुभद्रश्रवसे नमो नमः ॥ – *वही* २.४.१७ (मू.ग्र. पृ. १६१)

तप्तात्मनां पुरुषभूषण ! देहि दास्यम्। – *वही* १०.२९.३८ (मू.ग्र. पृ. १८८)

तमेव परमात्मानं जरा (लोक) बुद्ध्यापि सङ्गताः
जहुर्गुणमयं देहं सद्यः प्रक्षीण-बन्धनाः ॥ – *वही* १०.२९.११ (मू.ग्र. पृ. १८१)

तरणि-किरणसङ्गादेष पानीयपिण्डो दिनकरदिशि चञ्चच्चन्द्रिकाभिश्चकास्ते।
– उद्धृत, *लीलावती* (भास्कराचार्य), परिभाषा प्रकरण,
मङ्गलाचरण, *बुद्धिविलासिनी टीका* (मू.ग्र. पृ. १७८)

ता दृष्ट्वान्तिकमायाता भगवान् व्रजयोषितः।
अवदत्वदतां श्रेष्ठो वाचः पेशैर्विमोहयन् ॥ – *वही* १०.२९.१७ (मू.ग्र. पृ. १८३)

ताभिः समेताभिरुदारचेष्टितः प्रियेक्षणोत्फुल्लमुखीभिरच्युतः।
उदारहासद्विजकुन्द-दीधितिर्व्यरोचतैणाङ्क इवोडुभिर्वृतः ॥ – *वही* १०.२९.४३ (मू.ग्र. पृ. १८८)

ता वार्यमाणाः पतिभिः पितृभिर्भ्रातृ-बन्धुभिः।
गोविन्दापहृतात्मानी न न्यवर्तन्त मोहिताः ॥ – *वही* १०.२९.८ (मू.ग्र. पृ. १८१)

तासामाविरभूच्छौरिः स्मयमानमुखाम्बुजः।
पीताम्बरधरः स्रग्वी साक्षान्मन्मथमन्मथ ॥ – *वही* १०.३२.२ (मू.ग्र. पृ. १९०)

तासां तत्सौभगमदं वीक्ष्य मानं च केशव।
प्रशमाय प्रसादाय तत्रैवान्तरधीयत ॥ – *वही* १०.२९.४८ (मू.ग्र. पृ. १९०)

त्रयो वा इमे त्रिवृतो लोकाः। अस्ति वै चतुर्थो देवलोक आपः प्रजापतिस्तपोऽतप्यत। स तपस्तप्त्वा प्राणादेव इमं लोकं, अपानादन्तरिक्षलोकं, व्यानादमुं लोकं प्राबृहत्। सोऽग्निमेवास्माल्लोकात्-वायुमन्तरिक्षलोकात्-आदित्यं दिवः असृजत्। सोऽग्नेरेवर्चः, वायोर्यजूंषि, आदित्यात् सामानि-असृजत।
– *शाङ्खायनब्राह्मण* ६.१० (मू.ग्र. पृ. १५)

त्रिपादूर्ध्वं उदैत्पुरुषः, पादोऽस्येहाभवत् पुनः।
ततो विश्वग् व्यक्रामत् साशनानशने अभि ॥ – *यजुःसंहिता* ३२.४ (मू.ग्र. पृ. १३९)

त्रिंशद्धाम विराजति वाक्पतङ्गाय धीयते।
प्रति वस्तोरहद्युभिः ॥ – *ऋग्वेद* १०.१८९.३ (मू.ग्र. पृ. ४)

त्वामग्ने ! यजमाना अनु द्यून् विश्वा वसु दधिरे वार्याणि।
त्वया सह द्रविणमिच्छमाना व्रजं गोमन्तमुशिजो विवव्रुः ॥ – *यजुःसंहिता* १२.२८ (मू.ग्र. पृ. १६९)

द

दातारो नोऽभिवर्द्धन्तां वेदाः सन्ततिरेव च।
बहु देयं च नोऽस्तु, अतिथिंश्च लभेमहि।
श्रद्धा च मा नो व्यगमत्, याचितारश्च नः सन्तु।
मा च याचिष्म कञ्चन॥ – *अग्नि पु*॰ ११७.२५-२७ (मू॰ग्र॰ पृ॰ १९७)

दुष्टः शब्दः स्वरतो वर्णतो वा मिथ्याप्रयुक्तो न तमर्थमाह।
स वाग्वज्रो यजमानं हिनस्ति यथेन्द्रशत्रुः स्वरतोऽपराधात्॥ – *महाभाष्य*, पस्पशाह्निक पृ॰ ३० (मू॰ग्र॰ पृ॰ १२०)

दुहन्त्योऽभिययुः काश्चिद्दोहं हित्वा समुत्सुकाः।
पयोऽधिश्रित्य संयावमनुद्वास्यापरा ययुः॥ – *श्रीमद्भागवत* १०.२९.५ (मू॰ग्र॰ पृ॰ १८०)

दुःशीलो दुर्भगो वृद्धो जडो रोग्यधनोऽपि वा।
पतिः स्त्रीर्भिन हातव्यो लोकेप्सुभिरपातकी॥ – *वही* १०.२९.२५ (मू॰ग्र॰ पृ॰ २१८)

दुःसह-प्रेष्ठ-विरह-तीव्र-तापधुता-शुभाः।
ध्यान-प्राप्ताच्युताश्लेष-निर्वृत्या क्षीण-मङ्गलाः॥ – *वही* १०.२९. १० (मू॰ग्र॰ पृ॰ १८१)

दृष्टं वनं कुसुमितं राकेश-कर-कञ्जितम्।
यमुना-निल-लीलैत्तरुपल्ल-शोभितम्॥ – *वही* १०.२९.२१ (मू॰ग्र॰ पृ॰ १८४)

दृष्ट्वा कुमुद्वन्तमखण्ड मण्डलं रमाननाभं नवकुङ्कुमारुणम्।
वनं च तत्कोमल-गोभिरञ्जितं जगौ कलं वामदृशां मनोहरम्॥ – *वही* १०.२९.३ (मू॰ग्र॰ पृ॰ १८०)

देवाश्च वा असुराश्च उभये प्राजापत्याः पस्पृधिरे। तान्त्सर्द्धमानान् गायत्री अन्तरा तस्थौ। या वै सा गायत्री आसीत्, इयं वै सा पृथिवी। इयं हैव तदन्तरा तस्थौ। अग्निर्वै देवानां दूत आस। सा देवानुपावर्त्तत।
– *शत*॰ *ब्राह्मण* १.४.१.३४-३५ (मू॰ग्र॰ पृ॰ ३०)

द्वाविमौ पुरुषौ लोके क्षरश्चाक्षर एव च।
क्षरः सर्वाणि भूतानि कूटस्थोऽक्षर उच्यते॥ – *गीता* १५.१६ (मू॰ग्र॰ पृ॰ १३९)

द्वा सुपर्णा सयुजा सखाया समानं वृक्षं परिषस्वजाते।
तयोरन्यः पिप्पलं स्वाद्वत्त्यनश्नन्योऽभिचाकशीति॥ – *ऋक्संहिता* १.१६४.२० (मू॰ग्र॰ पृ॰ २१, ९१)

द्विधा कृत्वात्मनो देहमर्द्धेन पुरुषोऽभवत्।
अर्द्धेन नारी, तस्यां स विराजमसृजत् प्रभुः॥ – *मनु*॰ १.३२ (मू॰ग्र॰ पृ॰ ९४)

द्वे विद्ये वेदितव्ये इति ह स्म ब्रह्मविदो वदन्ति-परा चैव अपरा च। – *मुण्ड*॰ *उप*॰ १.१.४ (मू॰ग्र॰ पृ॰ १२४)

द्वे विद्ये वेदितव्ये शब्दब्रह्म परं च यत्।
शब्दब्रह्मणि निष्णातः परं ब्रह्माधिगच्छति॥ – *ब्रह्मबिन्दूपनिषद्* १७ (मू॰ग्र॰ पृ॰ ११६)

द्रुमाः सपुष्पाः सलिलं सपद्मंस्त्रियः सकामाः पवनः सौगन्धिः।
सुखा प्रदोषा दिवसाश्च रम्याः सर्वं प्रिये ! चारुतरं वसन्ते ॥ – *ऋतुसंहार* ६.२ (मू॰ग्र॰ पृ॰ १७७)

ध

धर्मः प्रोज्झित-कैतवोऽत्र परमो निर्मत्सराणां सतां-
वेद्यं वास्तवमत्र वस्तु शिवदं तापत्रयोन्मूलनम्।
श्रीमद्भागवते महामुनिकृते किं वा परैरीश्वरः-
सद्यो हृद्यवरुध्यतेऽत्र कृतिभिः शुश्रूषुभिस्तत्क्षणात् ॥ – *श्रीमद्भागवत* १.१.२ (मू.ग्र. पृ. १५९)

ध्यानेन याम पदयोः पदवीं सखे ते। – *वही* १०.२९.३५ (मू.ग्र. पृ. १८८)

न

न खलु गोपिकानन्दनो भवान् अखिल-देहिनामन्तरात्मदृक्।
विखनसाऽर्थितो विश्वगुप्तये-सख उदेयिवान्सात्वतां कुले ॥ – *वही* १०.३१.४ (मू.ग्र. पृ. १९१)

न चैवं विस्मयः कार्यो भवता भगवत्यजे।
योगेश्वरेश्वरे कृष्णे यत एतद्विमुच्यते ॥ – *वही* १०.२९.१६ (मू.ग्र. पृ. १८२)

न देहो न च जीवात्मा नेन्द्रियाणि परन्तप।
मन एव मनुष्याणां कारणं बन्ध-मोक्षयोः ॥ – *देवीभागवत पु*. १.१८.३९ (मू.ग्र. पृ. १०३)

न प्राणेन, नापानेन मर्त्यो जीवति कश्चन।
इतरेण तु जीवन्ति यस्मिन्नेतावुपाश्रितौ ॥ – *कठ उप*. २.२.५ (मू.ग्र. पृ. ४)

नमो नमस्तेऽस्त्वृषभाय सात्वतां विदूर-काष्ठायमुहुः कुयोगिनाम्।
निरस्त-साम्यातिशयेन राधसास्वधामनि ब्रह्मणि रंस्यते नमः ॥ – *श्रीमद्भागवत* २.४.१४ (मू.ग्र. पृ. १६१)

नमः परस्मै पुरुषाय भूयसे-सदुद्भव-स्थान-निरोध-लीलया।
गृहीत-शक्ति-त्रितयाय देहिनामन्तर्भवायानुपलक्ष्यवर्त्मने ॥ – *वही* २.४.१२ (मू.ग्र. पृ. १६०)

नमः तस्मै भगवते व्यासायामित-तेजसे।
पशुर्ज्ञानमयं सौम्या यन्मुखाम्बुरुहासवम् ॥ – *श्रीमद्भागवत* २.४.२४ (मू.ग्र. पृ. १६१)

न विश्व-मूर्तेरवधार्यते वपुः। – *कुमारसम्भव* ५.७८ (मू.ग्र. पृ. १४४)

न वै तत्र न निम्लोचनोदियाय कदाचन।
देवास्तेनाहं सत्येन मा विराधिषिं ब्रह्मणा। – *छा.उप*. ३.११.२ (मू.ग्र. पृ. ५१)

न सती सा नासती सा नोभयात्मा विरोधतः।
काचिद्विलक्षणा माया वस्तुभूता सनातनी ॥ – *देवीभागवत पु*. ७.३२.४ (मू.ग्र. पृ. १३४)

न सोऽस्ति प्रत्ययो लोके यः शब्दानुगमादृते।
अनुविद्धमिव ज्ञानं सर्वं शब्देन भाषते ॥ – *वाक्यपदीय*, ब्रह्मकाण्ड १ (मू.ग्र. पृ. ११८)

न ह वा अस्मा उदेति, न निम्लोचति।
सकृद्दिवा हैवास्मै भवति। – *छा.उप*. ३.११.३ (मू.ग्र. पृ. ५१)

नाकस्थविष्णोः परितस्तु वेदद्दगव्यासार्धजे सञ्चरति ध्रुवं ध्रुवः।
वृत्ते ततः क्वापि पुरा युगे स हि प्राङ्केरुखस्वस्तिकगोऽभिजित्यभृत् ॥ – *इन्द्रविजय* १.३१, पृ. ९ (मू. ग्र. पृ. ५३)

नायमात्मा प्रवचनेन लभ्यो न मेधया न बहुना श्रुतेन।
यमेवैष वृणुते तेन लभ्यस्तस्यैष आत्मा विवृणुते तनूं स्वाम् ॥ – *कठ. उप.* १.२.२३ (मू. ग्र. पृ. ८५)

नासत्यान्तक-वह्नि-धातृ-शशभृद्-रुद्रादितिज्योरगा-
ऋक्षेशाः पितरोऽर्य्यमा भगरवी त्वष्टा समीरः क्रमात्।
शक्राग्नी त्वथ इन्द्रमित्र-निऋति-क्षीराणि विश्वेविधि-
गोविन्दो वसुतोयपायचरणाहिर्बुध्न्यपूषाभिधाः ॥ – *मुहूर्तचिन्तामणि*, नक्षत्रप्रकरण १ (मू. ग्र. पृ. १७८)

नासूयन् खलु कृष्णाय मोहितास्तस्य मायया।
मन्यमाना स्वपार्श्वस्थान् स्वान् स्वान् दारान् व्रजौकसः ॥
– *श्रीमद्भागवत* १०.३३.३८ (मू. ग्र. पृ. १९४)

निगम-कल्पतरोर्गलितं फलं शुकमुखादमृतद्रवसंयुतम्।
पिबत भागवतं रसमालयं मुहुरहो रसिका भुवि भावुकाः ॥ – *वही* १.१.३ (मू. ग्र. पृ. १५९)

नित्यं छेदस्तृणानां, भुवि नखलिखनं पादयोरल्पपूजा
दन्तानामल्पशौचं, वसनमलिनता ग्रासहासातिरेकः।
द्वे सन्ध्ये चापि निद्रा, विवसनशयनं, रूक्षता मूर्द्धजानाम्
स्वाङ्गे पीठे च वाद्यं हरति धनपतेः केशवस्यापि लक्ष्मीः ॥ – *अष्टरत्नम्* ३ (मू. ग्र. पृ. ८८)

नियतविषयत्वमिन्द्रियत्वम्। – *न्यायभाष्य* १.१.१२ (मू. ग्र. पृ. १४८)

निवेशयन्नमृतं मर्त्यञ्च। – *ऋग्वेद* १.३५.२ (मू. ग्र. पृ. १५३)

निशम्य गीतं तदनङ्ग-वर्धनं व्रजस्त्रियः कृष्ण-गृहीत-मानसाः।
आजग्मुरन्योऽन्यमलक्षितोद्यमाः स यत्र कान्तो जवलोल-कुण्डलाः ॥
– *श्रीमद्भागवत* १०.२९.४ (मू. ग्र. पृ. १८०)

नूनं भगवतो ब्रह्मन् हरेरद्भुत-कर्मणः।
दुर्विभाव्यमिवाभाति कविभिश्चापि चेष्टितम् ॥ – *वही* २.४.८ (मू. ग्र. पृ. १६०)

नृणां निःश्रेयसार्थाय व्यक्तिर्भगवतो नृप !।
अव्ययस्याप्रमेयस्य निर्गुणस्य गुणात्मनः ॥ – *वही* १०.२९.१४ (मू. ग्र. पृ. १८२)

नैवास्तमनमर्कस्य नोदयः सर्वदा सतः।
उदयास्तमनाख्यं हि दर्शनादर्शनं रवेः ॥ – *विष्णु पु.* २.८.१५ (मू. ग्र. पृ. ५१)

नौमीड्य तेऽभ्रवपुषे तदिदम्बरायगुञ्जावतंस-परिपिच्छ-लसन्मुखाय।
वन्यस्रजे कवल-वेत्र-विषाण-वेणु-लक्ष्मश्रिये मृदुपदे पशुपाङ्गजाय ॥
– *श्रीमद्भागवत* १०.१४.१ (मू. ग्र. पृ. १६३, १७०)

प

पञ्चस्रोतोऽम्बुं पञ्चयोन्युग्रवक्रां-पञ्चप्राणोर्मि पञ्चबुद्ध्यादिमूलाम्।
पञ्चावर्तां पञ्चदुःखौघवेगां पञ्चाषद्भेदां पञ्चपर्वामधीमः॥ – *श्वेताश्वतरोपनिषत्* १.५ (मू.ग्र. पृ. ७१)

पञ्चेन्द्रियाणि मनःषष्ठानि मे हृदि। – *अथर्ववेद* १९.९.५ (मू.ग्र. पृ. १४९)

पराञ्चि खानि व्यतृणत्-स्वयम्भू-स्तष्मात् पराङ् पश्यति नान्तरात्मन्।
कश्चिद्धीरः प्रत्यगात्मानमैक्ष-दावृत्य चक्षुरमृतत्त्वमिच्छन्॥ – *कठ.उप.* २.१.१ (मू.ग्र. पृ. ७९)

परिवेषयन्त्यस्तद्धित्वा पाययन्त्यः शिशून्पयः।
शूश्रूषन्त्यः पतीन्काश्चिदश्नन्त्योऽपास्य भोजनम्॥ – *श्रीमद्भागवत* १०.२९.६ (मू.ग्र. पृ. १८१)

पवित्रं विततं ब्रह्मणस्पते प्रभुर्गात्राणि पर्येषि विश्वतः।
अतप्ततनूर्न तदामो अश्नुते शृतास इद्वहन्तस्तत्समाशत्॥ – *ऋक्संहिता* ९.८३.१ (मू.ग्र. पृ. ६७)

पूर्णमदः पूर्णमिदं, पूर्णात् पूर्णमुदच्यते।
पूर्णस्य पूर्णमादाय पूर्णमेवावशिष्यते॥ – *ईश.उप.*, शान्तिपाठ (मू.ग्र. पृ. ४६)

पृथिवी देव-यजन्योषध्यास्ते मूलं मा हिंसिषम्।
व्रजं गच्छ गोष्ठानं वर्षतु ते द्यौः। – *यजुःसंहिता* १.२५ (मू.ग्र. पृ. १६९)

प्रचोदिता येन पुरा सरस्वती-वितन्वताऽजस्य सतीं स्मृतिं हृदि।
स्वलक्षणा प्रादुरभूत् किलास्यतः स मे ऋषीणामृषयः प्रसीदताम्॥ – *श्रीमद्भागवत* २.४.२२ (मू.ग्र. पृ. १६१)

प्रजापतिश्चरति गर्भे अन्तरजायमानो बहुधा विजायते।
तस्य योनिं परिपश्यन्ति धीरास्तस्मिन् तस्थुर्भुवनानि विश्वा॥ – *यजुःसंहिता* ३१.१९ (मू.ग्र. पृ. ४४)

प्रथमं सर्वशास्त्राणां पुराणं ब्रह्मणा स्मृतम्।
अनन्तरञ्च वक्त्रेभ्यो वेदास्तस्य विनिर्गताः॥ – *मत्स्य पु.* ५३.३ (मू.ग्र. पृ. ४१)

प्रशासितारं सर्वेषाम् अणीयांसमणोरपि।
रुक्मभावं स्वप्नधीगम्यं तं विद्यात् पुरुषं परम्॥ – *मनु.* १२.१२२ (मू.ग्र. पृ. ७७)

प्रह्लाद-नारद-पराशर-पुण्डरीक-व्यासाऽम्बरीष-शुक-शौनक-भीष्म-दाल्भ्यान्।
रुक्माऽङ्गदाऽर्जुन-वसिष्ठ-विभीषणादीन् पुण्यानिमान् परम-भागवतान्नतोऽस्मि॥
– *पाण्डवगीता* १ (मू.ग्र. पृ. १६६)

प्राप्ता विसृज्य वसतीस्त्वदुपासनाशाः। – *श्रीमद्भागवत* १०.२९.३८ (मू.ग्र. पृ. १८८)

प्रायः श्रुतप्रिय-तमोदयकर्णपूरैर्यस्मिन् निमग्न-मनसस्तमथाक्षिरन्ध्रैः।
अन्तः प्रवेश्य सुचिरं परिरभ्य तापं-प्राज्ञं यथाभिमतयो विजहुर्नरेन्द्र!॥
– *श्रीमद्भागवत* १०.२३.२३ (मू.ग्र. पृ. १६४)

प्रेष्ठो भवांस्तनुभृतां किल बन्धुरात्मा। – *वही* १०.२९.३२ (मू.ग्र. पृ. १८८)

प्रेष्ठं प्रियेतरमिव प्रतिभाषमाणं कृष्णं तदर्थ-विनिवर्तित-सर्वकामाः।
नेत्रे विमृज्य रुदितोपहते स्म किञ्चित् संरम्भ-गद्गद्गिरोऽब्रुवतानुरक्ताः ॥ – *वही* १०.२९.३० (मू.ग्र. पृ. १८७)

ब

बहूनां जन्मनामन्ते ज्ञानवान्मां प्रपद्यते।
वांसुदेवः सर्वमिति स महात्मा सुदुर्लभः ॥ – *गीता* ७.१९ (मू.ग्र. पृ. १७४)

ब्रह्मरात्र उपावृत्ते वासुदेवानुमोदिताः।
अनिच्छन्त्यो ययुर्गोप्यः स्वगृहान् भगवत्प्रियाः ॥ – *श्रीमद्भागवत* १०.३३.३९ (मू.ग्र. पृ. १९४)

ब्रह्मवनं ब्रह्म स वृक्ष असीत्, यतो द्यावापृथिवी निष्ठतक्षुः।
मनीषिणो मनसा वि ब्रवीम् वो ब्रह्माध्यतिष्ठद् भुवनानि धारयन् ॥ – *तै. ब्राह्मण* २.८.७.९ (मू.ग्र. पृ. १४५)

ब्रह्मादि-जय-संरूढ-दर्प-कन्दर्प-दर्पहा।
जयति श्रीपतिर्गोपीरासमण्डल-मण्डनः ॥३५॥ – *श्रीमद्भागवत* १०.२९ श्रीधरीटीका (मू.ग्र. पृ. १६५)

बाहु-प्रसार-परिरम्भ-कराल-कोरु-नीवीस्तनालभन-नर्म-नखाग्रपातैः।
क्ष्वेल्याऽवलोक-हसितैर्व्रजसुन्दरीणां उत्तम्भयन् रतिपतिं रमयाञ्चकार ॥ – *वही* १०.२९.४६ (मू.ग्र. पृ. १८९)

बीभत्सूनां सयुजं हंसमाहुरपां यिव्यानां सख्ये चरन्तम्।
अनुष्टुभमनु चर्चूर्य्यमाणमिन्द्रं नि चिक्युः कवयो मनीषा ॥ – *ऋक्संहिता* १०.१२४.९ (मू.ग्र. पृ. ११९)

भ

भगवानपि ताः रात्रीः शरदोत्फुल्ल-मल्लिकाः।
वीक्ष्य रन्तुं मनश्चक्रे योगमायामुपाश्रिताः ॥ – *श्रीमद्भागवत* १०.२९.१ (मू.ग्र. पृ. १७६)

भरद्वाजो ह वै त्रिभिरायुभिर्ब्रह्मचर्यमुवास। तं ह जीर्णिं, स्थविरं, शयानं इन्द्र उपव्रज्य उवाच। भरद्वाज! यत्ते चतुर्थमायुर्दद्यां, किमनेन कुर्या इति? ब्रह्मचर्यमेवैनेन चरेयमिति होवाच। तं ह त्रीन् गिरिरूपानविद्यातानिव दर्शयाञ्चकार। तेषां हैकैकस्मान् सुष्टिमाददे। स होवाच – भरद्वाजेत्यमन्य वेदा वा एते। अनन्ता वै वेदाः। एतद्वा एतैस्त्रिभरायुभिरन्ववोचथाः। अथ त इतरदनूक्तमेव। – *तै. ब्राह्मण* ३.१०.११.३ (मू.ग्र. पृ. ३९)

भर्तुः शुश्रूषणं स्त्रीणां परो धर्मो ह्यमायया।
तद्बन्धूनां च कल्याण्यः प्रजानां चानुपोषणम् ॥ – *श्रीमद्भागवत* १०.२९.२४ (मू.ग्र. पृ. १८५)

भूतानां प्राणिनः श्रेष्ठाः, प्राणिनां बुद्धिजीविनः।
बुद्धिमत्सु नराः श्रेष्ठाः नरेषु ब्राह्मणाः स्मृताः ॥ – *मनु.* १.९६ (मू.ग्र. पृ. ८२-८३)

भूतैर्महद्भिर्य इमाः पुरो विभुर्निर्माय शेते यदमूषु पूरुषः।
भुङ्क्ते गुणान् षोडश षोडशात्मकः सोऽलङ्कृषीष्ट भवान् वचांसि मे ॥ – *श्रीमद्भागवत* २.४.२३ (मू.ग्र. पृ. १६१)

भूयो नमः सद्वृजिनच्छिदेऽसतामसंभवायाखिलसत्त्व-मूर्तये।
पुंसां पुनः पारमहंस्य आश्रमे-व्यवस्थितानामनुमृग्यदाशुषे ॥ – *वही* २.४.१३ (मू.ग्र. पृ. १६१)

म

मत्तः परतरं नान्यत् किञ्चिदस्ति धनञ्जय। – *गीता* ७.७ (मू.ग्र. पृ. १६२)

मन्मना भव मद्भक्तो मद्याजी मां नमस्कुरु।
मामेवैष्यसि युक्त्वैवमात्मानं मत्परायणः ॥ – *वही* ९.३४ (मू.ग्र. पृ. १५०)

मम योनिर्महद् ब्रह्म तस्मिन् गर्भं दधाम्यहम्।
सम्भवः सर्वभूतानां ततो भवति भारत॥ – *वही* ३.३ (मू.ग्र. पृ. १५०, १५१)

मल्लिका-मुकुले चण्डि ! भाति गुञ्जन् मधुव्रतः।
प्रयाणे पञ्चबाणस्य शङ्खमापूरयन्निव ॥
– *काव्यादर्शः* (मू.ग्र. पृ. २०७)

महतः परमव्यक्तः, अव्ययक्तात् पुरुषः परः।
पुरुषान्न परं किञ्चित्, सा काष्ठा सा परा गतिः॥ – *कठ.उप.* १.३. ११ (मू.ग्र. पृ. ५९, १६२)

मातरः पितरः पुत्रा भ्रातरः पतयश्च वः।
विचिन्वन्ति ह्यपश्यन्तो मा कृध्वं बन्धु-साध्वसम्॥ – *श्रीमद्भागवत* १०.२९.२० (मू.ग्र. पृ. १८४)

माता रुद्राणां दुहिता वसूनां स्वसादित्यानां अमृतस्य नाभिः।
प्राणु वोचं चिकितुषे जनाय मागामनागामदितिं बधिष्ट॥ – *ऋक्संहिता* ८.१०.१५ (मू.ग्र. पृ. ६६)

मृगो न भीमः कुचरो गरिष्ठाः। – *ऋग्वेद* १.१५४.२ (मू.ग्र. पृ. १७१)

मेघैर्मेदुरमम्बरं वनभुवः श्यामास्तमालद्रुमै-
र्नक्तं भीरुरयं त्वमेव तदिमं राधे ! गृहं प्रापय।
इत्थं नन्द-निदेशतश्चलितयोः प्रत्यध्व-कुञ्ज-द्रुमं
राधामाधवयोर्जयन्ति यमुनाकूले रहः केलयः ॥ – *गीतगोविन्द* १.१ (मू.ग्र. पृ. १७३)

मैवं विभोऽर्हति भवान् गदितुं नृशंसं !
सन्त्यज्य सर्वविषयांस्तव पादमूलम्।
भक्ता, भजस्व ! दुरवग्रह मा त्यजास्मान् !
देवो यथादिपुरुषो भजते मुमुक्षून् ॥ – *श्रीमद्भागवत* १०.२९.३१ (मू.ग्र. पृ. २२२)

य

य इमा विश्वा भुवनानि जुह्वदृषिर्होता न्यसीदत् पिता नः।
स आशिषा द्रविणमिच्छमानः प्रथमच्छदवराँ आ विवेश॥ – *ऋक्संहिता* १०.८१.१ (मू.ग्र. पृ. ५७)

यज्ञ इन्द्रमवर्द्धयत्, यद् भूमिं व्यवर्तयत्।
चक्राण ओपशं दिवि॥ – *वही* ८.१४.५ (मू.ग्र. पृ. ५२)

यत्कीर्तनं यत्स्मरणं यदीक्षणं यद्वन्दनं यच्छ्रवणं यदर्हणम्।
लोकस्य सद्यो विधुनोति कल्मषं तस्मै सुभद्रश्रवसे नमो नमः॥ – *श्रीमद्भागवत* २.४.१५ (मू.ग्र. पृ. १६१)

यत् पाद-पङ्कज-पराग-निषेवतृप्ता-योग-प्रभाव-विधुताखिल-कर्मबन्धाः।
स्वैरं चरन्ति मुनयोऽपि न नह्यमानास्तस्येच्छयात्तवपुषः कुत एव बन्धः ॥ – *वही* १०.३३.३५ (मू.ग्र. पृ. १९३)

यत् प्रज्ञानमुत चेतो धृतिश्च यज्ज्योतिरन्तरमृतं प्रजासु।
यस्मान्न ऋते किञ्च न कर्म क्रियते तन्मे मनः शिवसंकल्पमस्तु ॥ – *यजुःसंहिता* ३४.३ (मू.ग्र. पृ. ६१, १४९)

यतो वाचो निवर्तन्ते अप्राप्य मनसा सह। – *तै.उप.* २.४.१ (मू.ग्र. पृ. १४४)

यथा गुणांस्तु प्रकृतेर्युगपत् क्रमशोऽपि वा।
बिभर्ति भूरिशस्त्वेकः कुर्वन् कर्माणि जन्मभिः ॥ – *श्रीमद्भागवत* २.४.९ (मू.ग्र. पृ. १६०)

यथा वायुं समाश्रित्य वर्तन्ते सर्व जन्तवः।
तथा गृहस्वमाश्रित्य वर्तन्ते सर्व आश्रमाः ॥ – *मनु.* ३.७७ (मू.ग्र. पृ. ९७)

यदक्षरं पञ्चविधं समेति, युजो युक्ता अभि यत् संवहन्ति।
सत्यस्य सत्यमनु यत्र युज्यते तत्र देवाः सर्वं एकं भवन्ति ॥ – *ऐत.आरण्यक* २.३.८.२० (मू.ग्र. पृ. ११३)

यदङ्घ्र्यनुध्यानसमाधिधौतयाधियाऽनुपश्यन्ति हि तत्त्वमात्मनः।
वदन्ति चैतत् कवयो यथारुचं समे मुकुन्दो भगवान् प्रसीदताम् ॥ – *श्रीमद्भागवत* २.४.२१ (मू.ग्र. पृ. १६१)

यदस्ति किञ्चित्तदिदं प्रतीमो-विचालि-शश्वत्स्थमनाद्यनन्तम्।
प्रतिक्षणान्यान्यविकारस्रष्टु-प्रवाहि-तद्यद्द्विविरुद्धभावम् ॥
– *संशयतदुच्छेदवाद*, प्रथमखण्ड पृ. १, का. १ (मू.ग्र. पृ. १२८)

यदा स देवो जागर्त्ति तदेदं चेष्टते जगत्।
यदा स्वपिति शान्तात्मा तदा सर्वं निमीलति ॥ – *मनु.* १.५२ (मू.ग्र. पृ. १२५)

यदि हरिस्मरणे सरसं मनो यदि विलासकलासु कुतूहलम्।
मधुर-कोमल-कान्त-पदावलीं शृणु तदा जयदेव-सरस्वतीम् ॥ – *गीतगोविन्द* १.४ (मू.ग्र. पृ. १७३)

यदेतन्मण्डलं तपति-तन्महदुक्थं, ता ऋचः, स ऋचां लोकः, अथ यदेतदर्चिर्दीप्यते-तन्महाव्रतं, तानि सामानि, स साम्नां लोकः, अथ य एष एतस्मिन्मण्डले पुरुषः-सोऽग्निः, तानि यजूंषि, स यजुषां लोकः। सैषा त्रय्येव विद्या तपति, तद्धैतदप्यविद्वाँस आहुः – त्रयो वा एषा विद्या तपति इति। – *शत. ब्राह्मण* १०.५.२.१-२ (मू.ग्र. पृ. १३)

यदेवेह तदमुत्र यदमुत्र तदन्विह।
मृत्योः स मृत्युमाप्नोति य इह नानेव पश्यति ॥ – *कठ उप.* २.१.१० (मू.ग्र. पृ. १२७)

यस्मात् त्रयोऽप्याश्रमिणो ज्ञानेनान्नेन चान्वहम्।
गृहस्थेनैव वर्द्धन्ते तस्माज्ज्येष्ठाश्रयो गृही ॥ – *मनु.* ३.७८ (मू.ग्र. पृ. ९७)

यस्मात्परं नापरमस्ति किञ्चित्, यस्मान्नाणीयो न ज्यायोऽस्ति कश्चित्।
वृक्ष इव स्तब्धो दिवि त्यिष्ठत्येक-स्तेनेदं पूर्णं पुरुषेण सर्वम् ॥ – *श्वेत उप.* ३.९ (मू.ग्र. पृ. १३८)

यस्मान्न जातः परो अन्यो अस्तिय आविवेश भुवनानि विश्व।
प्रजापतिः प्रजया संरराणस्त्रीणि ज्योतींषि सचते स षोडशी ॥ – *यजुःसंहिता* ८.३६ (मू.ग्र. पृ. १३८, १६३)

यस्तद्वेद, स वेद सर्वं सर्वा दिशो बलिस्मै हरन्ति। – *छा.उप.* २.२१.४ (मू.ग्र. पृ. ५९)

या ते धामानि परमाणि, यावमा, या मध्यमा विश्वकर्मन्नुतेमा।
शिक्षा सखिभ्यो हविषि स्वधामः स्वयं यजस्व तन्वं वृधानः॥ – *ऋक्संहिता* १०.८१.५ (मू.ग्र. पृ. ५७)

या ते धामान्युश्मसि गमध्यै यत्र गावो भूरिशृङ्गा अयासः।
अत्राह तदुरुगायस्व विष्णोः परमं पदमवभारि भूरि॥ – *यजुःसंहिता* ६.३ (मू.ग्र. पृ. १६८)

यानि पञ्चधा त्रीणि, त्रीणि तेभ्यो न ज्याय परमन्यदस्ति। – *छा.उप.* २.२१.३ (मू.ग्र. पृ. ५९)

या राका शशिशोभना, गतघना, सा यामिनी यामिनी।
या सौन्दर्य-गुणान्विता पतिरता, सा कामिनी कामिनी॥
या गोविन्द-रस-प्रमोद-मधुरा सा माधुरी माधुरी।
या लोकद्वयसाधिनी तनुभृतां सा चातुरी चातुरी॥
– *गुणरत्नम्* १० (भवभूति विरचित *गुनरत्नमहाकाव्य*) (मू.ग्र. पृ. १५७)

यां यां शक्तिमुपाश्रित्य पुरुशक्तिः परः पुमान्।
आत्मानं क्रीडयन् क्रीडन् करोति विकरोति च॥ – *श्रीमद्भागवत* २.४.७ (मू.ग्र. पृ. १६०)

यो यज्ञो दिवि परमेष्ठिगोसवाख्यो विज्ञानं समुपदिदेश गीतया यः।
आनन्दं जनयतु विश्वतो ममायं-गोविन्दः स हि मयि सन्निधानमेतु॥
– *महर्षिकुलवैभव* (पूर्वार्द्ध), मङ्गलाचरण (मू.ग्र. पृ. १६५)

यो ब्रह्माणं विदधाति पूर्वं। – *श्वेत.उप.* ६.१८ (मू.ग्र. पृ. १७०)

यं प्रव्रजन्तमनुपेतमपेत्यकृत्यं द्वैपायनो विरहकातर आजुहाव।
पुत्रेति तन्मयतया तरवोऽभिनेदुस्तं सर्वभूतहृदयं मुनिमानतोऽस्मि॥ – *श्रीमद्भागवत* १.२.२ (मू.ग्र. पृ. १६०)

यः स्वानुभावमखिलश्रुतिसारमेकमध्यात्मदीपमतितितीर्षतां तमोऽन्धम्।
संसारिणां करुणयाऽह पुराणगुह्यंतं व्यास-सूनुमुपयामि गुरुं मुनीनाम्॥ – *वही* १.२.३ (मू.ग्र. पृ. १६०)

र

रजन्येषा घोररूपा घोरसत्त्व-निषेविता।
प्रतियात व्रजं नेह स्थेयं स्त्रीभिः सुमध्यमाः॥ – *वही* १०.२९.१९ (मू.ग्र. पृ. १८४)

रे वृक्षाः पर्वतस्था गिरि-गहन-लता वायुना वीज्यमानाः
रामोऽहं व्याकुलात्मा दशरथतनयः शोकशुक्रेण दग्धः।
बिम्बोष्ठी चारुनेत्री सुविपुल-जघना बद्धनागेन्द्रकाञ्ची-
हा! सीता केन नीता मम हृदयगता को भवान् केन दृष्टा॥ – *हनुमन्नाटकम्* ५.१० (मू.ग्र. पृ. १७५)

ल

लिम्पन्त्यः प्रमृजन्त्योऽन्या अञ्जन्त्यः काश्च लोचने।
व्यत्यस्त-वस्त्राभरणाः काश्चित्कृष्णान्तिकं ययुः॥ – *श्रीमद्भागवत* १०.२९.७ (मू.ग्र. पृ. १८१)

लोकवत्तु लीला-कैवल्यम्। – *ब्रह्मसूत्र* २.१.३३ (मू.ग्र. पृ. १४४)

व

वागर्थाविव सम्पृक्तौ वागर्थप्रतिपत्तये।
जगतः पितरौ वन्दे पार्वती-परमेश्वरौ॥ – *रघुवंश* १.१ (मू.ग्र. पृ. ११८)

विक्रिडीतं व्रजवधूभिरिदं च विष्णोः श्रद्धान्वितोऽनुशृणुयादथ वर्णयेद्यः।
भक्तिं परां भगवति प्रतिलभ्य कामंहृद्रोगमाश्वपहिनोत्यचिरेण धीरः ॥
– *श्रीमद्भागवत* १०.३३.४० (मू.ग्र. पृ. ११५)

विचक्षणा यच्चरणोपसादनात् सङ्गं व्युदस्योभयतोऽन्तरात्मनः।
विन्दन्ति हि ब्रह्मगतिं गतक्लमास्तस्मै सुभद्रश्रवसे नमो नमः ॥ – *वही* २.४.१६ (मू.ग्र. पृ. १६१)

विचिकित्सितमेतन्मे ब्रवीतु भगवान् यथा।
शाब्दे ब्रह्मणि निष्णातः परस्मिंश्च भवान् खलु॥ – *वही* २.४.१० (मू.ग्र. पृ. १६०)

विधुं दद्राणं समने बहूनां युवानं सन्तं पलितो जगार।
देवस्य पश्य काव्यं महित्वाद्या ममार स ह्यः समान॥ – *ऋक्संहिता* १०.५५.५ (मू.ग्र. पृ. २२)

विश्वतश्चक्षुरुत विश्वतोमुखो विश्वतोबाहुरुत विश्वतस्पात्।
सं बाहुभ्यां धमति सं पतत्रैर्द्यावाभूमी जनयत् देव एकः॥ – *वही* १०.८१.३ (मू.ग्र. पृ. ५७)

विरुद्धभावद्वयसन्निवेशात् सम्भाव्यते विश्वमिदं द्विमूलम्।
आभ्वभ्वसंज्ञे स्त इमे च मूले द्रष्टाभु, दृश्यं तु मतं तदभ्वम्॥२॥
– *संशयतदुच्छेदवाद*, प्रथमखण्ड पृ. १, का. २ (मू.ग्र. पृ. १२८)

विरूपास इदृषयस्ता इद्गम्भीरवेपसः।
तेऽङ्गिरसः सूनवस्ते अग्नेः परिजज्ञिरे॥ – *ऋक्संहिता* १०.६२.५ (मू.ग्र. पृ. २६)

वेदानधीत्य वेदौ वा वेदं वापि यथाक्रमम्।
अविप्लुतब्रह्मचर्यो गृहस्थाश्रममावसेत् ॥ – *मनु*. ३.२ (मू.ग्र. पृ. १७)

व्याख्यामुद्राक्षमाले कलशसुलिखिते बाहुभिर्भावपादं
बिभ्राणो जानुमूर्ध्ना पदतलनिहितापस्मृतिर्द्युद्रुमाघः।
सौवर्णे योगपीठे लिपिमयकमले सूपविष्टस्त्रिनेत्रः
क्षीराभश्चन्द्रमौलिर्वितरतु विबुधां शुद्धबुद्धिं शिवो नः॥ – *वेदान्तकौमुदी* १.१ (मू.ग्र. पृ. १२१)

श

शतं चैका हृदयस्य नाड्यः-तासां मूर्द्धानभिनिःसृतैका।
तयोर्ध्वमायन्नमृतत्त्वमेति विश्वङ्ङन्या उत्क्रमणे भवन्ति॥ – *छा.उप.* ८.६.६ (मू.ग्र. पृ. २८)

शैशवेऽभ्यस्तविद्यानां, यौवने विषयैषिणाम्।
वार्द्धक्ये मुनिवृत्तीनां, योगेनान्ते तनुत्यजाम्॥ – *रघुवंश* १.८ (मू.ग्र. पृ. ९६)

श्यामं हिरण्यपरिधिं वनमाल्तबर्हधातु-प्रवाल-नट-वेषमनुव्रतांसे।
विन्यस्त-हस्तमितरेण धुनानमब्जं कणोत्पललक-कपोल-मुखाब्जहासम्॥
– *श्रीमद्भागवत* १०.२३.२२ (मू.ग्र. पृ. १६४)

श्रवणाद्दर्शनाद्ध्यानान्मयि भावोऽनुकीर्तनात्।
न तथा सन्निकर्षेण, प्रतियात ततो गृहान्॥ – *वही* १०.२९.२७ (मू.ग्र. पृ. १८५)

श्रियः पतिर्यज्ञपतिः प्रजापतिर्धियांपतिर्लोकपतिर्धरापतिः।
पतिर्गतिश्चान्धक-वृष्णि-सात्वतां-प्रसीदतां मे भगवान् सतां पतिः॥ – *वही* २.४.२० (मू.ग्र. पृ. १६१)

स

स एष आत्माऽऽत्मवतामधीश्वरस्त्रयीमयो धर्ममयस्तपोमयः।
गतव्य-लीकैरजशङ्करादिभिर्वितर्क्य-लिङ्गो भगवान् प्रसीदताम्॥ – *वही* २.४.१९ (मू.ग्र. पृ. १६१)

स कथं धर्मसेतूनां वक्ता कर्ताभिरक्षिता।
प्रतीपमाचरद् ब्रह्मन्! परदाराभिमर्शनम् ॥ – *वही* १०.३३.२७-२९ (मू.ग्र. पृ. १९२)

सकृदिव वै पितरः। – *कौ.ब्रा.* ५.६, १०.४ (मू.ग्र. पृ. १५)

सत्यव्रतं सत्यपरं त्रिसत्यं सत्यस्य योनिं निहितं च सत्ये।
सत्यस्य सत्यं ऋतसत्यनेत्रं सत्यात्मकं त्वां शरणं प्रपन्नाः ॥ – *श्रीमद्भागवत* १०.२.२६ (मू.ग्र. पृ. ४८)

सदृशं त्रिषु लिङ्गेषु सर्वासु च विभक्तिषु।
वचनेषु च सर्वेषु यन्न व्येति तदव्ययम्॥
– *गोपथब्राह्मण*, पूर्वभाग १.२६ (मू.ग्र. पृ. १५०)

स प्रजापतिः – आपः, फेनं, मृदं, सिकतं शर्करा, अश्मानं अयः-हिरण्यं – असृजत्। अभूद्वा इयं प्रतिष्ठेति – तद्भूमिरभवत्। यदप्रथमयत् – सा पृथिव्यभवत्। सेयं सर्वा कृत्स्ना मन्यमाना अगायत्। यदगायत-तस्माद् गायत्री। त्स्मादु है – तद्यः सर्वः कृत्स्नो मन्यते, गायति, वैव वा, रमते। – *शत.ब्राह्मण* ६.११.१२-१५ (मू.ग्र. पृ. १२३)

स प्रजापतिः सर्वत्सरोऽभवत्। सर्वत्सरो ह वै नामैतत्-यत् सम्वत्सरः। – *वही* ११.१.६.१२ (मू.ग्र. पृ. ३१)

समानेन वो हविषा जुहोमि। – *ऋग्वेद* १०.१९१.३ (मू.ग्र. पृ. १५४)

समुद्रादर्णवादधि संवत्सरो अजायत।
अहोरात्राणि विदधद्विश्वस्य मिषतो वशी॥ – *ऋक्संहिता* १०.१९१.२ (मू.ग्र. पृ. ३९)

स यः स वैश्वानरः – इमे स लोकाः, इयमेव पृथिवी विश्वं, अग्निर्नरः, अन्तरिक्षं विश्वं, वायुर्नरः, द्यौरेव विश्वं, आदित्यो नरः। (विश्वेभ्यो नरेभ्यो जातः अग्निरेव यौगिकी वैश्वानरः)। स एष आधिदैविको वैश्वानराग्निः।
– *शत. ब्राह्मण* ९.३.१.३ (मू.ग्र. पृ. १९)

सर्गश्च प्रतिसर्गश्च वंशो मन्वन्तरस्तथा। – *विष्णु पु.* ३.६.२४ (मू.ग्र. पृ. ४२)

सर्वमापोमयं जगत्। – *मार्कण्डेय पु.* ८१.७५ (मू.ग्र. पृ. ४०)

सर्वयोनिषु कौन्तेय ! मूर्तयह् संभवन्ति याः।

तासाम् ब्रह्म महद्योनिरहं बीजप्रदः पिता ॥ – *गीता* ३.४ (मू॰ग्र॰ पृ॰ १५१)

सहनाववतु सह नौ भुनक्तु सह वीर्यं करवावहै। – *कठ उप॰*, शान्तिपाठ (मू॰ग्र॰ पृ॰ १५४)

सहयज्ञाः प्रजाः सृष्ट्वा पुरोवाच प्रजापतिः।
अनेन प्रसविष्यध्वमेव वोऽस्त्विष्टकामधुक् ॥ – *गीता* ३.१० (मू॰ग्र॰ पृ॰ ९४)

सहस्रशीर्षा पुरुषः सहस्राक्षः सहस्रपात्।
सभूमिं सर्वतस्पृत्वात्यतिष्ठद्दशाङ्गुलम् ॥ – *यजुःसंहिता* ३१.१ (मू॰ग्र॰ पृ॰ ५७)

स्वागतं वो महाभाग ! प्रियं किं करवाणि वः।
व्रजस्यानामयं कच्चित् ! ब्रूतागमनकारणम् ॥ – *श्रीमद्भागवत* १०.२९.१८ (मू॰ग्र॰ पृ॰ १८३)

संभूतिं च विनाशं च यस्तद्वेदोभयं सह।
विनाशेन मृत्युं तीर्त्वा सम्भूत्याऽमृतमश्नुते ॥ – *ईश॰उप॰* १४ (मू॰ग्र॰ पृ॰ १३०, १३६)

संस्थापनाय धर्मस्य प्रशमायेतरस्य च।
अवतीर्णो हि भगवान्-अंशेन जगदीश्वरः ॥ – *श्रीमद्भागवत* १०.३३.२७-२९ (मू॰ग्र॰ पृ॰ १९२)

साकञ्जानां सप्तथमाहुरेकजं षडिद्यमा ऋषयो देवजा।
तेषामिष्टामि विहितानि धामशः स्थात्रे रेजन्ते विकृतानि रूपशः ॥ – *ऋक्संहिता* १.१६४.१५ (मू॰ग्र॰ पृ॰ २७)

सूर्याचन्द्रमसौ धाता यथापूर्वमकल्पयत्।
दिवं च पृथवीं चान्तरिक्षमथो स्वः ॥ – *वही* १०.१९१.३ (मू॰ग्र॰ पृ॰ ४२)

स्वादु-पाकरसं-स्निग्धं-ओजस्य-धातुवर्द्धनम्।
प्रायः पयः तत्र गव्यं तु जीवनीयं रसायनम् ॥ – *अष्टाङ्गहृदय*, क्षीरवर्ग, ५.२०-२१ (मू॰ग्र॰ पृ॰ ६५)

सूर्यो बृहतीमध्यूढ़स्तपति। बृहद्ध तस्थौ भुवनेष्वन्तः। – *ऐत॰ आरण्यक* २.१.१ (मू॰ग्र॰ पृ॰ ५१)

सोमः पूषा च चेततुर्विश्वासां सुक्षितीनाम्।
देवत्रा रथ्योर्हिता। – *सामवेद*, पूर्वार्चिक, ऐन्द्रकाण्ड, द्वितीय प्रपाठक, चतुर्थ दशती,
मन्त्र संख्या १० (मू॰ग्र॰ पृ॰ ५१)

ह

हिता नाम नाड्यः – द्वासप्ततिः सहस्राणि हृदयात् पुरीततामभिप्रतिष्ठन्ते,
ताभिः प्रत्यवसृप्य पुरीतति शेते। – *बृ॰उप॰* २.१.१९ (मू॰ग्र॰ पृ॰ २९)

हृत्प्रतिष्ठं यदजिरं जविष्ठं तन्मे मनः शिवसंकल्पमस्तु। – *यजुःसंहिता* ३४.६ (मू॰ग्र॰ पृ॰ २३४)

हृदि ह्येष आत्मा। अत्रैतदेकशतं नाडीनां, तासां शतं शतमेकैकस्याम्,
द्वासप्ततिर्द्वासप्ततिः प्रतिशाखानाडीसहस्राणि भवन्ति, आसु व्यानश्चरति। – *प्रश्न उप॰* ३.६ (मू॰ग्र॰ पृ॰ २९)

Glossary of Vedic Terms

Āditya	sun; one of the numerous supraphysical energies emanating from sun; one of the many suns referred to in the Vedas
āgneya	produced from *agni*; full of *agni*
agni	fire; a supraphysical energy
Agnihotra	a Vedic ritual of making oblations to fire
Agnisoma *yajña*	the interaction or fusion of Agni and Soma which transforms into supraphysical energies like *agni*
ākāśa	space, one of the five *mahābhūta*s (gross elements); space generated by *antarikṣa* (the separation of heaven and earth), the principal space being a continuous, unbounded extension in every direction
amṛta	immortal; imperishable. In the technical sense, this term is used for the unchanging principle in an individual as distinguished from the ever-changing principles/factors
aṅgirā	the supraphysical energy from which *agni*, *vāyu* and *āditya* stem
annadā	which consumes *anna* (fire in relation to fuel).
antarikṣa (*loka*)	the space between heaven and earth; also translated as "interspace"
āpa (*āpaḥ*)	supraphysical variant of the physical entity, commonly known as water; also called *ambha* and *jala*
Aśvinīkumāra	generally identified as the father of the founder of Āyurveda. In Vedic usage, there are two Aśvinīkumāras among the thirty-three *deva*s.

asura	generally translated as demons or opponents of the *deva*s; a class of supraphysical energy. There are different types of *asura*s, namely *dasyu*s, *daitya*s, *dānava*s and *paṇi*s
ātmā	indivisible; unlimited; the all-pervasive and indestructible substratum of every individual, erroneously translated as "spirit"; the real self
Atri	a supraphysical energy, and the name of one of the seven seer-scientists (*ṛṣi*s) who discovered other supraphysical energies
bhuvaḥ	earth; second of the seven *vyāhṛti*s which are deeply meaningful utterances signifying seven "worlds": *bhū*, *bhuva*, *sva*, *maha*, *jana*, *tapa* and *satya*
Bhṛgu	a supraphysical energy, and a seer-scientist by that name
Brahmā	the foundation or basis of the totality of the created universe. This universe is another manifestation of Brahmā
brahma kalpa	a unit to measure the immeasurable span of time
Brāhmaṇa	a portion of the texts of the Vedas which elucidates the application of *yajña vijñāna* (scientific principles)
devāgni	a supraphysical energy called *agni*
devatā or *deva*	a specific class of supraphysical energies, as distinct from *asura* which emerges from the same source
dharma	this is a comprehensive term that reflects the blending of ethics, duty, characteristics and properties of an individual
dhātu	layer; stratum; ingredient; matter (generally used for metals); root (language)
divya yuga	the period related to the Partial Collapse (one year in the human time-scale is one-day night unit in the *divya* time-scale)
draṣṭa	seer; observer

gandharva	a class of entities; a species different from human beings, generally regarded as celestial musicians or singers
Hiraṇyagarbha	a golden foetus; the seed of elemental existence from which creation followed; a name of Brahmā
Īśvara	the supreme principle which regulates the universe, comprising all disparate individuals (*jīva* regulates individuals and *Īśvara* regulates *jīva*s)
itihāsa	historical episodes illustrating and explaining supraphysical forces and their functioning
jñāna	consciousness; knowledge; awareness; faculty of judgement; knowing how diversity ultimately coalesces into unity
Kṛṣṇa	a cosmic phenomenon; in the Purāṇas, Kṛṣṇa is the eighth *avatāra* of Viṣṇu; black or dark as a cloud
kṣatriya	one of the four sections in which ancient society was organized
madhyamā	between the two levels of speech (*vaikharī* and *paśyantī*) there is a middle level known as *madhyamā vāk* – the level of thought. Its association is chiefly with *buddhi* (the mind or intellect); sustenance
mana	one of three components of *ātmā*, the other two being *prāṇa* and *vāk*; also translated as "mind" or "heart"
mantra	a verse in the Vedas; the words in which the seer-scientists articulated their discoveries of the processes of nature, the cosmos and beyond
mleccha	outsider, inferior, language other than Sanskrit
parmeṣṭhi	the Prajāpati which orbits around Brahmā and is filled with *āpa*; also one dimension of the five-dimensional universe, the other four being *svayambhū*, *sūrya*, *candra* and *pṛthvī*

paṭhyasvasti	the language of the Vedas (Pandit Madhusudan Ojha has written a book with the same name)
pitṛ	"ancestors" or "forefathers". Technically it stands for one of the several unchangeable supraphysical energies
prajā	all created entities
prāṇa	supraphysical energy; breath
puruṣa	the ultimate manifested ocean of energy, which is observable as differentiated variegated nature
rajas	the second of the three *guṇa*s (qualities) (the other two being *sattva* – the most positive quality signifying goodness or peace; and *tamas* – the most negative quality signifying darkness or inertia). *Rajas* comes in-between these two and signifies vigour or activity
rasa	a supraphysical essence
ṛk	the fundamental *tattva* from which all forms evolve; one of the four Vedas
ṛṣi	a supraphysical energy which comes into motion spontaneously; a seer-scientist who discovers a specific supraphysical energy
rudra	the *agni* (supraphysical energy) emanating from *vāyu* (there are eleven Rudras); this supraphysical energy maintains a special relationship with Soma and Yama; also called Rudra *devatā*
sāma	the extent to which an individual or an entity can be seen; one of the four Vedas
saṁskāra	knowledge-impression; cognition residue
saṁvatsara	a year; the annual cycle; the aggregate of the seasons; the *yajña* from where the triadic worlds of *pṛthvī*, *antarikṣa* and *dyau* emanate
Savitā	the direct luminosity of the sun; luminous rays radiating from the mass of every indi-

vidual. Also known as "Savitra" and "Sāvitrī"

Śatapatha Brāhmaṇa — One of the Brāhmaṇa texts which has 100 chapters related to *Yajurveda*

śruti — another term for the Vedas (literally meaning "that which has been transmitted orally and heard by a disciple of the *guru*"); a direct statement

soma — the material cause of the universe; a specific category of supraphysical energy

sphoṭa — the sentence taken as an integral symbol

svāhā — one of the seven regions of the universe

svayambhū — that which comes into being on its own. This is the name given to the *yajña* which occurs at the very outset in the entire process of creation

tapa — intense endeavour, heat

tattva — essence; the fundamental factor from which something evolves

vāk — the substance in an object; the matter within the shell; speech

Veda — the fundamental *tattva* which goes into the evolution of the cosmos; the Vedas are the texts which elucidate and explain *veda-tattva*

Veda mantra — aphorisms in which the seer-scientists have articulated the principles of the Vedic sciences. These *mantras* cause vibration in the channels and help a seeker to realize the experienced reality

vedāṅga — a "limb" of the Vedas. There are six of these, namely phonetics, etymology, grammar, prosody, astronomy and rituals

vīrya — creative vitality

vijñāna — knowledge of how the variegated universe evolves from a unified, single harmonious *tattva*; science

vivasvān — one of the twelve states of the sun; one of the early recipients of the knowledge elucidated in *Śrīmadbhagavadgītā*

vāk prāṇa	the supraphysical energy that pulsates in matter
yajña	the interaction and fusion of supraphysical energies and/or material substances; the process of the acculturation of *agni*; the refinement and embellishment of *agni*
yama	generally understood as the "god of death"; ferocious wind

सन्दर्भ ग्रन्थ-सूची
For Further Reading

साक्षात् स्रोत
Direct Reference

अग्निपुराण, नाग पब्लिशर्स, दिल्ली, १९८५।
Agni Purāṇa, Nag Publishers, New Delhi, 1985.

अथर्ववेदसंहिता (भाग १-४), सम्पा॰ एवं अनु॰ श्रीपाद दामोदर सातवलेकर, स्वाध्याय मण्डल पारडी, १९८५।
Atharvaveda Saṁhitā (parts 1-4), ed. and tr. Sripad Damodar Satvalekar, Swadhyay Mandal, Paradi, 1985.

अमरकोश, अमरसिंह, *सुधाटीका सहित*, सं॰ शिवदत्त वासुदेव लक्ष्मण शास्त्री, राष्ट्रीय संस्कृत संस्थान, नई दिल्ली, पुनर्मुद्रण संस्करण, २००३, दिल्ली।
Amarakośa (with Amarsingh, *Sudhāṭīkā*), ed. Shivdutt Vasudev Lakshman Shastri, Rashtriya Sanskrit Sansthan, New Delhi, 2003.

अहोरात्रवाद, पण्डित मधुसूदन ओझा, सम्पा॰ आद्यादत्त ठाकुर, लखनऊ, १९२६।
Ahorātravāda, Pandit Madhusudan Ojha, ed. Adyadutt Thakur, Lucknow, 1926.

आधिदैविकाध्याय, पण्डित मधुसूदन ओझा, सम्पा॰ सुरजनदास स्वामी, वि॰सं॰ २००७।
Ādhidaivikādhyāya, Pandit Madhusudan Ojha, ed. Surjandas Swami, vs 2007 (publisher not known).

आवरणवाद, पण्डित मधुसूदन ओझा, सम्पा॰ दयानन्द भार्गव, हि॰अनु॰ अनन्त शर्मा, मधुसूदन ओझा शोध प्रकोष्ठ, जोधपुर, जयनारायण विश्वविद्यालय, १९९३।
Āvaraṇavāda, Pandit Madhusudan Ojha, ed. Dayanand Bhargav, Hindi tr. Anant Sharma, Madhusudan Ojha Shodh Prakoshtha, Jayanarayan University, Jodhpur, 1993.

आशौचपञ्जिका, पण्डित मधुसूदन ओझा, सम्पा॰ सुरजनदास स्वामी, वि॰सं॰ २००७।
Āśaucapañjikā, Pandit Madhusudan Ojha, ed. Surjandas Swami, vs 2007.

उपनिषत्संग्रह, सम्पा॰ पं॰ जगदीश शास्त्री, मोतीलाल बनारसीदास, दिल्ली, १९८४।
Upaniṣatsaṁgraha, ed. Pandit Jagdish Shastri, Motilal Banarsidass, Delhi, 1984.

ऋग्वेदसंहिता (भाग १-९) *सायणभाष्यसहित*, हि॰अनु॰ पं॰ रामगोविन्द त्रिवेदी, चौखम्भा विद्याभवन, वाराणसी, पुनर्मुद्रित संस्करण, १९९७।

Ṛgveda Saṁhitā (parts 1-9), with *Sāyaṇa-Bhāṣya*, tr. Pandit Ramgovind Trivedi, Chaukhamba Vidyabhawan, Varanasi, rev. edn, 1997.

ऐतरेयब्राह्मण, सम्पा॰ एवं हि॰ अनु॰ सुधाकर मालवीय, तारा बुक एजेन्सी, वाराणसी, २०१५।
Aitareya Brāhmaṇa, ed. and tr. Sudhakar Malaviya, Tara Book Agency, Varanasi, 2015.

कादम्बिनी, पण्डित मधुसूदन ओझा, सम्पा॰ गणेशीलाल सुथार, मधुसूदन ओझा शोध प्रकोष्ठ, जयनारायण विश्वविद्यालय, जोधपुर, २००३।
Kādambinī, Pandit Madhusudan Ojha, ed. Ganeshilal Suthar, Madhusudan Ojha Shodh Prakoshtha, Jainarayan University, Jodhpur, 2003.

कौषीतकि ब्राह्मण, सम्पा॰ बी॰ लिण्डर, जेना, हेर्मान, कोस्टेनोबल, १८८७।
Kauṣītaki Brāhmaṇa, ed. B. Lynder, Jena, Hermann, Costanoble, 1887.

गोपथब्राह्मण, सम्पा॰ प्रज्ञा देवी एवं मेधा देवी, चौखम्भा संस्कृत प्रतिष्ठान, दिल्ली, २००८।
Gopatha Brāhmaṇa, ed. Pragya Devi and Medha Devi, Chaukhamba Sanskrit Pratishtan, Delhi, 2008.

छन्दोभ्यस्ता, पण्डित मधुसूदन ओझा, सम्पा॰ प्रद्युम्न शर्मा, दी प्रिन्टर्स एण्ड पब्लिशर्स लि॰, जयपुर।
Chandobhyastā, Pandit Madhusudan Ojha, ed. Pradyumn Sharma, The Printers and Publishers Ltd, Jaipur.

छन्दःसमीक्षा, पण्डित मधुसूदन ओझा, सम्पा॰ सुरजनदास स्वामी, राजस्थान संस्कृत अकादमी, १९९१।
Chandaḥsamīkṣā, Pandit Madhusudan Ojha, ed. Surjandas Swami, Rajasthan Sanskrit Akademi, 1991.

जगद्गुरुवैभवम्, पण्डित मधुसूदन ओझा, सम्पा॰ प्रद्युम्न शर्मा, वि॰सं॰ १९९१।
Jagadguruvaibhavam, Pandit Madhusudan Ojha, ed. Pradyumn Sharma, vs 1991.

तैत्तिरीयब्राह्मण (सायणभाष्य सहित), सम्पा॰ गणेश उमाकान्त थिटे, न्यू भारतीय बुक कॉर्पोरेशन, दिल्ली, २०१२।
Taittirīya Brāhmaṇa (with *Sāyaṇa-Bhāṣya*), ed. Ganesh Umakant Thite, New Bharatiya Book Corporation, Delhi, 2012.

दशवादरहस्य, पण्डित मधुसूदन ओझा, सम्पा॰ अनन्त शर्मा, हि॰अनु॰ लक्ष्मी शर्मा, मधुसूदन ओझा शोध प्रकोष्ठ, जयनारायण विश्वविद्यालय, जोधपुर, १९९७।
Daśavādarahasya, Pandit Madhusudan Ojha, ed. Anant Sharma, tr. Lakshmi Sharma, Madhusudan Ojha Shodh Prakoshtha, Jainarayan University, Jodhpur, 1997.

देवतानिवित्, पण्डित मधुसूदन ओझा, सम्पा॰ आद्यादत्त ठाकुर, लखनऊ।
Devatānivit, Pandit Madhusudan Ojha, ed. Adhyadutt Thakur, Lucknow.

पञ्चभूतसमीक्षा, पण्डित मधुसूदन ओझा, सम्पा॰ प्रद्युम्न शर्मा।
Pañcabhūtasamīkṣā, Pandit Madhusudan Ojha, ed. Pradyumn Sharma.

पद्मपुराण (भाग १-४), नाग पब्लिशर्स, दिल्ली, १९८४।
Padma Purāṇa (part 1-4), Nag Publishers, Delhi, 1984.

पाणिनीयव्याकरणमहाभाष्य, पतञ्जलि (*कैयटप्रणीत-प्रदीप-नागेशभट्टविरचित-उद्योत-सहित*) सम्पा॰ श्री भार्गव शास्त्री, चौखम्भा संस्कृत प्रतिष्ठान, दिल्ली, पुनर्मुद्रित संस्करण, २०००।
Pāṇinīyavyākaraṇamahābāṣya, Patañjali (*Kaiyaṭapraṇīta-Pradīpa-Nāgeśabhaṭṭaviracita-Udyogatasahita*), ed. Shri Bhargav Shastri, Chaukhamba Sanskrit Pratishthan, Delhi, rev. edn, 2000.

पातञ्जलयोगसूत्र, सम्पा॰ रामशंकर भट्टाचार्य, हि॰अनु॰ स्वामी हरिहरानन्द, मोतीलाल बनारसीदास, दिल्ली, १९८७।
Pātañjalayogasūtra, ed. Ramshankar Bhattacharya, tr. Swami Hariharanand, Motilal Banarsidass, Delhi, 1987.

पितृसमीक्षा, पण्डित मधुसूदन ओझा, सम्पा॰ देवीदत्त शर्मा चतुर्वेदी, मधुसूदन ओझा शोध प्रकोष्ठ, जयनारायण विश्वविद्यालय, जोधपुर, १९९१।
Pitṛsamīkṣā, Pandit Madhusudan Ojha, ed. Devidutt Sharma Chaturvedi, Madusudan Ojha Shodh Prakoshtha, Jainarayan University, Jodhpur, 1991.

पुराणनिर्माणाधिकरण, पण्डित मधुसूदन ओझा, सम्पा॰ पद्मलोचन शर्मा, वि॰सं॰ २००९।
Purāṇanirmāṇādhikaraṇa, Pandit Madhusudan Ojha, ed. Padmalochan Sharma, VS 2009.

प्रत्यन्तप्रस्थानमीमांसा, पण्डित मधुसूदन ओझा, सम्पा॰ विनोद शास्त्री, हि॰अनु॰ रामप्रपन्न शर्मा, राजस्थान संस्कृत अकादमी, जयपुर, २००३।
Pratyantaprasthānmīmāṁsā, Pandit Madhusudan Ojha, ed. Vinod Shastri, tr. Ramprapanna Sharma, Rajasthan Sanskrit Akademi, Jaipur, 2003.

ब्रह्मपुराण, नाग पब्लिशर्स, दिल्ली, १९८५।
Brahma Purāṇa, Nag Publishers, Delhi, 1985.

बृहत्संहिता, वराहमिहिर (भाग १-२), हि॰व्या॰ पं॰ अच्युतानन्द झा, चौखम्भा विद्याभवन, वाराणसी, २०१०।
Bṛhat Saṁhitā, Varāhamihira (parts 1-2), tr. Pandit Achyutanand Jha, Chaukhamba Vidyabhavan, Varanasi, 2010.

बृहदारण्यकोपनिषद् (*शाङ्करभाष्यसहित*), गीताप्रेस, गोरखपुर, पुनर्मुद्रित संस्करण, २०१४।
Bṛhadāraṇyakopaniṣad (*Śāṅkarabhāṣyasahita*), Gita Press, Gorakhpur, rev. edn, 2014.

ब्रह्मचतुष्पदी, पण्डित मधुसूदन ओझा, सम्पा॰ प्रद्युम्न शर्मा, वि॰सं॰ २००९।
Brahmacatuṣpadī, Pandit Madhusudan Ojha, ed. Pradyumn Sharma, VS 2009.

ब्रह्मविनय, पण्डित मधुसूदन ओझा, सम्पा॰ वासुदेव शरण अग्रवाल, पृथिवी प्रकाशन, वाराणसी, १९६४।
Brahmavinaya, Pandit Madhusudan Ojha, ed. Vasudev Sharan Aggarwal, Prithvi Prakashan, Varanasi, 1964.

ब्रह्मसमन्वय, पण्डित मधुसूदन ओझा, सम्पा॰ प्रद्युम्न शर्मा, जयपुर, वि॰सं॰ २००१।
Brahmsamanvaya, Pandit Madhusudan Ojha, ed. Pradyumn Sharma, Jaipur, VS 2001.

ब्रह्मसिद्धान्त, पण्डित मधुसूदन ओझा, सम्पा॰ वासुदेव शरण अग्रवाल, सं॰टीका गिरिधर शर्मा चतुर्वेदी, काशी हिन्दू विश्वविद्यालय, वाराणसी, १९६१।

Brahmasiddhānta, Pandit Madhusudan Ojhan, ed. Vasudev Sharan Aggarwal with commentary by Giridhar Sharma Chaturvedi, Banaras Hindu University, Varanasi, 1961.

ब्रह्मसिद्धान्त, पण्डित मधुसूदन ओझा, हि॰अनु॰ देवीदत्त शर्मा चतुर्वेदी, राजस्थान पत्रिका प्रकाशन, जयपुर, २००५।

Brahmasiddhānta, Pandit Madhusudan Ojha, tr. Devidutt Sharma Chaturvedi, Rajasthan Patrika Prakashan, Jaipur, 2005.

ब्रह्मविज्ञान, पण्डित मधुसूदन ओझा, सम्पा॰ प्रद्युम्न शर्मा ओझा, राजस्थान पत्रिका प्रकाशन, वि॰सं॰ २०४४।

Brahmavijñāna, Pandit Madhusudan Ojha, ed. Pradyumn Sharma Ojha, Rajasthan Patrika Prakashan, vs 2044.

भविष्यपुराण (भाग १-३), नाग पब्लिशर्स, दिल्ली, १९८४।

Bhaviṣya Purāṇa (part 1-3), Nag Publishers, Delhi, 1984.

मत्स्यपुराण, मेहरचन्द लछमनदास, दिल्ली, १९८४।

Matsya Purāṇa, Meherchand Lachmandas, Delhi, 1984.

मनुस्मृति, सम्पा॰ एवं हि॰अनु॰ पं॰ रामेश्वर भट्ट, चौखम्भा संस्कृत प्रतिष्ठान, दिल्ली, २०११।

Manusmṛti, ed. and tr. Pandit Rameshwar Bhatt, Chaukhamba Sanskrit Pratishthan, Delhi, 2011.

मन्त्रमहोदधि, महीधर, सम्पा॰ एवं व्या॰ सुधाकर मालवीय, चौखम्भा संस्कृत प्रतिष्ठान, दिल्ली, २०१५।

Mantramahodadhi, ed. and tr. Sudhakar Malviya, Chaukhamba Sanskrit Prathishthan, Delhi, 2014.

महाभारत, वेदव्यास कृत, (भाग १-१८), सम्पा॰ विष्णु एस॰ सुक्थंकर, भण्डारकर ओरियण्टल रिसर्च इंस्टीट्यूट,पूना, १९९८।

Mahābhārata, Veda Vyāsa (parts 1-18), ed. Vishnu S. Sukthankar, Bhandarkar Oriental Research Institute, Pune, 1998.

महाभारत, वेदव्यास (भाग १-६), हि॰अनु॰ रामनारायणदत्त शास्त्री, गीता प्रेस, गोरखपुर, पुनर्मुद्रित संस्करण, २००६।

Mahābhārata, Veda Vyasa (parts 1-6), tr. Ramnarayan Shastri, Gita Press, Gorakhpur, rev edn, 2006.

मार्कण्डेयपुराण, चौखम्भा विद्याभवन, वाराणसी, १९९५।

Markaṇḍeya Purāṇa, Chaukhamba Vidyabhavan, Varanasi, 1995.

महर्षिकुलवैभव, पण्डित मधुसूदन ओझा, सं॰टीका गिरिधर शर्मा चतुर्वेदी, हि॰अनु॰ देवीदत्त शर्मा, राजस्थान प्राच्य प्रतिष्ठान, जयपुर, १९९४।

Maharṣikulavaibhava, Pandit Madhusudan Ojha, commentary by Giridhar Sharma Chaturvedi, tr. Devidutt Sharma, Rajasthan Prachya Prathishthan, Jaipur, 1994.

यज्ञसरस्वती, पण्डित मधुसूदन ओझा, सम्पा॰ प्रद्युम्न शर्मा ओझा।
Yajñasarasvatī, Pandit Madhusudan Ojha, ed. Pradyumn Sharma Ojha.

रजोवाद, पण्डित मधुसूदन ओझा, सम्पा॰ वी॰एस॰ अग्रवाल, बनारस हिन्दू विश्वविद्यालय, वाराणसी, १९६४।
Rajovāda, Pandit Madhusudan Ojha, ed. V.S. Agrawal, Banaras Hindu University, Varanasi, 1964.

रामायण, वाल्मीकि (भाग १-८), सम्पा॰ शास्त्री श्रीनिवास कट्टि मुधोल्कर,परिमल पब्लिकेशन, दिल्ली, १९८३।
Vālmīki Rāmāyaṇa (parts 1-8), ed. Shastri Srinivas Katti Mudholkar, Parimal Publication, Delhi, 1983.

वर्णसमीक्षा, पण्डित मधुसूदन ओझा, सम्पा॰ दयानन्द भार्गव, हि॰अनु॰ शिवदत्त शर्मा चतुर्वेदी, मधुसूदन ओझा शोध प्रकोष्ठ, जयनारायण विश्वविद्यालय, जोधपुर।
Varṇasamīkṣā, Pandit Madhusudan Ojha, ed. Dayanand Bhargav, tr. Shivdutt Sharma Chaturvedi, Madhusudan Ojha Shodh Prakoshtha, Jainarayan University, Jodhpur.

वायुपुराण, हि॰व्या॰ शिवजीत सिंह, चौखम्भा विद्याभवन, वाराणसी, २०१३।
Vayu Purāṇa, commentary Shivjit Singh, Chaukhamba Vidyabhavan, Varanasi, 2013.

वामनपुराण, सम्पा॰ आनन्दस्वरूप गुप्त, हि॰अनु॰ गोपालचन्द्र वेदान्तशास्त्री एवं नारायण सिंह, सर्वभारतीय काशीराज न्यास दुर्ग, रामनगर, वाराणसी, १९६८।
Vāmana Purāṇa, ed. Anandswarup Gupt, tr. Gopalchandra Vedantashastri and Narayan Singh, Sarvabharatiya Kashiraj Nyas Durg, Ramnagar, Varanasi, 1968.

विज्ञानविद्युत्, पण्डित मधुसूदन ओझा, हि॰अनु॰ शिवदत्त शर्मा चतुर्वेदी, राजस्थान पत्रिका प्रकाशन, १९९०।
Vijñānavidyut, Pandit Madhusudan Ojha, tr. Shivdutt Sharma Chaturvedi, Rajasthan Patrika Prakashan, 1990.

विष्णुपुराण, नाग पब्लिशर्स, दिल्ली, १९८५।
Viṣṇu Purāṇa, Nag Publishers, Delhi, 1985.

विष्णुस्मृति, सम्पा॰ जूलियस जॉली, चौखम्भा अमरभारती प्रकाशन, वाराणसी, २०१०।
Viṣṇusmṛti, ed. Julius Jolly, Chaukhamba Amarbharati Prakashan, Varanasi, 2010.

व्योमवाद, पण्डित मधुसूदन ओझा, सम्पा॰ दयानन्द भार्गव, हि॰अनु॰ अनन्त शर्मा, मधुसूदन ओझा शोध प्रकोष्ठ, जयनारायण विश्वविद्यालय, जोधपुर, १९९३।
Vyomavāda, Pandit Madhusudan Ojha, ed. Dayanand Bhargav, tr. Anant Sharma, Madhusudan Ojha Shodh Prakoshtha, Jainarayan University, Jodhpur, 1993.

शतपथब्राह्मण (भाग १-२), सम्पा॰ विद्याधर शर्मा, भारतीय विद्या प्रकाशन, दिल्ली, १९९४।
Śatapatha Brāhmaṇa (parts 1-2), ed. Vidyadhar Sharma, Bharatiya Vidya Prakashan, Delhi, 1994.

शारीरकविज्ञान, पण्डित मधुसूदन ओझा, हि॰अनु॰ शिवदत्त शर्मा चतुर्वेदी, राजस्थान पत्रिका प्रकाशन, १९९०।
Śārīrakavijñāna, Pandit Madhusudan Ojha, tr. Shivdutt Sharma Chaturvedi, Rajasthan Patrika Prakashan, 1990.

शारीरकविमर्श, पण्डित मधुसूदन ओझा, सम्पा॰ आद्यादत्त ठाकुर, वि॰सं॰ २००१।
Śārīrakavimarśa, Pandit Madhusudan Ojha, ed. Adyadutt Thakur, vs 2001.

शुक्लयजुर्वेदसंहिता (महीधरभाष्यसहित), हि॰व्या॰ रामकृष्ण शास्त्री, चौखम्भा विद्याभवन, वाराणसी, पुनर्मुद्रित संस्करण, १९९६।
Śuklyajurveda Saṁhitā (with *Mahīdhara-Bhāṣya*), tr. Ramakrishna Shastri, Chaukhamba Vidyabhavan, Varanasi, rev. edn, 1996.

श्रीमद्भगवद्गीताविज्ञानभाष्य, पण्डित मधुसूदन ओझा, हि॰अनु॰ गणेशी लाल सुथार, मधुसूदन ओझा शोध प्रकोष्ठ, जयनारायण विश्वविद्यालय, जोधपुर, २००६।
Śrīmadbhagavadgītāvijñānabhāṣya, Pandit Madhusudan Ojha, tr. Ganeshi Lal Suthar, Madhusudan Ojha Shodh Prakoshtha, Jainarayan University, Jodhpur, 2006.

श्रीमद्भगवद्गीताविज्ञानभाष्य, पण्डित मधुसूदन ओझा, सम्पा॰ नरेन्द्र अवस्थी, हि॰ अनु॰ आर॰टी॰ व्यास, मधुसूदन ओझा शोध प्रकोष्ठ, जयनारायण विश्वविद्यालय, जोधपुर, २००९.
Śrīmadbhagavadgītāvijñānabhāṣya, Pandit Madhusudan Ojha, ed. Narendra Awasthi, tr. R.T. Vyas, Madhusudan Ojha Shodh Prakoshtha, Jainarayan University, Jodhpur, 1991.

श्रीमद्भगवतगीता, सम्पा॰ वासुदेव लक्ष्मण शास्त्री पणशीकर, चौखम्भा संस्कृत प्रतिष्ठान, दिल्ली, १९९२।
Śrīmadbhagavadgītā, ed. Vasudev Lakshman Shastri Panashikar, Chaukhambha Sanskrit Pratishthan, Delhi, 1992.

श्रीमद्भागवतपुराण (भाग १-२), गीताप्रेस, गोरखपुर, १९९१।
Śrīmadbhāgavata Purāṇa (parts 1-2), Gita Press, Gorakhpur, 1991.

सदसद्वाद, पण्डित मधुसूदन ओझा, सम्पा॰ पद्मलोचन शर्मा।
Sadasadvāda, Pandit Madhusudan Ojha, ed. Padmalochan Sharma.

सामवेदसंहिता (सायणभाष्यसहित), सम्पा॰ एवं व्या॰ पं॰ रामस्वरूप शर्मा गौड, चौखम्भा विद्याभवन, वाराणसी, पुनर्मुद्रित संस्करण, १९९४।
Sāmaveda Saṁhitā (with *Sāyaṇa-Bhāṣya*), ed. and tr. Pandit Ramaswarup Sharma Gaur, Chaukhamba Vidyabhavan, Varanasai, rev. edn, 1994.

स्कन्दपुराण (भाग १-७), नाग पब्लिशर्स, दिल्ली, १९८६।
Skanda Purāṇa (parts 1-7), Nag Publishers, Delhi, 1986.

सिद्धान्तशिरोमणि, भास्कराचार्य, (भाग १-२), सम्पा॰ एवं व्या॰ सत्यदेव शर्मा, चौखम्भा सुरभारती प्रकाशन, वाराणसी, २०१६।
Siddhāntaśiromaṇi, Bhāskarācārya (parts 1-2), ed. and tr. Satyadev Sharma, Chaukhamba Surbharati Prakashan, Varanasi, 2016.

सुश्रुत संहिता, सुश्रुत, (भाग १-३) सम्पा० एवं व्या० अनन्तराम शर्मा, चौखम्भा सुरभारती प्रकाशन, वाराणसी, २०१३।

Suśruta Saṁhitā, Suśruta (parts 1-3), ed. and tr. Anantram Sharma, Chaukhamba Surbharati Prakashan, Varanasi, 2013.

सूर्यसिद्धान्त, सम्पा० एवं व्या० रामचन्द्र पाण्डेय, चौखम्भा सुरभारती प्रकाशन, वाराणसी, २०१४।

Sūryasiddhānta, ed. and tr. Ramchandra Pandey, Chaukhamba Surbharati Prakashan, Varanasi, 2014.

संशयतदुच्छेदवाद, पण्डित मधुसूदन ओझा, हि० भाष्य मोतीलाल शास्त्री, राजस्थान पत्रिका प्रकाशन, जयपुर, वि०सं० २०५०।

Saṁśayataducchedvāda, Pandit Madhusudan Ojha, tr. Pandit Motilal Shastri, Rajasthan Patrika Prakashan, Jaipur, vs 2050.

स्मार्तकुण्डसमीक्षाध्याय, पण्डित मधुसूदन ओझा, सम्पा० रामकृष्ण व्यास, हि० अनु० रामप्रपन्न शास्त्री, राजस्थान पत्रिका प्रकाशन, जयपुर, वि०सं० २०४४।

Smārtakuṇḍasamīkṣādhyāya, Pandit Madhusudan Ojha, ed. Ramakrishna Vyas, tr. Ramprapanna Shastri, Rajasthan Patrika Prakashan, Jaipur, vs 2044.

असाक्षात् स्रोत

Secondary Sources

ईशावास्योपनिषद्, हिन्दी विज्ञान भाष्य, पं० मोतीलाल शास्त्री, राजस्थान, वि०सं० १९९०।

Īśāvāsyopaniṣad, Hindī Vijñāna Bhāṣya, Pandit Motilal Shastri, Rajasthan, vs 1990.

कठोपनिषद्, हिन्दी विज्ञान भाष्य, पं० मोतीलाल शास्त्री, राजस्थान पत्रिका प्रकाशन, जयपुर, १९९७।

Kaṭhopaniṣad, Hindī Vijñāna Bhāṣya, Pandit Motilal Shastri, Rajasthan Patrika Prakashan, Japur, 1997.

गीताविज्ञानभाष्य, पं० मोतीलाल शास्त्री, जयपुर, १९३९।

Gītāvijñānabhāṣya, Pandit Motilal Shastri, Jaipur, 1939.

दिग्देशकालस्वरूपमीमांसा, पं० मोतीलाल शास्त्री, राजस्थान वैदिक शोध संस्थान प्रकाशन, जयपुर, वि०सं० २०१५।

Digdeśakālasvarūpamīmāṁsā, Pandit Motilal Shastri, Rajasthan Vaidik Shodh Sansthan Prakashan, Jaipur, vs 2015.

पुराण परिशीलन, गिरिधर शर्मा चतुर्वेदी, बिहार राष्ट्रभाषा परिषद्, पटना, द्वितीय १९९८।

Purāṇa Pariśīlana, Giridhar Sharma Chaturvedi, Bihar Rashtrabhasha Parishad, Patna, 1998.

प्रश्नोपनिषद्, हिन्दी विज्ञान भाष्य, पं० मोतीलाल शास्त्री, राजस्थान पत्रिका प्रकाशन, जयपुर १९९५।

Praśnopaniṣad, Hindī Vijñāna Bhāṣya, Pandit Motilal Shastri, Rajasthan Patrika Prakashan, Jaipur, 1995.

Bhāratavarṣa: The India Narrative, Pandit Madhusudan Ojha, tr. Kapil Kapoor, Shri Shankar Shikshayatan and Rupa & Co., Delhi, 2017.

भारती मानव और उसकी भावुकता, हिन्दी विज्ञान भाष्य, पं॰ मोतीलाल शास्त्री, राजस्थान वैदिक शोध संस्थान प्रकाशन, जयपुर, वि॰सं॰ २०१२।

Bhāratī Mānava aur usakī Bhāvukatā, Hindī Vijñāna Bhāṣya, Pandit Motilal Shastri, Rajasthan Vaidik Shodh Sansthan Prakashan, Jaipur, vs 2012.

मुण्डकोपनिषद्, हिन्दी विज्ञान भाष्य, पं॰ मोतीलाल शास्त्री, राजस्थान पत्रिका प्रकाशन, जयपुर, वि॰सं॰ २०४९।

Muṇḍakopaniṣad, Hindī Vijñāna Bhāṣya, Pandit Motilal Shastri, Rajasthan Patrika Prakashan, Jaipur, vs 2049.

वैदिक विज्ञान और भारतीय संस्कृति, गिरिधर शर्मा चतुर्वेदी, बिहार राष्ट्रभाषा परिषद्, पटना, द्वितीय संस्करण, १९७२।

Vaidika Vijñāna and Bhāratīya Saṁskṛti, Giridhar Sharma Chaturvedi, Bihar Rashtrabhasha Parishad, Patna, 2nd edn, 1972.

वैदिकविज्ञान, गिरिधर शर्मा चतुर्वेदी, श्रीलालबहादुरशास्त्री राष्ट्रीय संस्कृत विद्यापीठ, नई दिल्ली, द्वितीय संस्करण, २००५।

Vaidika-Vijñāna, Giridhar Sharma Chaturvedi, Shri Lal Bahadur Shastri Rashtriya Sanskrit Vidyapeeth, New Delhi, 2nd edn, 2005.

शतपथब्राह्मण, हिन्दी विज्ञान भाष्य (छह भाग), पं॰ मोतीलाल शास्त्री, मानवाश्रम, जयपुर, १९५९।

Śatapatha Brāhmaṇa, Hindī Vijñāna Bhāṣya (parts 1-6), Pandit Motilal Shastri, Manavashram, Jaipur, 1959.

सत्तानिरपेक्ष संस्कृति एवं सत्तासापेक्ष सभ्यता शब्द, पं॰ मोतीलाल शास्त्री, राजस्थान वैदिक शोध संस्थान प्रकाशन, जयपुर, वि॰सं॰ २०१५।

Sattānirapekṣa Saṁskṛti evam Sattāsāpekṣa Sabhyatā Śabda, Pandit Motilal Shastri, Rajasthan Vaidik Shodh Sansthan Prakashan, Jaipur, vs 2015.

सांस्कृतिकव्याख्यानपञ्चकम्, पं॰ मोतीलाल शास्त्री, राजस्थान पत्रिका प्रकाशन, जयपुर, १९९४।

Sāṁskṛtikavyākhyānapañcakam, Pandit Motilal Shastri, Rajasthan Patrika Prakashan, Jaipur, 1994.

Mishra, Rishi Kumar, 2000, *Before the Beginning and after the End*, Delhi: Rupa & Co.

———, 2001, *The Cosmic Matrix*, Delhi: Rupa & Co.

———, 2003, *The Realm of Supraphysics*, Delhi: Rupa & Co.

———, 2007, *The Ultimate Dialogue*, Delhi: Rupa & Co.

———, 2011, *The Whole Being*, Delhi: Rupa & Co.

कोश ग्रन्थ
Dictionaries

अंग्रेज़ी-हिन्दी शब्दकोश, कामिल बुल्के; कैथोलिक प्रेस, राँची, १९७२।

English-Hindi Dictionary, Camil Bulke, Catholic Press, Ranchi, 1972.

न्यायकोश, भीमाचार्य झलकीकर, भण्डारकर ओरिएन्टल रिसर्च इंस्टीट्यूट, पूना, १९७८।
Nyāyakośa, Bhimacharya Jhalkikar, Bhandarkar Oriental Research Institute, Pune, 1978.

पारिजातकोश, सं॰ पं॰ ईश्वरचन्द्र, परिमल पब्लिकेशन, दिल्ली, २००५।
Pārijātakośa, ed. Pandit Ishwarchand, Parimal Publication, Delhi, 2005.

भारतीय दर्शन बृहत्कोश, बच्चुलाल अवस्थी, शारदा पब्लिशिंग हाउस, २००४।
Bhāratīya Darśana Bṛhatkośa, Bacchulal Awasti, Sharada Publishing House, 2004.

भारतीय दर्शन परिभाषा कोश, दीनानाथ शुक्ला, प्रतिभा प्रकाशन, दिल्ली, १९९३।
Bhāratīya Darśana Paribhāṣā Kośa, Dinanath Shukla, Pratibha Prakashan, Delhi, 1993.

मीमांसाकोश, केवलानन्द सरस्वती, श्री सत्गुरु पब्लिकेशन्स, इण्डियन बुक सेंटर, दिल्ली, १९९२।
Mīmāṁsākośa, Kewalanand Saraswati, Sri Satguru Publications, Indian Book Centre, Delhi, 1992.

वाचस्पत्यम्, सङ्कलनकर्ता तारानाथ वाचस्पति, राष्ट्रीय संस्कृत संस्थान, नई दिल्ली, पुनर्मुदित संस्करण, २००२।
Vācaspatyam, Taranath Vachaspati, Rashtriya Sanskrit Sansthan, New Delhi, rev. edn, 2002.

शब्दकल्पद्रुम, राजा राधाकान्त देव, राष्ट्रीय संस्कृत संस्थान, नई दिल्ली, पुनमुद्रित संस्करण, २००२।
Śabdakalpadruma, Raja Radhakant Dev, Rashtriya Sanskrit Sansthan, New Delhi, rev. edn, 2002.

संस्कृत वाङ्मय कोश (परिभाषा-खण्ड), स॰ श्रीधर भास्कर वर्णेकर, भारतीय भाषा परिषद् कलकत्ता, १९३२।
Sanskrit Vāṅmaya Kośa, ed. Sridhar Bhaskar Varnekar, Bharatiya Bhasha Parishad, Calcutta, 1932.

संस्कृत-हिन्दी शब्दकोश, वामन शिवराम आप्टे, स॰ उमा प्रसाद पाण्डेय, कमल प्रकाशन, नई दिल्ली, १९९९।
Sanskrit-Hindī Śabdakośa, Vaman Shivram Apte, ed. Uma Prasad Pandey, Kamal Prakashan, Delhi, 1997.

Encyclopedia of Indian Philosophies, ed. Karl H. Potter, vols 1-2, Motilal Banarasidass, Delhi, 1995.

Oxford English-English-Hindi Dictionary, ed. Suresh Kumar and Ramanath Sahai, Oxford University Press, 2008.

Index